THE MUSIC VIDEO GUIDE

JOHN CHU and ELLIOT CAFRITZ

McGraw-Hill Book Company

New York   St. Louis   San Francisco   Auckland   Bogotá   Guatemala
Hamburg   Johannesburg   Lisbon   London   Madrid   Mexico
Montreal   New Delhi   Panama   Paris   San Juan
São Paulo   Singapore   Sydney   Tokyo   Toronto

THE MUSIC VIDEO GUIDE

1 2 3 4 5 6 7 8 9 DOC DOC 8 7 6 5

ISBN 0-07-010865-X

Library of Congress Cataloging in Publication Data

Chu, John.
    The music video guide.

    1. Music videos—Reviews.   I. Cafritz, Elliot.
II. Title.
PN1992.8.M87C48   1985   789.9'13645   85–7918
ISBN 0–07–010865–X

Sponsoring Editor: *Jeffrey McCartney*
Editing Supervisor: *Margery Luhrs*
Design by: *Paul Chevannes*

CONTENTS

iii

iv CONTENTS

x   CONTENTS

ACKNOWLEDGMENTS

We would like to thank the following people, without whose help this book would not have been possible:

We are grateful to Stan Goman of Tower Records, Sacramento, California, and Joe Medwick of Tower Video, New York City, for giving us full access to their vast store of video titles. We would also like to thank Michael Pollack for giving us similar access to titles at New Video in New York City.

Edd Griles of Ohlmeyer Communications, New York, Len Epand of Polygram Records, New York, and Ken Ross of CBS/Fox Video, New York, offered their professional wisdom in helping us understand the music video phenomenon and contributed their valuable time to the preparation of the Introduction.

The following individuals were instrumental in getting this book into production: Sid Holt, John Pickering of John Pickering Associates, and Jeff McCartney, our editor at McGraw-Hill.

Many distributors offered assistance to us in obtaining video titles. We'd like to thank Amy Alter, CBS/Fox Video; Jane Ayer, MCA Home Video; Hollis Brown, Paramount Home Video; Karen Cardell, Ken Baker Publicity Services; George Dassinger, Elektra Records; Ted Ewing, Blackhawk Films; Michael Finnegan, Warner Home Video; Ana Garrigo, Burson-Marsteller; Vicki Greenleaf, Media Home Entertainment; Jim

Gullo, Walt Disney Home Video; Denis Hedlind, Kultur Video; Danny Kopels, Continental Video; Cathy Mantegna, Vestron Video; Diane McGhee-Terry, Embassy Home Video; Bill Moss, Lippan and Grant; Meg Murphy, Sony Corp. of America; Gary Needle, Vid America; Bruce Ricker, Rhapsody Films; Vicky Rose, Howard Bloom Organization; Robin Schaffer, Unicorn Video; Stephanie Shulman, MGM/UA Home Video; Lynn Singer, International Video Entertainment; Richard Stadin, Mastervision; Andy Tannen, Ruder, Finn and Rotman; and Kimberley Wertz, MGM/UA Home Video.

Pamela Cafritz and Arnold Browne contributed photos to the book. We thank them. Finally, we'd like to gratefully acknowledge the profound debts we owe to our families. Without their support and love, this project would never have been completed.

INTRODUCTION

The Music Video Guide is the most complete and incisive handbook and reference guide to all concert, performance, and soundtrack titles in the following musical categories: rock, pop/adult, country/folk, classical, opera, ballet, black popular, and family entertainment. The reader will discover more than five hundred concise reviews. In addition, there are lavish photos of some of your favorite videos, and handy highlighted sections which spotlight the available video titles of notable recording artists, film stars, and performers. A four-star rating system provides a quick guide to our judgment of the tapes' artistic and entertainment value.

★★★★ = Excellent
★★★ = Good
★★ = Fair
★ = Poor

All in all, every effort has been made to provide an informative and discriminating overview of this rapidly growing entertainment field.

Although we are perfectly aware that divisions between musical styles are arbitrary and never ironclad, we have kept to these categories for the sake of clarity. The Rock

Video chapter includes all tapes which have been conceived and produced for home video and/or television promotion, whether singly or in compilations. The Rock Concert chapter heading is self-explanatory; the Rock Musicals chapter includes those titles which feature rock music prominently on their soundtracks. Movie Musicals, Jazz, and Black Artists are also self-explanatory. The Pop/Adult chapter includes artists whose music appeals to the twenty-five and older age group. Country/Folk features artists whose work draws upon the historical and traditional music primarily of the South and West. Family Entertainment is a grab bag of musical cartoons, children's movies with music, and other titles that can be viewed by the entire family. Finally, Performing Arts includes all titles featuring ballet, classical music, and opera.

It wasn't very long ago that pop music mavericks like David Bowie, Queen, and Todd Rundgren became the objects of skepticism for expending a great deal of time and money producing film and video companion pieces to their song compositions. With the wisdom of hindsight, they are now justly celebrated as the true pioneers of what has evolved into a major entertainment field: music on video. Up until recently, though, one could only enjoy promotional videos on such broadcast outlets as MTV and its various local and national imitators. With the proven success of MTV, many record companies began to license the concert and performance videos they had produced for MTV to prerecorded videocassette distributors, who now sell these video programs in record and video stores nationally and around the world. Added to the catalogues of the emerging home video industry, which already included a few hundred musicals and soundtrack films among its music-related titles, were such packaged-for-home-video million-dollar sellers as *Making Michael Jackson's Thriller, Video Rewind,* and *Do They Know It's Christmas?* These and other best-selling titles established the fact that there was a vast market for music on home video, not only rock music, but classical, opera, ballet, pop/adult, and country and western as well. In some of these musical categories, the potential has not even begun to be tapped. Following the lead of Sony's revolutionary video 45s and LPs, the major distributors have been engaged in a race to acquire, produce, and release short- and long-form music videos to meet the market's increasing demand.

The surprising boom in VCR sales, with industry estimates placing sales volume at almost a million VCR units per month in 1985–1986, has given credence to the predictions of the many industry analysts who have boldly stated that music video titles will garner a 25 percent share of cassette sales by 1988. Whereas for two or three years, major distributors trod carefully in regard to music video titles, fearing that there weren't enough VCRs out there to justify investing in the production and distribution of more music and music-related programs, they are now so sure of the potential market that record company-affiliated ventures like RCA/Columbia Musicvision, Warner Music, and Capitol-EMI are actively selling their programs in record stores as well as the traditional video stores.

In order to get a better idea of the inner workings and aspirations of the music video industry today, we canvassed three of the biggest names in the distribution, production, and creation of music on video. Kenneth Ross, who heads CBS/Fox's Video Music Division, a part of the largest distributorship of prerecorded videocassettes in the world, sees the road ahead for music titles on home video paved with gold. Although CBS/Fox was a relative latecomer to music video, under Mr. Ross' direction, its catalogue of exciting concert, performance, and conceptual titles is growing by leaps and bounds. One of the reasons for this movement is that musical artists who record for CBS Records, a subdivision of the CBS entertainment empire with which CBS/Fox Video is associated, will now be bringing their video productions to Mr. Ross and his staff, who can then exercise their right of first refusal. With the growing awareness of music on video's vast market potential on the part of record companies, CBS/Fox Video is in the enviable position of making great gains through an alliance with CBS Records, the leading purveyor of record albums, audio cassettes, and singles in the nation with over 25 percent of the musical market. Already, Mr. Ross has overseen the acquisition of video programs from such leading CBS artists as Billy Joel, Culture Club, Herbie Hancock, and Willie Nelson, available now to the home video consumer. In addition, CBS/Fox has compiled for home video release collections of short-form rock videos under the umbrella of its *Prime Cuts* series.

In the brief history of the rock video enterprise, Len Epand stands out as the first record company executive to recognize the limitless potential of what until then had been merely promotional films made by record companies for their artists to send overseas, where the films were shown on television shows like our own *American Bandstand* or *Soul Train.* In his work for Polygram Records as their chief of west coast publicity, Epand made the acquaintance of British rock video directors like Jon Roseman and Bruce Gowers and saw firsthand the usefulness of video in promoting many famed English groups. Between 1977 and 1981, he was able to place many of Polygram's artists on influential TV shows such as *Midnight Special* and *Rock Concert* via their innovative music videos. The artists include 10cc, Atlanta Rhythm Section, and Peaches and Herb.

When Epand moved into his current position of vice president and general manager of Polygram Music Video, he started to produce a long list of distinctive videos, both short-form and concert length. The artists with whom he's worked are: Def Leppard, Kool and the Gang, Rush, Rainbow, Donna Summer, John Cougar Mellencamp, Martin Briley, KISS, Pat Travers, Dr. Hook, the Scorpions, Golden Earring, Cameo, The Gap Band, and Stephanie Mills. Quite an impressive roster of musical talent.

Looking toward the future, Epand believes music video can evolve into an art form and will grow in popularity with the development of new video technology, technology that will improve upon the audio and video quality of today's equipment.

Edd Griles, who is among the leading rock video directors working in the field today, has won many awards for his breezy, fun-filled video treatments of songs like Cyndi Lauper's "Girls Just Wanna Have Fun" and Huey Lewis and the News' "If

This Is It." Like many of his colleagues, Griles' background is in advertising—he started out with Doyle Dane Bernbach, one of the top TV-commercial producers in the nation. What he brought to the rock video enterprise was technical facility and a grasp of the texture and content of the music he's been commissioned to work with.

Griles' first video, "I Had a Love," was created in 1980 for a group called Blue Angel. The group went nowhere fast, but its lead singer turned out to be Cyndi Lauper, who remembered Griles and called him to do the video for "Girls Just Wanna Have Fun," the breakthrough hit single off her platinum album, *She's So Unusual.* At this point, with the notoriety he was receiving from his "Girls" video, Griles' career started to zoom. Huey Lewis saw the Cyndi Lauper video and asked Griles to direct his videos from the *Sports* album, another huge seller from 1984. As with many of his projects, Griles acknowledges the creative input that comes from such diverse sources as the artist (or artists), the artist's personal manager, the record company, the executive producer, girlfriends and boyfriends of the artist, the artist's mother, etc. "It had to be talked out among all these different people. Everyone has to have some input but, in the end, only one person can guide the making of a video. That person is the director." Griles has been right almost every time out in his vision of what each song is about. When Cyndi Lauper first read his treatment for the "Time after Time" video, she was so touched that she cried. When Huey Lewis suggested a kind of *Airplane* approach to the "If This Is It" video, Griles was able to incorporate some refreshing silliness into his original concept of a sun, sand, and good times scenario. Recently, he's worked with Peter Wolf and Narada Michael Walden.

As for the future of music video, Griles foresees the strong possibility of advertiser-supported long-form video programs designed and produced specifically for home video. When record companies, video distributors, and advertisers realize that home video will be a reliable source of big income, such cooperative ventures will become commonplace.

If the confidence of the above movers and shakers in the industry is justified, then we are certainly at the threshold of a new medium in entertainment: music on video! We hope that this book can serve as your beacon to those music video titles that will become a treasured part of your leisure enjoyment and aesthetic pleasure.

John Chu
Elliot Cafritz

ROCK VIDEOS

ABC: MANTRAP ★★✦

ROCK. 1983. Artists: ABC (Martin Fry, David Palmer, Stephen Singleton, and Mark White). 60 min. Beta Hifi, VHS Stereo. RCA/Columbia ($29.95)

Rock video wunderkind Julien Temple, best known for his "Undercover of the Night" video for the Rolling Stones, which sparked a small controversy over its excessive violence, directed this hour-long video/film from the British art-rock group, ABC. It's an attempt at integrating the group's Roxy Music-derived sounds with a preposterous narrative about cold war espionage. Martin Fry, the group's lead singer, who consciously apes both David Bowie and Bryan Ferry, is the focal point of a plot to place a Russian agent look-alike in his stead. Shot in London, Paris, and Vienna, the look of this piece is all that really recommends it to viewers—take it as a travelogue of sorts. The music is eminently forgettable: "Mantrap," "Show Me," "Many Happy Returns," "Look of Love," "4 Ever 2 Gether," "All of My Heart," "Poison Arrow," and "Tears Are Not Enough." Except for the exotic locales and poor person's Roxy Music songs, this would come across as a third-rate BBC spy show.

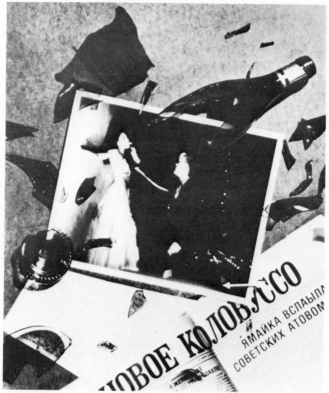

Mantrap, **featuring the British art-rock group ABC.**

ALICE COOPER: WELCOME TO MY NIGHTMARE ★

ROCK. 1975. Artists: Alice Cooper and Vincent Price. 67 min. Beta, VHS. Warner ($29.95)

Originally broadcast over network television, *Welcome to My Nightmare* is Alice Cooper's misguided attempt to provide his fans with a video counterpart to the horrific images invoked by his music. It is basically a string of rock videos shot on a single soundstage with lots of monochromatic effects—entire scenes bathed in blue, red, or white light. Vincent Price is Cooper's only guest, acting as his guide in the role of the Spirit of the Nightmare. Alice's rock and roll ghoulism had long ago worn thin and this additional assault on our sensibilities is certainly unwarranted. An incredibly stultifying one-man show. The songs heard are "Welcome to My Nightmare," "Devils Food," "Some Folks," "Only Women Bleed," "Cold Ethyl," "The Black Widow," "Years Ago," "Department of Youth," "Steven," "The Awakening," "Ballad of Dwight Fry," "Escape," and a reprise of "The Awakening."

THE BEAST OF I.R.S.   ★★♪

ROCK. 1983. Artists: The Go-Go's, R.E.M., Fleshtones, The Alarm, The English Beat, Howard DeVoto, Let's Active, Lords of the New Church, Wall of Voodoo, and The Cramps. 60 min. Beta Hifi, VHS Stereo. I.R.S. Video ($29.95)

I.R.S. Records, which records such hitmakers as The Go-Go's and R.E.M., had the bright idea of packaging many of their hit videos as a best-of compilation. For those who like the I.R.S. retro-rock sound—the sound of New Wave bands playing late

The English Beat, from *The Beast of I.R.S.*

sixties heavy guitar rock (not heavy metal!)—this tape will be quite a treat. The English Beat's "I Confess," Wall of Voodoo's "Mexican Radio," and The Alarm's "The Stand" are good representatives of British New Wave in the early eighties. Back in the U.S.A., The Fleshtones' college-mixer, good-time party music is well exemplified in the psychedelic Tex-Mex sound of "Right Side of a Good Thing." R.E.M., a group from Georgia that is fast becoming a legend in its own time, does "Radio Free Europe." Howard DeVoto offers scenes of rain and clouds in "Rainy Season." "Every Word Means No" by Let's Active, "Dance with Me" by Lords of the New Church, "Garbage Man" by The Cramps, and The Go-Go's' "Head over Heels" complete the program.

Mitch Weissman, Ralph Castelli, Tom Teely, and David Leon, stars of *Beatlemania.*

BEATLEMANIA ★★

ROCK. 1981. Cast: Mitch Weissman, Tom Teely, David Leon, and Ralph Castelli. 95 min. Beta Hifi, VHS Stereo. U.S.A. ($39.95)

Produced for the screen by Edie and Ely Landau, Steve Leber, and David Krebs, *Beatlemania* is the film adaptation of the Broadway multimedia extravaganza that had a long run at the Winter Garden Theater in New York City. The show is basically a tribute to the Beatles' biggest hits in America. As the title suggests, *Beatlemania* is a chronicle of how America in the sixties was reflected in the interaction between the Beatles' music and their fans. Using the legendary Beatles songbook to illustrate the moods of the tumultuous sixties, the viewer is treated to clever montages of such events as Vietnam War protests, the horrible political assassinations of the decade, the civil rights movement, the first landing on the moon, Woodstock, the mod look, and the emergence of a drug culture. Especially affecting is the elegant dissolve from an image of first lady Jackie Kennedy crying tears of grief at her husband's funeral to the ecstatic faces of teenage girls at a Beatles concert. In one image, the filmmakers capture the sorrows and joys of the Beatle generation. The Fab Four came to our shores at just the right time. The Beatles' songs are performed by four talented look-alikes and imitators. Mitch Weissman's portrayal of Paul McCartney, in particular, is right on. The film is divided into seven acts, more or less chronological, and, in each act, The Beatles are portrayed in a different stage of their musical and social development. Songs include: "Twist and Shout," "She Loves You," "I Wanna Hold Your Hand," "All You Need Is Love," "Strawberry Fields Forever," "A Day in the Life," "Get Back," "Helter Skelter," "Please Please Me," "Let It Be," "With a Little Help from My Friends," "Penny Lane," "The Long and Winding Road," and others.

BEST OF BLONDIE ★★

ROCK. 1981. Artists: Blondie. 48 min. Beta, VHS. Pacific Arts ($49.95)

This is a compilation by Chrysalis Records of Blondie's most popular videos, invariably tied to their hit singles. As the thematic thread used to tie all the videos together, we follow a cabbie driving through Manhattan at night. *American Gigolo's* theme song, "Call Me," is the soundtrack for the cabbie's meanderings. "In the Flesh," "X-Offender," and "Denis," three of Blondie's earliest efforts, immediately established Deborah Harry, the lead singer, as a rock sex symbol. In "Denis," she wears a striped, one-piece bathing suit under a man's jacket. Pat Benatar was later to make this particular clothing combination a staple of her early concerts. "Detroit 442," "I'm Always Touched by Your Pres-

Deborah Harry, lead singer of Blondie.

ence, Dear,'' and "Picture This" follow in rapid succession. The latter two were the first real Top 10 hits for Blondie. Then came the deluge. "Hanging on the Telephone" from *Parallel Lines,* "Heart of Glass," "Dreaming," "Union City Blue," and "Atomic" shot in rapid succession to the top of the charts. The final trio of songs are among the best: "The Tide Is High," "Rapture," and "Sunday Girl."

THE BEST OF THE KENNY EVERETT VIDEO SHOW   ★★

ROCK. 1981. Artists: Kenny Everett, Elvis Costello, David Essex, Dave Edmunds, Nick Lowe, Cliff Richard, Thin Lizzy, Darts, The Pretenders, Roxy Music, Rachel Sweet, David Bowie, and the Moody Blues. 104 min. Beta Hifi, VHS Stereo. Thorn-EMI ($59.95)

Long before rock videos were twinkles in the eyes of American recording executives, British television was already exploiting the promotional films that rock groups were making for export to Europe and elsewhere. Kenny Everett, a rather unfunny British TV comedian, utilized the look and attitude of techno-culture to give his weekly show a fast-paced appeal. Many of the leading lights of the British rock scene appeared on his show, usually in surreal sets. In today's context, it all seems a little extreme—especially the dancers in scanty costumes who bump and grind to The Rolling Stones and Nicky Gilder in nightmarishly tacky production numbers. David Mallet, one of the leading rock video directors in the world, was the technical mind behind all of this. If you ignore Everett's poor attempts at humor and concentrate on the array of musical talent presented here, you'll be pleasantly entertained. Elvis Costello ("Oliver's Army"), David Essex ("Imperial Wizard" and "Twenty Flights Up"), Dave Edmunds, Nick Lowe and Rockpile ("Trouble Boys"), Cliff Richard ("Green Light"), Thin Lizzy ("Waiting for an Alibi"), Darts ("Get It While You Can"), Pretenders ("Stop Your Sobbing"), Roxy Music ("Trash"), Rachel Sweet ("I Go to Pieces"), David Bowie ("Boys Keep Swinging"), and Moody Blues ("Nights in White Satin") are all present.

BILL WYMAN   ★★

ROCK. 1983. Artist: Bill Wyman. 11 min. Beta Hifi, VHS Stereo. Sony 45 ($19.95)

This is a collection of videos made by The Stones' bassist of songs that he recorded in his latest attempt at a solo career. The songs are: "Si, si, je suis un rock star," "A New Fashion," and "Come Back Suzanne." The locale for these videos is Wyman's home turf, the French Riviera. The problem with these videos, as with Bill's singing career in general, is that there's no discernible energy, no edge, absolutely no intensity. The crack about Wyman as a Stone was that he barely moved or twitched throughout an entire concert, standing stock still off to one side of the stage. He never took the rock star trip too seriously. We shouldn't take his solo career too seriously either.

If you want to see Wyman in another solo video effort, you may like his performance in *Digital Dreams,* where he appears with the actor James Coburn.

Metalhead, **a collection of three music videos by Blotto.**

BLOTTO ★★◗

ROCK. 1983. Artists: Blotto. 12 min. Beta Hifi, VHS Stereo. Sony ($16.95)

Weird Al Yankovic's recent successful parodies of Michael Jackson, Queen, and Greg Kihn notwithstanding, rock and roll and comedy are a rare combination. In an industry that takes itself oh so seriously, there isn't much room for performers who poke some good-natured fun at the pop music scene. Blotto is a garage band from Long Island, New York, with a decidedly satirical point of view. They are one of the hundreds of regional bands across the country who make a living catering to the particular musical tastes of their locale. In Blotto's case, it's a mixture of heavy metal and good-times beach music. The difference is that their songs are often witty reversals of the clichés of such music. In this compilation of their three music videos, we can see "Metalhead," which explores the suburban boredom that creates the need for heavy metal fantasies, "I Quit," which tells the story of some frustrated office workers, and "I Wanna Be a

Lifeguard," Blotto's anthem, a trenchant but hilarious depiction of what teenagers do during summer vacation as they wander aimlessly through shopping malls and cavort on the beach. What keeps Blotto from national recognition is the sad fact that their collective sense of humor surpasses their collective musicianship.

BRYAN ADAMS: RECKLESS ★★↗

ROCK. 1984. Artist: Bryan Adams. 30 min. Beta Hifi, VHS Stereo. A&M ($19.95)

When the impact of video on rock stardom is debated, the members of Duran Duran are quickly mentioned as the major beneficiaries of the rock video revolution. Add to that list the name of Bryan Adams, an obscure Canadian rocker whose video for "Cuts Like a Knife" managed to ingrain his rugged, blond good looks in the consciousnesses of teen fans everywhere. Otherwise, Adams is a run of the mill pub rocker with something close to a Rod Stewart rasp in his voice. In this long-form video directed by Steve Barron ("Billie Jean"), the mood and imagery of *Footloose* is openly borrowed: young love set against the bleakness and closed-in feeling of a small town. Laszlo Kovacs is the cinematographer. "This Time," "Summer of '69," and "Somebody" establish the story line, involving Adams and his childhood sweetheart, played by Lysette Anthony. Adams leaves the industrial ruins, suburban fences, and dying streams of British Columbia for the spotlight of rock stardom. "Kids Wanna Rock" and "Heaven" include concert footage, taking place some years later. In "Run to You" and "One Night Love Affair" (played over the credits), Adams and his sweetheart are reunited. The concert footage was shot in the Stanley and Orpheum Theaters in Vancouver and the Beverly Theater in Los Angeles.

CANNED HEAT BOOGIE ASSAULT ★★

ROCK. 1983. Artists: Canned Heat. 60 min. Beta Hifi, VHS Stereo. Monterey ($39.95)

Canned Heat was the ultimate boogie band of the late sixties, famous for their performances at both the Monterey and Woodstock rock festivals and noted for the hit singles "Goin' up the Country" and "Let's Work Together." Death and boredom have stripped the group of its original members (leaders Alan Wilson and Bob Hite both died of drug overdoses) and what remains today is Canned Heat in name only. Nevertheless, despite being reduced to the bar circuit in the San Francisco area of late, the band mounted a comeback attempt in 1983 with a double album and this long-form video. The tape is essentially a paean to the Hells Angels motorcycle gang, and those leather-clad ruffians of the road are extremely prominent in these clips. The best and most accessible video is "Hard Rider," which depicts the fantasies of a wholesome teenage girl whose fondest wish is to ride with the Angels. For the most part, these videos are crude and uninteresting, nor are they helped by the pallid music executed by the band. "Gimme That Money," "Stoned Bad Street Fightin' Man," "A Sleepy Hollow Baby," "Hell's on down the Line," "I Need a Hundred Dollars," "Boogie for the Bear," "You Lied," and "Let's Work Together" are performed.

CHRISTINE McVIE: THE VIDEO ALBUM   ★★★

ROCK. 1984. Artist: Christine McVie. 60 min. Beta Hifi, VHS Stereo. Vestron ($29.95)

Fleetwood Mac's emergence from obscurity to fame and fortune during the mid-seventies was predicated on the singing and songwriting of its two female members, Stevie Nicks and Christine McVie. While Stevie has embarked on a successful solo career, Christine's first solo effort didn't appear until late 1983, in the form of her eponymous

Christine McVie.

album. But like Nicks' albums, *Christine McVie* did well on the charts, propelled by the hit single "Got a Hold on Me." In this video companion piece to the album, Christine appears in two videos ("Love Will Show Us How" and "Got a Hold on Me") and is filmed in concert in December of 1983. The concert shows off her throaty, high-register voice and her talent for writing pop melodies with plenty of hooks. Backed by a band that includes Billy Burnette (son of rockabilly great Dorsey Burnette) on rhythm guitar, Christine sings "Why Are We Keeping Secrets?," "Love's a Challenge," "Who's Dreaming This Dream," "I'm the One," "I'm So Excited," "Don't Turn Him Down," "You Make Loving Fun" (with Mick Fleetwood sitting in on drums), "Yesterday's Gone," and "Songbird." Directed by Derek Burbidge.

THE COMPLEAT BEATLES ★★★✦

ROCK. 1982. Artists: The Beatles. 120 min. Beta, VHS. MGM/UA ($69.95)

Delilah Productions, an outfit that specializes in rock music subject matter, counts this docuvideo as their biggest success, both commercially and creatively. A tightly edited 2 hours of Beatle facts, memorabilia, songs, and interviews, *Compleat Beatles* is a must for fans of the Fab Four. The clips range from early black and white film of the quartet playing a gig at The Cavern in Liverpool to the promo films they made for "Strawberry Fields" and "Hey Jude" in the late sixties. George Martin, Marianne Faithfull, Billy Preston, and Beach Boy Bruce Johnston are just some of the interviewees. Of course, we hear a lot from John, Paul, George, and Ringo in various news conferences, rare interviews, and private reels. Our only quibble with this panoramic history of The Beatles is that more of their music could not have been played in its entirety. At times, Malcolm MacDowell, the narrator, seems to have been given too much text to read. Their music was much more eloquent. Some of the songs heard on the soundtrack are: "Hard Day's Night," "Help," "She Loves You," "I Wanna Hold Your Hand," "Please Please Me," "Yesterday," "Eleanor Rigby," "You Can't Do That," "Penny Lane," "All You Need Is Love," and "This Boy." Quite an experience despite its wordiness.

DANSPAK ★

ROCK. 1983. Artists: Man Parrish, Shox Lumania, Richard Bone, and Living. 20 min. Beta Hifi, VHS Stereo. Sony ($19.95)

Danspak features five videos by four New York underground artist-musicians. The most interesting video of the lot is presented by Man Parrish. His "Hip Hop, Be

Joe Tripician and Merrill Aldighieri, producers of *Danspak*.

Bop (Don't Stop)" is a flurry of fast-paced images of people dancing at breakneck speed, all cut to the beat of his techno-funk dance club hit. Richard Bone gives us a video version of his "Alien Girl." "Boat Talk," an irrelevant song about America, is performed by Living, a group of thirteen artists dressed in white robes. Shox Lumania closes the show with "Falling" and "Pointy Headgear."

DANSPAK II   ★↙

ROCK. 1983. Artists: The Jim Carroll Band, The Lenny Kaye Connection, Strange Party, Michael Musto and the Must, Go Ohgami, and Jason Harvey. 30 min. Beta Hifi, VHS Stereo. Sony ($19.95)

Danspak II presents six videos by New York City dance club performers that look as low-budget as they are amateurish. It appears the producers of this tape rented a

Lou Reed and Jim Carroll, featured in _Danspak II._

broadcast-quality video camera from a film rental supply house on Manhattan's Eleventh Avenue and shot off-the-cuff videos as visual ideas popped into the heads of the camera operator and performers. In the only video by a group known outside of New York, The Jim Carroll Band plays Lou Reed's "Sweet Jane." Whaddyaknow? Lou makes a cameo appearance as Jim's band plays a board game with some small children in an apartment on New York's Lower East Side. As the song continues on the soundtrack, Jim and Lou take a walk around the block. This man-on-the-street approach to videomaking might be some budding auteur's stab at cinema verité, but it is also very boring. _Danspak II_ includes a performance by Go Ohgami, a Tokyo pop singer who came to New York to cut an album and make a video. Go dances around the Big Apple's Upper West Side and sings his "Kids in the Street" in a phonetic English that bruises the language. The other videos included in this package are not worth discussing.

DAVID BOWIE ★★★

ROCK. 1984. Artist: David Bowie. 14 min. Beta Hifi, VHS Stereo. Sony ($16.95)

This 14-minute program includes three songs from Bowie's blockbuster 1983 album, *Let's Dance.* "Let's Dance" was shot in Australia—in the outback, in Sydney, and on Shark Island. Bowie appears as a singer in an outback pub, but the real concern of the video is the plight of aborigines, native Australians, in modern society. "China Girl," which was directed by David Mallet, appears in its unexpurgated entirety here (the BBC and U.S. network TV shows censored the final nude love scene on the beach). This video most successfully merges Bowie's lyrics with a series of visual images. About the relationship between the east and the west, most of it was shot in Sydney's Chinatown. "Modern Love," also directed by David Mallet, is straightforward, energetic film footage from a concert Bowie gave in Vancouver, British Columbia, Canada (it has been shown on HBO and is part of "Serious Moonlight," which is also reviewed in this book). It's well done and features the nice guitar work of Bowie's band director, Carlos Alomar. Directed by Jim Yukich. Bowie was one of the first rock artists to work seriously in video, and these clips are the culmination of his half decade of video exploration.

DAZZLEDANCIN' ★

ROCK. 1984. Cast: Rick Dees, Marine Jahan, Tommy Faragher, and Oz Rock and the Streetdance Wizards. 60 min. Beta Hifi, VHS Stereo. U.S.A. ($29.95)

Stumbling over themselves to jump on the bandwagon, the producers of this amateurish program display a mentality left over from the disco age in this sorry excuse for an introduction to breakdancing. Rick Dees, an L.A. disc jockey who seems to pop up in the unlikeliest places these days, Marine Jahan, who garnered fame for doing Jennifer Beals' dance steps in *Flashdance,* and Tommy Faragher, who was on screen for about thirty seconds in *Staying Alive,* are the supposed stars of the show. When you've finished scratching your head, wondering who these jokers are, you'll have to suffer through segments "demonstrating" breakdance steps and rapping. About the only authentic breaking, popping, and locking done here is courtesy of a decidedly bizarre little 8-year-old boy named Oz Rock and his troupe of b-boys, the Streetdance Wizards. Be forewarned that this is the west coast version of what hip-hop culture is all about. For what it's worth, Tommy Faragher sings "Dancing So Close to the Fire" and "Let's

Marine Jahan in *Dazzledancin'*.

Go Dancin'," Marine Jahan dances to "Rags or Flashface," and Rick Dees raps his way through "Break, Don't Stop."

D.O.A.: A RITE OF PASSAGE ★★★

ROCK. 1981. Artists: The Sex Pistols, X-Ray Specs, Rich Kids, Clash, Generation X with Billy Idol, Sham 69, Dead Boys, Augustus Pablo, and David Bowie and Iggy Pop. 90 min. Beta, VHS. Vestron ($39.95)

As good a documentary on British punk music and the reaction to it from both sides of the Atlantic as there is. The grainy look of its blown-up 16mm film stock is perfectly suited to the grimy reality represented by punk rock, here shown in graphic detail. Footage of the Sex Pistols' abortive tour of the U.S. in 1978 is interspliced with candid interviews of aspiring punk rockers in London and some painful moments with a spaced-out Nancy Spungeon and her Sex Pistol boyfriend, the drugged-up Sid Vicious, shot before their sordid deaths, in a Chelsea hotel and a New York City jail cell, respectively. Terry and The Idiots are the aspiring punk rockers whose need to escape the dead end of the British class system gives some perspective to the goings-on. In the age of mass media, rock stardom offers a quick release from the dull pain of everyday life—especially if you're washing dishes in some London pub. What the film also makes perfectly clear is the total lack of talent of such punk bands as the Sex Pistols ("Anarchy in the U.K.," "God Save The Queen," "Pretty Vacant," "Liar," and others), Generation X with a young Billy Idol ("Kiss Me Deadly"), Sham 69 ("Rip Off" and "Borstal Boy"), and the Dead Boys ("I Wanna Be a Dead Boy"). Helpful subtitles make the lyrics intelligible; there's something that's worth listening to here but the music is intentionally awful. Therein lies the dilemma of the punk enterprise—crying out to be taken seriously and yet incredibly self-loathing. The Sex Pistols tour footage shows why they never caught on here. Americans have never felt truly defeated as the British currently do. In addition to the live performances on camera, one can hear David Bowie and Iggy Pop's "Nightclubbing" and "Lust for Life" as well as reggae artist Augustus Pablo's "A.P. Special."

THE DOORS: TRIBUTE TO JIM MORRISON   ★★★

ROCK. 1981. Artists: The Doors. 60 min. Beta, VHS. Warner ($29.95)

In 1980, Danny Sugarman and Jerry Hopkins released a biography of Jim Morrison that ignited a revival of interest in Morrison and his seminal sixties rock group, The Doors. This video relies heavily on that book in painting a portrait of an anguished poet and rock singer whose brief life epitomized his own lyric, "No one here gets out alive." Along with interviews with other Doors, Ray Manzarek, Robby Krieger, and John Densmore, as well as their producer, Paul Rothschild, we get to see lots of footage of Morrison and the band in concert. The point that's put across most forcefully about the enigmatic Morrison is that, as Manzarek claims, he was "the last beatnik," a rock singer by accident who used drugs, booze, and emotional upheaval in an attempt to transcend what he viewed as a mundane reality devoid of spontaneity. It was a heart attack that finally did him in, in Paris, at the age of 27. We see and hear The Doors perform "5 to 1," "Back Door Man," "The End," "Moonlight Drive," "People Are Strange," and "Light My Fire" on *The Ed Sullivan Show,* and "Touch Me" on *The Smothers Brothers Show.* In addition there is never before seen film of The Doors in concert doing "Changeling," "Unknown Soldier," "Celebration of the Lizard," "Crawlin' King-

The Doors: Robby Krieger, John Densmore, Jim Morrison, and Ray Manzarek.

snake," and "When the Music's Over." A strong, entertaining look at a puzzling and charismatic rock pioneer.

DURAN DURAN   ★★

ROCK. 1983. Artists: Duran Duran. 60 min. Beta Hifi, VHS Stereo. Thorn-EMI ($29.95)

The Record Industry Association of America (RIAA) gave the group Duran Duran a gold award for busting up the video charts with what has been called the first video album. Comprised of eleven songs taken from their audio albums *Duran Duran* and *Rio,* the video *Duran Duran* sold over a million copies in 1983! "The band made in videoland" readily admits success in America has been due to its national exposure

Duran Duran.

on MTV. The group has a knack for hiring directors who have the ability to tape striking yet fleeting images that captivate one's attention and soon disappear from memory. Naked women, boys in makeup, and exotic locations, the stuff of fashion magazines, are presented as illustrations for the catchy dance rhythms and silly lyrics of their hit songs. The hour-long tape includes the hit title song from the band's second album, *Rio,* along with "Planet Earth," "Lonely in Your Nightmare," "Careless Memories," "My Own Way," "Hungry Like the Wolf," "Night Boat," "Girls on Film," "Save a Prayer," "The Chauffeur," and "Is There Something I Should Know?"

DURAN DURAN (ed.)   ★★✦

ROCK. 1983. Artists: Duran Duran. 10 min. Beta Hifi, VHS Stereo. Sony ($16.95)

This pair of rock videos, "Hungry Like the Wolf" and "Girls on Film," proved to be the most popular on the band's historic million-seller video album, *Duran Duran* (available in its entirety on Thorn-EMI). Part fashion show, part androgynous fantasy, "Girls on Film," shown in its original unexpurgated version, perfectly matches the cryptic lyrics and driving beat of the hifi audio track. The highlight of the video "Hungry Like a Wolf" shows one of the members of the band running through lush tropical jungle in pursuit of an exotic, dark, mysterious love priestess. This one was very big on MTV when released.

DURAN DURAN: DANCING ON THE VALENTINE   ★★★

ROCK. 1984. Artists: Duran Duran (Roger Taylor, Nick Rhodes, Andy Taylor, Simon le Bon, and John Taylor). 15 min. Beta Hifi, VHS Stereo. Sony ($16.95)

Birmingham's own Duran Duran can add yet another title to their burgeoning list of videos. *Duran Duran: Dancing on the Valentine* is a compilation of three video clips, the first of which is a concert piece called "The Reflex." Directed by Russell Mulcahy, this well-shot clip puts the band on an enormous stage in front of a large and very enthusiastic audience. Behind them, surrounding the stage, are Doric columns of tremendous size. As Duran Duran performs its tune, an animated waterfall gushes out over the audience. Very exciting. One of the best concert clips around. In "Union of the Snake," directed by Simon Milne, the band appears in a desert setting populated by lizard people. From there, they take an elevator down into a subterranean world that holds a high-tech underground city. A sort of *Road Warrior* crossed with *The Mole People,* the classic *bad* science fiction film. Completely ridiculous. In Brian Grant's "New Moon on Monday," the members of Duran Duran star as underground freedom fighters in a totalitarian fascist state. After passing out forbidden leaflets, they lead the city's population to freedom.

DYNAMITE CHICKEN   ★

ROCK. 1969. Cast: Richard Pryor, Lenny Bruce, Ace Trucking Company, Joan Baez, Sha Na Na, Paul Krassner, Jimi Hendrix, John Lennon, Yoko Ono, Michael O'Donoghue, Fred Willard, B. B. King, Nina Simone, Andy Warhol, Al Goldstein, Al Kooper, and Malcolm X. 75 min. Beta, VHS. Monterey ($39.95)

Dynamite Chicken is an aimless trip across a patchwork of comedy skits (including a very young Richard Pryor doing his urban shtick). Add to this some bits of music, a couple of shots of semicelebrities mouthing off about social concerns that were important in the late sixties, and a couple of self-appointed radicals lecturing about the coming revolution. John Lennon can be seen on the screen for less than a minute. If one concentrates, one can hear music on the soundtrack. Jimi Hendrix plays "Foxy Lady." Cat Mother and the All-night Newsboys, a group Hendrix produced, plays "Track in A." Eric Dolphy, the jazz alto sax player, blows a tune called "Ironman." Al Kooper sings his "Magic in My Sox." The Velvet Underground plays Lou Reed's electric "White Light/White Heat."

EARLY ELVIS ★★★

ROCK. 1956. Artist: Elvis Presley. 56 min. Beta, VHS. Video Yesterday ($39.95)

This is a black and white compilation tape of kinescopes from fifties television shows that featured musical appearances by the young Elvis. First up is an episode of *Stage Show with the Dorsey Brothers* from the 1955–1956 TV season. The June Taylor Dancers open the show with a production number that dissolves into the Dorsey Brothers introducing a then-unknown Elvis. He sings "Money Honey" and "Heartbreak Hotel." Elvis appears on a *Steve Allen Show* episode, also from 1956, in top hat and tails (to counter detractors who criticized him for being a "savage"). He sings "I Want You, I Need You, I Love You" and "Hound Dog." Elvis also participates in a country and western skit entitled "Range Round-up." Finally, Elvis appears in a selection of clips from his three *Ed Sullivan Show* appearances during the 1956–1957 season. He does some excellent versions of his big hits of the time, including "Don't Be Cruel," "Love Me Tender," "Ready Teddy," "Hound Dog," "Love Me," and "Too Much."

EAT TO THE BEAT ★★♪

ROCK. 1979. Artists: Blondie. 42 min. Beta Hifi, VHS Stereo. Warner ($29.95)

This was one of the first video albums, released to coincide with Blondie's record album of the same name for Chrysalis Records. *Eat to the Beat* was a follow-up to their smash hit album, *Parallel Lines,* which established them as consistent hitmakers. Although, at the time, this was an audacious undertaking for any rock group, *Eat to the Beat* generally failed to come up to the standard of success reached by their previous album, both critically and financially. "Eat to the Beat" leads off the video album, featuring Deborah Harry performing before an enthusiastic studio crowd perched on building scaffolding—highly reminiscent of sixties TV dance shows like *Shindig* and *Hullabaloo.* This backdrop is also seen in "Living in the Real World" and "Dreaming." "The Hardest Part" shows off Deborah in a black wig and tattered black dress. She plays a street-tough chanteuse who likely will whip her fans into a frenzy. "Union

Deborah Harry of Blondie in *Eat to the Beat*.

City Blue," which was intended to be the theme song for Harry's film debut, *Union City,* but was never used, has the group performing the song on a pier on the New Jersey side of the Hudson River facing Manhattan. Other songs are: "Slow Motion," "Shayla," "Die Young Stay Pretty" (one of the first American reggae-influenced pop hits), "Accidents Never Happen," "Atomic," "Sound-A-Sleep," and "Victor."

ELEPHANT PARTS ★★★

ROCK. 1981. Cast: Michael Nesmith, William Dear, and William Martin. 60 min. Beta, VHS. Pacific Arts. ($39.95)

This won a Grammy Award for best video album. In fact, it was the first video of any sort to be awarded a Grammy. On a second viewing this melange of music and satire masterminded by ex-Monkee Mike Nesmith has more historical than true entertainment value. While much of *Elephant Parts* is quite funny (credit for this goes to the comic inventiveness of William Martin, the head writer and costar), the consistently low-budget quality of the acting, props, and conceptualization ultimately does it in. Indeed, compared to the minioperettas pulled off by Queen and David Bowie in Britain even before this project was thought up, *Elephant Parts* is a poor relation. Still, there is a lot to laugh at and marvel at here. Nesmith's video clips include his look at L.A. street people, "Lucy and Romona," and "Magic," "Cruisin'," "Light," "Tonight," and "Rio," this last a slapstick glance at California high times. The comedy skits include a game show where contestants guess the names of drugs ("I can name that drug in three tokes"), Elvis Drugs (Blue Suede Ludes, Love Me Tenderizers, and All Shook Uppers), a rock and roll hospital, and a talk show featuring a "battered" wife (as in cake batter). Rates three stars because Mike Nesmith was a Monkee, it's funnier than 99 percent of all other music video productions, and Nesmith's mother was the woman who invented Liquid Paper, without which modern society would be unthinkable.

ELTON JOHN: VISIONS ★↙

ROCK. 1982. Artist: Elton John. 45 min. Beta Hifi, VHS Stereo. Embassy ($29.95)

With the help of director Russell Mulcahy, another in the long line of pioneering British rock video auteurs, Elton John filled a temporary lull in his musical fortunes

Visions, featuring singer/songwriter Elton John.

with this long-form video effort. Supposedly, the videos are based on autobiographical material ("Elton's Song" caused a small controversy when it was first offered to MTV, BBC, etc.) but it doesn't engage the viewer in any important respect at all. In fact, much of this is quite inaccessible, perhaps filled with inside jokes and private allusions. Among the weirder videos are: "Heart in the Right Place" (wherein Elton vents his anger at gossipmongers), "Just Like Belgium" (which has Elton playing piano in a gay bar), "Fanfare" (featuring dancers made up to look like geishas), "The Fox" (in which Elton is a tramp invited into a farm woman's house for a gluttonous meal), and "Elton's Song" (a young boy at a British boarding school has a crush on an older upperclassman). Other songs are "Breaking Down Barriers," "Nobody Wins," "Fascist Faces," "Carla Etude," "Chloe," and "The Hunter and the Haunted."

ELTON JOHN: VISIONS (ed.)   ★★↲

ROCK. 1982. Artist: Elton John. 14 min. Beta Hifi, VHS Stereo. Sony ($16.95)

The best three songs from the complete *Visions,* distributed by Embassy Home Entertainment. While the complete video is too diffuse and esoteric to be enjoyed by most viewers, the Sony version manages to keep things down to an acceptable time span. "Breaking Down Barriers," "Elton's Song," and "Just Like Belgium" not coincidentally received the most airplay of the videos in the *Visions* package. Shot in the famous Shepperton Studios in London by director Russell Mulcahy.

EURYTHMICS: SWEET DREAMS   ★★★↲

ROCK. 1983. Artists: Eurythmics (Annie Lennox and Dave Stewart). 60 min. Beta Hifi, VHS Stereo. RCA/Columbia ($29.95)

Lennox and Stewart, an improbable-looking pop music duo, had one of the loudest debuts in recent memory with their megahit album, *Sweet Dreams,* in 1982. While, in truth, the pair had drifted in and out of numerous rock alliances for almost a decade in their native Scotland, *Sweet Dreams* seemed the arrival of a full-blown concept— the sound of synthesizer-assembled pop music framed in an androgynous context. Annie Lennox's R&B voice and mannish look took British New Wave and hung a mysterious but highly sophisticated image on it. Multi-instrumentalist and composer Dave Stewart's silent, equally androgynous looks completed a chic, catchy image. And the music itself was glorious; full of lush melodies and tonal nuance, it spotlighted

Dave Stewart and Annie Lennox—the Eurythmics.

Lennox's back to basics vocals. In this video album, Derek Burbidge, a rock video pioneer, mixes live performances at a London club called Heaven with video clips and some intriguing stop-action animation. At the club, Eurythmics perform a lively set including "This Is the House," "Never Gonna Cry Again," "Take Me to Your Heart," "I've Got an Angel," "Satellite of Love," "Jennifer," "Sweet Dreams," "I Could Give You a Mirror," "Somebody Told Me," "Wrap It Up," and "Tous les Garçons et les Filles." The clever and stylish videos include "Love Is a Stranger," "Who's That Girl," "This City Never Sleeps," and "Sweet Dreams."

THE EVERLY BROTHERS' ROCK AND ROLL ODYSSEY ★★★

ROCK. 1984. Artists: The Everly Brothers. 73 min. Beta, VHS. MGM/UA ($59.95)

The maker of *The Compleat Beatles* and *Girl Groups,* Delilah Films, seems to have cornered the market on rockumentaries—documentary films about rock and roll subjects. Commemorating the reunion of the Everly Brothers after a decade of bitter separation,

The Everly Brothers.

this video program takes a good stab at tracing the musical roots, careers, and personal conflicts of Phil and Don Everly, the sons of a white blues musician who moved the family from Kentucky to Chicago to pursue better career prospects. Performing from a very young age, the brothers soon caught the attention of Chet Atkins, who arranged their signing to a recording contract. Singing the songs of Felice and Boudleaux Bryant ("Bye Bye Love," "Wake Up Little Susie," "Bird Dog," "Problems," "All I Have to Do Is Dream," and "Poor Jenny"), they rapidly became million-selling recording artists. Moreover, their close harmony vocals influenced later artists like The Beatles, The Beach Boys, and dozens of folk revival acts. As the hits got fewer and farther between in the late sixties, the first signs of tension emerged. In 1973, in the middle of a concert at Knotts Berry Farm, Phil put an end to their partnership by smashing his guitar on the floor of the stage and walking off. The documentary ends with Don and Phil, at their reunion concert in London's Royal Albert Hall, singing "Let It Be Me." Celebrities interviewed include Linda Ronstadt, Chet Atkins, Tom Petty, Andrew Lloyd Webber, Brian Setzer, and Charlotte Rampling.

FLEETWOOD MAC   ★★★

ROCK. 1980. Artists: Fleetwood Mac (Mick Fleetwood, John McVie, Christine McVie, Stevie Nicks, and Lindsey Buckingham). 60 min. Beta, VHS. Warner ($29.95)

In 1980, Fleetwood Mac was riding high atop the pop music world, shipping platinum once again with their new album, *Tusk,* a rather adventurous concept LP for a group known for nothing more complex than Christine McVie's boogie-band love songs, Stevie Nicks' spaced-out arias about witches and woodland spirits, and Buckingham's teen heartbreak ballads. This documentary attempts to fill us in on the making of the album, the attendant concert tour, and the state of the band in general. For its behind-the-scenes peeks at Christine and Stevie's creative moments, Mick's aggressive management of the group, and Lindsey's production zeal in the studio, *Fleetwood Mac* manages to distinguish itself from the run of the mill puff piece. Very clearly, we come to understand that the group is first and foremost a business enterprise—*Tusk's* artistic failure attests to the group's lack of a unified vision. Since Nicks and Buckingham came aboard, Mac has been a singles band, masters of the pop hook. Mick Fleetwood's candid comments on the band's rather diffuse output and the picture we get of John McVie, the bassist and a founding member with Fleetwood of the original band, a legendary electric blues outfit responsible for classics like "Black Magic Woman," left with nothing to do in the studio, say it all. The group performs "Sisters of the Moon," "Walk a Thin Line," "Go Your Own Way," "Tusk," "Angel," "Never Make Me Cry," "Think about Me," "Not That Funny," "Sara," "The Chain," and "Songbird," at places like St. Louis' Checkerdome.

A FLOCK OF SEAGULLS   ★★

ROCK. 1983. Artists: A Flock of Seagulls. 13 min. Beta Hifi, VHS Stereo. Sony ($16.95)

The British have always been more susceptible to the blandishments of Continental fashion than they'll admit, their long-standing enmity with the French and Germans notwithstanding. Thus, one can explain the movement in English pop music known as the New Romanticism. It is the marriage of a fashion mentality with rock star images. Adam and the Ants were too musically extreme with their amateurish use of African rhythms, but Duran Duran and Wham have since brought home the bacon with their manicured looks and sound. Earlier, A Flock of Seagulls had garnered some small successes with the formula of foppish couture and synthesizer pop music. Their best known song, "Wishing" ("If I Had a Photograph of You"), was a Top 10 hit in the U.S. Appropriately enough for a group that relies heavily on image, Flock's videos

FLEETWOOD MAC

Stevie Nicks was born May 26, 1948, in Phoenix, Arizona. Lindsey Buckingham was born October 3, 1947, in Palo Alto, California. Christine McVie was born July 12, 1943, in Birmingham, U.K. Mick Fleetwood was born June 24, 1942, in London, U.K. John McVie was born November 26, 1945, in London, U.K.

After an earlier incarnation as one of Britain's hardest-rocking blues bands in the late sixties, the new Fleetwood Mac didn't emerge until it moved to Los Angeles in 1974. Several personnel changes later, with Buckingham and Nicks aboard to lead them in a pop-rock direction, they produced an album, *Rumours,* which was, in 1977, the biggest-selling LP of all time with over ten million copies sold. Nicks' songs like "Rhiannon," "Dreams," and "Sara" propelled Fleetwood Mac into the upper echelon of music stardom.

In addition to Christine McVie's hook-filled love ballads, it was Stevie's gypsy rhetoric and gossamer clothing that etched Mac's image in the mind of the record buyer. Both Christine McVie and Stevie Nicks have had very successful solo careers as well. Lindsey Buckingham's solo efforts have not fared well by comparison.

Though they are currently inactive, we can look forward to another album from this supergroup soon. Reaction to their concept album of 1979, *Tusk,* was not good critically and has caused Mac to record at a snail's pace ever since.

Video Resume

Christine McVie, (1984), Vestron.

Fleetwood Mac, (1980), Warner.

Fleetwood Mac in Concert, (1983), RCA/Columbia.

Stevie Nicks in Concert, (1982), CBS/Fox.

are carefully produced, cinematically derivative objects. For "Wishing," the group is placed on board a spaceship amidst futuristic props. "Nightmares" focuses on a Hitch-cockian treatment of a little girl's bad dream. "I Ran (So Far Away)" has the group performing in a manner very reminiscent of German expressionist films.

THE GIRL GROUPS: THE STORY OF A SOUND ★★★

ROCK. 1983. Artists: The Angels, Darlene Love, The Dixie Cups, The Exciters, Martha and the Vandellas, Mary Wells, The Shangri-Las, Ronnie Spector, The Ronettes, and the Supremes. 65 min. Beta, VHS. MGM/UA ($59.95)

The documentary *The Girl Groups: The Story of a Sound* traces the history of the phenomenon of "girl groups," all-female popular singing groups that swept the American charts

The Supremes, one of the acts featured in
The Girl Groups.

in the early sixties. Interviewing many of the most successful singers, songwriters, and producers of the day and inserting old kinescopes of television dance shows of the period, the film not only faithfully depicts the creation of the girl group sound, but also the time in which it became the national rage.

The film starts in the early days of the sound in New York, interviewing Jerry Lieber, Mike Stoller, and Ellie Greenwich, and spotlighting such hits as "My Boyfriend's Back" by The Angels, "Maybe" by The Chantels, "Mashed Potato" by Dee Dee Sharp, "Loco-Motion" by Little Eva, "Chapel of Love" by The Dixie Cups, and "Tell Him" by The Exciters. Continuing with Motown Records' entry into the girl group field, the documentary features the songs "Dancing in the Streets" by Martha and the Vandellas, "My Guy" by Mary Wells, and "Please, Mr. Postman" by the Marvellettes.

Girl Groups covers the contributions of sometime eccentric record producer Phil Spector by interviewing his ex-wife, Ronnie, and leading star, singer Darlene Love, before launching into the story of the most successful female vocal group of all time, the Supremes. This section of the film includes the Holland-Dozier-Holland monster hits that Diana Ross and the Supremes made famous: "Baby Love," "Come See about Me," and "Stop! In the Name of Love."

HALL AND OATES VIDEO COLLECTION ★★★

ROCK. 1984. Artists: Hall and Oates. 30 min. Beta Hifi, VHS Stereo. RCA/Columbia ($19.95)

This is a compilation of their videos made originally for MTV and other rock video programs, now packaged for the home video collector. The videos directed by Mick Haggerty and C. D. Taylor, "Say It Isn't So," "Family Man," "Maneater," and "One on One," are all well-shot, highly narrative clips, sticking pretty closely to the lyrical content of each song. Unfortunately, Hall and Oats sought something a bit more "profound" in their next few videos. Jay Dubin's videos, "Private Eyes" and "I Can't Go for That" ("No Can Do"), reach for clichés from cinema history, like the Bogie fedoras and trenchcoats used in the former clip. But Tim Pope (that eccentric Brit) places Hall and Oates in an embarrassing tour de farce in "Adult Education." A conceptual video, as they say in the business, which defies easy explanation and limits the duo to standing around, mouthing the words to the song, and modeling apparel straight out of *Road Warrior.* They ought to revoke Mr. Pope's artistic license.

Hall and Oates.

HEARTBEAT CITY: THE CARS   ★★↓

ROCK. 1984. Artists: The Cars (Ric Ocasek, Benjamin Orr, Greg Hawkes, Elliot Easton, and David Robinson). 48 min. Beta Hifi, VHS Stereo. Warner ($29.95)

Like New York's Blondie, Akron's Devo, and San Francisco's The Tubes, Boston's The Cars emerged in the late seventies with a punk rock sound owing more to legendary sixties punkers like Lou Reed, Iggy Pop, and Bryan Ferry than seventies avatars such as Johnny Rotten. True to their arty origins, The Cars approached Andy Warhol with the idea of directing a rock video for their new single, "Hello Again." True to *his* principles, Andy gave them their requisite 15 minutes of fame and ordered his assistant, Don Munroe, to concoct an appropriately bizarre clip for the group. "Hello Again" features a parade of New York underground types, including Dianne Brill, a woman

The Cars in *Heartbeat City*.

with an enormous bust wearing a T-shirt that reads "Hello," and a transvestite with a rather friendly boa constrictor. Other videos presented include "Magic," "Drive," "Panorama," "Heartbeat City," "Shake It Up," "Why Can't I Have You?," and the very popular "You Might Think," easily the most embarrassing if not repellent video ever made by a major rock group—Ric Ocasek's head on the animated body of a fly as he buzzes around a pretty model! Quick! Someone throw a boulder at it!

HOT ROCK VIDEOS, VOLUME I ★★★

ROCK. 1984. Artists: Eurythmics, The Kinks, Alan Parsons Project, Jefferson Starship, Rick Springfield, Lou Reed, and Icicle Works. 28 min. Beta Hifi, VHS Stereo. RCA/ Columbia ($19.95)

A compilation of some of your favorite rock videos from seven artists ranging from Rick Springfield to Eurythmics. If anything, the selection here might be too eclectic; it's debatable whether Mr. Springfield and, say, Lou Reed have any fans in common. That reservation aside, this collection is okay. The highlights are: "Sweet Dreams (Are Made of This)" by Eurythmics; The Kinks' "Come Dancing," a video by Julien Temple which borrows a good idea from Italian director Ettore Scola (see *Le Bal*); "No Way Out" by Jefferson Starship, in which Mickey Thomas discovers all sorts of weird sights in a strange mansion; and Lou Reed's "I Love You Suzanne," which follows the plight of the crestfallen Reed when he realizes that his girlfriend "does what she gotta do," which doesn't include him.

Further editions of the *Hot Rocks* series are not as electric as this one. Apparently, consumer tastes in the rock video field are becoming clearer to video producers.

IRON MAIDEN: VIDEO PIECES ★★♪

ROCK. 1984. Artists: Iron Maiden. 17 min. Beta Hifi, VHS Stereo. Sony 45 ($16.95)

Jim Yukich and David Mallet, two of the most talented and prolific gentlemen directing rock videos today, directed the four videos by Iron Maiden, a British heavy metal band, included in this Sony Video 45. "Run to the Hills," directed by Mallet, is a song about the plight of the vanquished native Americans whose nations were decimated by the invading Europeans. Using silent film footage from old cowboys and Indians flicks to illustrate the story line, the video comes off as unintentionally funny. "The Number of the Beast" features the band in performance, standing onstage beneath a skull very much like Black Sabbath's skull logo except for the addition of devil's horns. "The Flight of Icarus" borrows imagery from Ingmar Bergman, depicting Death as a cloaked figure lurking about. Finally, "The Trooper" is a video, again from Mallet, which intercuts clips from the film *The Charge of the Light Brigade* with the group's performance of "The Trooper."

JAZZIN' FOR BLUE JEAN ★★★♪

ROCK. 1984. Artist: David Bowie. 20 min. Beta Hifi, VHS Stereo. Sony ($19.95)

In *Jazzin' for Blue Jean,* David Bowie takes the long-form music video, the most famous example of which is Michael Jackson's 14-minute tape, *Thriller,* to a level of perfection that makes this "minimovie" more than just a promotional tool. A complete work in itself, the video tells an old story with a new twist. Boy finds girl. Boy loses girl to aging rock star. David plays both Vic, the smooth-talking sign painter who is playing for the affections of the unnamed girl, and Screamin' Lord Byron, a worn out, decadent rock performer who sings "Blue Jean" while wearing makeup that is reminiscent of that worn by ballet dancer Vaslav Nijinsky in the 1913 production of Stravinsky's *L'Après-midi d'un Faune.* The video's soundtrack also contains two other songs from Bowie's *Tonight* album, "Don't Look Down" and "Warszawa." Perhaps other musical

Jazzin' for Blue Jean, **featuring David Bowie.**

performers will follow Michael and David's lead and create longer videos with more story content.

JEFFERSON STARSHIP   ★★

ROCK. 1983. Artists: Jefferson Starship (Craig Chaquico, David Freiberg, Pete Sears, Danny Baldwin, Paul Kantner, Mickey Thomas, and Grace Slick). 60 min. Beta Hifi, VHS Stereo. RCA/Columbia ($29.95)

Looking like a heavy metal band that's a little long in the tooth, Jefferson Starship stars in a video program which is ultimately quite embarrassing for Starship veterans Slick and Kantner. Wrapping segments featuring a space-age disc jockey, Shortwave Mike (Mike MacDonald), around footage of a concert at the Queen Elizabeth Theater

Jefferson Starship.

in Vancouver, Canada, the producers came up with an hour of tape that is only fitfully entertaining. While one can hear such songs as "Winds of Change," "Stranger," "Find Your Way Back," and "Jane" performed, it's sad to watch Grace and Paul with really very little to do on stage. Starship is now basically Mickey Thomas and Craig Chaquico's band, spotlighting keening vocals and heavy metal guitar flashes. The young audience at the concert probably doesn't know the Airplane numbers the group also does: "Ride the Tiger," "Somebody to Love," and "White Rabbit." Directed by Stanley Dorfman.

J. GEILS BAND   ★★

ROCK. 1983. Artists: J. Geils Band (J. Geils, Peter Wolf, Magic Dick, Seth Justman, Danny Klein, and Stephen Jo Bladd). 12 min. Beta Hifi, VHS Stereo. Sony ($16.95)

The J. Geils Band is a continuing throwback to the generation-old electric blues concept that went out with the sixties. (Even lead singer Peter Wolf, with his exaggerated swagger and hoarse voice, has always been a pallid imitation of Mick Jagger.) They've struggled to get a sound that would be commercially successful. With the album *Freeze-*

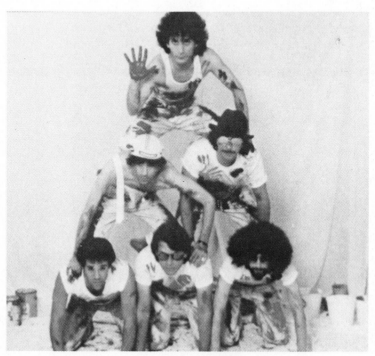

The J. Geils Band.

Frame, they added more synthesizer from Seth Justman and broke through with the hits "Centerfold," and "Angel in Blue." This video contains clips for four songs in all, directed by Paul Justman. "Centerfold" takes place in a high school classroom where a bevy of scantily clad beauties parade around in negligees, sweaters, and pompoms. "Angel in Blue" is a montage about a girl with an identity problem. "Love Stinks" pokes fun at the song's lyrics as everyone appears wearing a gas mask. Finally, "Freeze-Frame" presents another montage intercut with the group having fun with cans of paint.

JIMI HENDRIX   ★★★★

ROCK. 1973. Cast: Jimi Hendrix, Al Hendrix, Pete Townshend, Little Richard, Mick Jagger, Lou Reed, Eric Clapton, Buddy Miles, Mitch Mitchell, Billy Cox, Alan Douglas, Dick Cavett, and Germaine Greer. 103 min. Beta, VHS. Warner ($39.95)

Of all the Hendrix videotapes available, *Jimi Hendrix* is the best. Using a variety of interviews with Jimi's army buddies and friends and with famous rock musicians along

Jimi Hendrix performing in San Francisco's Golden Gate Park.

JIMI HENDRIX

Jimi Hendrix was born November 27, 1942, in Seattle, Washington; he died September 18, 1970, in London, England. The most important electric guitarist since jazz master Charlie Christian, Hendrix played backup guitar behind Little Richard, Ike and Tina Turner, Sam Cooke, Jackie Wilson, The Isley Brothers, Curtis Knight, and James Brown on the "chitlin' circuit" after being discharged from the Army in 1961.

In 1965, under the pseudonym of Jimmy James, he played with his band The Blue Flames at the Cafe Wha? in Greenwich Village in New York. There he was discovered by Chas Chandler of the Animals, who convinced Jimi to travel to London to form the Jimi Hendrix Experience in 1966 with Noel Redding on bass and Mitch Mitchell on drums. Their British hit (Number 6 on the U.K. charts) "Hey Joe" was turned into one of the first rock promo films, starring Jimi, Noel, and Mitch as psychedelic cowboy-outlaws. Soon they released their milestone *Are You Experienced?* album and Jimi was on his way back to the U.S.A. to wow an American audience at the Monterey Pop Festival in 1967 in a performance that has been recorded for all time in D. A. Pennebaker's film *Monterey Pop.*

Jimi piled success on top of success, toured constantly, opened his own Electric Lady recording studios in New York City, and released six albums over a 3-year period, including *Axis: Bold as Love* and *Electric Ladyland.* Jimi was recorded in performance in a number of films, including *Rainbow Bridge, Woodstock,* and the posthumous *Jimi Hendrix.*

The pressures of touring, recording schedules, and battles with his management resulted in his death in London, two months before his twenty-eighth birthday.

Video Resume

Dynamite Chicken, (1969), Monterey.

Jimi Hendrix, (1973), Warner.

Jimi Hendrix Videogram, (1983), Videogram International.

Jimi Plays Berkeley, (1971), Vestron.

Rainbow Bridge, (1971), Independent United Distributors.

Woodstock II, (1970), Warner.

with a fine collection of concert footage, the film clearly paints a portrait of the shy, generous man from Seattle who was a twentieth-century American genius. Using a guitar and a rudimentary recording studio, he was able to create sounds and use them in a way that is far beyond the capabilities of even the most talented musicians and most sophisticated machinery today. The film traces his life from his childhood to his first successes as a pop idol, his stardom, his battles with his business managers, and his untimely death. In addition to the well-known performances of "Rock Me Baby," "Wild Thing," "Hey Joe," and "Like a Rolling Stone," recorded during the first American appearance of the Jimi Hendrix Experience at the Monterey Pop Festival in June of 1967, *Jimi Hendrix* includes rare footage of Jimi playing "Purple Haze" at London's Marquee Club in 1967, and Band of Gypsies performing "Machine Gun" at the Fillmore East on New Year's Eve, 1969. Jimi's only acoustic recording, "Hear My Train A'Coming," is featured in the film. Additional footage includes "The Star-Spangled Banner" from Woodstock, 1969, and "Red House" and "In from the Storm" from the Isle of Wight Concert, 1970. Highly recommended.

JIMI HENDRIX VIDEOGRAM   ★★

ROCK. 1983. Artist: Jimi Hendrix. 38 min. Beta Hifi, VHS Stereo. Vestron ($59.95)

This tape, which has been shown on various rock video networks, is a video homage by several video artists to the music of Jimi Hendrix. All of the music is Jimi's; the images are not. Keep that in mind. Dara Birnbaum's video interpretation of "Fire" centers around the ritual behavior of teenagers in the suburbs, hanging around fast-food restaurant parking lots. "Little Wing" by W.T.V. is given an abstract reading in *chroma-key* (a video technique for super-imposing images on other images using a key color), video-processed images. "Wild Thing" by Kit Fitzgerald and John Sanborn seems to mount a tale about gender confusion and androgyny onto Jimi's incredible rendition of The Troggs' cult hit. "Hey Joe" by Dan Reeves, "Hear My Train" by Shalom Gorewitz, and Gorewitz's "Star-Spangled Banner" all try to make social and political statements through montages of urban decay and blight. "Voodoo Chile" by Stephen Beck and "Bleeding Heart" by Woody Wilson complete the videogram.

THE JOHN LENNON INTERVIEW   ★★

ROCK. 1975 and 1980. 60 min. Beta, VHS. Karl Video ($39.95)

In 1975, John Lennon appeared on Tom Synder's late-night interview show, *Tomorrow*, on the NBC network. In its time, this was quite a coup for Snyder and NBC because

John rarely appeared on television, much less sat still for a protracted discussion. Although Snyder tries to explore Lennon's Beatle past with him, John offers little cooperation, claiming that he is no longer interested in that period of his life. The rest of the interview is a hodgepodge of topics: contemporary rock music, drugs and groupies, John's marijuana bust in England and his subsequent immigration problems in America. At the time, he was trying to obtain resident alien status from the U.S. government. John's radical alliances made it difficult for him to gain the favor of several government agencies. Wrapped around this interview is an introduction and commentary taped a few days after John's death. Lisa Robinson, a rock journalist, provides her insight into John's last days, drawing upon her exclusive interview with John done only a week or two before his death. Recommended only for those Lennon fans out there who have to see everything John appeared in.

KAJAGOOGOO ★★

ROCK. 1983. Artists: Kajagoogoo. 11 min. Beta Hifi, VHS Stereo. Sony ($16.95)

Another British band with wild looks and synthesizer-based music, Kajagoogoo had a hit single in the U.S. with "Too Shy." Nothing much has been heard from them since, due in large part to the defection of their androgynous lead singer from the band. In these three videos directed by Simon Milne, "Too Shy," "Ooh to Be Ahh," and "Hang On Now," the group shows itself to be capable of making some archly humorous statements in their music, aided enormously by their bizarre clothing and appearance. They came before Boy George and Culture Club, exploring much the same territory, but faded quickly away.

KIDS ARE ALRIGHT   ★★★

ROCK. 1979. Artists: The Who (Pete Townshend, Roger Daltrey, John Entwhistle, and Keith Moon). 96 min. Beta, VHS. Thorn-EMI ($29.95)

This is a fascinating and very thorough compendium of clips of The Who, covering the entire span of their career. From the opening clip of The Who on *The Smothers Brothers Show*, doing "My Generation" and "I Can't Explain" before totaling Tommy Smothers' acoustic guitar, to their *Shindig* appearance, their concerts at Monterey and Woodstock, their BBC-TV interviews, promo shorts, and, finally, a seventies concert version of "I Won't Get Fooled Again," the film holds countless moments of sheer joy for the true Who fan. Besides destroying a BBC-TV interview show hosted by Russell Harty with their bizarre antics and sarcasm, Pete Townshend and Keith Moon smash what seems like a hundred guitars and drum kits along the way. Other songs heard are: "Baba O'Riley," "Shout and Shimmy," "Young Man Blues," "Tommy," "Pinball Wizard," "See Me, Feel Me, Touch Me," "Substitute," "Anywhere, Anyway, Anyhow," "Pictures of Lily," "Magic Bus," "Happy Jack," "A Quick One," "Barbara Ann," "Roadrunner," "Who Are You?," and "I Won't Get Fooled Again."

LET IT BE ★★★♪

ROCK. 1970. Artists: John Lennon, Paul McCartney, George Harrison, Ringo Starr. 80 min. Beta, VHS. CBS/Fox ($69.95)

Michael Lindsay-Hogg (*Brideshead Revisited*) was asked by The Beatles to film their recording sessions for an album that was intended to be an exploration of their rock and

The Beatles in *Let It Be*.

roll roots in R&B. What the film turned out to be, much to their own surprise, was a chronicle of the group's impending breakup. Although it would be two years and another album, *Abbey Road,* before their official split, *Let It Be* reveals the tensions hidden just below the surface. With Yoko Ono as the constant and inseparable companion of John, the four members seem to spar with one another at the drop of a hat. Despite all this, lots of great music can be heard, including a jam session in which The Beatles (and Billy Preston) play "Besame Mucho," "Kansas City," and "Lawdy Miss Clawdy." The climax takes place on the rooftop of their Abbey Road studios, where they perform a live set: "Get Back," "I've Got a Feeling," "One After the 909," "Don't Let Me Down," and "I Dig a Pony." The set and the film end when London policemen order the group to cease and desist because of complaints from their neighbors. Other songs are: "Two of Us," "I Me Mine," "For You Blue," "The Long and Winding Road," and "Across the Universe." The mix, by the way, is different (and we think better) than the mix on the album, which was reengineered by Phil Spector with his "wall of sound" technique.

MADONNA ★★★

ROCK. 1984. Artist: Madonna. 17 min. Beta Hifi, VHS Stereo. Warner Music ($19.95)

If Prince was the male pop music story of 1984, then Madonna must be considered the female pop music story of that same year. From the Motor City originally, ex-dancer with the Alvin Ailey troupe in New York, Madonna died her hair blonde and, after an Island Records Artists and Repertoire man, Mark Kamins, heard her demo tapes, teamed up with producer Nile Rodgers (Chic) to record an album of danceable funk laced with materialistic lyrics. That album, *Madonna,* was a platinum best-seller, and her next album, *Like a Virgin,* duplicated the first's success. In many ways, Madonna could be seen as the dark, knowing side of Cyndi Lauper's "just wanna have fun" image. Making no bones about it, Madonna has stated that she's "a material girl," intrigued by wealth and power, willing to pursue it aggressively and unabashedly. This attitude and her fondness for New York haute couture fashions, jewelry, and the high life make her a dubious symbol for contemporary women. These four videos really show off her patented slithery, slinky sensuality. In *Burning Up,* directed by Steve Barron, Madonna writhes about in a white minidress in the middle of a road. *Borderline* immerses her in the arty, chic New York setting that she's adopted; she plays a street urchin plucked off the curb by a photographer to do some modeling. *Lucky Star* is a simple video of Madonna and two other dancers showing off some dance floor gyrations. Finally, *Like a Virgin,* directed by Mary Lambert, features Madonna in a gondola on a canal in Venice.

Madonna.

MICHAEL NESMITH IN RIO AND CRUISIN' ★★★

ROCK. 1983. Artist: Michael Nesmith. 11 min. Beta Hifi, VHS Stereo. Sony ($16.95)

Culled from *Elephant Parts,* Nesmith's Grammy-winning video album, these two video shorts are probably his best work, filled with humor, good camerawork, and distinctive melodies. "Cruisin' " is a song about L.A.'s street people. Lucy and Romona are two roller-skating runaways who are cruising the streets looking for a good time when they meet up with bodybuilder Sunset Sam, who sells jewelry. The three of them team up, "trying to find a plan, looking for the land." "Rio" is a wonderfully wry comment on California life, choosing to depict the state of mind of someone in Lotus Land rather than his or her real surroundings. Nesmith, the dreamer, is carried off to the Rio de Janeiro of his imaginings—looking suspiciously like the beach communities up and down the California coast. In a funny climax, three Carmen Miranda types "fly" down to Rio with him and Nesmith comically reenacts the Astaire-Rogers dance numbers from *Flying Down to Rio.* A humorous counterpart to the subject matter of Rupert Holmes' "Escape."

THE MOTELS ★★

ROCK. 1984. Artists: The Motels. 14 min. Beta Hifi, VHS Stereo. Sony ($16.95)

In each of the four videos presented here, The Motels try to create images that are as atmospheric and haunting as the sound of their songs. With the use of dreamlike

Martha Davis, lead singer of The Motels.

flashbacks, fifties automobiles, and antique clothing, the band puts lead singer Martha Davis in settings that are supposed to be romantic, but fails to generate the same nostalgic mood that is so appealing in their audio work. In their big hit, "Suddenly Last Summer," a girl reads a romance novel in bed. She remembers the lost love she met at the beach. In "Only the Lonely," Martha Davis casually walks through a closed restaurant singing her song. The video for "Take the L" brings the characters of a True Love comic to life. "Remember the Nights" was filmed in L.A.'s Chinatown.

MR. MIKE'S MONDO VIDEO   ★★

ROCK. 1979. Cast: Michael O'Donoghue, Teri Garr, Deborah Harry, Sid Vicious, Dan Aykroyd, Bill Murray, Carrie Fisher, Margot Kidder, Gilda Radner, etc. 75 min. Beta, VHS. Pacific Arts ($59.95)

Rarely does one get the chance to catch a glimpse of the ravings of a deranged mind on broadcast television (hold the snide remarks now), but *Mr. Mike's Mondo Video* almost sneaked in under the nose of the NBC censors in 1979. Originally slated to appear in place of *Saturday Night Live* during it's monthly week of hiatus, this abortive brainchild of Michael O'Donoghue, ex-mastermind of *National Lampoon* magazine and spiritual father of *Saturday Night Live,* managed to offend everyone in almost every way.

Never shown on TV, it was banished to cult movie houses where it never caught on either. *Mondo Video* is the personal comedy testament of a sick mind. What one has to remember is that seventies humor may well have been O'Donoghue's creation; its mixture of Catholic guilt, nose-thumbing attitudes, and wacky self-absorption was the basis for the comic performances of SNL's greater lights like Belushi, Aykroyd, and Chase.

Some of the skit premises here verge on true comic genius: Julius La Rosa singing "The Haunting Theme from Mondo Video" (remember "More" from *Mondo Cane?*), the worshippers of the Jack Lord in the Mainland Temple of the Perfect Wave, the Café No Americain in Paris, and Marcel Cousteau, the swimming mime. But in execution and approach all of it reeks of a sleazy contempt for the audience as well as society at large. Sid Vicious sings "My Way" . . . silently! Root Boy Slim's singing of "Boogie 'Til You Puke" is a funny parody of Meatloaf's gargantuan performances. Ultimately, the most succinct thing one can say about *Mondo Video* is that Michael O'Donoghue hasn't written a page for television or the movies since. Small wonder.

NAKED EYES ★★

ROCK. 1983. Artists: Naked Eyes. 14 min. Beta Hifi, VHS Stereo. Sony ($16.95)

The British have been into music video since the early seventies, seeing the potential for promotion and exposure long before American recording executives did. One of the reasons music video flourished first in the British Isles rather than here was the American disregard for stage apparel, especially during the Woodstock era, when jeans and T-shirts ruled the day. At the same time, in England, David Bowie's glitter theatrics were already quite popular. Pop sensibility has dictated the British concern for image above all else in rock and roll. As an alternative to the punk scene, there were always bands who crooned love songs and dressed in the latest teenage fashions. Naked Eyes is one of those bands. Taking songs with Beatles-derived melodies and attaching a steady drum-machine beat to them, they have also made videos which parallel their sophisticated image. In "When the Lights Go Out," director Marcello Anciano borrows dwarves from the movie *Time Bandits* to depict a young girl's midnight fantasy. "Promises, Promises" is a slick narrative about broken promises and murderous rage directed by Simon Milne, who also directed "Always Something There to Remind Me," in essence an elaborate short film about missed romantic opportunities. Finally, in a video directed by Marek Kaniewski, "Voices in My Head," Kabuki masks and shrouded figures add up to an indecipherable mystery.

PAT BENATAR: HIT VIDEOS ★★

ROCK. 1984. Artist: Pat Benatar. 25 min. Beta and VHS Hifi. RCA/Columbia ($19.95)

Feet planted firmly on the Fem-rock plank of the New Wave platform, Pat Benatar has fashioned an incredibly successful career as yet another of rock's favorite icons: the child-woman diva. Often seen on stage wearing only a man's jacket over a revealing bathing suit, Benatar delivers music that's the tough-girl equivalent of her wardrobe: sinewy guitar lines supporting aggressive lyrics sung in a Broadway-size voice. Viewing this compilation of videos for her more recent hits, one cannot help but be puzzled by their unnecessary elaborateness. "Anxiety" ("Get Nervous") correctly conveys Pat's apprehension about her visit to the dentist but gets thoroughly sidetracked when the dentist becomes a mad scientist straight out of an old horror flick. "Lipstick Lies," in depicting the plight of the working woman, specifically a factory worker, borrows heavily from the mood established in *Flashdance.* "Shadows in the Night" is an absurd video made up of equal pieces of such movies as *Wings, God Is My Co-Pilot,* and *Swing*

Shift! Ultimately, we suppose, the video was inspired by a visit to one of those boutiques that specializes in retro clothing. Finally, "Love Is a Battlefield" is an epic production by video director Bob Giraldi that traces the story of a runaway girl who ends up as a hooker in the big city. Pat looks silly trying to dance in a barroom scene. A minidocumentary concludes the tape, giving us some behind-the-scenes peeks at the making of "Battlefield."

PAT TRAVERS: JUST ANOTHER KILLER DAY ★★

ROCK. 1984. Artists: Pat Travers Band (Pat Travers, Barry Dunaway, Pat Marchino, and Jerry Riggs). 30 min. Beta Hifi, VHS Stereo. RCA/Columbia ($19.95)

Len Epand, the head of Polygram Music Video, who produced this long-form video, tells us that he wished they could have done more with the concept but that budget

Pat Travers in *Just Another Killer Day.*

considerations were the ultimate constraints. What *Just Another Killer Day* attempts may or may not be beyond the limits of music video anyway. Can one assemble an interesting narrative that is autonomous of the music yet perfectly able to exploit it at the same time? In the middle of a sci-fi plot that concerns the movements of "sex sirens" from outer space who have come to earth for our music (music cannot be heard in public on their planet), the Pat Travers Band performs "Killer," "Women on the Edge," "Louise," and "Hot Shot." Because of the poor quality of the acting and writing, much of what is going on is simply indecipherable. A bizarre idea with some merits, but clumsy execution managed to obscure the Pat Travers music—certainly not what was intended.

THE PAUL SIMON SPECIAL ★★

ROCK. 1977. Artists: Paul Simon, Art Garfunkel, The Jesse Dixon Singers, Lily Tomlin, Chevy Chase, and Charles Grodin. 50 min. Beta, VHS. Pacific Arts ($29.95)

An uninspired attempt to put the usually sensitive and thought-provoking performances of Paul Simon and his songs into the structure of an ill-conceived comedy show. The special supposedly shows Paul in rehearsal for his upcoming television special. Along the way, he is dragged by a bumbling director (Charles Grodin) through camera set-ups, mike cues, and set changes and is forced to act as the lone sane body in the middle of a crazed, comedic whirlwind of activity. Paul tries to rise to the occasion, but his talents are not in comedic acting; they lie elsewhere. He is an excellent songwriter and interpreter of his own songs. The comedians give Paul the opportunity to sing eight of his compositions. Art Garfunkel joins him to sing a tune appropriately titled "Old Friends." Paul joins the Jesse Dixon Singers to sing "Loves Me Like a Rock," and "Amazing Grace." "Toots" Thielemans backs up Paul on harmonica on "I Do It for Your Love." Drummer Steve Gadd and pianist Richard Tee accompany Paul on "Still Crazy after All These Years" and "Something So Right." Paul closes the show on solo guitar singing "The Boxer."

PETE TOWNSHEND ★★

ROCK. 1982. Artist: Pete Townshend. 30 min. Beta Hifi, VHS Stereo. Sony ($19.95)

A man who has been acclaimed as one of rock's all-time geniuses, Pete Townshend, the guiding light behind The Who for almost twenty years, has made a series of idiosyncratic solo albums since his *Who Came First* opus of 1972. This video is based on his 1982 album, *The Best Cowboys Have Chinese Eyes.* All in all, it is, like the album, quite depressing. Townshend's always been a morose, easily misunderstood man. Here, we are given ample evidence of why. Recovering from a long battle with alcoholism and saddened by the havoc it has caused in his family, Pete holds forth on camera. His ramblings are framed by a series of rock videos produced for seven cuts off the *Best Cowboys* album: "Preludes," "Face Dances, Part II," "Communicate," "Stardom in Action," "Slit Skirts," "Exquisitely Bored," and "Uniform." The most interesting of these is "Stardom in Action," wherein Pete and a group of teenage would-be rock musicians cross paths on a London street. It perfectly conveys Townshend's misgivings about the whole rock star trip as well as his dismay at his new image, no longer a Young Turk but rock's Old Man. "Uniform," the most bizarre clip, features an offhand comment on the class system in England with Pete as a harried waiter in a country club filled with well-dressed mannequins. Somber and slow-moving, the video is recommended only for real Townshend fans. Lighten up, Pete!

PHIL COLLINS   ★★◗

ROCK. 1983. Artist: Phil Collins. 17 min. Beta Hifi, VHS Stereo. Sony ($16.95)

Since he began to divide his time between Genesis and his own solo career in 1982, Phil Collins has parlayed a love of Motown soul and a knack for Beatles-derived lyrical hooks into something of a one-man musical force. With four hit albums, several hit singles (including the theme from the film *Against All Odds,* a best-selling collaboration with Earth, Wind, and Fire's Philip Bailey, and his album filled with "top ten singles," *No Jacket Required,* which was a Number 1 LP in the spring of 1985), and with high visibility in the music video world, Collins is, astonishingly, one of the hottest performers in the world today. Ironically, he is a prime argument for the relative insignificance of rock videos in determining an artist's success. As these four Stuart Orme-directed videos clearly show, Phil's best assets as a performer reside in his vocal chords and his resourceful mind—not in a matinee idol face or physique. Simple but efficient, his videos emphasize the strong narrative content of his love songs without having to resort to unwieldy symbolism and embarrassing images. And in "I Missed Again" and "You Can't Hurry Love," Phil plays all the parts himself with a flip sense of humor. "In the Air Tonight" and "Through These Walls" are more dramatic in tone.

PICTURE MUSIC   ★★✦

ROCK. 1983. Artists: Kim Carnes, Strange Advance, Naked Eyes, America, J. Geils, Kim Wilde, Red Rider, Talk Talk, Thomas Dolby, George Thorogood, Eddie Jobson, Billy Squier, Burning Sensations, and Steve Miller. 60 min. Beta Hifi, VHS Stereo. Vestron ($29.95)

One of the first successful compilation tapes, *Picture Music* offers the viewer many Capitol-EMI artists, all of whom are recognizable and accessible. With this package, you are assured of getting your money's worth. There are no unknown bands trying to ride on the coattails of a monster group. Each video has been seen on MTV and elsewhere, and they include a couple of the best rock videos ever produced. Kim Carnes' "Bette Davis Eyes" is immediately familiar to rock video fans, but Strange Advance's "She Controls Me" with its high-tech scenery might be entertaining to those who haven't seen it. Naked Eyes' "Always Something There to Remind Me," America's "The Border," and J. Geils' "Freeze-Frame" are favorite videos that follow

Featured performers from the video compilation *Picture Music*.

in succession. The trio of videos that come next are all somber, heartfelt studies, each in its own way: Kim Wilde's "Kids in America" is about runaways and disillusionment, "Light in the Tunnel/Human Race" by Red Rider spotlights the grimness of the urban landscape, and Talk Talk's signature hit, "Talk Talk," lampoons the theatricality of stage performance. Eddie Jobson's "Turn It Over," Billy Squier's "Everybody Wants You," and Burning Sensations' happy, Caribbean-inflected "Belly of the Whale" round out the tape. But the highlight of *Picture Music* is undoubtedly the string of videos that begins with Thomas Dolby's "She Blinded Me with Science," runs through George Thorogood's wonderful "Bad to the Bone" (which costars blues legend Bo Diddley), and culminates in Steve Miller's exciting, spectacular "Abracadabra."

PINK FLOYD AT POMPEII ★★★

ROCK. 1972. Artists: Pink Floyd (Roger Waters, Dave Gilmour, Nick Mason, and Richard Wright). 90 min. Beta Hifi, VHS Stereo. Vestron ($29.95)

In 1972, Pink Floyd, those purveyors of space music for sky-high listeners, played a concert to empty seats in an ancient amphitheater amidst the ruins of Pompeii, Italy. The occasion was a film to be shot by a French director, Adrian Maben, and his crew. Made just before their breakthrough album was released (*Dark Side of the Moon,* which stayed on the Top 100 album chart for a record 10 consecutive years!), *Pink Floyd at Pompeii* offers glimpses of the group in their recording studio in London, having a meal in their hotel, and performing in the amphitheater. Maben presents Roger Waters, the leader and lyricist, as some sort of master technician—directing the recording sessions and fiddling around with all the electronic equipment through which their music is processed. In interviews, none of the group members seem to articulate although Waters' scowl and Gilmour's good-natured smirk speak volumes. Parts of this film could easily qualify as the earliest examples of conceptual rock videos. The Floyd play "Echoes, Part I and Part II," "Careful with That Axe, Eugene," "A Saucerful of Secrets," "One of These Days I'm Going to Cut You into Little Pieces," "Set the Controls for the Heart of the Sun," and "Mademoiselle Nobs." An intriguing look at the group before it became legendary.

PRIME CUTS ★★♪

ROCK. 1984. Artists: Journey, Quiet Riot, The Romantics, Toto, Cyndi Lauper, Matthew Wilder, Bonnie Tyler, and Men At Work. 37 min. Beta Hifi, VHS Stereo. CBS/Fox ($17.95)

This compilation of hit videos by CBS Records artists starts off with Journey's "Chain Reaction," which features a checkerboard set, tuxedoes, mannequins, blonde wigs, and evening gowns. Quiet Riot's heavy metal anthem, "Cum On Feel the Noize," originally done by a proto-heavy metal band, Slade, introduces the notion that music can cause natural upheavals like earthquakes and hurricanes. The Romantics' "Talking in Your Sleep," Toto's megahit, "Roseanna," Cyndi Lauper's breakthrough single, "Girls Just Wanna Have Fun," with its Edd Griles-directed insanity, and Matthew Wilder's "The Kid's American" are all loads of fun to watch. Good examples of rock videos that appropriately treat the songs they illustrate. Bonnie Tyler's "Total Eclipse of the Heart" made it as a hit record but the video is incomprehensible. Finally, Men At Work, one of the biggest recording acts of the eighties, takes a funny look at Australia's outback in "Down Under."

PRIME CUTS II: HEAVY METAL   ★★✚

ROCK. 1984. Artists: Ozzy Osbourne, Slade, Fastway, and Judas Priest. 34 min. Beta Hifi, VHS Stereo. CBS/Fox ($19.95)

Much of today's best heavy metal music is produced by British bands from industrial towns in the English midlands like Manchester and Birmingham: Black Sabbath, Ozzy Osbourne, Nazareth, Judas Priest, and Iron Maiden. Unlike American heavy metal bands, who seem to be primarily motivated by good, clean adolescent fun, these British practitioners of the black arts foster an image on stage and in their lyrics of pseudo-satanic or Druidic, pre-Christian paganism. Hence their tribal and ritualistic approach to their unique, earsplitting sound. In Volume II of CBS/Fox's *Prime Cuts* series, Ozzy Osbourne's hit songs, "Bark at the Moon" and "So Tired," open the proceedings. The ex-lead singer of Black Sabbath, who often causes observers to question his tenuous grasp on sanity, gets to dress up in the latter video as Abe Lincoln, the Hunchback of Notre Dame, the Phantom of the Opera, someone we imagine to be the evil Dr. Caligari (from the classic German horror film, *The Cabinet of Dr. Caligari,* made in 1919), and the most terrifying creature of all, the Ozz himself! Slade performs "Cum On Feel the Noize" and "Run Runaway." Fastway, a new heavy metal band, does "All Fired Up," a video which features drag racing, and "Tell Me," wherein the band holds up a bank. Finally, Judas Priest, perhaps the foremost heavy metal group today, are seen in videos for "You've Got Another Thing Comin'" and "Freewheel Burning." Rob Halford, their lead singer, sums up both the operatic vigor and adolescent ludicrousness of heavy metal.

Other editions in this series are even more adventurous. In *Prime Cuts—Jazz and Beyond,* there are videos from masters of the genre like Miles Davis, Herbie Hancock, Chuck Mangione, Al Dimeola, and Andreas Vollenweider.

QUEEN'S GREATEST FLIX ★★★

ROCK. 1981. Artists: Queen (Freddie Mercury, Roger Taylor, Brian May, and John Deacon). 60 min. Beta, VHS. Thorn-EMI ($29.95)

The original "pomp rock" band, Queen, has careened through the last decade assimilating everything in its path from classical rock to disco to rap music. One of the smarter rock groups around (two of the members have graduate degrees in medicine and astronomy), they early on saw the advantages of doing extensive rock videos to accompany and promote their records. Their first entries into the Top 10 were semioperatic melanges of classical and rock music styles. The seminal "Bohemian Rhapsody," with its posed faces and stark, atmospheric lighting, and the vision of Freddie Mercury crooning in eye makeup and white satin matador pants, is still, for its budget, unsurpassed by today's rock videos. Obviously, image was very important for the group. "You're My Best Friend," "Somebody to Love," "Tie Your Mother Down," and "We Are the Champions" continued to present the group in a combination of mist, glitter, and leather. Searching for other icons, Queen toned down the pomp for "We Will Rock You" (still played at sports stadia across the country to exhort the local teams), "Spread

Queen.

Your Wings," "Bicycle Race," and "Fat-bottomed Girls." Under director Dennis De Vallance's guidance, their videos involved more and more animation and computer graphics: "Don't Stop Me Now," "Love of My Life," "Crazy Little Thing Called Love," "Save Me," "Play the Game," "Another One Bites the Dust" (which inadvertently started Weird Al Yankovic's career), and "Flash" (the theme song from the movie *Flash Gordon*). The earlier, ground-breaking videos were directed by Brian Grant, Bruce Gowers, and Derek Burbidge.

RALPH VIDEO, VOLUME I   ⟩

ROCK. 1982. Artists: The Residents, Tuxedomoon, MX-80, Snakefinger, and Renaldo and the Loaf. 35 min. Beta, VHS. Ralph Video ($49.95)

The Residents are a cult rock group who reside in San Francisco. Their minimalist electronic sounds have captured a small but loyal following among art-rock connoisseurs. Their music is not for everyone—nor, certainly, are their videos, which range from the simply bizarre to the confoundingly inane. With Graeme Whifler as their video director, The Residents churn out easily the most arcane rock videos you'll ever run across. The adventurous among you might find this tape, featuring The Residents and other artists who record on the Ralph label, intriguing. Others will be left baffled. Tuxedomoon, led by singer Winston Tong, mixes "Jinx" with images of bondage and destruction. MX-80's "Why Are We Here?" explores the possibilities of visual monotony. The centerpiece of this compilation is The Residents' series of videos made from 1975 to 1981. "One Minute Movies," "Moisture," "Act of Being Polite," "Perfect Love," and "Simple Song" are all exercises in surreal, twisted style without content. "Hello Skinny" and "Land of a Thousand Dances" are early efforts done without Whifler. Finally, Snakefinger's *Road Warrior*-like video for "Man in the Dark Sedan" and Renaldo and the Loaf's "Songs for Swinging Larvae" reiterate The Residents' message: we are heading for a society in which chaos reigns over order and where human impulses are systematically perverted.

RUBBER RODEO: SCENIC VIEWS   ★★★⟩

ROCK. 1984. Artists: Rubber Rodeo (Trish Milliken, Bob Holmes, Barclay Holmes, "EZ" Mark Tomeo, Gary Leib, and Hal Cragin). 18 min. Beta Hifi, VHS Stereo. Sony ($16.95)

A superb little video program from the immensely attractive country rock group Rubber Rodeo, featuring songs written by Bob Holmes and Trish Milliken and sung by the same duo, who could be country music's answer to Ashford and Simpson. For all their sweet chemistry on screen, Rubber Rodeo displays a flip sense of humor and a keen eye for the details of southwestern life. The three videos presented here are miniature movies, humorously treating such icons of the southwestern experience as truckers, roadside diners, laundromats, beauty parlors, hoedowns, bars, and the stereotypical roles played by southwestern men and women. "Need You, Need Me" is heard over the opening titles. In "Anywhere with You," Trish plays the girl trucker Bob left behind. Using the motif of a postcard sent from Bob to Trish, the video works toward their happy reunion. "It's the Hardest Thing," shot in Banning and Cabazon, California, scopes the action between Bob and Trish at a country hoedown. "How the West Was Won" juxtaposes old silent film footage of cowboy exploits with the realities of today's west. Trish, in a blonde wig, has to retrieve her ne'er-do-well husband, Bob, from his favorite neighborhood bar. Bob stops her singing complaints with a kiss. These little gems were directed by David Greenberg and produced by Len Epand of Polygram Music Video.

SATURDAY NIGHT LIVE: CHARLES GRODIN ★★꜀

ROCK. 1977. Cast: Charles Grodin, John Belushi, Dan Aykroyd, Bill Murray, Jane Curtin, Laraine Newman, Gilda Radner, Garrett Morris, and Paul Simon. 67 min. Beta, VHS. Warner ($39.95)

In this Halloween show from 1977, the SNL cast is joined by guest host Charles Grodin and musical guests Paul Simon and The Persuasions. Grodin, who's made an entire career out of playing ineffectual, laconic bumblers, is true to form here as he pretends to mess up every skit that he's in, incurring Belushi's wrath and vitriol. This works at times but gets old toward the second half of the show. Here again, the SNL crew shows its debt to such British zanies as *Monty Python* and *The Goon Show,* who used this device years beforehand.

Among the skits are: the Coneheads, unfamiliar with Earth customs, handing out six-packs of beer to trick-or-treaters on Halloween; Samurai Dry Cleaner (Belushi); the Judy Miller Show, featuring Gilda Radner as an overactive 11-year-old; and the Killer Bees playing trick-or-treat on an unsuspecting couple. Paul Simon, one of producer Lorne Michaels' favorite people, sings "Slip Sliding Away" (with The Persuasions) and "Goodbye" (with "Toots" Thielemans on harmonica).

SATURDAY NIGHT LIVE: ERIC IDLE I ★★⌐

ROCK. 1976. Cast: Eric Idle, Chevy Chase, John Belushi, Richard Belzer, Dan Aykroyd, Gilda Radner, Jane Curtin, Laraine Newman, Garrett Morris, Joe Cocker, and Stuff. 64 min. Beta, VHS. Warner ($39.95)

One of two episodes available on home video in which Eric Idle of Monty Python fame guest hosted. Here, Lorne Michaels and his crew of aggressive zanies attempt to ape the Monty Python trait of cutting away from skits midway through. The Pythons did this, they'll admit, because often they couldn't think of a way to end a given skit. SNL tries the gimmick of having Eric mess up his lines, thereby halting skits and, supposedly, alienating the cast. The timing in live shows is so tricky that it doesn't come off well at all—it all seems so phoney. They later tried the same gimmick when Charles Grodin hosted. Grodin was slightly better because he has those Jack Benny-like slow takes. Highlights of the show include: Aykroyd as a d.j. performing *both* AM and FM duties in the respective styles simultaneously, the Killer Bees entering a Swine Flu Inoculation Center and wreaking comic havoc, Baba Wawa (Gilda Radner) announcing her departure from NBC to go to rival ABC, Eric Idle's original film short of The Rutles, and Eric and Aykroyd as drag racers (in women's clothing). Joe Cocker, backed by Stuff, sings "You Are So Beautiful" and is a good sport while Belushi does a hilarious impression of him as they both sing "Feelin' Alright."

SATURDAY NIGHT LIVE: MICHAEL PALIN ★★★

ROCK. 1979. Cast: Michael Palin, John Belushi, Jane Curtin, Dan Aykroyd, Gilda Radner, Bill Murray, Garrett Morris, Laraine Newman, Don Novello, Franken and Davis, and the Doobie Brothers. 67 min. Beta, VHS. Warner ($39.95)

From the 1978–1979 season, this SNL episode was one of the funnier shows in the original series. The main reason for that is the presence of Monty Python member Michael Palin, whose odd humor seems to inject the whole cast with some needed enthusiasm (the show had been on the air for almost five years by now). The comedy highlights include: Aykroyd as Jimmy Carter giving the State of the Union address, making pointed references to his famous case of hemorrhoids; Aykroyd again, as "Klaus Kent," in a skit that asks the question, what if Superman had grown up in Nazi Germany?; Don Novello as Father Guido Sarducci, the gossip columnist for the Vatican newspaper; Palin leading the cast through his wacky version of a Dickens novel, *Miles Copperthwaite;* and Franken and Davis giving us their version of made-for-TV porno.

There is also an episode of the *Mr. Bill Show.* The Doobie Brothers appear doing two songs, "What a Fool Believes" and "Taking It to the Streets." Catch this one for the *Miles Copperthwaite* skit. It's hilarious.

SATURDAY NIGHT LIVE: RICHARD BENJAMIN ★★

ROCK. 1979. Cast: Richard Benjamin, Dan Aykroyd, Jane Curtin, Garrett Morris, Bill Murray, Laraine Newman, Gilda Radner, Rodney Dangerfield, and Rickie Lee Jones. 64 min. Beta, VHS. Warner ($39.95)

In an episode from the original *Saturday Night Live* series, Richard Benjamin, now primarily a film director (*Racing with the Moon*) although best known for his series, *He and She,* is the guest host alongside wife Paula Prentiss, and Rickie Lee Jones is the musical guest. This was the show in 1979 that John Belushi was inexplicably AWOL from (he was actually filming part of *Blues Brothers*) and some pointed jokes are made about that. The comedy highlights include: "The Pepsi Syndrome," a parody of *The China Syndrome* in which President Jimmy Carter (Aykroyd) becomes a 50-foot-tall giant because of radiation exposure; the Nerds, Radner and Murray, getting their "noogies"; Garrett Morris' impression of an Hispanic ex-ballplayer turned sportscaster, Chico Escuela; Gilda's Roseanne Roseannadanna discussing another "one of those things"; and Benjamin and Laraine Newman as a couple who eat dinner at a Scottish restaurant. Rickie Lee Jones, noted for her jazzy, sultry chanteuse image, performs "Chuck E.'s in Love" and "Coolsville." Not one of the best SNL episodes.

SATURDAY NIGHT LIVE: RODNEY DANGERFIELD ★★

ROCK. 1980. Cast: Rodney Dangerfield, Don Novello, Jane Curtin, Laraine Newman, Gilda Radner, Garrett Morris, Bill Murray, Harry Shearer, Paul Shaffer, Brian Doyle-Murray, and J. Geils Band. 68 min. Beta, VHS. Warner ($39.95)

During the original SNL's last season under the aegis of producer Lorne Michaels, after the departure of John Belushi and Dan Aykroyd, the show was carried by an ever-increasing cast of unknowns and hangers-on. It was the season when nepotism reared its ugly head, so to speak, as Bill Murray's older brother Brian and Dan Aykroyd's younger brother Peter became regulars on the show. This particular episode has the always funny Rodney Dangerfield as its host but is otherwise a good example of why SNL entered a long period of comic doldrums, with its scattershot humor and incredibly narrow concerns. After Dangerfield's "no respect" monologue, the show goes downhill, hitting bottom with an interminably long, black and white (!) parody of Woody Allen's *Manhattan,* here retitled *Manhasset* (a small community on New York's Long Island). The only good skit concerns a "substitute" judge who takes over the bench in a courtroom full of mischievous, schoolboy-like adults, who toss spitballs at the judge when his back is turned, etc. J. Geils Band plays "Love Stinks" and "Sanctuary."

SCROOGE'S ROCK 'N' ROLL CHRISTMAS   ★↲

ROCK. 1983. Artists: Jack Elam, Bobby Goldsboro, Mary MacGregor, The Association, Mike Love, Dean Torrence, Paul Revere and the Raiders, Three Dog Night, Bridget, and Lee Benton. 44 min. Beta Hifi, VHS Stereo. Sony ($24.95)

This tape might have been more appropriately titled *Your Favorite Golden Oldies Meet Your Favorite Christmas Album.* It stars mellow rock stars you haven't seen in at least fifteen years. Where have these guys been? Why are they singing Christmas songs? The producers gathered a bunch of hitmakers from the sixties and the seventies and a new act they wanted to introduce, Bridget, and asked them to sing Christmas carols somewhere in the high Sierra of California. The results are less than startling. Three Dog Night opens the program with "Rocking around the Christmas Tree." "Jingle Bells" is performed by Paul Revere and the Raiders in their traditional Revolutionary War uniforms. "Some Children See Him" is performed by a young woman who is presented only as "Bridget." The Beach Boys' Mike Love and singer Mary MacGregor sing a duet on "Do You Hear What I Hear." Mike then teams up with Jan and Dean's Dean Torrence to do a mellow cover of "Jingle Bell Rock." The Association perform "Sleigh Ride" before Bobby Goldsboro's version of "Winter Wonderland." In a wrap-around that is used to tie all of the songs together, Jack Elam, a character actor who has appeared in countless television westerns as an old coot, is grossly miscast as Dickens' Ebenezer Scrooge.

SHEENA EASTON   ★★↲

ROCK. 1983. Artist: Sheena Easton. 15 min. Beta Hifi, VHS Stereo. Sony ($16.95)

Scotland's contribution to the pop music world of late, Sheena Easton, has certainly been more successful in America than those other Scots, the Bay City Rollers. Her adaptability to the currents of Top 10 taste indicates an affinity between her and

Olivia Newton-John, both of whom swing from soft rock to pop to punk rock with nary a difficulty. In the four videos presented here, several versions of Sheena's musical image can be discerned. In "Telefone" ("Long Distance Love Affair") she is cast in the role of a Gothic heroine hounded by classic movie monsters like Frankenstein, Dracula, King Kong, and the Hunchback of Notre Dame. "Machinery" offers Sheena as a working woman who rebels against the automation in her office. "Ice Out in the Rain" plumbs the emotional depths of lost love in the wistful eyes of our subject, Sheena. These three videos were directed by Steve Barron (Michael Jackson's "Billie Jean"). In the final video, Sheena is shown in concert, belting out "Morning Train" ("9 to 5") in Vegas stage show style. This was directed by David G. Hillier.

SLIPSTREAM: JETHRO TULL   ★★♪

ROCK. 1981. Artists: Jethro Tull (Ian Anderson, Martin Barre, Dave Pegg, and Mark Craney). 60 min. Beta Hifi, VHS Stereo. Pacific Arts ($49.95)

Here's an early, award-winning long-form video directed by David Mallet for Jethro Tull, a progressive rock group that combined contemporary rhythms with traditional folk instruments and melodies. Several years after their last real hit single, the group, led by flautist and woodland satyr Ian Anderson, have made a video that defies summarization. Mallet's avowedly bizarre images are diverting to look at but hardly accessible to those who are not entirely familiar with Anderson's complex set of mythic allusions. The one distinctive thing about this video is that live sound, from the interspersed concert at Hammersmith Odeon in London, is used over each of the clips—something that hasn't, unfortunately, been imitated by more recent video directors. The songs, admirably executed by Anderson with a band full of newcomers to Jethro Tull, are "Black Sunday," "Dun Ringill," "Flyingdale Flyer," "Songs from the Wood," "Heavy Horses," "Sweet Dreams," "Too Old to Rock 'n' Roll, Too Young to Die," "Skating Away," "Aqualung," and "Locomotive Breath." It's a shame that Anderson's unique music is now completely foreign to the contemporary scene.

SOFT CELL   ★♪

ROCK. 1982. Artists: Soft Cell. 58 min. Beta Hifi, VHS Stereo. Thorn-EMI ($49.95)

Self-titled a "nonstop exotic video show," this video by the British art-rock duo, Soft Cell, is little more than a compilation of home movies substituting shock value for entertainment value. Much of this is of interest only to Soft Cell, their immediate families, and the misguided who are their fans. Marc Almond, the one that sings, is an ugly young man wearing liberal amounts of mascara on his eyes. Unfortunately, he is on camera most of the time. Their one hit in America, "Tainted Love," is the only song that's worth listening to in this collection. Fitting in with what seems to be their image, the other videos are glum exercises in sophomoric, asexual hijinks. For those interested in travel, there are glimpses of London sights in "Bedsitter," a tour through Clubland at night ("Seedy Films"), a look at London's underworld, and "Memorabilia," wherein the duo go shopping at a flea market. The other songs, "Entertain Me," "Frustration," "Torch," "Secret Life," "Youth," "Sex Dwarf," "What," and "Say Hello Wave Goodbody," are eminently forgettable.

STRAY CATS   ★★

ROCK. 1983. Artists: The Stray Cats. 13 min. Beta Hifi, VHS Stereo. Sony ($16.95)

The Stray Cats (Brian Setzer, Slim Jim Phantom, and Lee Rocker) originally left their native New York to make it big in England with their unique rockabilly sound. They returned home to hit the American charts with the loud rockers "Rock This Town," "Stray Cat Strut," and "(She's) Sexy + 17," the videos of which are all included in this package. Showing a softer side of the band, Brian Setzer sings the atmospheric ballad "I Won't Stand in Your Way" in a video shot at night beneath the Brooklyn Bridge.

THIS IS ELVIS   ★★★

ROCK. 1981. Artist: Elvis Presley. 144 min. Beta, VHS. Warner ($69.95)

This 1981 documentary was authorized by Colonel Tom Parker, Elvis' manager and promoter, as the first in-depth account of the King's life, death, and career. It surrounds a whole treasure chest of Elvis clips with some dramatic scenes illustrating parts of his life. The scenes were especially shot for this film, using professional actors like David Scott, who plays the young Elvis in the early sections. The narration used throughout is Ral Donner's adequate impersonation of Elvis' own speaking voice. This device becomes quite ludicrous at times and detracts from one's enjoyment of the rare Elvis clips. For instance, the narrator's voice cuts into songs like "Jailhouse Rock" and "Hound Dog." The clips used are taken from such diverse sources as newsreel

Elvis from 1957 to 1977, as seen in the documentary *This Is Elvis.*

footage, television interviews, concert films, home movies, and ancient kinescopes. There are all the songs that the Elvis fan will want to hear and then some. However, unlike the other tapes we've discussed, this one forces you to put up with assorted narrators cutting in and with sequences being shortened for the needs of the film's pacing. But, *This Is Elvis* does present a good overview of Elvis' life and accomplishments along with a compendium of all the clips available on other titles. As such, it resembles a good reference book for the Elvis admirer or aficionado.

THOMAS DOLBY ★★★

ROCK. 1984. Artist: Thomas Dolby. 16 min. Beta Hifi, VHS Stereo. Sony ($16.95)

In these four videos, Thomas Dolby displays not only an ability to write danceable techno-rock tunes with snappy lyrics, but a full command of the vocabulary of the

Thomas Dolby.

video medium and a grasp of the medium's potential for creating images that cannot be generated any other way. In "Hyperactive," Thomas visits a psychiatrist. As he describes his problems to the doctor, Thomas' head is graphically replaced on the video screen by a box. Each side of the box projects a different image: one side shows photos of Dolby; others show cartoons that are conjured by words in the song. The video is more striking than the lyrics or the music of the tune. In "Europa and the Pirate Twins" and "Radio Silence," Dolby tries to tackle the conflict between technology and humanity. The well-known "She Blinded Me with Science" video is a short film structured around the slapstick of old silent film comedies.

TODD RUNDGREN: VIDEOSYNCRACIES ★★♪

ROCK. 1983. Artist: Todd Rundgren. 12 min. Beta Hifi, VHS Stereo. Sony ($16.95)

Todd Rundgren has probably been making rock videos longer than any other major American pop music star, yet he's garnered very little notoriety, respect, or adulation for his efforts. And there is a reason for this. As evidenced in the three videos showcased here, Todd's use of the medium leaves something to be desired. The unpredictability of his music has been a hindrance (audiences have never known quite how to take him), and the surreal logic of his video imagery further complicates matters. In "Hideaway," for instance, we look into Todd's reflector shades and discover Todd climbing the contours of a giant female torso. In "Can We Still Be Friends?", a tiny ballerina dances atop Todd's grand piano. Finally, in "Time Heals," a montage of surrealistic paintings by Dali, Magritte, and others is a tour de force of animation. But, the brilliance of these rather odd images aside, they do very little to communicate the substance of the songs to the viewer. After all, the purpose of any music video, from a practical standpoint, is to promote sales of records. By offering objects rather than engaging in a dialogue with the viewers (prospective record buyers), Todd has invited his own failure.

TONI BASIL: WORD OF MOUTH ★★★

ROCK. 1981. Artist: Toni Basil. 30 min. Beta Hifi, VHS Stereo. Pacific Arts ($29.95)

By the time Toni Basil hit the Top 10 in 1981 with "Mickey," she had already had a long and illustrious career as a dancer, choreographer, and actress. Perhaps her most notorious work was with the group of street dancers from Los Angeles that she named the Lockers. Years before breaking, popping, and locking became household dance

Toni Basil in *Word of Mouth.*

steps, the Lockers appeared on national television doing outrageous robotics and contortions. Basil even joined them on occasion. With her background in dance, Toni felt she was a natural to exploit the burgeoning possibilities of music video. *Word of Mouth* was one of the first video EPs released to coincide with a record album. If anything in this imaginative production can be faulted, it might be Basil's own proclivity to ham it up like some silent screen star from the twenties. Her dancing and singing are marvelous; her acting is too contrived. The numbers presented are: "Mickey," "Nobody," "Little Red Book," "Time after Time," "Be Stiff," "Space Girls," and "You Gotta Problem" (which is the funniest, featuring Toni in a poodle skirt walking two cantankerous dancers in poodle costumes). Directed and choreographed by Basil as "a total video concept," *Word of Mouth* is worth seeing.

UTOPIA SAMPLER ★★♪

ROCK. 1983. Artists: Utopia (Todd Rundgren, Kasim Sulton, Roger Powell, and John Wilcox). 11 min. Beta Hifi, VHS Stereo. Sony ($16.95)

Alternately solo artist, record producer, film scorer, and front man for the group Utopia, Todd Rundgren, the boy genius from Upper Darby, Pa., has had a rather strange and meandering musical career. Rundgren's rather eclectic tastes have both made him notorious and kept him from the commercial success he deserves. Wavering between highly technological rock doodlings (early Utopia) and patently pop derivations (*Something/Anything* is probably his best album), Todd has always had an interest in video, and was a video pioneer in rock music. His stuff now seems archaic, but remember that, at one time, he was the only serious American rocker playing around with a video camera at all. This sampler features four videos made for Utopia: "Hammer in My Heart," "Feet Don't Fail Me Now," "You Make Me Crazy," and "The Road to Utopia." The last one is the most interesting. It's a variation on the concept of utopia depicted in H. G. Wells' classic sci-fi novel, *The Time Machine.*

VIDEO REWIND—THE ROLLING STONES GREAT VIDEO HITS ★♪

ROCK. 1984. Artists: The Rolling Stones (Mick Jagger, Keith Richards, Bill Wyman, Ron Wood, Charlie Watts, and Mick Taylor). 60 min. Beta Hifi, VHS Stereo. Vestron ($29.95)

Those aging bad boys The Rolling Stones present *Video Rewind,* a collection of old and new promo clips that are intended to shock the sensitive and amuse the legions

THE ROLLING STONES

Mick Jagger was born July 26, 1943, in Dartford, U.K. Keith Richards was born December 18, 1943, in Dartford, U.K. Bill Wyman was born October 24, 1936, in London, U.K. Charlie Watts was born June 2, 1944, in Islington, U.K. Ron Wood was born June 1, 1947, in London, U.K.

The Rolling Stones were formed when Jagger and Richards bumped into each other in a London subway in 1960 and discovered their common interest in American blues music. By 1964, the year the Beatles became a worldwide phenomenon, the Stones were well known in England for their intense cover versions of songs by black artists like Muddy Waters and Chuck Berry.

The end of the sixties saw the Stones survive the end of the British Invasion to become "the greatest rock and roll band in the world." The controversial nature of their music, epitomized by "Under My Thumb," "Midnight Rambler," and "Sympathy for the Devil," was tragically underlined by the events that took place at their free concert in Altamont, California, in 1969.

A spotty but often brilliant roster of recordings was put out by the Stones in the seventies despite two personnel changes and a growing feeling of disinterest among the group's members. Most recently, rumors of their breakup were squelched when they announced plans to tour again in 1986. They continue to hold the position of the number one rock and roll band in the world.

Video Resume
The Rolling Stones
Gimme Shelter, (1970), RCA/Columbia.

Let's Spend the Night Together, (1982), Embassy.

Ready, Steady, Go, Vols. I and II, (196-), Thorn-EMI.

Sympathy for the Devil, (1970), CBS/Fox.

That Was Rock, (1965), Media.

Video Rewind, (1984), Vestron.

Mick Jagger
Jimi Hendrix, (1973), Warner.

The Nightingale, (1983), CBS/Fox.

Performance, (1970), Warner.

Bill Wyman
A.R.M.S. Concert, Parts I and II, (1984), Media.

Bill Wyman, (1983), Sony.

Charlie Watts
A.R.M.S. Concert, Parts I and II, (1984), Media.

Ron Wood
The Last Waltz, (1978), CBS/Fox.

Singer Mick Jagger in _Video Rewind._

of Stones fans who believe that Mick and the band can do no wrong. A wraparound, written and directed by boy video genius Julien Temple, serves to glue the various tapes together. In the wraparound, bassist Bill Wyman acts as a security guard in a large metropolitan museum who breaks into an off-limits storage closet filled with rock and roll memorabilia. There Bill finds Mick Jagger, dressed for a concert performance, held in suspended animation in a glass display case. Bill frees Mick. After seeing that he's been left to gather dust in a museum closet, Mick, with a calculated, sardonic smirk on his face, sits down to watch a number of old Stones film clips and videos on an old television set. They see the unexpurgated versions of Temple's "Too Much Blood" and "She's Hot" that were not seen on MTV. On a studio set, the Stones sing "Emotional Rescue" and "She's So Cold." Mick and Bill sit around and talk about rock and roll debaucheries of the past like a bunch of superstar has-beens before returning to the television set to see a series of videos that were popular on the cable and broadcast video shows. They watch "Undercover of the Night," the

Stones' video about the violence in Central America, "Waiting on a Friend," filmed on New York's St. Mark's Place, and "Neighbors," a recording that features the saxophone playing of jazz master Sonny Rollins. The real boon to Stones fans is the inclusion of rarely seen early promo clips from the early seventies. Guitarist Mick Taylor can be seen in films of "Brown Sugar," "Angie," and "It's Only Rock and Roll."

WE'RE ALL DEVO   ★★★✦

ROCK. 1983. Cast: Devo, Laraine Newman, and Robert Mothersbaugh, Sr. 54 min. Beta Hifi, VHS Stereo. Sony ($29.95)

Devo, that bunch of fun-loving boys from Ohio who hit the national scene in 1977 with their well-conceived art-rock concept band, was one of the first rock groups to use the visual media of film and video to illustrate the content of their songs. While still only known within the confines of metropolitan Akron, the band declared that not only was Darwin's theory of evolution wrong, but it was a cover-up! The human race was not evolving as speculated, but actually "devolving." In order to get the point across they called themselves Devo, and started to make films with director Chuck Statler that at times are more entertaining and effective than their music. In *We're All Devo,* the home video audience can see the group's "evolution" from a highly original garage band to a highly paid tongue in cheek rock stage show. With use of great costumes (copies of which you can buy through their fan club), a strong command of video and film special effects, and a collective fertile imagination, Devo entertains with songs that get you dancing even though you are just a "spud." Devo's first video efforts were "Satisfaction," their cover version of the Stones' classic, and "The Day My Baby Gave Me a Surprise," both of which were performed by the band in white jump suits and dark sunglasses on a dark and eerie television stage set. In the video for their superhit, "Whip It," Devo appears in their patented ziggurat hats and calf-length skintight bodysuits on a western cowboy set. "Beautiful World" is an amalgam of revolting images. "Through Being Cool" presents a group of teenagers wearing plastic John F. Kennedy pompadour helmets (which are also available from Devo's fan club) and dancing around with laser guns in their hands that they use to shoot innocent bystanders. *We're All Devo* includes the band's promo piece for Dan Aykroyd's movie *Dr. Detroit.* In a video excerpted from Neil Young's as yet unreleased film, *The Human Highway,* the members of Devo and their mascot, Boogie Boy, play nuclear reactor workers who are exposed to massive amounts of radiation and sing "Worried Man." This tape also includes the group's videos for several of their songs:

"The Girl U Want," "Freedom of Choice," "Peek-A-Boo," "That's Good," "Love without Anger," and "Jocko Homo."

WILD RIDES   ★★★

ROCK. 1982. Artists: The Who, Steve Miller, Steely Dan, The Cars, Jimi Hendrix, and Dave Mason. 27 min. Beta Hifi, VHS Stereo. Warner ($29.95)

Teen heartthrob Matt Dillon is your host for a rock video look at famous roller coaster rides across the nation, ranging from Magic Mountain's Colossus in Los Angeles to Astroworld's Texas Cyclone in Houston. The Who's "You" is heard over your ride on the Colossus, the Great American Scream Machine's thrills and spills in the Six Flags Over Georgia Park in Atlanta are viewed to the strains of Dave Mason singing "Nothing to Fear," and Steve Miller's classic "Living in the U.S.A." accompanies the Roaring Tiger at Barnum and Bailey's Circus World in Florida as it undulates with dramatic effect. Steely Dan's synthesizer rendition of the Duke Ellington-Bubber Miley standard, "East St. Louis Toodle-oo," is played over a capsule history of the roller coaster, its genesis and development. The Cars' "Don't Cha Stop" is your mood music for the Triple Loop Mindbender at Six Flags Over Georgia, and the Texas Cyclone, purportedly the best roller-coaster ride in the world, slings the viewer around to the tune of "Fire" by Jimi Hendrix. Written and directed by Robert C. Hughes.

YOKO ONO: THEN AND NOW   ★★★✦

ROCK. 1984. Artists: Yoko Ono, John Lennon, Paul McCartney, George Harrison, and Lena Lovich. 56 min. Beta, VHS. Media ($39.95)

Documentary director Barbara Graustark examines the life and times of one of the most controversial, most public, and least understood women of pop culture, Yoko Ono. From the alienation of her privileged upbringing to her life as one of the first conceptual artists in the early sixties, Graustark underlines the idea that Yoko had been an artistic maverick before her marriage to John Lennon. If not well known outside the small circle of the avant-garde before her courtship with John, Yoko's name soon became a household word and her photograph and accounts of her exploits and work soon filled the pages of the world's newspapers. Yoko and John's marriage coincided with the breakup of the Beatles, and Yoko was vilified by Beatles fans and critics for urging John to experiment with musical forms and media outside of the pop field. She weathered the storms of public controversy with the stoicism that would give her strength after John's death. After John was arrested for possession of marijuana in England, the Lennons moved to New York, had a son, Sean, and set up housekeeping in the Dakota, the famous apartment building on Central Park West. They began to feel complacent in married life and broke up for a period of almost two years. After their well-publicized separation, Yoko and John made up and solved the problems that had plagued them in the past. They celebrated this renewal with the release of their album, *Double Fantasy,* and specifically in John's hit song from that album, "Starting Over." This short period of bliss was ended tragically in December of 1980 when an assassin's bullet took John's life. Still Yoko persevered with her work. Today she records as before and maintains in such efforts as the dedication of Strawberry Fields, in Central Park, as a memorial to John. Yoko had been overshadowed by John's fame during his life. Ironically, his death brought public and critical recognition of her conceptual work before her marriage and the Kabuki-influenced primal scream recordings she made with John in the early seventies. These records influenced such New Wave singers as Lena Lovich and Nina Hagen. *Yoko Ono: Then and Now* is a very thoughtful and provocative documentary. On the tape are numerous songs by John and Yoko, including "Imagine," "Give Peace a Chance," "Thin Ice," "Watching the Wheels," "Beautiful Boy," "Starting Over," "Let It Be," and "I Want You."

ROCK CONCERT VIDEOS

ADAM AND THE ANTS: PRINCE CHARMING REVUE ★

ROCK. 1982. Artists: Adam and the Ants. 76 min. Beta Hifi, VHS Stereo. CBS/Fox ($39.95)

The only significant thing about Adam and the Ants, a curiosity from the days of British pop music's New Romanticism, is that they were the first rock band to use the African double-drum rhythms of Burundi. Otherwise, they were quite bad. As all fads dissipate, so did the vogue for Adam and the Ants. This is a video concert of a date in London on their Prince Charming tour in 1982. The scenery, which looks like the interior of a seventeenth-century manor, and Adam's pitiful singing may hold your attention for about thirty seconds. It is clear that Adam's major achievement in life must have been dating Jamie Lee Curtis for a short time in 1982. One can hear "Five Guns West," "Sex to Sex," "Ant Music," "Dirk Wears White Sox," "Prince Charming," "Stand and Deliver," "Ranchero," "Christian Dior," and many others.

ALCHEMY: DIRE STRAITS LIVE   ★★♪

ROCK. 1983. Artists: Dire Straits (Mark Knopfler, John Illsly, Alan Clark, Hal Lindes, Terry Williams, Tommy Mandel, Mel Collins, and Joop de Korte). 95 min. Beta Hifi, VHS Stereo. Media ($29.95)

Mark Knopfler is an unusual British rock star. Until Dire Straits hit it big in 1979 with "Sultans of Swing," Knopfler had spent most of his adult life teaching English at various London public colleges. Not only did fame come to him at a later age (for a rock star), but the life of a professional musician was not his until he was almost thirty years old. The time that he spent in obscurity, as it were, enabled him to come up with a guitar sound that, while not original, was unlike anything anyone was producing on the pop/rock scenes. Essentially, Knopfler's plangent, pickless style is a combination of acoustic blues (Lightnin' Hopkins, J. J. Cale) and electric blues (Albert King). Add to that his obvious admiration for Bob Dylan and Bruce Springsteen and you come up with a music that has defied categorization. This video of a concert at London's Hammersmith Odeon in July 1983 was recorded at the same time as Dire Straits' double live album, *Alchemy.* In concert, Dire Straits indulges in long instrumental passages, making some cuts 10 minutes in length. The strangeness of Knopfler's guitar style is lost in such repeated application; one can clearly hear the real limitations in range and expression that are inherent in his style. Also, on this outing, his nasal, slightly garbled vocals are painful to endure—he is not a master of phrasing as his hero Dylan was and perhaps still is. Finally, what makes the concert dull is part and parcel of the Dire Straits program for success. It's the catch 22 of Knopfler's artistry: the extreme stylization of his music made Dire Straits popular but it's also the reason why *every* song sounds the same! Simply put, Mark Knopfler comes up with more lyrics than he has music to back up. The songs: "Once Upon a Time in the West," "Expresso Love," "Romeo and Juliet," "Private Investigations," "Sultans of Swing," "Two Young Lovers," "Tunnel of Love," "Telegraph Road," "Solid Rock," and "Going Home" (Knopfler's instrumental theme for the film *Local Hero*).

ALICE COOPER AND FRIENDS   ★★

ROCK. 1977. Artists: Alice Cooper, Nazareth, Sha Na Na, The Tubes. 60 min. Beta, VHS. Media ($44.95)

Originally produced for syndicated television, this 1-hour program chronicles an all-day rock concert held in the summer of 1977 at Anaheim Stadium, Anaheim, California. An old-looking, overweight Alice Cooper opens the video with "School's Out." Nazareth, one of the standard bearers of heavy metal, performs "Love Is Just Physical,"

"Love Hurts," and "Better to Have Loved and Lost." Sha Na Na's stage hijinks can try one's patience if one isn't into fifties rock and roll, but greasers in the audience will like their versions of "Yakety Yak," "Jailhouse Rock," "Leader of the Pack," and "Blue Moon." The Tubes follow with their own brand of theatrics as they lampoon The Captain and Tenille and Frank Sinatra in "Love Will Keep Us Together" and "This Town." Alice Cooper concludes the concert with a long set that includes "Who I Really Am," "Under My Wheels," "Billion Dollar Babies," "You and Me," "Only Women Bleed," "Lace and Whiskey," and "I Love the Dead."

THE ALLMAN BROTHERS BAND: BROTHERS OF THE ROAD ★★♪

ROCK. 1982. Artists: Allman Brothers Band. 90 min. Beta Hifi, VHS Stereo. RCA/Columbia, Pioneer ($29.95)

Recorded at an outdoor concert on the campus of the University of Florida at Gainesville, the Allmans (featuring Greg Allman, Dicky Betts, Butch Trucks, Dan Toler, and Mike Lawler) perform most of their biggest hits in the first half. The second half is given over to more concert footage from a gig at the Capitol Theater in New Jersey and

The Allman Brothers Band in *Brothers of the Road.*

some rehearsal footage shot in a television studio. The program, then, gives one a rounded picture of the band, onstage and off. In the Gainesville concert, the band plays "Jessica," "You Don't Love Me Anymore," "Blue Skies," "Melissa," "Statesboro Blues," and the almost-symphonic "Whipping Post." At the Capitol Theater, after an intervening jam session filmed in a motel room on the road (Dicky Betts and Dan Toler playing acoustic blues guitar), the Allmans do "Come and Go Blues," "You Can't Take It with You," "Crazy Love," "In Memory of Elizabeth Reed," "One Way Out," "Southbound," "The Judgement," and "Ramblin' Man." Betts' electric guitar work is still thrilling to hear but, on the whole, especially in the case of Greg Allman's deteriorating vocals, the years have not been too kind to the Allmans' once-classic southern rock sound.

APRIL WINE LIVE IN LONDON ★★

ROCK. 1981. Artists: April Wine. 60 min. Beta Hifi, VHS Stereo. Thorn-EMI ($59.95)

By 1978, Myles Goodwyn, April Wine's leader and guitarist, was the only original member still left in the group. Coincidentally, the Canadian hard-rock band began to get more airplay outside of their native country, here and in Britain, at the same time. By January of 1981, when this video concert at London's Hammersmith Odeon took place, April Wine was riding high on their most successful LP of all time, *Nature of the Beast.* Their sound, pretty much a throwback to late sixties Guess Who sides, with perhaps a little more active guitar work, was rather dated even in 1981. The video is also quite dated: slo-mo effects and belated psychedelia along with some gratuitous videogame graphics. Considering that Derek Burbidge directed this (he later did *Eurythmics*), it's a pretty disappointing program. Songs: "Big City Girls," "Crash and Burn," "Tellin' Me Lies," "Future Tense," "Ladies' Man," "Caught in the Crossfire," "Sign of the Gypsy Queen," "Just between You and Me," "Bad Boys," "One More Time," "21st Century Schizoid Man," "Roller," "I Like to Rock," "All over Town," and "Wanna Rock."

THE A.R.M.S. CONCERT, PART I ★★★↓

ROCK. 1984. Artists: Eric Clapton, Steve Winwood, Bill Wyman, Charlie Watts, Kenny Jones, Andy Fairweather-Low, Ray Cooper, Fernando Saunders, and James Hooker. 60 min. Beta Hifi, VHS Stereo. Media ($29.95)

Ronnie Lane, ex-Small Face guitarist, suffers from multiple sclerosis, and with the help of his musical friends, has instituted a foundation for assistance to other victims

Featured performers from *The A.R.M.S. Concert.*

of this disease, A.R.M.S. (Action for Research into Multiple Sclerosis). In a series of concerts given in Britain and in the U.S.A., Lane and some of the biggest names in the history of British rock and roll were able to raise a considerable amount of money for the foundation. The occasion also made possible a meeting of rock legends unlike anything since Woodstock. When virtuosos like Eric Clapton, Jimmy Page, Jeff Beck, Steve Winwood, and Rolling Stones Bill Wyman and Charlie Watts get together to play, you know it's worth your attention. This particular concert, recorded at the Royal Albert Hall in London, has been divided into two parts, two tapes. In Part I, Eric Clapton and Steve Winwood serve as the focal points. Clapton performs "Everybody Ought to Make a Change," "Rita Mae," "Lay Down Sally," "Ramblin' on My Mind," "Have You Ever Loved a Woman?," and "Cocaine." Eric is in fine form and looks very healthy. Andy Fairweather-Low, a veteran of the U.K. rock scene, sings the ska classic, "Man Smart, Woman Smarter." Steve Winwood's set includes "Roadrunner," "Slowdown Sundown," "Take Me to the River," and "Gimme Some Lovin'," his Spencer Davis Group standard from 1965. It will bring a smile to your face and a spring to your step.

THE A.R.M.S. CONCERT, PART II   ★★★★

ROCK. 1984. Artists: Jeff Beck, Eric Clapton, Ray Cooper, Andy Fairweather-Low, Kenny Jones, Ronnie Lane, Jimmy Page, Charlie Watts, Steve Winwood, and Bill Wyman. 59 min. Beta Hifi, VHS Stereo. Media ($29.95)

In the second part of this recorded benefit concert for Ronnie Lane's Action for Research into Multiple Sclerosis at the Royal Albert Hall in London, two guitar legends share the same stage for the first time in 15 years—Jeff Beck and Jimmy Page, who last jammed together in the old Yardbirds. And in the final segment, the two are joined on stage by Eric Clapton. An entire generation of British electric blues is summarized in this trio. Beck, accompanied by his usual sidemen (James Hooker, Tony Hymas, Simon Phillips, and Fernando Saunders), displays the guitar pyrotechnics that make him, in the light of Clapton's current mellow, J. J. Cale-influenced style, perhaps the premier rock guitarist living today. "Pump" ("The Pump"), "Led Boots," and "Goodbye Porkpie Hat" (the Charlie Mingus composition) are all instrumental gems. With the help of Winwood and Fairweather-Low, Jeff attempts to sing "Hi Ho Silver Lining." Jimmy Page, ex of Led Zeppelin and currently in The Firm, rekindles the spirit of his early blues mysticism in the passionate "Who's to Blame" and "City Sirens," aided by Steve Winwood on vocals. The capper is an instrumental version of "Stairway to Heaven," reputed to be the most heavily played FM radio cut of all time. Joined by the full complement of A.R.M.S. concert musicians, Eric Clapton sings out on "Tulsa Time" and "Layla," trading licks with Page and Beck. Finally, Ronnie Lane comes out to lead the assembled cast in singing "Goodnight Irene." Directed by Stanley Dorfman. Music produced by veteran recording engineer Glyn Johns. A musical event!

ASIA IN ASIA   ★★ﾉ

ROCK. 1983. Artists: Asia (Greg Lake, Carl Palmer, Steve Howe, Geoff Downes). 60 min. Beta Hifi, VHS Stereo. Vestron ($29.95)

Originally broadcast over MTV, this concert video of the supergroup Asia at the Budokan Arena in Japan points up both Asia's virtuosity and their lack of focus. A gathering of players from art-rock legends of the early seventies (Lake and Palmer were in Emerson, Lake, and Palmer; Steve Howe and Geoff Downes were in Yes), Asia resembles a classic chamber jazz quartet more than a rock and roll band. While fully capable of fashioning exquisite songs like "Only Time Will Tell," the group seem more interested in parceling out equal time to their four superstar egos in the form of long solos. If it were not for the commercial demands of the rock medium, I'm sure the typical Asia concert would be one extended jam. They have achieved platinum record status with brilliantly played throwbacks to the art rock of a decade

Asia.

ago. In this particular concert, they concentrate on their individual virtuosity. "The Heat Goes On," "Here Comes That Feeling," and "Eye to Eye" lead to Steve's guitar solo on the instrumental "Time and Time Again." "Only Time Will Tell," "Open Your Eyes," and "The Smile Has Left Your Eyes" cue Geoff Downes' keyboard pyrotechnics. Carl Palmer takes his drum solo on "Wildest Dreams" seated inside a revolving drum kit. Finally, Asia does encores of "Heat of the Moment" and "Sole Survivor." Directed by video master David Mallet.

THE BAND REUNION ★★★

ROCK. 1983. Artists: The Band (Levon Helm, Richard Manuel, Garth Hudson, and Rick Danko). 87 min. Beta Hifi, VHS Stereo. Media ($29.95)

Without lead guitarist and songwriter Robbie Robertson, The Band staged a reunion tour in 1983. This concert at Vancouver's Queen Elizabeth Theater is the culmination of that tour, and the viewer is treated to a reasonable facsimile of those old, characteristically intense Band performances of a decade ago. The absence of Robertson, here replaced by guitarist Earl Cate of the Cate Brothers Band, Helm's touring group, is felt heavily as the concert progresses. It was Robbie's consummate musicianship (blending various styles of blues guitar into a concise, extremely expressive mode of playing) that made The Band a legendary concert act. But, for most of the 87 minutes, Levon Helm's singing and the enthusiasm of the Canadian audience divert your attention from Robbie's disconcerting absence. "Rag Mama Rag," "Up on Cripple Creek," "The Shape I'm In," "It Makes No Difference," "Milk Cow Boogie," "The Weight," "King Harvest," "Nobody Knows but Me," "W. S. Walcott's Medicine Show," "Mystery Train," "Ophelia," "Don't Start Me Talkin'," "Java Blues," "Chest Fever," "Going Back to Memphis," "In a Blaze of Glory," and "Willie and the Hand Jive" are performed.

BIG COUNTRY LIVE ★★✚

ROCK. 1984. Artists: Big Country (Stuart Adamson, Mark Bryezicki, Tony Butler, and Bruce Watson). 75 min. Beta Hifi, VHS Stereo. Media ($29.95)

MTV broadcast Big Country's New Year's Eve 1983 concert from Barrowland in Glasgow, Scotland, live over its cable network to an American public which had made

The Scottish band Big Country.

Big Country one of the major musical groups of 1983. The odd-sounding combination of electric guitars and bagpipes had a distinct appeal, especially in their hit single, "In a Big Country." But the extended use or abuse of that motif, as in this concert, can grate on one's ears. Big Country has not shown anyone that they are more than a one-hit gimmick band, no matter the appeal of that one hit. Stuart Adamson's thick Scottish accent helps him in his singing but is quite an impediment when speaking to American audiences.

The concert itself features a rowdy but celebratory audience of partisans, some brick back-wall coffeehouse atmosphere, and the appearance of a fife and drum regiment replete with bagpipes during the break after "The Storm." Songs are: "1000 Stars," "Angle Park," "Close Action," "Lost Patrol," "Wonderland," "The Storm," "Porroh Man," "Chance," "Inwards," "Fields of Fire," "Harvest Home," "Tracks of My Tears," "In a Big Country," and "Auld Lang Syne." Directed by Nigel Gordon.

BILLY JOEL LIVE ON LONG ISLAND ★★★

ROCK. 1983. Artist: Billy Joel. 80 min. Beta Hifi, VHS Stereo. CBS/Fox ($29.95)

Billy Joel, native son, returns to Long Island to give a concert for his most rabid fans. The Nassau Coliseum is jam-packed for this 1983 date (recorded, strangely enough, just months before Joel was to climb out of a minor career slump with his platinum album, *An Innocent Man*). The always buoyant, energetic Joel delivers a number of his biggest hits in bravado fashion, jumping away from his piano stool often for calisthenics on stage and forays into the audience. The six cameras used provide a panoramic view of the indoor arena, bathed in light for video. Because the arena is unusually well lit, we are able to see the faces of practically everyone in the audience. Disconcerting as this is, it doesn't detract from the performance on stage, which is simply delightful. Joel opens with "Allentown" and slides into his semiautobiographical songs—"My Life," "The Angry Young Man," "Piano Man," and "The Stranger." "Scandinavian Skies" introduces some obligatory stage effects as a cloud-mottled sky is projected onto the backdrop, giving the proceedings an unintentionally eerie atmosphere. But "Moving Out," "Pressure," "Scene from an Italian Restaurant," "Just the Way You Are," "It's Still Rock and Roll to Me," "Sometimes a Fantasy," and "Big Shot" are all straight-ahead rock and roll, served with generous dollops of Billy Joel's Little Richard act. His three encores are: "You May Be Right," "Only the Good Die Young," and "Souvenir."

BILLY SQUIER   ★★

ROCK. 1982. Artist: Billy Squier. 60 min. Beta Hifi, VHS Stereo. Thorn-EMI ($49.95)

Billy Squier, a rocker from Boston, has the look and sound that appeals to America's suburban teenagers. Although he is 30 years old, Squier's long, curly hair, his wiry, thin body, and his penchant for writing soft heavy metal songs make him a safe alternative to the harsher, more flamboyant images of Judas Priest and the like. Whereas teenage boys may prefer the psychodramatic antics of the cartoonish heavy metal brigade, teenage girls see in Squier something a little closer to a matinee idol. In a video concert directed by Keef, Billy plays to a crowd at the Santa Monica Civic Center, in a minimalist stage show that features nothing more spectacular than Billy switching electric guitars. "In the Dark," "Rich Kids," "My Kinda Lover," "What Do You Want from Me?," "Lonely Is the Night," "Young Girls," "I Need You," "The Stroke," "Should Be My Love," "Two Days Gone," "Big Beat," and "You Know What I Like" are the songs performed.

Billy Squier.

BLACK SABBATH LIVE! ★★⌐

ROCK. 1983. Artists: Black Sabbath with Ozzy Osbourne. 60 min. Beta Hifi, VHS Stereo. Media Home ($29.95)

Black Sabbath, whose act was centered around insistent imagery reminiscent of different strains of occultism, satanism, pre-Christian rites, and general all-around ghoulism, had four gold albums in the seventies. Ozzy Osbourne, their front man, was the main reason for their popularity. He was the incarnation of Black Sabbath's menacing demeanor in voice and attitude. In 1980, Osbourne left the group to pursue a solo career. This tape, recorded before Osbourne's departure, is an exciting concert video featuring Ozzy at his best. As the logo of Black Sabbath, a huge, grinning skull, appears in the backdrop of the stage, Ozzy and the group step forward to perform many of their best-selling hits from the past decade. Included are: "War Pigs," "Never Say Die," "Paranoid," "Black Sabbath," "Dirty Women," "Symptom of the Universe," "Snowblind," "Rock and Roll Doctor," "Electric Funeral," and "Children of the Grave." A cheerful, good time to be had by all!

BLONDIE LIVE! ★★★

ROCK. 1983. Artists: Blondie. 55 min. Beta Hifi, VHS Stereo. MCA ($29.95)

Blondie is the name of the group; Deborah Harry the name of the blonde siren who fronts the band. Originally from New Jersey, Harry traveled quite a long and meandering road to rock superstardom in the late seventies. From Greenwich Village folksinger to New Wave pop vocalist and sex symbol, Harry's transformation was in large part the work of Chris Stein, who is also Harry's longtime live-in lover. Together, they epitomized the sound of New York New Wave music, with its arty lyrics, amphetamine beat, and fashion magazine sensibility. This, *Blondie Live!,* is perhaps their most satisfying *musical* video program. Taped at a concert in Toronto during Blondie's last tour (before Chris Stein's lengthy bout with a mystery ailment), the concert is surprisingly good because of some excellent additions to the band and new arrangements of their old hits. A horn section adds soulfulness to many of Blondie's otherwise coldly calculated songs. A new guitarist, Eddie Martinez, trades licks with Chris Stein and adds depth to their sometimes superficial rhythm section. If one wanted to view only one title of Blondie's, this would be the one. The concert is packed with a lineup of all their most popular hits. The songs performed are: "Rapture," "Island of Lost Souls," "Dance

Deborah Harry in *Blondie Live!*

Way," "The Tide Is High," "Heart of Glass," "Hanging on the Telephone," "Dreaming," "One Way or Another," "War Child," "Start Me Up," and "Call Me."

CONCERT FOR BANGLADESH ★★★♪

ROCK. 1972. Artists: George Harrison, Eric Clapton, Billy Preston, Ringo Starr, Leon Russell, Bob Dylan, Dave Mason, Ravi Shankar, and many others. 99 min. Beta Hifi, VHS Stereo. Thorn-EMI ($39.95)

This star-studded benefit concert for the relief of the Bangladeshi refugees who were displaced by the Indian-Bangladeshi War of 1971 took place in New York's Madison Square Garden on August 1, 1971. George's "friends" appeared for free in order to help him raise funds for much-needed food and medical supplies. Ravi Shankar, a noted classical Indian musician, asked George to help him help his people. *This* is what George came up with in a matter of days. Some of the musicians who flew thousands of miles to make the gig were: Eric Clapton, Leon Russell, Ringo Starr, Dave Mason, Billy Preston, Klaus Voorman, Badfinger, and special guest star Bob Dylan. George and the band play "Wah-Wah," "My Sweet Lord," "Awaiting on You All," "Beware of Darkness," and "While My Guitar Gently Weeps" (featuring Clapton's bristling guitar solo). Leon Russell does a medley of "Jumping Jack Flash" and "Young-blood." Billy Preston performs "That's the Way God Planned It." Bob Dylan is joined by George and Leon for "A Hard Rain's Gonna Fall," "It Takes a Lot To Laugh," "Blowing in the Wind," "Mr. Tambourine Man," and "Just Like a Woman." The finale has George doing "Here Comes the Sun," "Something," and "Bangladesh." A scintillating experience!

CROSBY, STILLS AND NASH: DAYLIGHT AGAIN ★★★

ROCK. 1983. Artists: Crosby, Stills, and Nash. 108 min. Beta Hifi, VHS Stereo. MCA ($39.95)

Affectionately known to their fans as the Law Firm, Crosby, Stills, and Nash have entertained a generation of young urban professionals since 1969, long before their fans had any inkling they would soon become yuppies. Neil Young left the group when he realized that CS&N did not want to abandon its signature close-harmony vocals or to rock harder. Later developments have borne out Young's suspicions. While

Crosby, Stills and Nash in *Daylight Again.*

their music has never challenged the very foundations of the recording industry, much less society at large, CS&N has always managed to reflect the tastes and concerns of their core audience. Typical subject matter for the group: chemical waste, whales, Vietnam veterans, gothic architecture, raising kids, and post-sixties disillusionment. Live in concert at the Universal Amphitheater in Los Angeles, Crosby, Stills, and Nash deliver a mellow performance that is strangely elegiac rather than celebratory. It is an informal and laid-back response to an older, less restless audience, one that is willing to listen to the lyrics of their songs carefully, as Graham Nash clearly demands. The songs: "Lonely Days and Lonely Nights," "Chicago," "Just a Song Before I Go," "Wooden Ships," "Dark Star," "Barrel of Pain," "Wind on the Water," "You Don't Have to Cry," "Blackbird," "Wasted on the Way," "Whistling Down the Wire," "Treetop Flyer," "Magical Child," "Suite: Judy Blue Eyes," "Cathedral," "For What It's Worth," "Love the One You're With," and "Teach Your Children."

CULTURE CLUB: A KISS ACROSS THE OCEAN ★★★

ROCK. 1984. Artists: Culture Club. 60 min. Beta Hifi, VHS Stereo. CBS/Fox ($29.95)

Much has been written about the immensely popular Culture Club and its bizarre, androgynous lead singer, Boy George, but one thing is immediately clear from a careful hearing of their work: they are very talented. George owes debts to such soulful crooners as Marvin Gaye and Smokey Robinson; when backed by the eclectic rhythmic underpinning provided by Club mates Jon Moss, Roy Hay, and Mikey Craig, his voice is clear, romantic, and compelling. Never mind the lyrics, which alternate between amorphous claptrap and syrupy sentiment, Culture Club is exciting. Eleven cameras capture the Club live at an engagement in London where the group performs hits from their two albums (at the time), *Colour by Numbers* and *Kissing to be Clever.* "I'll Tumble 4 Ya," "Mr. Man," "It's a Miracle," "Kharma Chameleon," "Black Money," "Do You Really Want to Hurt Me?," "Miss Me Blind," "Church of the Poisoned Mind," "Victims," "Time," "White Boys," and "Melting Pot" are all impeccably reproduced live. It takes some time to realize that they aren't lip-syncing; this is a well-rehearsed, extremely capable band. As is usual with British rock and roll, the audience has to wade through the thick pop sensibility which pervades every new act in order to get to the real core of a group's sound—if there is one. Culture Club may be around for some time, with or without Boy George's outrageous appearance, but certainly not without his immense talent.

DAVID BOWIE—SERIOUS MOONLIGHT   ★★★★

ROCK. 1984. Artist: David Bowie. 90 min. Beta Hifi, VHS. Media ($39.95)

David Bowie takes center stage in this tape shot as an HBO special at the P.N.E. Grandstand in Vancouver, British Columbia, with a relaxed confidence that guarantees a solid performance right from the start. Aided by emphatic arrangements of his hits both old and new, Bowie launches into such classics as "Fashion," "Let's Dance," "Rebel, Rebel," and "Life on Mars." David and his band of formidable musicians electrify such Bowie standards as "Young Americans" and "Fame." Guitarists Carlos Alomar and Earl Slick run around stage and trade explosive licks on "Cat People." The whole show is so well planned and the musicians so well rehearsed that the concert seems completely spontaneous. But Bowie, the rock star, movie star, and actor, leaves nothing to chance, and is in complete command of his stagecraft. He even makes fun of his role-playing when he dons cloak and dark sunglasses and holds a skull at arms reach in a pose reminiscent of Hamlet to sing the satirical "Cracked Actor." Also conscious of the home video audience, Bowie hired director David Mallet

David Bowie performing in *Serious Moonlight*.

and sound engineer Bob Clearmountain to record this section of the 1983 Serious Moonlight World Tour with no less than nine cameras. The result is an aural and visual accomplishment that should be used as the standard for concert videos of all types for many years to come. This concert includes eleven other songs. Highly recommended.

DAVID GILMOUR ★★★

ROCK. 1984. Artist: Dave Gilmour. 101 min. Beta Hifi, VHS Stereo. CBS/Fox ($29.95)

True to the Pink Floyd tradition of long-windedness, this video on the life, times, and music of David Gilmour, ex-lead guitarist of the Floyd, is about a half hour too long. Otherwise, Gilmour's superb guitar pyrotechnics in concert at the Hammersmith Odeon in London and his genuinely likeable personality make this an entertaining music video, worth seeing even if you've never been a Pink Floyd fan. The first half of the video is straightforward concert footage. Backed by a band including Mick Ralphs on guitar and former Floyd drummer Nick Mason, Gilmour performs a mixture of original solo material and old Floyd nuggets. "Until We Sleep," "All Lovers Are Deranged," "There's No Way out of Here," "Short and Sweet," "Run Like Hell," "Out of the Blue," "Blue Light," "Murder," and "Comfortably Numb" fill out the concert's agenda. This concert material is followed by Gilmour's two rock videos, "Blue Light" and "All Lovers Are Deranged," both hard rock tunes significantly lighter in tone than Pink Floyd's material. The video concludes with a documentary on Gilmour's solo European tour. The biggest laugh comes when Gilmour explains why Pink Floyd finally broke up. It seems that Roger Waters couldn't come up with any more "depressing, fatalistic lyrics" for a new album. It's obvious from Gilmour's sly smile that he was getting a little tired of Waters' gloom and doom songs.

DEXY'S MIDNIGHT RUNNERS: THE BRIDGE ★★⌁

ROCK. 1982. Artists: Dexy's Midnight Runners (Kevin Rowlands, Billy Adams, Helen O'Hara, Mickey Billingham, Spike Edney, Johnny Edwards, Nick Gatfield, Andy Hamilton, Seb Shelton, Steve Brennan, and Kevin Gilson). 52 min. Beta Hifi, VHS Stereo. RCA/ Columbia ($29.95)

Dexy's Midnight Runners, led by Kevin Rowlands, broke onto the scene with their Top 10 hit single, "Come On Eileen," a rave-up Irish rockabilly/folk tune. After capturing the fans' attention with that rather intriguing combination of musical dialects, the Runners surprised them even more with their rustic, Li'l Abner clothes and Irish farmland demeanor. In concert, at the Shaftesbury Theatre in London on October

10, 1982, the Runners make clearer the basic tenets of their musical philosophy, and it appears that, "Eileen" notwithstanding, there's more depth to their sound than one might at first suspect. As all British rock music is deeply indebted to American currents (blues, rockabilly, bubble gum, whatever), it is a pleasant surprise to hear the Runners doing a version of "Respect," the Otis Redding-Aretha Franklin standard, right after a cover of Van Morrison's homage to soul music, "Jackie Wilson Said." The other songs, all originals, fit snugly into the band's special musical niche—Irish R&B with a heavy folk component (lots of violins and traditional Irish instruments). The final tune, "Celtic Soul Brothers," sums up their music in its title. Other songs are: "Old," "All in All" ("This One Last Wild Waltz"), "Let's Make This Precious," "Until I Believe in My Soul," and "Kevin Rowland's Band." Directed by Steve Barron.

DIO ★★♪

ROCK. 1984. Artists: Dio (Ronnie James Dio, Vinny Appice, Jimmy Bain, Vivian Campbell, and Claude Schnell). 51 min. Beta Hifi, VHS Stereo. Warner Music ($29.95)

Ronnie James Dio first reached prominence in the rock world as the lead singer of Richie Blackmore's Rainbow. A heavy metal maven from upstate New York, Dio cut loose from Rainbow and established himself with a string of solo successes under

Dio: Ronnie James Dio, Vinny Appice, Jimmy Bain, and Vivian Campbell.

the banner of a new group, cleverly named Dio. This was, of course, after a brief stint in the granddaddy heavy metal band of them all, Black Sabbath, replacing the legendary Ozzy Osbourne. In his new group, Dio combines high-energy Vegas-style showmanship with some good-natured heavy metal music. The obligatory laser effects, Egyptian motif, and skull and crossbones trimmings are all present at this Dio concert, shot at The Spectrum in Philadelphia, but you don't get the feeling they *really* mean it. Dio won't menace you the way Black Sabbath used to or Judas Priest tries to. Phil Tuckett, under the supervision of Steve Sabol's NFL Films, directs this straightforward concert footage. Dio performs "Stand Up and Shout," "Don't Talk to Strangers," "Mystery," "Egypt" ("The Chains Are On"), "Heaven and Hell," "The Last in Line," "Rainbow in the Dark," "The Mob Rules," and "We Rock."

ELTON JOHN IN CENTRAL PARK ★★

ROCK. 1980. Artist: Elton John. 59 min. Beta, VHS. Media ($39.95)

For several years now, Elton John has been seeking a grip on the pop music fan's shifting tastes. In the mid-seventies, John was one of the giants of the music industry,

Elton John.

but the end of the decade saw his career in rapid decline. Though he has recently recouped some of his losses, in August of 1980 Elton felt he needed the publicity that a free concert in New York's Central Park might give him. By 3 P.M., more than four hundred thousand spectators were in place waiting for Elton's show to begin. Backed by his regular touring band (Dee Murray, James Newton Howard, Nigel Olsson, Tim Renwick, and Richie Zito), John turns in a concert performance that is strangely sedate, almost detached. Director Mike Mansfield positions his cameras appropriately to catch the action but there just isn't any. Wearing a bell captain's uniform festooned with a keyboard motif, Elton sleepwalks his way through "Saturday Night's Alright for Fighting," "Little Jeannie," "Bennie and The Jets," "Imagine," "Somebody Saved My Life Tonight," "Goodbye Yellow Brick Road," "Philadelphia Freedom," and "Sorry Seems to Be the Hardest Word." The highlight of the concert comes when Elton changes into a Donald Duck costume and has to endure the company of a young woman from out of the audience who plops herself down on the piano bench next to him while he's singing "Your Song."

The free concert did not give Elton the career boost he had sought. Despite some recent successes, his better days seem to be behind him.

ELVIS ON TOUR ★★★♪

ROCK. 1972. Artist: Elvis Presley. 92 min. Beta, VHS. MGM/UA ($59.95)

This film, originally released theatrically in 1972, is an account of Elvis' fifteen-city tour in the spring of 1972. Although Elvis purists may be disappointed by the fact that the film is not a straightforward performance film, it is an invaluable record of the phenomenon that was the King on tour in the seventies. Lots of backstage views and dialogue are interspersed with the twenty-nine songs sung in concert or on the soundtrack. Split-screen technique offers the viewer a panorama of Elvis concerts in cities like Detroit, Dayton, Roanoke, Greensboro, and Memphis (his home town). Songs include: "C. C. Rider," "Polk Salad Annie," "Proud Mary," "Burnin' Love," "Suspicious Minds," "Bridge over Troubled Water," "American Trilogy," "Mystery Train," "That's Alright," "Hunk of Love," "Lawdy Miss Clawdy," and "I Can't Help Falling in Love." Some montage sequences use songs like "Johnny B. Goode" and "Memories" to good effect. In a rehearsal studio, we see and hear Elvis and his backup singers do gospel songs including "Rock O' My Soul." Much of the film's look and pacing can be attributed to Martin Scorcese, later director of *Raging Bull* and *Taxi Driver*, who is credited as the supervising editor.

ELVIS! 68 COMEBACK SPECIAL   ★★★★

ROCK. 1968. Artist: Elvis Presley. 76 min. Beta, VHS. Media ($29.95)

This is the *best* performance recorded on video or film that Elvis ever gave! Backed by great production values and an empathetic director-writer tandem (Steve Binder, Chris Beard, and Allan Blye), Elvis' musical special delivers something few if any of today's television specials do: charisma and spontaneity. Much of the program is just Elvis, wearing a black leather outfit, in an extended jam session with some of the original Sun session musicians who helped him record his first songs. This is the high-

Elvis in his *68 Comeback Special.*

light of the special. Conveying spontaneity and intensity at the same time, the jam session shows off not only Elvis' unparalleled singing and guitar-playing talents but his off-the-cuff wit and personality as well. Look at this lineup of songs: "Lawdy Miss Clawdy," "Baby, What You Want Me to Do?," "Heartbreak Hotel," "Hound Dog," "All Shook Up," "I Can't Help Falling in Love," "Jailhouse Rock," "Don't Be Cruel," "Love Me Tender," "Are You Lonesome Tonight?," "That's All Right," "Tiger Man," "Tryin' to Get to You," "One Night," and "Memories." In the two production numbers, Elvis is first seen to good advantage singing a medley of gospel tunes: "Motherless Child," "Up above My Head" ("There Is Music in The Air"), "Where Could I Go?," and "I'm Saved." The leitmotif of the show, initiated in an opening sequence which features Elvis against a backdrop of silhouetted guitarists perched on scaffolding singing "I'm Evil," is Elvis as "Guitar Man." In this mini-rock operetta, Elvis dramatizes the story of a country boy who goes off to make his fortune as a musician, only to meet with failure and disillusionment at every turn. Songs include: "Let Yourself Go," "Nothingville," "Big Boss Man," "Someone Like You," "Little Egypt," and "I'm Evil." In the rousing, inspirational finale, Elvis sings "If I Can Dream," a song of peace and understanding in a time of great strife and turmoil.

AN EVENING WITH UTOPIA ★★♩

ROCK. 1983. Artists: Utopia (Todd Rundgren, Kasim Sulton, Roger Powell, and Willie Wilcox). 85 min. Beta Hifi, VHS Stereo. MCA ($39.95)

The first thing that should be said about this tape is that it's about thirty minutes too long. The second thing is that Todd Rundgren should really seriously sit down and ask himself why he's bent upon recreating his original group, Nazz, endlessly. In this stripped-down version of the earlier Utopia, which featured more keyboards than you could find in a music store, Rundgren is essentially trying to prove to his audience that he is not Paul McCartney—and succeeding. Wearing narrow-lapeled sharkskin suits, the band look as if they had just stepped out of *A Hard Day's Night.* Although their Beatle parody album of a few years back, *Deface the Music,* was both clever and right on target, there's no excuse for the charade to persist. Utopia sounds best when they're doing Todd's characteristically sweet pop tunes and awful when they deviate from that into such experiments as mechano-rock and garage rock. Simply put, Todd is better off as a solo act. Of the twenty-one songs presented here, too many (eight) are sung by other members of the band. The attempt at a Beatles-like variety of musical styles fails miserably. It is no surprise that the best performances in the concert occur when Todd sings such numbers as "Couldn't I Just Tell You,"

Utopia.

"Hammer in My Heart," "Rock Love," "The Road to Utopia," "Caravan," and "Love Is the Answer," all well within the parameters of Rundgren's pop capabilities.

THE EVERLY BROTHERS REUNION CONCERT ★★★

ROCK. 1983. Artists: The Everly Brothers. 60 min. Beta Hifi, VHS Stereo. MGM/UA ($59.95)

After a 10-year separation due to pent-up frustrations, drug problems, and general mid-life crisis, Phil and Don Everly announced their reunion in 1983. Their first concert together would take place at the Royal Albert Hall in London in September of 1983. Veteran rockabilly maven Albert Lee, who had played with Dave Edmunds, Emmylou Harris, and Jackson Browne, put together a band to back the Everlys and, as is clear from the concert, plays the Everly Brothers catalogue with evident joy. The concert promised to be emotional, and during the finale, "Let It Be Me," tears well up in Phil and Don's eyes as they sing the song to each other as well as the audience. Rick Gardner's competent direction allows the viewer to concentrate on the Everlys on stage, still masterful performers after almost three decades. In fact, Don Everly's lead vocals sound even better now than in the past, and the pair's intricate country harmonies are as good as they sound on record. Songs performed are: "Claudette," "Walk Right Back," "Cryin' in the Rain," "Cathy's Clown," "Love Is Strange," "When Will I Be Loved?," "Good Love Gone Bad," "Bird Dog," "Be Bop A Lula," "Barbara Allen," "Long Time Gone," "Step It Up and Go," "Bye Bye Love," "Wake Up Little Susie," "Devoted to You," "Ebony Eyes," "Love Hurts," "Until I Kissed Ya," "Dream," and "Lucille."

FLEETWOOD MAC IN CONCERT ★♪

ROCK. 1983. Artists: Fleetwood Mac. 60 min. Beta Hifi, VHS Stereo. RCA/Columbia ($29.95)

Filmed at the end of their 1982 concert tour in support of the *Mirage* album, Fleetwood Mac is captured live, but unflatteringly so. Due to a combination of factors (the end of a long, exhausting tour, the evident decline of the group's creative impetus, and Stevie Nicks' chronic throat problems), the concert presented here lacks energy and commitment from the players. Other than Mick Fleetwood's demonic drumming and Christine McVie's always professional demeanor, there is little here for anyone other than a real Mac fan. The choice of songs performed indicates how much Lindsey Buckingham had come to dominate the group's output at this point. Of the thirteen tunes heard, Buckingham sings lead on seven, leaving only three songs from Stevie and three for Christine. This is not a good mix. Indeed, throughout most of the concert, it appears that the band is backing up Buckingham, what with Stevie flitting on and off stage, obviously having trouble with her voice. If the arena looks familiar to veteran basketball watchers, it should. It's the Forum in Los Angeles. Songs include: "The Chain," "Gypsy," "Love in Store," "Not That Funny," "You Make Loving Fun," "I'm So Afraid," "Blue Letter," "Rhiannon," "Tusk," "Eyes of the World," "Go Your Own Way," "Sister of the Moon" (on which Lindsey has to finish the last verse for the sore-throated Stevie!), and "Songbird."

GARY NUMAN: THE TOURING PRINCIPLE '79 ★★♪

ROCK. 1979. Artist: Gary Numan. 52 min. Beta Hifi, VHS Stereo. Warner ($29.95)

Several years ahead of his time, Gary Numan introduced mechano-rock to the pop music world with his hit song, "Cars," in 1979. An extreme obsession with automation, expressed in repetitive rhythmic synthesizer runs, a pyramidal-design stage show with a dehumanized look, and his own robotlike movements, marked Numan's emergence onto the musical horizon. In England, where fans saw him as the sophisticated version of punk ideology (we're all being turned into automatons), he reached superstar status. Here in the States, audiences, at first attracted to his odd theatrics, were repelled by Numan's intellectual glee at his bleak vision of the future. The fantasy that recession-torn young Brits enjoyed was definitely not shared by Americans. With the perspective of time, it's clear that only the robotic rhythms of Numan's music have survived to permeate contemporary sounds. His stage moves and attitude, borrowed from David Bowie, and his horror film facial makeup, borrowed from Lou Reed's Transformer guise, have not. Songs: "Cars," "Me! I Disconnect from You," "M.E.," "We Are So Fragile," "Every Day I Die," "Conversations," "Remember I Was Vapour," "On Broadway," "Down in the Park," "My Shadow in Vain," "Are Friends Electric?," and "Tracks."

GENESIS: THREE SIDES LIVE ★★★

ROCK. 1982. Artists: Genesis (Phil Collins, Tony Banks, Mike Rutherford, Darryl Stuermer, and Chester Thompson). 90 min. Beta, VHS. Thorn-EMI ($49.95)

This could easily have been retitled *A Weekend in New York* or *Three Brits in the Big Apple* since the two concerts used in compiling this on-the-road documentary about Genesis both take place in the New York area, at the Nassau Coliseum on Long Island and the Savoy in New York City. Shot on film and transferred to video, *Three Sides Live* presents the group at the apex of its popularity after almost ten years of art-rock obscurity. Not since Peter Gabriel left the group after *The Lamb Lies Down on Broadway* had Genesis had a more successful American tour. The reason for this was the new sound they had come up with: R&B-derived dance music.

Phil Collins, the lead singer, has also had a hugely successful solo career, and in many ways, the Genesis road show *is* Phil Collins. In interviews, Banks and Rutherford sound like two Oxford lads, cerebrally picking apart the music they make, offering philosophical bromides. Collins, on the other hand, with his slight cockney accent and day laborer looks, keeps the whole business in perspective and also seems to be having a lot of fun. Songs are: "Behind the Lines," "Duchess," "Misunderstanding," "Dodo," "Abacab," "No Reply at All," "Who Dunnit," "In the Cage," "Afterglow," "Me and Sarahjane," "Man on the Corner," and "Turn It On Again." Directed by Stuart Orme.

GIMME SHELTER ★★★★

ROCK. 1970. Artists: The Rolling Stones, Ike and Tina Turner, The Grateful Dead, Jefferson Airplane, and The Flying Burrito Brothers. 90 min. Beta Hifi, VHS Stereo. RCA/Columbia ($29.95)

Acclaimed documentary filmmakers Al and David Maysles, along with Charlotte Swerin, directed this film record of The Rolling Stones' American tour of fall 1969. What originally looked like a very straightforward concert film about the so-called bad boys of rock turned into a nightmare when the band decided to put on a free rock festival at the Altamont Speedway near San Francisco, the last stop on their tour. Their big mistake was hiring the Hells Angels motorcycle gang to police the crowd at the festival. Things got ugly when the bikers started using knives and brass knuckles to control a crowd of 300,000 drug-crazed hippies. The Maysles captured poignant looks of disgust and derision on the faces of the Angels as they watched the mob of "flower children" turn on, tune in, and drop acid. And the Angels were no bargains either. What turned a bad situation into a horror show that Don MacLean would later refer to as "the day the music died " was the killing of a young black man in the audience, knifed to death on camera by a Hells Angel during The Stones' rendition of "Sympathy for the Devil." All at once, the sham satanism of their bad-boy image rose up to haunt them with a vengeance. The final freeze-frame on Mick Jagger's face, as he shows real fear and trembling while watching the footage of the killing, is an apt image to end the sixties with. Despite the depressing nature of the film's climax, a lot of good music can be heard from beginning to end. The Stones, in good form, do "Satisfaction," "Jumpin' Jack Flash," "Wild Horses," "Brown Sugar," "Honky Tonk Woman," "Street Fighting Man," "Under My Thumb," and "Gimme Shelter."

GOLDEN EARRING LIVE FROM THE TWILIGHT ZONE ★★

ROCK. 1984. Artists: Golden Earring (George Kooymans, Barry Hay, Rimus Gerritsen, and Cesar Zuiderwijk). 60 min. Beta Hifi, VHS Stereo. RCA/Columbia ($29.95)

If you visit the Netherlands, you will discover that most of that country's popular music is sung in English and that, indeed, many of their most popular singers sound exactly like Bob Dylan, Neil Diamond, Bob Seger, etc. Thus, it's no surprise that, once in a while, a rock group from the Netherlands will actually show up on the American Top 100 charts. Golden Earring plays Dutch heavy metal music, singing entirely in English, sounding almost exactly like a typical American or British hard-rock band. This video concert was recorded at the Groenoordhallen in Leiden, Holland, on June 23, 1984. Before the group appears on stage, we see a video about a spy who is hit by a car and brought to a hospital, where he has plastic surgery performed on him to alter his features. This, I suppose, is an introduction to their hit song, "Twilight Zone." When the group arrives on stage, they do "Mission Impossible," "When the Lady Smiles," "Long Blonde Animal," "The Devil Made Me Do It," "Radar Love," and "Twilight Zone." The show comes complete with two leather-clad dancing girls.

GRAHAM PARKER   ★★★

ROCK. 1982. Artists: Graham Parker and The Rumour (Brinsley Schwarz, Kevin Jenkins, Carlos Alomar, Michael Braun, and George Small). 60 min. Beta Hifi, VHS Stereo. Sony ($29.95)

Four or five years ago, it seemed that British rocker Graham Parker was on the verge of superstardom. Gathering praise from all corners of the pop music world (Bruce Springsteen said Parker was the only act he'd pay money to see), Parker's no-nonsense, hard R&B sound was waiting to break into the Top 10 charts. The breakthrough never materialized. Perhaps the intense, often unremitting lyrical content of Parker's bluesy songs militated against across-the-board popularity. But he is still a strong concert attraction, touring the States frequently. Here, captured live at Park West in

Graham Parker.

Chicago during June of 1982, Parker delivers a characteristically hard-edged performance, backed by The Rumour. The concert, originally broadcast on MTV, features "Jolie Jolie," "Fear Not," "White Honey," "Thankless Task," "Howling Wind," "Stick to Me," "Passion Is No Ordinary Word," "Can't Waste a Minute," "No More Excuses," "Heat Treatment," "Dark Side of the Bright Lights," "You Hit the Spot," "Empty Lives," and "Nobody Hurts You."

THE GRATEFUL DEAD: DEAD AHEAD ★★✦

ROCK. 1980. Artists: Grateful Dead (Bob Weir, Jerry Garcia, Mickey Hart, Phil Lesh, Bill Kreutzmann, and Brent Mydland). 90 min. Beta, VHS. Warner ($29.95)

The Grateful Dead are the ultimate cult group, loved by millions of followers around the world for their uncanny music, characterized by a looseness in live performance that suggests the improvisatory nature of modern jazz. Originally formed to play at Ken Kesey's "acid-test" weekend retreat/orgies, the Dead quickly became San Francisco's most prominent rock group, though they've never sold a lot of records. Favorites of the Hells Angels, they are notorious for playing long, narcotic-tinged jams which may very well be the American equivalent of Jamaican reggae music—tunes to toke up by. Caught live in concert on Halloween night at New York's Radio City Music Hall, they are introduced by ex-Saturday Night Live comics Franken and Davis. As is their custom, the Dead open the concert with an acoustic set, playing very long versions of "To Lay Me Down," "On the Road Again," and "Ripple." They reappear after a short break to play an electric set. "Don't Ease Me In," "Lost Sailor," "Saint of Circumstance," "Franklin's Tower," "Rhythm Devils" (an excruciatingly drawn-out drum/percussion solo by Hart and Kreutzmann), "Fire on the Mountain," "Not Fade Away," and "Good Lovin'" (the old Rascals nugget) complete the evening's performance. While this may satisfy Deadheads, the group's musical stagnation and self-satisfaction are all too obvious to the unprejudiced eye.

HALL AND OATES: ROCK'N SOUL LIVE   ★★★

ROCK. 1983. Artists: Hall and Oates. 90 min. Beta Hifi, VHS Stereo. RCA/Columbia ($29.95)

With most other groups, the paying fan risks going to a concert and not hearing any of the songs the group is famous for. Not so with Daryl Hall and John Oates. Their

DARYL HALL AND JOHN OATES

Daryl Hall was born in Pottstown, Pennsylvania, in 1949. John Oates was born on April 7, 1949, in New York City. The two met as teenagers in Philadelphia doo-wop groups, went to different colleges, experienced some early setbacks in brief solo stints, and reteamed in 1969 back in Philadelphia.

Although Hall and Oates had a hit with "She's Gone" in 1973 (a much bigger hit for the soul group Tavares), it wasn't until 1976, after switching record labels, that they had their first Number 1 single, "Rich Girl." Then, as soon as they seemed to find the magic formula, they lost it. They went through three lean years, during which time they tried a New Wave sound that failed and Hall embarked on a very brief solo interlude, before filling the airwaves with pop hooks again.

"Kiss on My List" in 1980 started a string of Top 10 hits that hasn't stopped yet. Surpassing even the Everly Brothers, Hall and Oates are now the most successful recording tandem in the history of the pop music charts. Their blend of soul music and pop rock distinguishes them from the harsher sounds of their contemporaries, forming a bridge to the music of the sixties when white artists and black artists learned a great deal from each other's musical styles.

Video Resume

Hall and Oates: Rock'n Soul Live, (1983), RCA/Columbia.

Hall and Oates Video Collection, (1984), RCA/Columbia.

Rock, Rhythm, and Blues, (1984), Disney.

string of hits is so long that there is absolutely no danger of coming up empty-handed at a typical Hall and Oates concert. Starting out as a blue-eyed soul duo from Philadelphia, a hotbed of pop music in the early seventies, Hall and Oates have made several adjustments in their musical approach over the years. A few years ago, they were in danger of losing their recording contract, having gone years between hits and having failed at a New Wave sound. Then the hook-filled, eminently danceable gold singles started to avalanche. For more than three years, Hall and Oates have been consistent Top 10 artists. It is difficult to explain where they got their newfound hitmaking power from. Perhaps someone sold his soul to the devil, but neither Hall nor Oates is telling. On their H$_2$O tour of 1983, they stopped by at the Montreal Forum in Canada to record this live video. Taken from two performances, March 10 and 11, what Hall and Oates deliver here is essentially a greatest-hits concert. Songs include "Family Man," "Diddy Doo Wop," "Italian Girls," "Kiss on My List," "She's Gone," "Art of a Heartbreak," "One on One," "You've Lost That Loving Feeling," "I Can't Go for That" ("No Can Do"), "Sara Smile," "Wait for Me," "Maneater," "Private Eyes," "Open All Night," "You Make My Dreams," and "Room to Breathe."

IN OUR HANDS   ★★✦

ROCK. 1982. Artists: James Taylor, Carly Simon, Holly Near, Peter, Paul, and Mary, Rita Marley, Pete Seeger, Meryl Streep, and Orson Welles. 90 min. Beta, VHS. Continental ($29.95)

A concert film made to document the music made at the largest antinuclear rally in the history of the United States. On June 12, 1982, approximately a million people gathered in New York's Central Park to demonstrate against the proliferation of nuclear weaponry and to listen to the performances of a number of musical guests. Between musical segments, the viewer can spot such celebrity participants as Dr. Benjamin Spock, Dr. Helen Caldicott, Meryl Streep, Orson Welles, Roy Scheider, Ellen Burstyn, Christopher Reeve, and many others. Actually appearing in concert are Holly Near ("Singing for Our Lives"), Rita Marley ("That's the Jury" and "My Kind of World"), Peter, Paul, and Mary ("Where Have All the Flowers Gone?"), James Taylor ("You've Got a Friend"), Jon Hall ("Children's Cry"), House of the Lord Choir ("We Cry Disarmament"), Are and Be Ensemble ("If There Is No Struggle"), and Pete Seeger ("It's the Bomb That Has to Die" and "If I Had a Hammer"). Carly Simon's "Turn of the Tide" is heard over the opening sequence but she does not actually appear in the film.

JAMES TAYLOR IN CONCERT   ★★↵

ROCK. 1979. Artists: James Taylor and The Section. 90 min. Beta, VHS. CBS/Fox, Pioneer ($29.98)

Much of James Taylor's music evokes the movement of daylight toward calm, cool evening, and in this concert taped at the Blossom Music Center in July 1979, that mood is startlingly captured. As evening draws closer, Taylor and his backup band, that group of crack L.A. session players called The Section (featuring Waddy Wachtel, Danny Kootch, and David Sanborn), make a small world out of the modern amphitheater where a few thousand mellow fans have gathered. James opens the concert quite unassumingly, emerging onstage alone to sing "Blossom," "Millworker," "Carolina on My Mind," "Handy Man," "Brother Trucker," and "Secret O' Life." Then the band appears, revealed by the stagelights, and the concert begins to rock a little harder. "Your Smiling Face," "Up on the Roof," "Steamroller Blues," "Don't Let Me Be Lonely Tonight," "Long Ago and Far Away," "I Will Not Lie for You," and "Walking Man" feature his band's precise, recording-studio style of playing. In the darkness of late evening, Taylor closes with "Mexico," "Honey, Don't Leave L.A.," "Sweet Baby James," and the encores, "How Sweet It Is," "Summertime Blues," and "Fire and Rain." Much good music from the failed troubadour of California high times and Nixon's first administration.

JIMI PLAYS BERKELEY   ★★

ROCK. 1971. Artists: Jimi Hendrix Experience. 55 min. Beta, VHS. Vestron ($59.95)

This is the only video program that consists almost entirely of concert footage of the great Jimi Hendrix. Here, he plays a gig at the Berkeley Community Center in Berkeley, California, on Memorial Day, 1970. The band he has with him includes Mitch Mitchell on drums and Jimi's old Army buddy, Billy Cox, on bass. The opening shots show Jimi arriving for rehearsal at the concert hall in a chauffeur-driven limousine. Across town, at the same time, college students from the local campus are picketing a theater where *Woodstock,* the movie, is playing. "I'm not going to pay $3.50 to see this movie," a young woman tells the camera. "It should be free because the people made the movie, man." When the film does finally settle down to showing us the concert, we are treated to a fine set from Hendrix, displaying both his musical prowess and his stage charisma. "Johnny B. Goode" starts off the performance. A highlight of any Hendrix concert was a move he picked up while playing the chitlin' circuit with the Isley Brothers and Little Richard. He would "eat" his guitar, picking the strings with his teeth while fretting the guitar with his right hand. "Hear My Train,"

"Star Spangled Banner," "Purple Haze," "I Don't Live Today," "Little Wing," "Lover Man," "Machine Gun," and "Voodoo Chile" complete the songs in his concert. Recommended solely because it is the most complete visual record of a *single* Hendrix concert.

JOE COCKER LIVE ★★✔

ROCK. 1984. Artist: Joe Cocker. 59 min. Beta Hifi, VHS Stereo. TWE ($29.95)

Captured live at a free outdoor concert in Tokyo, Joe Cocker, master of the spastic gesture on stage, delivers a competent performance to a rain-soaked audience. The tape shows Cocker standing beneath a canopy that shields him from the hard-driving afternoon shower; his reputation as a blues shouter (*Mad Dogs and Englishmen*) is what protects him from serious criticism now that he's past his prime. He's still able to give expression to some songs, and the concert is not a washout for fans of boogie band music. Highlights of the performance are "You Are So Beautiful," "The Letter," and "With a Little Help from My Friends," songs which lend themselves thoroughly to Joe's kick-out-all-the-jams style of singing. Also on the agenda are "What Is He to You?," "Look What You Done," "Fun Time," "Whiter Shade of Pale," "I'm So Blue," "Sweet Little Woman," "Seven Days," "Watching the River Flow," "Sweet Forgiveness," and "Hitchcock Railway." For the definitive Joe Cocker performance, we'll have to wait until someone releases his concert film of the Mad Dogs tour on home video.

JOHNNY WINTER LIVE ★★

ROCK. 1983. Artist: Johnny Winter. 45 min. Beta Hifi, VHS Stereo. Media ($29.95)

Raised in Beaumont, Texas, with his younger brother Edgar, Johnny Winter learned the blues during sojourns to Louisiana's delta region and a long stay in Chicago. Fusing the rural blues of the Delta and the electric, urban blues of Chicago's South Side, Winter emerged as America's foremost white blues guitarist in the late sixties. Although his career has had its ups and downs, overshadowed by his younger brother's more commercially oriented music ("Frankenstein"), the fast-fingered technique that made him a youthful legend hasn't diminished in the least. In this live concert shot at Massey Hall in Toronto, Canada, Winter, backed by Jon Paris on bass and Bobby Turello on drums, plays a satisfying set of electric blues standards and original compositions. One can hear a similarity in pitch and tempo between Johnny's work on guitar and that of the new Texas blues guitar hero, Stevie Ray Vaughan. "Jumping Jack Flash," "Rock and Roll Hoochie Koo," "Stranger," "Unseen Eye," "Sweet Papa John," "High-

Blues guitarist Johnny Winter.

way 61 Revisited" (Winter's version is better than Dylan's own), "Mean Town Blues,"
"Johnny B. Goode," and "It's All Over Now." Directed by Stan Jacobson.

KANSAS ★★⌐

*ROCK. 1982. Artists: Kansas (Bobby Steinhardt, Kerry Livgren, Dave Hope, Phil Ehart,
Rich Williams, Warren Hamm, and John Elefante). 87 min. Beta Hifi, VHS Stereo. Sony
($29.95)*

Originally broadcast over MTV, Kansas' tenth anniversary concert from the Omaha
Civic Auditorium in Omaha, Nebraska, is a greatest hits package, displaying the qualities
that made Kansas, at one time, the most popular rock band in the country. They
reached the apex of their success in 1977 with their best-selling single, "Dust in the
Wind." Another American group deeply influenced by the majestic art-rock sound
of such British bands as Yes, ELO, Emerson, Lake, and Palmer, and Roxy Music,

Kansas' live concert video.

Kansas spent a few years in obscurity before the trademark guitar heroics of Kerry Livgren, the quasi-classical violin of Bobby Steinhardt, and Steve Walsh's archetypal vocals broke through on the charts. (With most of the group's biggest hits already behind them, Walsh left in 1981 and was replaced by John Elefante, whose voice is almost identical to Walsh's.) Another, less sanguine, aspect of Kansas' art-rock music is a tendency toward half-baked philosophizing. Be forewarned and take a hint from some of these titles: "Paradox," "Windows," "Right Away," "Portrait," "Diamonds and Pearls," "Mysteries and Mayhem," "No One Together," "Hold On," "Dust in the Wind," "Chasing Shadows," "Crossfire," "Face It," "Play the Game Tonight," "Carry On Wayward Son," "Sparks of the Tempest," and "Down the Road."

KATE BUSH LIVE AT HAMMERSMITH ODEON ★★★

ROCK. 1981. Artist: Kate Bush. 52 min. Beta, VHS. Thorn-EMI ($49.95)

One of the more pleasant oddities of the British pop music scene is Kate Bush, a brunette beauty with a little girl soprano voice who has combined modern jazz dance steps with electric folk-rock music. She caused quite a stir in her native land with her one-woman stage revue at the Hammersmith Odeon in London. Part mime show, part operetta, and part glitter-rock spectacle, Bush's musical extravaganza is like nothing you have seen or will likely see soon. Using a vocal style that relies on coos, hiccups, and a four-octave range, Kate presents a dozen set pieces, many of which, for all their silly panache, could easily have been thought up by Andrew Lloyd Webber. "Moving," "Them Heavy People," "Violin," "Strange Phenomena," "Hammer Horror," "Don't Push Your Foot on the Heartbrake," "Wow," "Feel It," and "Kite" are just the appetizers for the climax, "James and the Cold Gun." This last piece is almost indescribable. It involves a sci-fi, space-age shootout between Kate, dressed in slinky leather chaps and gun belt, and a male dancer dressed similarly. This turns into an erotic ballet (Freud would have choked on his cigar). "Oh, England My Lionheart" and "Wuthering Heights" conclude the revue. Directed by Keef. American audiences might have some difficulty with the numerous references to British pop culture.

The legendary Kinks.

THE KINKS: ONE FOR THE ROAD   ★★★

ROCK. 1980. Artists: The Kinks (Ray Davies, Dave Davies, Mick Avory, Ian Gibbons, and Jim Rodford). 60 min. Beta, VHS. Vestron ($29.95)

Another of the sixties' lost geniuses of rock and roll, Ray Davies has made a startling comeback, pulling himself and The Kinks up from the depths of obscurity and back into the limelight. Always recognized as a wonderfully talented songwriter (his songs are askance looks at contemporary themes), Ray was never noted for being a strong stage performer. Indeed, his fabled drinking bouts often made him too incoherent to deliver a complete concert.

The eighties have discovered a new Ray Davies, Mr. Showman. Captured live here at the Providence (Rhode Island) Civic Center, Ray and The Kinks are in fine form. Jumping about the stage and acting out the songs, Ray certainly gives his audience their money's worth. The opening number has Ray, alone on stage with an acoustic guitar, directing the audience to sing along on "Lola." Joined by the rest of the band, Ray goes through the catalogue: "All Day and All of the Night," "Low Budget," "Superman," "Attitude," "Celluloid Heroes," "Hardway," "Where Have All the Good Tunes Gone," "You Really Got Me," "Pressure," "Catch Me Now I'm Falling," and "Victoria."

LET'S SPEND THE NIGHT TOGETHER   ★★

ROCK. 1982. Artists: The Rolling Stones (Mick Jagger, Keith Richard, Bill Wyman, Charlie Watts, and Ron Wood). 100 min. Beta Hifi, VHS Hifi. Embassy ($39.95)

Hal Ashby, who directed *Coming Home,* filmed The Stones on tour in 1981 in North America. The concerts used in this movie are an outdoor extravaganza in Tempe, Arizona, and an indoor performance in the Brendan Byrne Arena in New Jersey. It's a breezy, straightforward concert flick that shows off twenty-five Stones classics. Dressed in football pants and colorful knee pads and standing against a backdrop of murals, Mick struts his stuff, bumping and grinding to the delight of packed houses. But the performance, although spirited, is blunted by the inept camerawork under Ashby's leadership—it's fairly obvious he did not map out the camera positions for each concert site. Ashby's considerable directorial talent did not translate well into the concert film genre, and Stones fans will have to battle against that in their enjoyment of this picture. The Stones do "Shattered," "Neighbors," "Black Limousine," "Just My Imagination," "Beast of Burden," "Miss You," "Going to A Go-Go," "Tumbling Dice," "Hang Fire," "Under My Thumb," "Let's Spend the Night Together," "Start Me Up," "She's So Cold," "Honky Tonk Woman," "Satisfaction," "Twenty Flight Rock," and many other favorites.

LIVE INFIDELITY: R.E.O. SPEEDWAGON IN CONCERT ★★

ROCK. 1981. Artists: R.E.O. Speedwagon. 87 min. Beta, VHS. MGM/UA ($29.98)

R.E.O. Speedwagon, the band named after a fire engine, was founded in 1968 on the campus of the University of Illinois at Champaign. After recording nine albums, none of which sold well, and spending years as an opening act for such national groups as Kansas and Bob Seger during their tours through the midwest, the Speedwagon struck gold with their album *Hi-Infidelity*, which held the Number 1 position on the charts three different times and sold over six million copies. With their combination of pop hooks and rock riffs, the band entertains an enthusiastic SRO crowd at the McNichols Arena in Denver, Colorado, in a concert that can be seen on this tape. Starting with "Don't Let Him Go," the band kicks into "I Never Seen a Woman Who Made Me Feel the Way You Do," before a version of "Tough Guys" that features a searing two-note solo by lead guitarist Gary Richrath. R.E.O. Speedwagon brings the auditorium to its feet with their big hit, "Take It on the Run," and then "Time to Fly," "Ridin' the Storm Out" (the title tune from their 1972 album), and "157 Riverside Avenue."

MEN AT WORK: LIVE IN SAN FRANCISCO
OR WAS IT BERKELEY? ★★★

ROCK. 1983. Artists: Men At Work (Colin Hay, Ron Strykert, Greg Ham, John Rees, and Jerry Speiser). 58 min. Beta Hifi, VHS Stereo. CBS/Fox ($29.95)

Men At Work, the most successful of the Australian Invasion bands, is captured live in concert in the Berkeley Amphitheater on the campus of the University of California at Berkeley during their initial tour of the U.S. in 1983. With an odd sound that blends reggae and New Wave tempos, Men At Work scored numerous chart successes, including "Down Under," "Dr. Heckle and Mr. Jive," and "Who Can It Be Now." The most interesting bit of business during the concert, and the reason behind the title, is that odd-looking lead singer Colin Hay keeps referring to San Francisco even though they're actually in Berkeley—quite a difference to the audience although Hay probably figured that crossing the bay didn't mean that much. Finally, near the end of the concert, the audience's insistent shouts get through to Hay and he corrects his mistake. The rest of the tape, directed by rock video veteran Bruce Gower, is dominated by the music hall-type banter and antics of Colin Hay (with his spooky, zombielike eyes) and keyboardist Greg Ham and includes sections from their videos for "Down Under," "High Wire," and "It's a Mistake." They also perform "Overkill," "Dr. Heckle and Mr. Jive," "Underground," "The Longest Night," "Blue for You," "No Sign of Yesterday," "Who Can It Be Now," "Helpless Automation," "Mr. Entertainer," and "Be Good Johnny."

NO NUKES: THE MUSE CONCERT   ★★★

ROCK. 1980. Artists: Jackson Browne, Carly Simon, James Taylor, Bruce Springsteen, Doobie Brothers, Crosby, Stills, and Nash, Gil Scott-Heron, Bonnie Raitt, John Hall, and Jesse Colin Young. 103 min. Beta, VHS. CBS/Fox, Pioneer ($59.95)

In October of 1979, Jackson Browne gathered together an all-star cast of musical artists under the banner of nuclear disarmament to play a benefit concert at New York's Madison Square Garden.

While Browne may not have been completely successful in bringing back the idealism and activism of the sixties, *No Nukes* is a rewarding concert film, filled with good performances and, for the most part, engaging camerawork. The concert features some of the staple performers of this kind of gathering: Carly Simon and James Taylor ("Mockingbird," "The Times They Are A-Changing," "Your Smiling Face," and "Stand and Fight"), Bonnie Raitt (Del Shannon's "Runaway"), CS&N ("Suite: Judy Blue Eyes" and "Barrel of Pain"), and John Hall ("Power" and "Get Together," with Jesse Colin Young). But, musically, the film is noteworthy for the contributions of the Doobie Brothers ("Depending on You," "What a Fool Believes," and "Taking It to the Streets") and such rarely lensed artists as Jackson Browne ("Running on Empty" and "Before the Deluge"), Gil Scott-Heron ("We Almost Lost Detroit"), and Bruce Springsteen, whose bravura performance ("The River," "Thunder Road," and Gary U.S. Bonds'

"Quarter to Three") is the highlight of this event. Haskell Wexler is the director of photography.

THE OUTLAWS ★★

ROCK. 1982. Artists: The Outlaws. 81 min. Beta Hifi, VHS Stereo. Sony LP ($29.95)

This concert, recorded live at the Tower Theater in Philadelphia, in July of 1982, was originally broadcast over MTV. The Outlaws, a veteran band whose albums go back as far as 1974, are a good example of how southern rock has gained mainstream acceptance. While keeping in touch with the blues-based sound of the Allman Brothers Band, The Outlaws' music can best be described as a cross between country rock and heavy metal. With this mix, they have remained popular over a decade amidst shifting commercial tastes. The first two-thirds of the concert is given over to the music they've been making most recently. "Devil's Road," "Hurry Sundown," "Don't Stop," "Long Gone," "You Are the Show," "Easy Does It," "Goodbye," and "Foxtail Lily" are all done in the heavy, distorted guitar style that has helped them reach out to an audience that wouldn't normally go to see a southern band. But it is in the final third of the concert that The Outlaws' real talent and country roots reappear as they do stirring, heartfelt renditions of their early classics, "Green Grass and High Tides," "Ghost Riders," and "There Goes Another Love Song." Artificial fog streams onto the stage as the band finishes up some stirring licks in their final number.

PAUL SIMON IN CONCERT ★★↓

ROCK. 1981. Artist: Paul Simon. 54 min. Beta, VHS. Warner ($29.95)

After a few years' absence, Paul Simon returned to the concert stage in October of 1980 to play a date at the Tower Theatre in Philadelphia. He brought with him a collection of fine New York studio musicians, including Richard Tee on piano, Eric Gale on guitar, and Steve Gadd on drums. Together they run through a set of twelve of Paul's best-loved songs. Starting with his 1971 hit, "Me and Julio Down by the Schoolyard," they move into the title song from his smash album, "Still Crazy after All These Years," and continue with "Ace in the Hole." Paul plays his acoustic guitar

Paul Simon.

on "Something So Right," and then sings the title tune from his film, *One Trick Pony*. Paul adds "Johan," "Fifty Ways to Leave Your Lover," "Late in the Evening," and "American Tune." In closing the concert, he performs two songs he made famous with Art Garfunkel, "The Boxer" and "The Sound of Silence."

PHIL COLLINS LIVE AT PERKINS PALACE ★★⁺

ROCK. 1983. Artist: Phil Collins. 56 min. Beta Hifi, VHS Stereo. Thorn-EMI ($29.95)

Best described as a no-frills rock star, Phil Collins has been an amazingly successful performer since stepping out for a solo career away from his duties as drummer for Genesis. Collins chooses to play a funkier, more R&B-inflected brand of music than

PHIL COLLINS

Born January 31, 1951, in London, U.K., Phil Collins joined the progressive rock group Genesis in 1970. For the first few years, Phil was basically an outsider to the group's creative core, Peter Gabriel and Tony Banks. After Gabriel's departure for a solo career in 1974, Collins took over as lead singer, and, to all intents and purposes, Genesis became Collins' backup band as he steered it farther and farther away from its neoclassical, oddly theatrical sound toward R&B and pop/rock.

With the release of *Face Value* in 1982, Phil's solo career got an auspicious launching. He's had Top 10 hits with "I Missed Again," "I Don't Care Anymore," "You Can't Hurry Love," "Behind the Lines," and "Against All Odds."

Phil's love for Motown soul standards has permeated his own music. His association with The Phoenix Horns, who back up Earth, Wind, and Fire, led to his producing Philip Bailey's *Chinese Wall* album and dueting with him on their smash hit, "Easy Lover." In a way, he is largely responsible for the current revival in R&B sounds, both here and in the United Kingdom. He is also reputed to be one of the best rock drummers in the world. Despite his less-than-matinee idol looks, Phil makes consistently interesting rock videos, and in a time of increasing emphasis on the visual, Collins is the proof that music is the ultimate criterion, not flashy clothes or tons of makeup.

Video Resume

Do They Know It's Christmas?, (1984), Vestron.

Genesis: Three Sides Live, (1982), Thorn-EMI.

Phil Collins, (1983), Sony.

Phil Collins Live At Perkins Palace, (1983), Thorn-EMI.

Prince's Trust Rock Gala, (1982), MGM/UA.

Secret Policeman's Other Ball, (1982), MGM/UA.

Secret Policeman's Private Parts, (1984), Media.

Genesis had always been noted for, and his reedy, thin voice has an appeal few could have predicted. As he steps out center stage at Pasadena's Perkins Palace to a packed house, the balding, dumpy-looking Collins is no one's vision of a rock and roll idol. Yet, as the concert progresses, he wins you over with his earnestness, exuberance, and marvelous songwriting skills. Singing tunes from his two albums, *Face Value* and *Hello, I Must Be Going,* Collins is backed by The Phoenix Horns, who also back Earth, Wind, and Fire, as he seems to want to start a soul music revival. The mixed results are predictable (Collins neither has the voice nor the stage moves to be convincing as, say, Smokey Robinson or Marvin Gaye, two performers to whom his current sound is deeply indebted), but the man does write some good songs. He performs "I Don't Care Anymore," "I Cannot Believe It's True," "Through These Walls," "I Missed Again," "Behind the Lines," "The Roof Is Leaking," "The West Side," "In the Air Tonight," "You Can't Hurry Love," "It Don't Matter to Me," and "People Get Ready."

In his most recent work, Collins seems to be leaning toward a more sophisticated dance sound, leaving behind his re-workings of Motown masterpieces.

POLICE AROUND THE WORLD   ★★★

ROCK. 1982. Artists: The Police (Sting, Andy Summers, and Stewart Copeland). 77 min. Beta Hifi, VHS Stereo. I.R.S. ($33.98)

The Clash and The Police are the two most important bands to have emerged from the British punk scene of the late seventies. Taking reggae motifs and adding jazz-derived elements, The police have come up with a highly original and compelling sound, spearheaded by Sting's distinctive vocals and evocative lyrics. However, back in 1980, although well known in their native Britain, The Police were anonymous elsewhere, especially in the U.S. where they desperately wanted to make it. Miles Copeland, Stewart's brother and the group's manager, decided to send them on a world tour—even though there wasn't really a clamoring demand for them. Playing in small clubs and truly out of the way venues, The Police established a foundation for their current multimillion-dollar worldwide market. This combination travelogue and concert film presents the viewer with an unusually entertaining look at the group and its music. Japan, Hong Kong, Australia, India (where they play a gig at a Ladies' Social Club), Egypt, Greece, Argentina, France, and the U.S.A. (Los Angeles) form the itinerary for their voyage. Songs include: "Next to You," "Man in a Suitcase," "Walking on the Moon," "Born in the Fifties," "So Lonely," "Can't Stand Losing You," "Bring On the Night," "Canary in a Coal Mine," "When the World Is Running Down,"

The Police.

"Shadows in the Rain," "Da Do Do Do De Da Da Da," "Don't Stand So Close to Me," "Truth Hits Everybody," "Roxanne," and "Message in a Bottle."

THE POLICE SYNCHRONICITY CONCERT ★★★♪

ROCK. 1984. Artists: The Police. 76 min. Beta Hifi, VHS Stereo. A&M/I.R.S. ($39.95)

The Police have deserved all the superlatives thrown their way. They are one of the most daring, innovative, and assured pop music bands in the world. The charisma of Sting, their lead singer, is, strangely enough, not in his sexy demeanor but in the attitude of high seriousness and sincerity that he is able to convey. That, combined with the group's vaunted experiments in African rhythms and exotic instruments, has translated into millions in record sales internationally. Caught live at The Omni in Atlanta by Godley and Creme, ex-10 CC members who've developed a video studio of sorts, The Police deliver a spirited performance to an SRO crowd. "Synchronicity 1," "Walking in Your Footsteps," "Message in a Bottle," "Walking on the Moon,"

"Wrapped around Your Finger," "Hole in My Life," "King of Pain," "One World," "Da Do Do Do De Da Da Da," "Every Breath You Take," "Can't Stand Losing You," "Spirits in the Material World," and "So Lonely" fill out the concert program. Also included are previously unreleased songs, "Tea in the Sahara" and "Oh My God."

PRINCE'S TRUST ROCK GALA ★★♪

ROCK. 1982. Artists: Pete Townshend, Phil Collins, Gary Brooker, Joan Armatrading, Robert Plant, Ian Anderson, Midge Ure, Madness, and Unity. 60 min. Beta Hifi, VHS Stereo. MGM/UA ($39.95)

The Prince's Trust is a charity benefit concert presented each year in London, England. In the 1982 concert, an unparalleled array of British rock and pop stars gave freely of their time and talents; the concert was recorded for this videocassette. Prince Charles himself is seen early on, presenting an award to the reggae group Unity. Basically a taped stage show, with lots of good performances: Madness doing "Madness Song" and "Baggy Trousers," Unity doing "Crab Race," Ian Anderson singing "Jack in the Green" and "Pussy Willow," Joan Armatrading performing "Give Me Love," Phil Collins doing "In the Air Tonight," Midge Ure singing "No Regrets," Pete Townshend performing "Let My Love Open the Door" and "Slit Skirts," Kate Bush doing "Wedding List," Robert Plant singing "I Don't Know," and the whole entourage getting back on stage for the finale, "Let Me Take You Higher," the old Sly and The Family Stone nugget. Very viewable in terms of video technique and an earful of British rock at its best.

THE PUNK ROCK MOVIE FROM ENGLAND ★★

ROCK. 1978. Artists: Sex Pistols, The Clash, Billy Idol and Generation X, Siouxsie and the Banshees, Slaughter and the Dogs, The Slits, Subway Sect, Alternative T.V., Wayne County and the Electric Chairs, and X-Ray Specs. 115 mins. Beta, VHS. Sun Video ($39.95)

A title at the beginning of *The Punk Rock Movie From England* declares boldly that it was shot completely on Super-8 film, the stock used in home movie cameras. Although this might seem unbelievable to film professionals, it seems very in keeping with punk aesthetics. The film looks awful. It's dark and grainy, just the right medium to record the dynamics of London's punk scene in the early years of 1976–1978. The soundtrack is equally bad and sounds as though it had been recorded on a Walkman. Most of

The Punk Rock Movie is made up of concert footage taken at London's Roxy Club, later known as the 100 Club. The Clash performs an almost unintelligible version of "White Riot." A very young Billy Idol and Generation X run through "Walking in the City" and "Kleenex." Subway Sect sings its "Why Don't You Shoot Me?" Siouxsie and the Banshees scream out the lyrics of their "Bad Shape." The movie also inserts footage of The Clash and Siouxsie and the Banshees on tour in the British Midlands. Reserved for the hardcore fan.

RAINBOW BRIDGE ★┙

ROCK. 1971. Cast: Pat Hartley, Jimi Hendrix Experience, and members of the Rainbow Bridge commune. 51 min. Beta, VHS. Independent United ($49.95)

What you should immediately know about this video-repackaged version of a 1971 movie is that Jimi Hendrix is seen for only 20 minutes, performing seven songs. The rest of this "story" involves a young woman, Pat Hartley, who leaves sunny California to join a commune in sunny Maui, Hawaii. She becomes a member in good standing of something called the Rainbow Bridge Occult Research Meditation Center. Mitch Mitchell and Billy Cox join Jimi on stage as the group plays in front of members of the commune. In comparison to *Jimi Plays Berkeley*, the vibes are really sedate. Jimi's performance is, accordingly, subdued. "Dolly Dagger," "E-Z Rider," "In from the Storm," "Foxy Lady," "Get My Heart Back Together," "Purple Haze," and "Roomful of Mirrors" are performed by Jimi with fewer pyrotechnics than expected. This is not the definitive Hendrix concert tape. For those who can tolerate the non-Hendrix footage, and it is rather inane, one can hear and see performed Hendrix rarities like "In from the Storm" and "Roomful of Mirrors."

RAINBOW LIVE BETWEEN THE EYES ★★

ROCK. 1982. Artists: Rainbow (Richie Blackmore, Roger Glover, Joe Lynn Turner, Bob Rondinelli, and David Rosenthal). 76 min. Beta Hifi, VHS Stereo. RCA/Columbia ($29.98)

Richie Blackmore was the driving force behind the original Deep Purple, heavy metal pioneers in the age of bubblegum music, with his searing blues guitar licks that seemed a portent of things to come. But success and fame were short-lived for the group, which disbanded a year or so after their biggest hit, "Smoke on the Water." Blackmore

Richie Blackmore, lead guitarist of Rainbow.

formed Rainbow in 1975 and achieved some gold records through the rest of the decade. In late summer, 1982, Rainbow brought its heavy metal act to San Antonio for a concert to be broadcast over MTV. Playing in front of a gimmicky set of giant eyes which shoot beams of light into the audience, Joe Lynn Turner, who had replaced Ronnie Dio as lead singer, does the honors on "Spotlight Kid," "Miss Mistreated," "It Can't Happen Here," "Tearin' Out My Heart," "All Night Long," "Stone Cold," "Power," "Long Live Rock and Roll," and "Smoke on the Water." Blackmore indulges in a long guitar solo entitled "Blues Interlude" and can be heard playing snippets of Beethoven's Ninth Symphony before smashing his guitar against the floor of the stage in a gesture that is perhaps lost on an eighties audience that never saw Pete Townshend of The Who do the same schtick 15 years ago. Recently, of course, the original members of Deep Purple, including Blackmore and Roger Glover, reunited. That's good because Richie appears to have been pretty bored in this concert.

RICK DERRINGER'S ROCK SPECTACULAR ★★

ROCK. 1982. Artists: Rick Derringer, Karla De Vito, Southside Johnny, Carmine Appice, Tim Bogert, and Ted Nugent. 58 min. Beta Hifi, VHS Stereo. Sony ($29.95)

Rick Derringer hosts a strange ensemble of rock artists in this video program, shot live at The Ritz in New York. Derringer, ex-lead singer of The McCoys ("Hang on Sloopy"), guitarist for Edgar Winter in the mid-seventies, and an active record producer, opens the show with "Easy Action" and then introduces Karla De Vito, Meatloaf's touring girl singer. De Vito, at the time doing *Pirates of Penzance* on Broadway, enters with a parasol to sing "Is This a Cool World or What?" and "Just Like You." Southside Johnny, whom many may know as Bruce Springsteen's Asbury Park buddy, sings the Carl Perkins classic "Honey Hush," and the low-down blues, "Five Long Years." On the latter number, Derringer displays some surprising blues licks on his Fender. Rick then sings his one hit, "Rock and Roll Hoochie Koo." Carmine Appice and Tim Bogert, ex-members of early heavy metal pioneer Vanilla Fudge and frequent collaborators with Jeff Beck, play "Have You Heard?" and "Lady." The next segment features gonzo rock madman Ted Nugent, whose odd grimaces and funny expressions make listening to "Cat Scratch Fever" and "Oh, Carol" bearable if not enjoyable. In the finale, the ensemble joins in on "Party at the Hotel" and "Hang on Sloopy."

ROCKSHOW ★★ノ

ROCK. 1980. Artists: Paul McCartney and Wings, featuring Linda McCartney, Denny Laine, Joe English, and Jimmy McCulloch. 120 min. Beta, VHS. Thorn-EMI ($69.95)

Paul McCartney, whose career, in many ways, has outstripped even The Beatles' farflung popularity, can be seen to good advantage here, before his recent duets with Stevie Wonder and Michael Jackson added yet another notch to his belt of hit records. *Rockshow* is a filmed concert that is quite disappointing visually, as it shows no imagination whatsoever in its choice of camera angles, or in pace and cutting. However, if you are a McCartney fan, the twenty-six songs from the entire McCartney catalogue (Beatles and post-Beatles until 1980) should more than satisfy. To a sellout crowd of 67,000 in Seattle's Kingdome, Paul delivers: "Rock Show," "Jet," "Spirits of Ancient Egypt," "Medicine Jar," "Maybe I'm Amazed," "Live and Let Die," "Bluebird," "Falling," "Yesterday," "Magneto and Titanium Man," "Go Now," "Listen to What the Man Says," "Let Him In," "Silly Love Songs," "Beware My Love," "Letting Go," and "High, High, High." This is all rather too bland for us, but you certainly can't argue with Paul's multimillion-dollar record sales.

ROD STEWART LIVE AT THE LOS ANGELES FORUM ★★♪

ROCK. 1979. Artist: Rod Stewart. 60 min. Beta, VHS. Warner ($29.98)

In the annals of home video, Rod Stewart can stake a claim to being the first artist to present essentially the same show on two different video programs. This Warner tape and the later (1981) Embassy tape differ only in the slightest ways. Many of the same songs are performed, practically the same wardrobe is displayed by Rod, and the venue is the L.A. Forum. This one is rated lower because the later tape does have a guest appearance by Tina Turner. Dressed in a green satin warm-up suit, Rod bumps and grinds his way about the stage, strutting through his hoarse-voiced classics like a bantam rooster. Never the genteel type, Rod enters to the brassy sound of "The Stripper" and launches right into "Hot Legs," "Tonight's the Night," "Do Ya Think I'm Sexy?," "I Just Wanna Make Love to You," "Blondes Have More Fun," "Maggie May," and "If Loving You Is Wrong (I Don't Want to Be Right)." The spike-haired one concludes the concert with "The Wild Side of Life," "You're in My Heart," "Sweet Little Rock 'n' Roller," "Stay with Me," "Twistin' the Night Away," and "Every Picture Tells a Story." An early video concert by the team of director Bruce Gowers and producer Len Epand of Polygram Music Video.

ROD STEWART: TONIGHT HE'S YOURS ★★★

ROCK. 1981. Artists: Rod Stewart and Tina Turner. 90 min. Beta Hifi, VHS Stereo. Embassy ($39.95)

A companion piece to the Warner concert title, *Tonight He's Yours* returns Rod Stewart to his favorite arena, the Forum in Los Angeles, for another high-powered evening of boogie band music. His new touring band is tighter and hotter than the group from 2 years back, making for a more propulsive dance beat underpinning to the occasion. The added attraction of Tina Turner's brief appearance is also a treat. When the two are together, performing "Get Back" and "Hot Legs," it's tempting to wonder who influenced whom. On stage in leopard spot tights, purple satin baseball jacket, and a T-shirt that reads "Cruel But Fair," Rod performs "Give Me Wings," "Sweet Little Rock 'n' Roller," "Tear It Up," "Passion," "She Won't Dance with Me," "You're in My Heart," "Rock Your Plimsoul" (from his Jeff Beck days), "Young Turks" (including his video for the song), "Tora Tora Tora," "If Loving You Is Wrong," "Maggie May," "Do Ya Think I'm Sexy?," "I Was Only Joking," "You Wear It Well," and "The Wild Side of Life." Directed by Bruce Gowers.

ROXY MUSIC: THE HIGH ROAD ★★★

ROCK. 1983. Artists: Roxy Music (Bryan Ferry, Phil Manzanera, Andy Mackay, Neil Hubbard, Andy Newmark, Alan Spenner, and Guy Fletcher). 75 min. Beta Hifi, VHS Stereo. RCA/Columbia ($29.95)

Formed in 1971 in London, Roxy Music has succeeded, and has gone on to survive a decade of changes in musical taste by accomplishing what other British art-rock groups would or could not do. Spurred by the self-irony of lead singer Bryan Ferry and the smoking guitar of Phil Manzanera, Roxy Music added a highly danceable beat to otherwise lyrically inaccessible songs and logged a number of hit singles and albums here as well as in the U.K. In this concert film shot in a large outdoor arena in Frejus, France, on their 1982 world tour, the band has seemingly perfected its characteristic, now oft-imitated sound—best heard in such gems as "Avalon," "Jealous Guy," and "Dance Away." It is lush, dense, full of instrumental runs, and rhythmically compelling.

The High Road, featuring Roxy Music.

By now, the typical Roxy Music show has become iconic: Ferry, dressed in white tuxedo jacket and black bow tie, self-mocking yet nobly aloof, backed by a big-band-size rock orchestra, and singing complex narratives about the modern condition while acting as if he were Frank Sinatra on stage in a forties ballroom. Aided by unobtrusive camerawork (though the outdoor space was badly underlit for filming), the concert comes off quite well for the viewer. Ferry's French fans thrill to "The Main Thing," "Out of the Blue," "Both Ends Burning," "A Song for Europe," "Can't Let Go," "While My Heart Is Still Beating," "Love Is the Drug," "Like a Hurricane," "Do the Strand," and others.

RUSH: EXIT STAGE LEFT   ★★♪

ROCK. 1981. Artists: Rush (Geddy Lee, Alex Lifeson, and Neil Peart). 60 min. Beta Hifi, VHS Stereo. RCA/Columbia ($29.95)

A veteran power-rock trio from Canada, Rush has enjoyed steady if unspectacular sales in the U.S. for a decade. Geddy Lee, the shrill-voiced lead singer with the goblinlike

A scene from the Rush concert video *Exit Stage Left*.

appearance, gained his greatest notoriety for singing on Rick Moranis and Dave Thomas' 1982 McKenzie Brothers comedy single, "Take Off," which stayed in the Top 10 for some time. In this early video concert, Rush is caught live at the Montreal Forum, performing before an enthusiastic sold-out Canadian audience. They play a sort of pre-heavy metal hard rock which reminds one alternately of Yes and Led Zeppelin. Alex Lifeson's twelve-string electric guitar is a major component of their odd sound, but it is Geddy Lee's high, keening voice which distinguishes Rush from the run of the mill rock band. A pall of blood-red light over the screen gives the video a disturbing look. Needless to say, the arena could have been better lit for the cameras. Songs heard are: "Limelight," "Tom Sawyer," "The Trees," "Instrumental," "Xanadu," "Red Barchetta," "Free Will," "Closer to the Heart," "XYZ," "By-Tor and the Snow Dog," "In the End," "In the Mood," and "2112 Finale."

RUST NEVER SLEEPS ★★

ROCK. 1979. Artist: Neil Young. 111 min. Beta Hifi, VHS Stereo. Vestron ($29.95)

Neil Young's career in rock and roll has been puzzling. He seems to want to avoid success at all costs (he left Crosby, Stills, Nash, and Young at its commercial height), alternating albums that are introspective and personal with others that are calculatedly populist. Despite his efforts to elude stardom, many of his least likely to sell albums have shipped gold and platinum, including his starker collaborations with Crazy Horse, a band he discovered playing bars in southern California. Full of contradictions and ironies, it often appears Young is chasing his own tail, so to speak. This concert film, directed by Young under the pseudonym Bernard Shakey, is further proof that he enjoys living his musical life on the edge, somewhere between exasperating the audience and holding it securely within his grasp. The stage show Neil presents has elements of *Star Wars* and *Gulliver's Travels;* stagehands in shrouds, like the creatures of the desert planet in the original *Star Wars,* move giant-size microphones and speakers on and off. The first part of the concert features Neil alone with acoustic guitar and stand-up piano, singing "Sugar Mountain," "I Am a Child," "Comes a Time," "After the Gold Rush," and "My My, Hey Hey" ("Out of the Blue"). During his electric set with Crazy Horse (Billy Talbot, Ralph Molina, and Frank Sampedro), Neil performs "He's a Loner," "Welfare Mothers," "The Needle and the Damage Done," "A Lotta Love," "Powderfinger," "Sedan Delivery," "Cortez the Killer," "Cinnamon Girl," "Like a Hurricane," and "My My Hey Hey" ("Out of the Blue"). It's difficult to read Young sometimes—he has a strange sense of humor, undoubtedly. This tape is often stupefying.

THE SECRET POLICEMAN'S OTHER BALL ★★✦

ROCK. 1982. Artists: Pete Townshend, Sting, Eric Clapton, Jeff Beck, Phil Collins, Dono-
van, John Cleese, Michael Palin, Terry Jones, and Peter Cook. 101 min. Beta, VHS.
MGM/UA ($69.95)

The Secret Policeman's Ball has become an annual benefit concert event for Amnesty International in London, England. The first ball reunited the members of the *Beyond the Fringe* satirical revue with old friends Monty Python and The Goodies, thus bringing together the major comic talents of Britain's post-cold war generation. At this, the second ball, members of Monty Python and Not the Nine O'Clock News perform comedy skits in between musical sets. Pete Townshend's acoustic versions of "Pinball Wizard" and "Won't Get Fooled Again" are startling. You feel as if you are hearing these songs for the first time. Sting, of The Police, sings "Roxanne" and "Message in a Bottle," mesmerizing the audience with his nearly a capella renditions (he is chording an electric guitar that is very softly amplified). Jeff Beck and Eric Clapton trade blues licks on "Further On up the Road." Donovan does his first big hit, "Catch the Wind," and Phil Collins sings "In the Air Tonight." For the musical finale, everyone gets on stage to support Sting's lead vocals on Eric Clapton's "Anyday."

THE SECRET POLICEMAN'S PRIVATE PARTS ★✦

ROCK. 1983. Artists: Pete Townshend, Bob Geldof, Donovan, Phil Collins, Graham Chap-
man, John Cleese, Michael Palin, Terry Jones, Terry Gilliam, and Peter Cook. 77 min.
Beta Hifi, VHS Stereo. Media ($59.95)

Essentially outtakes from *The Secret Policeman's Ball* and *Other Ball, Private Parts* is a collage of comedy skits and musical numbers from the Amnesty International benefit shows given in London from 1976 to 1983. What we have here are the drips and drabs of programs that were inconsistently entertaining in the first place. Edited together by Roger Graef and Julien Temple (he *does* get around), the film will probably satisfy Monty Python fans but leave all others wanting more than they'll get in its brief 77 minutes. Among the comedy bits are "The Pet Shop," with Cleese and Palin arguing about a dead parrot; Peter Cook as a mass murderer on trial; Cleese and ex-wife Connie Booth (*Fawlty Towers*) having an odd literary conversation in a book store; and "The Lumberjack Song," Monty Python's classic routine about sexual confusion. Musical spots include Pete Townshend singing "Drowning in Love," Donovan performing "Sunshine Superman," the ubiquitous Phil Collins doing "The Roof Is Leaking," Bob Geldof

Members of the Monty Python troupe and friends in
The Secret Policeman's Private Parts.

of the Boomtown Rats and chief organizer of the much heralded worldwide Live Aid concert broadcasts in July of 1985 singing "I Don't Like Mondays," and comic Neil Innes (*The Rutles*) doing his Dylan impression on "Down with Everything."

SIMON AND GARFUNKEL: THE CONCERT IN CENTRAL PARK ★★★★

ROCK. 1982. Artists: Simon and Garfunkel. 87 min. Beta Hifi, VHS Stereo. CBS/Fox ($29.98)

One of the best music video titles ever produced. Michael Lindsay-Hogg's wonderful direction and the superb sound quality capture all the excitement of the original concert in Central Park where, in the spring of 1982, Simon and Garfunkel launched their reunion tour. Lindsay-Hogg, whose credits include *Let It Be, Brideshead Revisited,* and countless others, placed three overhead cameras in cherrypickers in order to let video viewers see just how huge the audience was—some four hundred thousand fans took advantage of the free concert in the Sheep Meadow. The stage is made up to resemble a typical industrial New Jersey town with water towers and metal siding. The excellent band consists of several famous New York session musicians, including Richard Tee on piano, Pete Carr on guitar, Steve Gadd and Grady Tate on drums, and Howard Johnson on trumpet.

You'll marvel at the smoothness of presentation here and you'll thrill to the audio quality (the vocal tracks were sweetened in the studio after the concert because of some microphone problems). Simon and Garfunkel are in excellent form, singing "Mrs. Robinson," "Homeward Bound," "America," "Me and Julio," "Scarborough Fair," "April Come She Will," "Wake Up Little Susie," "Still Crazy after All These Years," "American Tune," "Late in the Evening," "Slip Sliding Away," "A Heart in New York," "The Late Great Johnny Ace," "Kodachrome," "Maybelline," "Bridge over Troubled Water," "Fifty Ways to Leave Your Lover," "The Boxer," "Old Friends," "59th St. Bridge Song," and "Sounds of Silence." This was originally seen over Home Box Office.

SIOUXSIE AND THE BANSHEES: NOCTURNE   ★★

ROCK. 1983. Artists: Siouxsie and the Banshees. 60 min. Beta, VHS. Media ($29.95)

Siouxsie and the Banshees met as fans of the Sex Pistols back in London in 1976. Banshee original Sid Vicious left the band to join the ranks of their idols, the Sex Pistols, before Siouxsie Sioux and the rest of the band carried on to release the single "Hong Kong Garden" and album *The Scream.* Never really developing a widespread U.S. following, the Banshees have had a couple of U.K. hits such as "Christine" and "Happy House" and have maintained their garage band musicianship intact over the last 9 years. In this tape of their best performances, taken from a 3-day gig at London's Royal Albert Hall at the end of September 1983, Siouxsie proves she's the "Queen of Nightmare Rock" by appearing on stage in black shrouds and screaming the lyrics of twelve songs to the band's piercing three-note guitar accompaniment. The Banshees perform "Israel," "Cascade!", "Melt!", "Pulled to Bits," "Nightshift," "Sin in My Heart," "Painted Bird," "Switch," "Eve White/Eve Black," "Voodoo Dolly," "Spellbound," and the Beatles' "Helter Skelter."

STARS ON 45 ★★✦

ROCK. 1983. Cast: John Prophet, Bethany Owen, Gaille Heidemann, George Solomon, David Dash, Sy Gorieb, Forrest Gardner, Monica Francene Pege, Donna Garcia, Jeffrey Douglas Thomas, Debbie Bell, and Tony Abruzzo. 71 min. Beta Hifi, VHS Stereo. MCA ($39.95)

This stage revue tracing the history of American rock and roll was based on the novelty records, "Stars on 45," on which studio musicians imitated the songs of the Beatles, Stevie Wonder, the Four Seasons, and others. Over fifty songs are performed in part or in their entirety by a repertory group of talented mimics and dancers. The show is divided into nine roughly chronological segments: early rockers, doo-wop, teen idols, Elvis, folk revival, The Beatles, Woodstock, disco, and New Wave. Among the songs heard are: "Rock around the Clock," "Lucille," "Shake, Rattle, and Roll" (early rockers); "Little Darling," "The Great Pretender," "Earth Angel" (doo-wop); "Swingin' School," "Venus," and "Where the Boys Are" (teen idols); "Jailhouse Rock" and "Are You Lonesome Tonight?" (Elvis); "Blowing in the Wind," "Hey, Mr. Tambourine Man," "Sounds of Silence" (folk revival); "Do You Want to Know a Secret?," "Nowhere Man," "I Want to Hold Your Hand," and "Hey Jude" (The Beatles); "Foxy Lady,"

Performers from the stage revue *Stars on 45.*

"Somebody to Love" (Woodstock); "Hot Stuff" and "Macho Man" (disco); and "My Sharona," "Whip It," and "Hit Me with Your Best Shot" (New Wave). Entertaining if you don't try to take it too seriously.

STEVE MILLER BAND LIVE   ★★★

ROCK. 1983. Artists: Steve Miller Band (Steve Miller, Norton Buffalo, Kenny Lee Lewis, John Massaro, Gary Mallaber, Byron Allred, and Gerald Johnson). 50 min. Beta, VHS. Thorn-EMI ($29.95)

Every two or three years, it seems, rock veteran Steve Miller emerges from his farm in Oregon with yet another catchy, hook-filled hit single. Miller is one of those fortunate

The Steve Miller Band.

musicians who may really have a Midas touch which turns anything he produces into gold records. This from a man whose start in music would have militated against popular success; he formed one of the first modern electric blues bands in San Francisco in 1966. Early on, though, Miller displayed an adaptability to pop tastes which has minted him a small fortune. In this concert film shot at The Pine Knob Club in Detroit (Miller attended the University of Michigan), the band offers many of their biggest hits in a rewarding performance. If nothing else, this concert proves that one can play honest, hard-driving rock and roll and still pay the rent. Steve and the band play "Macho City," "Gangster of Love," "Rock'n Me," "Living in the U.S.A.," "Fly Like an Eagle," "Jungle Love," "The Joker," "Mercury Blues," "Take the Money and Run," "Abracadabra," "Jet Airliner," and "Buffalo Serenade."

STEVIE NICKS IN CONCERT ★★✈

ROCK. 1981. Artist: Stevie Nicks. 60 min. Beta Hifi, VHS Stereo. CBS/Fox ($39.95)

It is not hard to explain Stevie Nicks' success in the world of popular music. Combining a penchant for fairytale lyrics sung in a throaty voice with blonde good looks, Nicks catapulted Fleetwood Mac into the higher circles of rock stardom with songs like "Rhiannon" and "Dreams." Her first solo album, *Belladonna,* was so successful that it left no doubt that Mac fans were drawn to the group because of her special talents above all else. In 1982, despite recurring throat problems, Stevie put together a brief tour. This video program presents the last concert on that tour (in Los Angeles, her adopted home). Stevie's father introduces her at the beginning of the concert, and Stevie appears on stage in her typical swirl of capes, shawls, and formfitting leotards. Although her voice sounds rather hoarse and slightly off-key at first, Stevie's singing improves as the concert progresses. The conclusion is rather funny. A veritable shower of flowers, gifts, and stuffed animals from the audience is carried offstage by a teary-eyed Stevie. The songs: "Gold Dust Woman," "Don't Hide behind Your Hair," "I Need to Know," "Belladonna," "Dreams," "Stop Draggin' My Heart Around," "Sara," "The Edge of Seventeen," and "Rhiannon."

STYLE COUNCIL: FAR EAST AND FAR OUT ★★★

ROCK. 1984. Artists: Style Council (Paul Weller, Mick Talbot, Chris Lawrence, Stewart Prosser, Steve White, Anthony Harty, Steve Sidelmyk, Billy Chapman, Julia Williamson, and Helen Turner). 80 min. Beta Hifi, VHS Stereo. Media ($29.95)

Paul Weller, ex-leader of The Jam, has always been drawn to the music made by Motown artists in the sixties. His own singing style is indebted to Curtis Mayfield and Marvin Gaye's crooning soul tenors. In his new group, Style Council, which made its debut with the Top 10 hit "My Everchanging Moods," Weller has dedicated himself to reproducing the various soul music styles of the sixties. The horn section and the Booker T. Jonesian organ runs recall the Memphis Sound, the double-tracked bass and wah-wah guitar lines are the signature of numerous Temptations and Four Tops classics, and the soul falsetto vocals remind one so much of Mayfield and Smokey Robinson.

Promoted as a dance band to fit in with current record trends, Style Council really proffers a soul revival smorgasbord. Their concert here at the Nakano Sun-plaza Hall in Tokyo (May 4, 1984) is a little ragged but funky and upbeat nevertheless. Songs are: "The Big Boss Groove," "Here's One That Got Away," "You're the Best Thing," "Pieces," "Mick's Up," "Dropping Bombs on the White House," "Long Hot Summer," "My Everchanging Moods," "Le Depart," "The Whole Point of No Return," "Paris Match," "Party Chambers," "Money Go Round," "Speak Like a Child," "Head Start for Happiness," and "Me Ship Came In." Directed by Kensaku Yasuda.

STYX: CAUGHT IN THE ACT ★★✦

ROCK. 1983. Artists: Styx (Tommy Shaw, Dennis DeYoung, Chuck Panozza, John Panozza, and James Young). 87 min. Beta Hifi, VHS Stereo. RCA/Columbia ($29.95)

Styx, an American version of Queen, the original pomp-rock band, toured America in 1983 with a live show that interwove the story presented on their *Kilroy Was Here* album with hits from past albums. Like Kansas, only more successful, Styx prides itself on lavishly produced, lushly instrumentalized miniature rock arias that tell a slender wisp of a story—enough to engage their mostly teenage audiences. *Kilroy Was Here* rips off the story line of *1984*, George Orwell's classic novel about totalitarian politics, transforming it into a tale about a future society where Dr. Righteous, a media Big Brother, has outlawed rock and roll music. Dennis DeYoung plays Kilroy, the former rock star who liberates his people from the shackles of Dr. Righteous' oppressive rule. Starting off with a slickly produced video showing Kilroy's escape from prison, the concert is partly an acting out of this rock opera. "Mr. Roboto," "Rockin' the Paradise," "Blue Collar Man," "Snowblind," "Too Much Time on My Hands," "Don't Let It End," "Heavy Metal Poisoning," "Cold War," "Best of Times," "Come Sail Away," "Renegade," "Haven't We Been Here Before," and a reprise of "Don't Let It End" fill out the list of tunes played. Superbly lit and well shot, this concert in Dallas, Texas, was directed by Jerry Kramer. The Kilroy video was directed by Brian Gibson.

Styx.

THOMAS DOLBY: LIVE WIRELESS ★★★

ROCK. 1983. Artist: Thomas Dolby. 58 min. Beta Hifi, VHS Stereo. Thorn-EMI ($29.95)

Thomas Dolby's hit, "She Blinded Me with Science," managed to combine the mechano-rock trend in New Wave with thoughtful and clever lyrics. Here was a synthesizer-based composition that lyrically played with the idea of technocracy and the mechanization of human feelings. The thinking person's dance music? In this concert shot at a small club in London, Dolby performs his original brand of techno-rock in front of a bank of television monitors which continually display a running film and video accompaniment to the performance on stage. The program itself, written and directed by Dolby, betrays the strong arty streak in his overall image: German expressionist lighting and fin de siècle black humor which point up the demise of the British Empire. "One of Our Submarines" delivers that latter point rather blatantly. "Europe," "Windpower," and "Radio Silence" extend that analysis to the continent in general. Lena

Techno-rock artist Thomas Dolby.

Lovich, another eccentric British New Waver, once Dolby's employer, joins Thomas on stage for "New Toy." "Urban Tribal," "Flying North," "Jungleline," "Puppet Theatre," "Samson and Delilah," the video for "Science," and "Airwaves" continue his musings on the state of western civilization. If this all sounds a bit too abstract for your taste, it might be noted that, more recently, Dolby has been playing less allusive, even more danceable music.

THOMPSON TWINS: SIDE KICKS ★

ROCK. 1983. Artists: Thompson Twins (Tom Bailey, Alannah Currie, Joe Leeway). 60 min. Beta Hifi, VHS Stereo. Thorn-EMI ($29.95)

The Thompson Twins are a testament to blind ambition in rock and roll—British style. Originally conceived as an all-percussion dance band by a group of squatters in some abandoned London tenements, The Thompson Twins' marriage of black rap music and New Wave mechano-rock has taken the minimalist sound into the Top 10 charts. In this concert shot at the Royal Court Theater in Liverpool, England, they are augmented by a bassist, a vibraphonist, two synthesizer players, and a non-mechanical, human drummer. Yet they still sound like an all-percussion band. Those fans hoping to hear their smash hit, "Hold My Heart," will be disappointed since the concert predates the release of that record and, indeed, predates their popularity in the United States. Songs heard are: "Kamikaze," "Love Lies Bleeding" (not the Elton John composition), "Judy Do," "Tears," "Watching," "If You Were Here," "All Fall Out," "Lucky Day," "Lies," "Detectives," "In the Name of Love," "Beach Culture," and "Love on Your Side." Here's a video program that can be enjoyed just as much with the sound turned down.

TO RUSSIA . . . WITH ELTON ★★★

ROCK. 1979. Artist: Elton John. 80 min. Beta, VHS. CBS/Fox ($39.95)

While Elton John was suffering through a brief slump in his musical fortunes, he busied himself with a number of odd projects, including a long-form video (*Visions*), his cricket team, and a state-sponsored concert tour of the Soviet Union. This is a documentary film of that tour. While it is, at first, surprising to learn that Russians even know who Elton John is, what is more surprising is the Russian decision to allow John to play his music in Leningrad and Moscow for packed houses of comrades. There was one stipulation, however. Elton would not be allowed to bring a full band with him. Ray Cooper, that maniacal drummer with the banker's demeanor, provides percussion for Elton's piano-backed vocals. *To Russia* is as much travelogue as concert film (and it's really more interesting as a travelogue), but we hear Elton perform "Pinball Wizard," "Saturday Night's All Right for Fighting," "Back in the U.S.S.R.," "Get Back," "Your Song," "Daniel," "The Man Who Wants to See You Smile," "Part-time Love," "Bennie and the Jets," "Sixty Years On," "Candle in the Wind," "Better Off Dead," "Rocket Man," "I Think I'm Gonna Kill Myself," and others. Soviet officials constantly exhort Elton to tone down his concerts and, in the end, Elton resembles a folk singer in loud clothing more than a pop-rock star.

TOTALLY GO-GO'S! ★★✦

ROCK. 1981. Artists: The Go-Go's. 75 min. Beta, VHS. Thorn-EMI ($25.95)

At a Los Angeles high school, the Go-Go's put on a show that combines their two musical influences: the all-female vocal groups of the sixties and the heavy-guitar

THE GO-GO'S

Belinda Carlisle was born August 17, 1958, in Hollywood, California. Charlotte Caffey was born October 21, 1953, in Santa Monica, California. Kathy Valentine was born January 7, 1959, in Austin, Texas. Gina Schock was born August 31, 1957, in Baltimore, Maryland. Original members Belinda Carlisle and Jane Wiedlin formed the group in 1978 to play the club scene in Los Angeles.

When Madness, the British New Wave band, asked the Go-Go's to tour Britain with them, the Go-Go's discovered their first real audience. "We Got the Beat," released on the famous Stiff label, was a hit with British teens who immediately grasped the surf-rock inspiration behind their sound. Two months after they signed with I.R.S. Records, their debut album, *Beauty and the Beat,* established them as a major new force in rock and roll . . . But 1981 and 1982, years of continued chart success, were followed by a couple of down years as injuries to Charlotte Caffey's left wrist, Gina Schock's health problems, and some musical soul searching put a halt to their steady advance. Their successful "Prime Time Tour" in 1984 set the stage for renewed activity both on vinyl and on videotape in 1985.

However, the Go-Go's legion of fans were saddened to learn of the group's sudden split in the summer of 1985. Belinda Carlisle and Jane Wiedin expect to record together some time soon.

Video Resume

The Beast of I.R.S., (1983), I.R.S. Video.

The Go-Go's: Prime Time, (1985), RCA/Columbia Musicvision.

The Go-Go's Wild at the Greek, (1985), RCA/Columbia Musicvision.

Prime Cuts: Too Hot to Handle, (1985), CBS/Fox.

Totally Go-Go's, (1981), Thorn-EMI.

sound of California surf music of the same period. They jump on stage eager to kick off their concert with their hits "Skidmarks on My Heart," "Fading Fast," and "Automatic," all taken from their monster debut album, *Beauty and the Beat.* They cover the up-tempo R&B classic by the Capitols, "Cool Jerk," and the Shangri-La's "(Remember) Walking in the Sand." Without skipping a beat, they launch into more hits from their *Beauty and the Beat* and *Vacation* albums. Lead singer Belinda Carlisle sings "Lust to Love," "Can't Stop the World," "You Can't Walk in Your Sleep," the Top 10 "Our Lips Are Sealed," and the megahit "We Got the Beat." The audience loves it. Also included in this tape are interviews with members of the Go-Go's who talk about rock and roll, their lives, and the founding and history of the band.

THE TUBES: LIVE AT THE GREEK ★★½

ROCK. 1979. Artists: The Tubes. 60 min. Beta, VHS. FHE ($39.95)

In *The Tubes: Live at The Greek,* the rock group cum burlesque troupe put on a show that contains just as much live theater as music. Taped during their Remote Control

The Tubes.

tour in 1979, The Tubes perform a number of songs that illustrate the tour's theme: how television is dehumanizing the population of America. Each song is acted out on stage with a healthy dose of buffoonery by lead singer Fee Waybill, who goes through a number of costume changes to present the images of the lyrics of each song. During his performance of "No Way Out" Fee places a television set over his head like some giant mask to put across the point that we are all tubes, mindless receivers of pop culture. It seems that the group Devo with its "spudboys" already has this area of rock performance covered. Fee sings "Don't Touch Me There" while riding a Harley-Davidson motorcycle across stage. The Tubes run through "T.V. Is King," "What Do You Want from Life?," and "Telecide" before the highlight of the show. Fee walks in front of the microphone in a Rod Stewart blonde fright wig, Elton John-style illuminated glasses, snakeskin trousers, and 24-inch heel boots. In a cockney accent he rouses the audience to sing The Tubes' only hit, "White Punks on Dope," the Isley Brothers' "Shout," The Who's "Ba Ba O'Reilly," and "The Kids Are Alright." Silly, Stupid, and Sophomoric. Just the ticket for Tubes fans.

U2 LIVE AT RED ROCKS   ★★★

ROCK. 1983. Artists: U2 (Adam Clayton, The Edge, Larry Mullen, Jr., and Bono). 55 min. Beta Hifi, VHS Stereo. MCA ($29.95)

Take a band which leans heavily on stage theatrics and lyrical messages and place them in a naturally dramatic setting. Dynamite? The combination of U2 and a rainy, cloud-enshrouded day in the elemental outskirts of Denver, Colorado, make this concert video a cut above average. Obviously, the whole thing could not have been planned, but even David Lean (*Passage To India*) wouldn't have been able to stage the concert with more visual appropriateness and atmosphere. On their tour of America in 1983, U2 stopped off on an uncharacteristically raw June day in Denver to give a concert at Red Rocks, a natural amphitheater carved out of a red granite hillside. Given the subject matter of much of the Irish group's material, the existential nature of being in the middle of a civil war, the wind and rain could have arrived with them from across the Atlantic. The music itself, phenomenally popular in the U.S., where they are bigger than they are at home, is top-drawer hard rock, influenced by The Police and American punk pioneers like Iggy Pop. What is truly amazing here though is the setting: the canyon seems awesome in the darkening twilight; the redness of the rocks, awash in the stagelights, is eerie. Watch the guitar work of The Edge and the driven singing of Bono (no relation to Sonny) as U2 performs "Surrender," "Seconds," "Sunday, Bloody Sunday," "October," "New Year's Day," "I Threw a Brick," "A

Irish hard rockers U2.

Day without Me," "Gloria," "Party Girl," "11 O'Clock Tick Tock," "I Will Follow," and "40."

WARREN ZEVON ★★

ROCK. 1982. Artist: Warren Zevon. 68 min. Beta Hifi, VHS Stereo. Sony ($29.95)

Originally shot for broadcast over MTV, this video concert of one of rock's true wild men/philosophers is disappointing. Perhaps it was the venue, Passaic, New Jersey's Capitol Theater on a date in November 1982, or a lack of rehearsal on the band's part, but Zevon's efforts here are quite muddled. Emerging from the "Hotel California" era of west coast songwriters, Zevon's vision has always been a savage and unremitting one, filled with fin de siècle black humor. Until the success of singles like "Excitable Boy" and "Werewolves of London," Zevon was more noted for having written songs for Linda Ronstadt than for his performing. In this concert, one can see clearly that he is not at ease in the spotlight, fronting a band. It starts off wildly enough with

Zevon being brought onto the stage in handcuffs but fails to deliver on its promise of mean rock and roll. Warren sings: "Johnny Strikes Up the Band," "The Overdraft," "A Certain Girl," "Jeannie Needs a Shooter" (cowritten with Bruce Springsteen), "Roland the Headless Thompson Gunner," "Play That Dead Man's Song," "Accidentally Like a Martyr," "Poor Pitiful Me," "Cadillac Ranch" (another Springsteen song), "An Excitable Boy," "Werewolves of London," and many others.

WHO ROCKS AMERICA ★★✦

ROCK. 1983. Artists: The Who (Roger Daltrey, Pete Townshend, Kenny Jones, John Entwhistle). 118 min. Beta Hifi, VHS Stereo. CBS/Fox ($39.95)

On their final tour of North America, in 1982, The Who visited Toronto's Maple Leaf Gardens to present a powerful concert with laser effects. Kenny Jones, once the drummer for The Faces, stands in well for the late Keith Moon and, on the whole, The Who acquit themselves superbly in this final go-round. This video is of a high quality because the concert hall was lit for the cameras rather than the audience. Thus, the viewer gets a clear picture of what happened on stage that night. The Who perform "My Generation," "It's So Hard," "Baba O'Rilley," "Boris the Spider," "I Am the Sea," "Love Ain't for Keeping," "Pinball Wizard," "Overture to Tommy," "Who Are You?," "5:15," "Love Reign on Me," "Long Live Rock," "I Won't Get Fooled Again," "Naked Eye," "Squeezebox," "Young Man Blues," and more.

ZIGGY STARDUST AND THE SPIDERS FROM MARS: THE MOTION PICTURE ★★✦

ROCK. 1973–84. Artists: David Bowie, Ringo Starr, Mick Ronson, and Trevor Bolder. 91 min. Beta Hifi, VHS Stereo. RCA/Columbia ($29.95)

Released for the first time theatrically in the United States in 1984, *Ziggy Stardust and the Spiders from Mars: The Motion Picture,* filmed at the end of his 1973 Ziggy Stardust tour, was intended to be a record of Bowie's final stage performance. Bowie hired director D. A. Pennebaker to record the momentous occasion. (Of course, David returned to the stage without the guise of Ziggy after producing a number of albums and starring as an actor in a number of movies.) D. A. Pennebaker is known for shooting music films (*Don't Look Back, Monterey Pop*) in the "direct cinema" documentary style of filmmaking, producing movies that are more of a document, a record of a musical

THE WHO

Peter Townshend was born May 19, 1945, in London, U.K. Roger Daltrey was born March 1, 1944, in London, U.K. John Entwistle was born October 9, 1944, in London, U.K. Keith Moon was born August 23, 1947, in London, U.K., and died September 7, 1978. Kenny Jones was born September 16, 1948, in London, U.K.

The group that symbolized mod London in the mid-sixties, The Who featured Roger Daltrey's soaring vocals (he's one of the few singers who can stay on key while practically shouting) and Pete Townshend's sensitive bad-boy lyrics. Townshend was particularly infamous for his wholesale destruction of guitars, amps, and bandstands as he acted out the teen-age rage his songs portrayed. Moon followed suit by destroying his drum kit at every opportunity.

Tommy, the first rock opera, prompted critics to take Townshend very seriously. From that point on, until their breakup in 1982, The Who were considered among the grand old men of rock and roll—an image that bothered the innately rebellious Townshend no end. Some of their most loved songs include "I Can't Explain," "My Generation," "Happy Jack," "I Can See for Miles," "Magic Bus," "Pinball Wizard," "Baba O'Reilly," "Won't Get Fooled Again," and "Who Are You?" Their masterpiece, *Who's Next* (1971), contained some of the first extensive use of synthesizers in mainstream rock and roll.

Even before their breakup, Pete had released several solo albums and Roger had not only been pursuing a solo recording career but also dabbling in film acting. The Who, maybe with the exception of The Rolling Stones, were the most important rock group to come out of England and survive into the eighties.

Video Resume

Cool Cats, (1984), MGM/UA.

Jimi Hendrix, (1973), Warner.

Kids Are Alright, (1979), Thorn-EMI.

Lisztomania, (1975), Warner.

McVicar, (1980), Vestron.

Pete Townshend, (1982), Sony.

Prince's Trust Rock Gala, (1982), MGM/UA.

Quadrophenia, (1979), RCA/Columbia.

Ready, Steady, Go, Vols. I and II, (1965), Thorn-EMI.

Secret Policeman's Other Ball, (1982), MGM/UA.

Secret Policeman's Private Parts, (1984), Media.

That'll Be The Day, (1974), Thorn-EMI.

Tommy, (1975), RCA/Columbia.

Woodstock I, (1970), Warner.

event, than the concert videos made today with "sweetened" audio tracks as promotional tools to recreate the concert experience for the home viewer. Pennebaker's *Ziggy Stardust* is removed, distant, and analytical, showing not only the art, Ziggy on stage in his extraterrestrial performance piece, but also the artifice, David chatting with Ringo Starr backstage while undergoing a costume change. With its jerky camera movements and grainy filmstock, *Ziggy Stardust* might not be all that satisfying to every Bowie fan, but it does stand on its own as a celluloid document of Bowie's Ziggy period. The film features seventeen songs, including "Ziggy Stardust," "Changes," "Space Oddity," "Time," "White Light/White Heat," "Hang onto Yourself," "Wild-eyed Boy from Freecloud," "All the Young Dudes," "Oh! You Pretty Thing," "Moonage Daydream," "Cracked Actor," "Width of a Circle," "Let's Spend the Night Together," "Suffragette City," and "Rock 'n' Roll Suicide."

ROCK MUSICALS

ALICE'S RESTAURANT ★★

ROCK. 1969. Cast: Arlo Guthrie, Pat Quinn, James Broderick, and Pete Seeger. 111 min. Beta, VHS. CBS/FOX ($59.95)

Folk singer Arlo Guthrie's famous 22-minute talking blues, "The Alice's Restaurant Massacree," was celebrated as the anthem of the youth generation of the sixties. Arthur Penn based his 1969 film *Alice's Restaurant* on the folk-rock favorite and made what was to become the swan song for a generation. In this semiautobiographical seriocomedy, Arlo plays himself and the real Alice Brock of the song's title can be seen in a bit role as Suzy. The film was shot in and around Stockbridge, Massachusetts, the town where Alice, Arlo, and their friends celebrated Thanksgiving in 1965. To evade the draft Arlo enrolls in a college in Montana, but soon leaves to be closer to his father, the famous folk singer Woody Guthrie, who is hospitalized in New York City, and to live with Alice (Pat Quinn), her husband Ray (James Broderick), and a commune of hippies in a converted church in Stockbridge. Ray travels to New York to pick up Shelley, a member of the commune who has shaken a drug habit in a treatment center in the city. The commune decides to set Alice up in the restaurant business to help

136

defray expenses. For Thanksgiving Ray and his friends decide to throw a bash in their church to celebrate their togetherness. But Shelley, back on drugs, spoils the party by running out, hopping on his motorcycle, and killing himself. In a very moving cemetery scene, Ray, Alice, Arlo, and the group bury Shelley and their hopes for a perfect world to the sounds of "Song to Aging Children," Joni Mitchell's composition. Pete Seeger guest stars and sings Woody Guthrie's "Car Car Song" and his "Pastures of Plenty."

BIKINI BEACH   ★★

ROCK. 1964. Cast: Frankie Avalon, Annette Funicello, Martha Hyer, Don Rickles, Keenan Wynn, Harvey Lembeck, Meredith MacRae, Little Stevie Wonder, The Pyramids, and The Exciters Band. 100 min. Beta, VHS. Embassy ($59.95)

Further adventures with Frankie and Dee Dee on the beach. Not the best in the series by a long shot. Indeed, the underlying cynicism of the whole project shows itself in the ridiculous plot thought up by those American International Pictures (AIP) lackeys for this third beach film. Frankie plays two roles; he is Frankie and he is also the Potato Bug, a long-haired, "yeah-yeahing" British rock star. The Beatles and other British groups were coming overseas and putting an end to the age of the teen idol, hence the absurdity of the portrayal by Avalon, who obviously could see his own career beginning a steep decline. Keenan Wynn and Martha Hyer are the "adults" caught up in the escapades of our little beach commune. Harvey Lembeck, as Eric Von Zipper, returns as the kids' nemesis, and Don Rickles plays Big Drag, the owner of the local youth bistro by the beach. After you've gotten tired of listening to Avalon drift in and out of his bad English accent, there's some interesting music from some unusual acts to occupy your time. The Pyramids, an interracial, all-bald surf-rock band, play "Record Run" and "Bikini Drag." The Exciters Band does "Gotcha Where I Want You." Little Stevie Wonder (all of 14 years old) sings "Dance and Shout." Of course, Frankie and Annette sing too. Those are the breaks.

BLOW-UP   ★★★♪

ROCK. 1966. Cast: David Hemmings, Vanessa Redgrave, Sarah Miles, Verushka. 102 min. Beta, VHS. MGM/UA ($59.95)

Michelangelo Antonioni's first English language film, *Blow-Up,* is a fascinating example of a movie that both entertains and enlightens. Many films are attempted that marry dramatic and philosophical content, but this one manages to be successful on both levels. David Hemmings plays a swinging fashion photographer in the mod London society of the mid-sixties who has his private little world invaded by a possible murder. Vanessa Redgrave is the mysterious young woman he photographs with an older man in Hyde Park one afternoon. When he develops the film at home, he begins to suspect that the man with Vanessa was killed while he was talking to her for a brief two or three minutes. What ensues is a fruitless but frenetic search through London's rock and roll underbelly, where drug orgies and dance clubs proliferate. The Yardbirds, with double lead guitars Jimmy Page and Jeff Beck, are seen in a club, performing "Stroll On." Beck smashes his guitar to bits in an open imitation of Pete Townshend's notorious rite of mod rebellion. Finally, in a scene which was much talked about when the film was first released, Hemmings is left to ponder his unresolved puzzle while a group of mimes plays tennis without a ball on a public court in Hyde Park. Antonioni's subtext here is the place of the artist in relation to reality—both in terms of simple perception (remember op art?) and political responsibility. Hemmings, the very model of a modern artist, both visionary and businessperson, must be certain that what he thinks he sees in the photos is real and then he must fulfill his social obligation to report the alleged crime. Hemmings, Redgrave, and Miles, as the married woman drawn to Hemmings' stylish charms, are all excellent. Herbie Hancock composed the acoustic jazz score.

Antonioni later went on to shoot *Zabriskie Point,* an effort to encapsulate parallel issues in American culture (*see* p. 195).

BLUE HAWAII   ★★

ROCK. 1961. Cast: Elvis Presley, Angela Lansbury, Joan Blackman, and Jenny Maxwell. 101 min. Beta, VHS. CBS/Fox ($59.95)

The well-scrubbed, completely sanitized Elvis, once again playing a returning G.I., comes home to Hawaii and rekindles an old romance with a real Hawaiian princess. However, he can't deal with the pressure he's getting from his plantation-owning parents, who want him to run the family pineapple-growing business. Instead, he decides to join his girlfriend in working for a tourist-guide agency. By becoming very successful as a tourist guide, Elvis establishes his independence from his parents and is able to marry his sweetheart in a climactic Hawaiian wedding ritual. Gets two stars for the scenery. Elvis sings "The Hawaiian Wedding Song," "Ku-U-I-Po," "Beach Boy Blues," "Ito Eats," the title tune, and others. Elvis flick number eight.

BREAKING GLASS   ★★

ROCK. 1980. Cast: Phil Daniels, Hazel O'Connor, Gary Tibbs, Peter-Hugo Daly. 94 min. Beta, VHS. Paramount ($49.95)

Brian Gibson's film about a rock group named Breaking Glass tries to provide an insight into the rise of punk rock in England during the late seventies. Hazel O'Connor is the ambitious young singer with a penchant for protest lyrics who meets up with Phil Daniels (*Quadrophenia*), an aggressive young manager, and rises to the top of the pop charts through a series of fortuitous as well as calculated events. Gibson does a good job of portraying the recession mentality among Britain's underclass youth that spawned punk rock—the glimpses of working class pubs and dance clubs speak volumes about the state of British morale today. What Gibson doesn't do really well is make us care all that much about O'Connor and Daniels, neither of whom is a sweetheart. O'Connor is an egotistical chanteuse with delusions of grandeur and Daniels is a pushy

Hazel O'Connor and Phil Daniels in *Breaking Glass*.

opportunist at bottom. The satirical portraits of recording executives and "genius" producers are on target but are merely potshots, not part of some general critique. The latter part of the film develops into a rock version of *A Star Is Born*, but, by that time, the viewer is glad to see everyone get what they deserve. O'Connor sings her own songs: "Writing on the Wall," "Give Me an Inch," "Black Man," "Big Brother," "Who Calls the Tune?," and "Amen."

BREATHLESS   ★

ROCK. 1983. Cast: Richard Gere, Valerie Kaprisky, and Art Metrano. 105 min. Beta, VHS. Vestron ($79.95)

Going back to Raymond Chandler and Nathaniel West in the thirties, the underworld of Los Angeles, the hidden city that comes alive only after the working world is safely back inside the look-alike houses that line the residential streets, has always attracted the curiosity and creative energy of novelists and filmmakers. In *Breathless,* transplanted New York independent "auteur" Jim McBride (*Mike's Murder*) continues his love affair with the outcasts and criminals of the Los Angeles nightworld. Richard Gere plays Jesse, a car thief who seems to have walked into the frame from 1957, and Valerie Kaprisky, a French soft-porn actress, plays an exchange student attending U.C.L.A. The relationship between the two, based, of course, on the Jean-Paul Belmondo–Jean Seberg duet in Godard's original *Breathless,* runs into problems with Jesse's rather shady colleagues and creditors, who chase them all the way to the Mexican border. Gere and Kaprisky show a lot of skin but don't rate highly in the Bonnie and Clyde mold. The soundtrack includes two versions of "Breathless," Jerry Lee Lewis' own original and that of L.A. punk-art band, X. The rest of the score is indeed eclectic, including Fripp and Eno's "Wind On Water/Wind On Wind," Sam Cooke's "Wonderful World," Eddie Palmieri's "No Me Hagas Sufrir," King Sunny Ade's "365 Is My Number/ The Message," Dexy's Midnight Runners' "Celtic Soul Brothers," The Pretenders' "Message of Love," and Joe 'King' Corrasco's "Caca de Vaca."

BRIMSTONE AND TREACLE   ★★

ROCK. 1982. Cast: Sting, Denholm Elliott, Joan Plowright, and Susanna Hamilton. 85 min. Beta Hifi, VHS Stereo. MGM/UA ($59.95)

This is something they used to do much better on the old anthology TV series like *Alfred Hitchcock* and *Twilight Zone.* Sting, of The Police, stars as a pathological liar and con man in a bizarre little British film that also stars Denholm Elliott and Joan Plowright as the middle-aged parents of an autistic college-age daughter. Sting wins over Joan Plowright and leads her to believe that her daughter's condition can be reversed (it was caused by an auto accident the daughter had after she witnessed her father and his secretary making love). The texture of the movie is correct, but the bareness of the story ultimately leads to boredom. In a shorter, condensed form, the story might have worked quite splendidly. Sting sings "Spread a Little Happiness" on the soundtrack and is heard with The Police on "Only You" and "I Burn for You." The Go-Go's sing "We Got the Beat" and Squeeze does "Up the Junction."

CAT PEOPLE ★★

ROCK. 1983. Cast: Nastassia Kinski, John Heard, Malcolm McDowell, and Annette O'Toole. 118 min. Beta Hifi, VHS Stereo. MCA ($79.95)

This wrong-headed remake of the classic Val Lewton horror fantasy was given to us by Paul Schrader (*Hardcore*) and schlock horror veteran Alan Ormsby. (Schrader directed; Ormsby wrote the screenplay.) Despite having the advantage of Nastassia Kinski's talents to exhibit throughout the film, Schrader and Ormsby forgot to make it thought-provoking, scary, and worth your time. Nastassia is a young woman who doesn't know that she's a cat person but finds out quite shockingly when her long lost brother (Malcolm McDowell) starts making sexual advances toward her and chewing up prostitutes left and right. It seems cat people revert to their feline form when sexually aroused. John Heard is the zookeeper in New Orleans who unwisely falls in love with Nastassia. Hoo boy! The second half of this picture is simply a continual parade of scenes in which Schrader gets Nastassia to walk around buck naked. Perhaps he thinks that's pretty scary. The first half is very atmospheric and very stylishly executed. What happened to the movie from there on in is quite inexplicable. "Cat People" ("Putting Out Fire"), written by David Bowie and Giorgio Moroder, is sung by Bowie. Ella Fitzgerald's "Sunday Kind of Love" and Jimmy Hughes' "Why Not Tonight" are also on the soundtrack.

CAVEMAN ★★★♪

ROCK. 1981. Cast: Ringo Starr, Barbara Bach, Shelley Long, Dennis Quaid, John Matuszak, Avery Schreiber, and Jack Gilford. 92 min. Beta, VHS. CBS/Fox ($59.95)

Ringo Starr has appeared in ten films at last count, all flops except for his Beatles epics and *Caveman*. In this comedy farce written by Rudy DeLuca and Carl Gottlieb and directed by Gottlieb, Ringo plays a bumbling but inventive caveman who is banished from his tribe by the tribe's leader (John Matuszak, the football player), after Ringo tries to seduce Matuszak's mate, Barbara Bach. In exile, Ringo gathers together a group of ne'er-do-wells including Dennis Quaid, Jack Gilford, and Gilford's lovely daughter, Shelley Long (*Cheers*). By discovering fire and taming a dinosaur, Ringo overthrows Matuszak as leader of the tribe. Wildly funny. There is no dialogue per se, as everyone communicates in a sort of primitive double-talk. Ringo does not sing.

CHRISTIANE F. ★★

ROCK. 1981. Cast: Natja Brunckhorst, Thomas Haustern, Jens Kuphal, and David Bowie. 130 min. Beta Hifi, VHS Stereo. Media ($39.95)

This West German film explores in numbing detail the descent into hell of a teenage drug addict. Christiane F., played by Natja Brunckhorst with convincing earnestness, is a 15-year-old middle class girl whose aimless boredom pushes her to try heroin.

David Bowie appearing as himself in *Christiane F.*

Once hooked, her life rapidly degenerates until she is a prostitute patrolling Berlin's Zoo Railroad Station with her addict boyfriend, Detlef (Thomas Haustern), a male hustler. When this film was first released in the U.S., reviewers were impressed by its "realism." Actually, there is an intentional air of surrealism in the movie that manages somehow to rip the situation of the protagonists completely out of its social context. What we have here in reality is an evil fable which is carried forward by an underlying moral concern far larger than its subjects justify. *Christiane F.* should be seen as a science fiction allegory similar to *The Village of the Damned,* where the children symbolized the hidden evils of their parents' society. David Bowie appears as himself in concert, singing "V2 Schneider," "TVC 15," "Heroes," "Look Back in Anger," "Stay," "Sense of Doubt," "Boys Keep Swinging," and "Warszawa," on stage and on the soundtrack. Directed by Ulrich Edel. Dubbed in English.

COMEBACK   ★↩

ROCK. 1983. Cast: Eric (Rocco) Burdon, Julie Carmen, Michael Cavanaugh, and Soleil Moonfry. 105 min. Beta, VHS. MGM/UA ($59.95)

One of the drawbacks of rock and roll's acceptance by mainstream culture has been the increasing use of rock themes and personalities in pretentiously self-indulgent films which try to make serious statements about life, the pursuit of the American dollar, and male-female relationships. *Comeback,* which stars British rock legend Eric Burdon, is a recent and exceptionally mediocre example of this trend. Written and directed by Christel Buschmann, obviously a German who takes rock and roll very seriously, this film concerns the personal odyssey of Rocco (Burdon), a disillusioned rock star, from the fleshpots of Los Angeles to the ghettoes of West Berlin, where he rediscovers for a fleeting time the spiritual meaning of his musical calling. If it sounds really heavy, that's because it is. As an actor, Burdon is a pretty good singer. Julie Carmen is delectable as his confused and confusing wife, and Soleil Moonfry (Punky Brewster) plays their daughter. Almost two hours of Teutonic solemnity end the way most of these rock epics end—with a gratuitous killing. The songs performed by Burdon are "Do You Feel," "House of the Rising Sun," "Sweet Blood Call," "No More Elmore," "Crawling King Snake," "It Hurts Me Too," "Take It Easy," "Bird on a Beach," "The Road," "Lights Out," "Streetwalker," "Devil's Daughter," "Where Is My Friend?," and "Kill My Body."

Eric Burdon as rock star Rocco in *Comeback.*

COMING HOME   ★★★

ROCK. 1978. Cast: Jane Fonda, Jon Voight, Bruce Dern, Penelope Milford, Robert Carradine, and Robert Ginty. 128 min. Beta, VHS. CBS/Fox ($69.95)

Director Hal Ashby gathered together all of the threads of liberal thought in the late seventies, especially feminism, in this much-heralded film about the Vietnam War's effect upon a group of well-meaning people in 1968. Jane Fonda is the Marine wife whose husband, Bruce Dern, has just shipped out to Nam for his first overseas duty. Jon Voight plays the disabled veteran she meets while doing volunteer work in a Veterans Administration hospital near Camp Pendleton in southern California. The inevitable occurs between the embittered but sensitive Voight and the lonely, suddenly blossoming Fonda. They have an affair. When Bruce Dern returns home because of shot nerves, the last thing he expects is to find his wife carrying on with a "gimp." Tragedy ensues and many critics have called *Coming Home* a triumph of the sixties spirit over the moral lethargy of the seventies. Viewers ought to take a second look; they might think differently. The soundtrack is a parade of great music from the period depicted in the movie. It includes The Rolling Stones ("Out of Time," "No Expectations," "Jumping Jack Flash," "My Girl," "Ruby Tuesday," and "Sympathy for the Devil"), The Beatles ("Hey Jude" and "Strawberry Fields Forever"), Bob Dylan ("Just Like a Woman"), Jefferson Airplane ("White Rabbit"), Jimi Hendrix ("Manic Depression"), Chambers Brothers ("Time Has Come Today"), and much more.

DINER ★★★♪

ROCK. 1982. Cast: Mickey Rourke, Steve Guttenberg, Kevin Bacon, Timothy Daly, Daniel Stern, and Ellen Barkin. 110 min. Beta, VHS. MGM/UA ($79.95)

Barry Levinson left behind a decade and more of writing comedy for television, most visibly for *The Carol Burnett Show,* with his critically praised directorial debut in *Diner,* a semiautobiographical look at a group of college-age buddies in the Baltimore suburbs circa 1959. The ensemble comedy of manners formulated by George Lucas in *American Graffiti* has proven to be the most imitated vehicle for first-time filmmakers in the

Cast of *Diner.*

seventies and eighties. In most other directors' hands, this nostalgic material would have been maudlin and boring, but Levinson's perceptive eye and thorough knowledge of his subjects make this film a stunning actors' exercise. The cast of young performers has since gone on to successful careers of their own—Mickey Rourke being the foremost talent in the group. His portrayal of Boogie, the suave but aimless leader of this band of buddies, touches the reality that we all know. Always looking for that angle, always making plans, eternally chasing the perfect woman, Rourke's character gives thematic coherence to Levinson's portrait of the end of the fifties and the dawn of the sixties in one of the nation's heartlands. Look for the fine work of Ellen Barkin and Kevin Bacon also. The soundtrack is one of the best rock and roll anthologies ever used in a movie and includes Jerry Lee Lewis' "Whole Lotta Shakin' Goin' On," Bobby Darin's "Dream Lover" and "Beyond the Sea," the Del-Vikings' "Come Go with Me," Jimmy Reed's "Take Out Some Insurance," Chuck Berry's "Run Rudolph, Run" and "Merry Christmas Baby," Dion's "Teenager in Love" and "I Wonder Why," Carl Perkins' "Honey Don't," Clarence "Frogman" Henry's "Ain't Got No Home," Howling Wolf's "Smokestack Lightning," Lowell Fulson's "Reconsider Baby," Eddie Cochran's "Something Else," and Elvis Presley's "Don't Be Cruel," among others.

DOUBLE TROUBLE   ★★

ROCK. 1966. Cast: Elvis Presley, Annette Day, John Williams, Yvonne Romaine, and Michael Murphy. 92 min. Beta, VHS. MGM/UA ($39.95)

In this opus, Elvis plays a rock singer named Guy Lambert who is on tour in Europe. In London, he meets Jill (Annette Day), the heiress to an enormous fortune, who has a rather protective uncle. The uncle turns out to be quite a bounder. It seems that Elvis can't shake the girl loose, even as he heads for Antwerp, Brussels, and his next gig. Soon enough, he becomes involved not only in the struggle between Jill and her uncle but in an international diamond-smuggling caper. The songs include such forgettable tunes as the title song, "Give Me All Your Love," "Could I Fall in Love," "Long-legged Girl with the Short Dress On," "The City by Night," "Old Mac-Donald," "I Love Only One Girl," and "There's So Much World to See." If the foreign locales like London and Antwerp look familiar, it's because they are. The film was shot entirely on a back lot in exotic Hollywood, U.S.A.

ELVIS: ALOHA FROM HAWAII   ★★★

ROCK. 1973. Artist: Elvis Presley. 75 min. Beta Hifi, VHS Stereo. Media (29.95)

It is probably true that the majority of Elvis' fans see no difference between the young man from Memphis who fused black rhythm and blues and white hillbilly music into what has come to be called rock and roll and the Las Vegas-style glitter entertainer that he became in his later years. The other thing that is ignored about this intriguing dichotomy is the fact that he set the standard for both performing types. He was the original rocker *and* the man who brought Vegas into the modern era, leaving Sinatra and Bennett behind in his wake. On January 14, 1973, *Aloha from Hawaii* was transmitted live throughout the world via satellite from Honolulu, Hawaii. This unprecedented television event finds the King in a later stage of his career, about where the constant touring and the tensions of his dissolving marriage to Priscilla were starting to take their toll on him, both physically and emotionally. Despite feeling understandably depressed over his broken marriage (he had just filed divorce papers the week before), Elvis gives one of his better performances of that period (see also *Elvis on Tour*). In his famous white, sequined suit with the eagle motif on front and back, flowing cape, and oversized belt buckle, Elvis looks and acts the part of the king of rock and roll. The packed auditorium goes wild over Elvis' renditions of old hits and new standards like: "Hawaii, U.S.A.," "C. C. Rider," "Burning Love," "Something," "You Gave Me a Mountain," "Early Morning Rain," "Steamroller Blues," "My Way," "Love Me," "Johnny B. Goode," "It's Over," "Blue Suede Shoes," "So Lonesome I Could Cry," "I Can't Stop Loving You," "Hound Dog," "Blue Hawaii," "What Now My Love," "Fever," "Welcome to My World," "Suspicious Minds," "I'll Remember You," "Hawaiian Wedding Song," "Long Tall Sally," "Ku-U-I-Po," "American Trilogy," "Hunk of Love," and "I Can't Help Falling in Love." Directed by Marty Pasetta.

EDDIE AND THE CRUISERS ★★

ROCK. 1983. Cast: Michael Pare, Tom Berenger, Ellen Barkin, Helen Schneider, and John Cafferty. 100 min. Beta Hifi, VHS Stereo. Embassy. ($79.95)

The cable-TV surprise of 1984 and the launching pad for Beaver Brown, the band whose music was used as the Eddie and The Cruisers sound in the movie *Eddie and The Cruisers*, failed miserably when released theatrically in 1983. What seemed pointless and amateurish on the big screen became soap opera-ish enough to be swallowed on the small screen. The idea, not altogether original but potentially intriguing, goes like this: 20 years after Eddie Wilson's supposed death, his last, unreleased album, *A Season in Hell*, is released to critical and commercial acclaim. A TV reporter, Ellen Barkin, believes that Wilson is still alive somewhere, hiding out for his own secret reasons. Michael Pare, another in the mumbler school of acting, essays the role of Wilson, serious rocker ahead of his time. Tom Berenger plays the graduate student turned rock lyricist who matches his Rimbaud-derived poetry to Wilson's allegedly advanced music. Quite silly really. Beaver Brown, with front man John Cafferty, provided the music for the group and, to everyone's amazement, had a hit album with the movie's soundtrack. Songs are "On the Dark Side," "Wild Summer Nights," "Boardwalk Angel,"

"Tender Years," "Down on My Knees," "I Don't Wanna Hang Up My Rock and Roll Shoes," and "Season in Hell (Pre-Suite)." Sort of like The Doors meeting Bruce Springsteen and making a terrible film together.

FAST TIMES AT RIDGEMONT HIGH   ★★★

ROCK. 1982. Cast: Ray Walston, Sean Penn, Jennifer Jason, Phoebe Cates, and Judge Reinhold. 92 min. Beta Hifi, VHS. MCA ($79.95)

Yes! It's another one of that long list of California teenage coming-of-age-at-the-nearby-mall-and-the-high-school pictures. But, instead of the usual predictable plot with cookie-cutter characters, *Fast Times at Ridgemont High* is an entertaining romp packed with characters who breathe. You might not personally know people like these, but you'll enjoy meeting them. Director Amy Heckerling's fast-paced debut plays Ray

Sean Penn in *Fast Times at Ridgemont High.*

Walston's tough and concerned high school history teacher, Mr. Hand, against Sean Penn's very funny and memorable portrayal of the perpetually stoned surfer and student, Spicoli. Linda Barlett (Phoebe Cates) and Stacy Hamilton (Jennifer Jason Leigh) play two teenage girls who are always watching the guys. Judge Reinhold plays Stacy's brother Brad, a frustrated teenage guy who is always watching the girls. The music that fills the soundtrack from start to finish is used for maximum effect. The Go-Go's tune "We Got the Beat," to which the opening titles are cut, is followed by Jackson Browne's "Somebody's Baby," Joe Walsh's "Waffle Stomp," Poco's "I'll Leave It Up to You," The Cars' "Moving in Stereo," Stevie Nicks' "Sleeping Angel," Louise Coffin's "Uptown Boys," Gerard McManon's "The Look in Your Eyes," another Go-Go's tune, "Speeding," Led Zeppelin's "Kashmir," Graham Nash's "Love Is the Reason," Jimmy Buffet's "I Don't Know" (Spicoli's Theme), and Reeves Nevo and the Cinch's "Life in the Fast Lane."

FLASHDANCE   ★★★

ROCK. 1983. Cast: Jennifer Beals, Michael Nouri, Belinda Bauer, Lilia Skala, and Cynthia Rhodes. 95 min. Beta Hifi, VHS Stereo. Paramount ($39.95)

This was one of the major events and one of the genuine surprises of 1983. Adrian Lyne's grooved vision of the way music and the me generation commingle in contemporary culture proved to be his ticket to the top of the film world. Jennifer Beals, as Alex Owens, welder by day and "flash" dancer by night in a seedy Pittsburgh bar, made a sensational debut (even though she didn't do much of the dancing in the film—it was Marine Jahan, uncredited) playing a female Rocky of the barre. Although she does get into a relationship, sort of, with her boss at the steel foundry (Michael Nouri), the image that stays in the mind is of her practicing her steps all alone in the vastness of her loft apartment, the grayness of the walls matching her own stolid determination. This is goal-oriented America, made attractive with appealing doe eyes and an iron, self-obsessed will. Lyne's work shimmers with straightforward narrative power and anticipates the look of today's best rock videos. Emotionally, this film caught the currents of social belief, which explains much of its great success, but, cinematically, it deserves attention as a prototypical synthesis of story and music that is a step ahead of the traditional musical. The notable score includes Laura Branigan's smash hit, "Gloria," her "Imagination," Irene Cara's platinum "Flashdance" ("What a Feeling"), Michael Sembella's hit, "Maniac," Kim Carnes' "I'll Be Where the Heart Is," Joan Jett's "I Love Rock and Roll," and Jimmy Castor Bunch's "It's Just Begun."

Marine Jahan in *Flashdance*.

FOOTLOOSE ★★♪

ROCK. 1984. Cast: Kevin Bacon, Lori Singer, Dianne Wiest, John Lithgow, Chris Penn, and Sarah Jessica Parker. 107 min. Beta Hifi, VHS Stereo. Paramount ($39.95)

Herbert Ross, one of Hollywood's major directors (*Turning Point, California Suite, Goodbye Girl,* etc.), teamed up with writer Dean Pitchford to produce one of the hit movies of 1984, a deceptively simple narrative about teenagers in a small midwestern town who just want to have some fun. Kevin Bacon plays the Chicago native who moves with his recently divorced mother to Beaumont, a rural roadstop where John Lithgow, a minister, has convinced the elders to ban dancing within the town limits. Bacon gets involved, of course, with the minister's less than innocent daughter, Lori Singer, and, eventually, gets the town to rescind its ban. Ross' attempt at a serious teen pic exceeded even his own expectations of popular success. Two things contributed to its box office power: the performances of Bacon, Singer, and a very funny Chris Penn and a soundtrack filled with Top 10 hits. The producers showed shrewd judgement

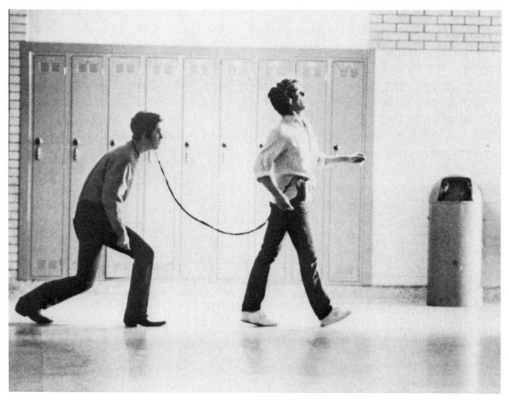

Scene from *Footloose*.

in their choice of music; five of the songs heard in the film became gold records ("Foot-loose" by Kenny Loggins, "Let's Hear It for the Boy" by Deniece Williams, "Holding Out for a Hero" by Bonnie Tyler, "Almost Paradise" by Mike Reno and Ann Wilson, and "Hurts So Good," by John Cougar Mellencamp). Other songs heard are "The Girl Gets Around" by Sammy Hagar, "Dancing in the Sheets" by Shalamar, "Some-body's Eyes" by Karla Bonoff, "I'm Free" by Kenny Loggins, "Waiting for a Girl Like You" by Foreigner, and "Mind Your Head" by Quiet Riot.

FOXES ★★★

ROCK. 1980. Cast: Jodie Foster, Sally Kellerman, Cherie Currie, Randy Quaid, and Scott Baio. 106 min. Beta, VHS. Key ($59.95)

In an early film by Adrian Lyne (*Flashdance*), Jodie Foster delivers a sensitive, complex performance as a teenager living in suburban Los Angeles who acts as a mother figure to her troubled girlfriends. Although Jodie's wisdom is a bit farfetched for her age (her mother, played by Sally Kellerman, at one point calls her "a short 40-year-old"), Lyne's apparent empathy for his lost teenage protagonists makes it all seem plausible. More recent films about high school kids don't pack the power that this film does. Among the problems the girls face are: Cherie Currie's psychotic cop father, Randy Quaid's professional photographer, having an affair with Jodie's best friend, whose house is totaled by Jodie's overzealous friends during an "intimate little dinner party," and Scott Baio's confrontation with an angry biker. Above all, the concept of "family" is the focus in this film, as the girls form their own support group in the face of the overwhelming indifference of their spaced-out, weary parents. Paints a picture of L.A. middle class neighborhoods as tract housing for the well-to-do. The soundtrack includes "Fly Too High" by Janis Ian, "Twentieth Century Foxes" and "Virginia" by Angel, Boston's "More Than a Feeling," "Bad Love" by Cher, "Ship of Fools" by Bob Seger, and Donna Summer's "Foxes" and "On the Radio."

FUN IN ACAPULCO ★♪

ROCK. 1963. Cast: Elvis Presley, Ursula Andress, and Paul Lukas. 97 min. Beta, VHS. CBS/Fox ($59.95)

This is the thirteenth film made by Elvis Presley, his ninth after being discharged from the army in 1960. In the spectrum of Elvis musicals, *Fun in Acapulco* fits snugly in the middle. What it has going for it are the Mexican landscape (it was shot in and around the famous Mirador Hotel in Acapulco) and Ursula Andress (straight from her debut in *Dr. No*). Elvis plays a former trapeze artist who has come to Mexico to forget the accidental death of his brother in a fall. As he learns to conquer his fear of heights, two women, a bullfighter and a hotel social director (Andress), vie for his affections. The slow pace of the film, done in the Elvis formula "perfected" by producer Hal Wallis in the sixties, is only occasionally accelerated by songs like "El Toro," "The Bullfighter Was a Lady," "Bossa Nova, Baby," "Guadalajara," and the title tune. For Elvis fans only.

GET CRAZY ★★♪

ROCK. 1983. Cast: Allen Goorwitz, Malcolm McDowell, Daniel Stern, Gail Edwards, Franklyn Ajaye, Bill Henderson, Ed Begley, Jr., Bobby Sherman, Fabian Forte, Lou Reed, and Paul Bartel. 98 min. Beta, VHS. Embassy ($69.95)

In the tradition of the "Gosh kids! Let's put on a show and show 'em" musicals of the forties, *Get Crazy* is a hit-and-miss eighties comedy update that did not deserve to close as soon as it opened in limited theatrical release across the country in 1983. The writers of the film wrapped a thin plot around a theater full of wonderful comedic characters. In the film, Allen Goorwitz plays Max Wolfe, the owner of the Saturn Theater in Los Angeles, who every year puts on a rock and roll spectacular on New Year's Eve just for the fun of it. To ring in 1984 he wants to put on his biggest show ever with the biggest names in rock.

Ed Begley, Jr. (St. Elsewhere) stars as Colin Beverly, the head of Serpent Records and an all-around meanie and no-goodnik, who wants to blow up the Saturn and build his world headquarters on its site. Daniel Stern (*Diner, Blue Thunder*) acts the role of the Saturn's stage manager, Neil Allen, who organizes the mayhem of the New Year's Eve bash. Malcolm McDowell (*O Lucky Man, Cat People*) stars as rock legend Reggie Wanker, a thinly veiled comedic portrait of Mick Jagger. The bad boy of New York rock himself, Lou Reed, portrays the very funny character of Auden, a takeoff on Reed's fellow rock poet Bob Dylan. Bill Henderson (the AT&T commercials) appears on stage as King Blues, in an imitation of and tribute to Bo Diddley, and sings Muddy Waters' "Hootchie Coochie Man" and Elmore James' "The Sky Is Crying." Will Max put on his concert? Will Colin Beverly and the forces of evil be thwarted? Will the kids have fun? Hmm . . . could be.

G.I. BLUES ★♪

ROCK. 1960. Cast: Elvis Presley, Juliet Prowse, Robert Ivers, and James Douglas. 104 min. Beta, VHS. CBS/Fox ($59.95)

Two years away in the army, Elvis returned to the screen in *G.I. Blues,* an attempt to cleverly exploit his status as a homecoming hero/soldier. The wait was not worth it, by the looks of this movie. This is a weak, completely inane "entertainment" which lacks any continuity with the Elvis of the fifties. Here, cleaned up, patriotized, and hung out to dry, Elvis can only smirk and sing silly songs while cinematic inanity is cut loose.

The makers of this film, producer Hal Wallis and director Norman Taurog (who were to perpetrate more crimes of this nature in the Elvis films of the sixties), didn't even bother to shoot this story of a G.I. in Berlin who tries to win a bet by dating a nightclub dancer (Juliet Prowse) on location in Germany. Rather, Elvis and Juliet are matted into some stock footage of Berlin taken by an anonymous film crew. All in all, a waste of time. Elvis doesn't even sing a hit tune. What one hears instead are: "Wooden Heart," "Pocketful of Rainbows," "Big Boots," and many others.

GIRLS, GIRLS, GIRLS ★★

ROCK. 1962. Cast: Elvis Presley, Laurel Goodwin, Stella Stevens, and Jeremy Slate. 106 min. Beta, VHS. CBS/Fox ($59.95)

Elvis, in his eleventh film, plays a tuna-boat skipper whose prize possession, his boat, is sold without his knowledge to Jeremy Slate, a boorishly aggressive fleet owner. Enter spoiled rich girl Laurel Goodwin, who can't understand all this fuss about a little boat but is willing to buy it back for Elvis with her daddy's money. Although the film has its lighter moments, especially a scene in which Elvis sings a song in Chinese, it's pretty slow going. Stella Stevens is a bright spot, playing a nightclub chanteuse who can't quite divert Elvis' attentions from his rich girlfriend. For those who care, Elvis sings "Return to Sender" near the beginning of the film. That and the title tune, an old Coasters nugget, are the only songs worth hearing in this mélange of music and comic drama.

GIVE MY REGARDS TO BROADSTREET ★★

ROCK. 1984. Cast: Paul McCartney, Ringo Starr, Bryan Brown, Barbara Bach, Linda McCartney, Tracy Ullman, and Ralph Richardson. 109 min. Beta Hifi, VHS Stereo. CBS-Fox ($29.95)

Paul McCartney wrote the screenplay for what amounts to a 109-minute music video. Paul falls asleep in the back of his limo while being driven to work. He dreams that the master soundtrack mix of his soon-to-be-released album has been stolen by an employee and must be recovered by midnight or else all of his worldly property will pass by default into the hands of a large multinational conglomerate. This mystery is set against the daily busy schedule of Paul McCartney. Paul should stick to songwriting. We have the opportunity to see Paul and Ringo perform a number of songs recorded by the Beatles. Paul sings "Good Day, Sunshine," "Yesterday," "Here, There, and Everywhere," "For No One," "Eleanor Rigby," and "The Long and Winding Road." In addition, Paul and his wife, Linda, sing "Silly Love Songs," "No More Lonely Nights," "So Bad," "No Values," and "Not Such a Bad Boy."

A HARD DAY'S NIGHT ★★★★

ROCK. 1964. Cast: John Lennon, Paul McCartney, George Harrison, Ringo Starr, Victor Spinetti, Wilfred Brambell, Norman Rossington. 90 min. Beta Hifi, VHS Stereo. MPI ($64.95)

When this film, The Beatles' celebrated screen debut, was released, more prints of it were made and distributed internationally than had been made of any other film ever produced in the history of motion pictures! The film was not only a revelation in box office terms but a surprising critical success as well. Richard Lester, a young but veteran film director in mod London, was able to cull the most refreshing and charming performances of The Beatles' careers. In an inventive mix of music and narrative, Lester weaves a tale of pop music success and pop-idol tribulations around the appearance of The Beatles on a fictional British TV variety program. Playing the harried TV director in bravura style is Victor Spinetti. But the real star of this film turned out to be Ringo, whose freshness and comic timing signaled the arrival of a new comic talent on the silver screen. Among the funniest scenes are: George stumbling into an advertising agency where a mod executive is disturbed by "typical young bloke" George's replies to his well-researched campaigns designed to anticipate the youth market; and John being stopped by a woman who swears that she recognizes him from somewhere but can't quite put her finger on it. The Beatles sing: "A Hard Day's Night," "I Should Have Known Better," "If I Fell," "I'm Happy Just to Dance with You," "And I Love Her," "Tell Me Why," "Can't Buy Me Love," "Anytime at

Paul, George, Ringo, and John in *A Hard Day's Night.*

All," "I'll Cry Instead" (added to the original film in its 1981 re-release in Dolby stereo), "Things We Said Today," "When I Get Home," and "I'll Be Back."

HAROLD AND MAUDE ★ʲ

ROCK. 1971. Cast: Bud Cort, Ruth Gordon, Vivian Pickles, and Cyril Cusack. 91 min. Beta, VHS. Paramount ($59.95)

This sardonic black comedy bombed at the box office when it was originally released but has found an enduring audience in cult movie houses and at midnight showings. Hal Ashby (*Coming Home, Let's Spend the Night Together*) has since settled for less eccentric material but this film may never be surpassed for its decidedly outré subject matter. Bud Cort is a millionaire's son with a necrophiliac orientation and a gallows sense of humor who falls in love with Ruth Gordon, an octogenarian who is a kindred spirit. They meet at a series of funerals and ride around together in Harold's custom-built hearse. Bizarre! Before Harold can pop the question to Maude, she poisons herself and puts an end to their preposterous May-December romance. Bud Cort is absolutely hideous as Harold and Ruth Gordon must have done it for a quick buck. As for Ashby's excuse, there is, I suppose, no telling what skeletons any of us may have locked away in our closets. Colin Higgins, who wrote this, later went on to write and direct light comedies (*Nine to Five, Foul Play*). On the soundtrack, there are some well-known songs by Cat Stevens, including "Tea for the Tillerman," "Where Do the Children Play," "Wild World," "Hard Headed Woman," and "Sad Lisa."

HARUM SCARUM ★★

ROCK. 1965. Cast: Elvis Presley, Mary Ann Mobley, Fran Jeffries, and Michael Ansara. 86 min. Beta, VHS. MGM/UA ($59.95)

Another of Elvis' back-lot epics, shot well within the lifespan of the average fruit fly. At this point in the mid-sixties, he was churning out these flicks at the rate of three a year, for which he got paid a million per. The rest of the time he spent doing what has been exhaustively documented since his demise by relatives, "best" friends, and professional biographers. In this youth programmer, Elvis plays Johnny Tyronne, an American film star on a publicity tour of the middle east. He is kidnapped by the evil Arab (Michael Ansara), escapes, and enlists the help of an Arab princess (Mary Ann Mobley) to foil Ansara's plan to overthrow the legitimate government of his country. All in a day's work for this diplomatically inclined American screen idol.

Elvis in *Harum Scarum*.

Elvis sings "Harum Holiday," "Desert Serenade," "Go East, Young Man," "Mirage," "It's Kismet," "Shake That Tambourine," "Hey, Little Girl," "All the Pleasures of Love," and "So Close Yet So Far from Paradise."

HIGH SCHOOL CONFIDENTIAL ★★

ROCK. 1958. Cast: Russ Tamblyn, Mamie Van Doren, Jan Sterling, Jackie Coogan, Michael Landon, John Drew Barrymore, and Jerry Lee Lewis. 85 min. Beta, VHS. NTA ($39.95)

A black and white film directed by Jack Arnold (*The Incredible Shrinking Man*) and produced by B-movie king Albert Zugsmith, *High School Confidential* was one of the first attempts at a youth exploitation picture, with its formula of rock and roll, drugs, and teenage sex. For its first forty minutes or so, it's a real scream. Jive-talking teens slinging hepcat phrases and beatnik conceits around in a high school classroom makes for an entertaining time. Hear Russ Tamblyn say "I'm puttin' it down and you ain't pickin' it up" to the Lord Buckley-spouting John Drew Barrymore, before he witnesses Barrymore delivering a "cool" lecture on Christopher Columbus in history class. "What a wild cat, man!" But then it gets tediously conventional as the serious side of this narrative unfolds and we find out that Tamblyn is an undercover narc out to infiltrate a drug gang selling dope to school kids. Mamie Van Doren is his aunt, Jan Sterling is the teacher who wants to show him the correct path, and Michael Landon is the do-gooder classmate who's too squeaky clean to believe. Jerry Lee Lewis sings "High School Confidential" on a flatbed truck driving across the school grounds.

HOW I WON THE WAR ★★

ROCK. 1967. Cast: Michael Crawford, John Lennon, Roy Kinnear, Jack McGowran, and Michael Hordern. 111 min. Beta, VHS. MGM/UA ($59.95)

After the successes of *A Hard Day's Night* and *Help!*, director Richard Lester, an expatriate American in Britain, had carte blanche and he abused the privilege, setting back his career for many years. One of the projects that received scathing critiques and played before empty houses was 1967's *How I Won the War.* Conceived as a biting satire on World War II and the British stiff upper lip, the most noteworthy thing about it, finally, is that John Lennon of The Beatles has a supporting role as Private Gripweed.

John Lennon in *How I Won the War.*

Plagued by its *Goon Show* scattershot humor and the often unintelligible mélange of British accents, the film fails to draw anything funny out of the bleakness of the war. Much of it, in fact, is squirmingly repellent: blood and gore splashed about, death discussed endlessly, and the feeling of suffocating hopelessness. Michael Crawford is the leader of a squad of soldiers sent to North Africa on a reconnaissance mission—that is, to construct a cricket field in the desert for British officers. One by one, his men die off, leaving the eternally deceived Crawford to fend for himself in a prisoner-of-war camp. Lennon, actually, is quite good in his small role but the rest of the film will remain impenetrable to American sensibilities.

HOW TO STUFF A WILD BIKINI ★

ROCK. 1965. Cast: Annette Funicello, Frankie Avalon, Buster Keaton, Mickey Rooney, Harvey Lembeck, Dwayne Hickman, and The Kingsmen. 90 min. Beta, VHS. Warner ($39.95)

One of the weaker entries in a mediocre series, *How to Stuff a Wild Bikini* again stars Annette and Frankie as Dee Dee and Frankie, your favorite beach party couple. This time, Frankie is away in the south Pacific with the Naval Reserve and Dee Dee is trying to fend off the advances of Dwayne Hickman (*Dobie Gillis*). When witch doctor Buster Keaton sends a mysterious beauty in a leopard-spot bikini to spy on Dee Dee on Frankie's behalf, Mickey Rooney, an advertising executive, decides to sign her up to represent a motorcycle manufacturer in a new national campaign. Obviously, this causes some problems. Happily, everything is resolved in the end after a wild cross-country motorbike race. The Kingsmen appear midway through the picture, singing "Give Her Loving." Other songs performed by the cast are "How About Us?," "Mad Madison Avenue," "A Healthy Girl," "The Boy Next Door," "You Better Be Ready," "The Perfect Boy," "Follow Your Leader," "Here We Are," and "After the Party."

THE HUNGER ★★

ROCK. 1983. Cast: David Bowie, Catherine Deneuve, and Susan Sarandon. 100 min. Beta, VHS. MGM/UA ($79.95)

Director Tony Scott, whose brother Ridley Scott brought to the screen *Alien* and *Blade Runner,* uses many current TV-commercial and music video techniques to tell this story of stylish horror set in modern day New York. Bowie plays the 400-year-old lover of ageless vampire Catherine Deneuve, who must drink human blood in order to survive and sustain her eternal beauty. When Bowie's character begins to age rapidly,

David Bowie and Susan Sarandon in _The Hunger._

he turns to Susan Sarandon, who plays a research scientist investigating the aging process. Deneuve gradually takes Sarandon on as her lover to replace the dying Bowie. Some horrific twists and lots of carefully crafted shots of the three superbly lit stars fill out this kinky movie. Bowie does not sing.

THE IDOLMAKER ★★★

ROCK. 1980. Cast: Ray Sharkey, Tovah Feldsuh, Peter Gallagher, and Paul Land. 119 min. Beta Hifi, VHS Stereo. MGM/UA ($59.95)

Taylor Hackford (_Officer and a Gentleman_) made his feature film directorial debut with _The Idolmaker,_ an inconsistent but sometimes powerful portrayal of a rock and roll manager-promoter in the early sixties who lives vicariously through his clients. Ray Sharkey, in the title role of Vincent Vicarri, turns in a fine performance as the failed Philadelphia singer who, in turning his energies toward building the careers of others, finds that he is no longer living fully himself. Tovah Feldsuh plays the woman who

Scene from *The Idolmaker*.

loves him, Peter Gallagher plays his first discovery, and Paul Land plays the discovery who becomes a paranoid superstar, ultimately ditching the man who taught him all he knew. In spots, this film is quite well done. The songs performed are: "Sweet Little Lover," "A Boy and a Girl," "Forever Dark the Night," "Where Is My Love," "Come and Get It," "Shelley," "I Know Where You're Going," "It's Never Been Tonight Before," "Oo Wee Baby" (sung by Darlene Love), "I Can't Tell," and "Baby."

IT HAPPENED AT THE WORLD'S FAIR ★★♪

ROCK. 1963. Cast: Elvis Presley, Gary Lockwood, Joan O'Brien, Ginny Tiu. 105 min. Beta, VHS. MGM/UA ($39.95)

In this Norman Taurog-Hal Wallis Elvis film, another formula movie based on tried and true television sitcom material, the standard for post-Army Elvis films, Elvis is once again involved in a triangle involving a little girl, a big girl, and a duplicitous buddy. He's an itinerant airplane pilot whose partner, played by Gary Lockwood, can't seem to stay away from poker games and crap shoots. When their plane is repossessed in lieu of payment of some steep debts, they head for Seattle (site of the 1963 World's Fair) to look for work. Along the way, a Chinese truck driver and his little niece, Su Ling, pick them up. Complications arise when Su Ling's uncle disappears, leaving her in the care of Elvis. A nurse at the World's Fair dispensary, played by Joan O'Brien, becomes Elvis' romantic interest. The convoluted but entertaining movie rambles on, as Elvis wins the girl, finds Su Ling's uncle, and cures his buddy's gambling fever once and for all. Songs: "Rainbow beyond the Bend," "Relax," "Take Me to the Fair," "Remind Me Too Much of You," "One Broken Heart for Sale," "I'm Falling in Love," "Cotton Candy Land," "A World of Our Own," "Tra-La-La," and "Happy Ending."

JAILHOUSE ROCK   ★★★

ROCK. 1957. Cast: Elvis Presley, Judy Tyler, Dean Jones, Vaughn Taylor, and Mickey Shaughnessy. 97 min. Beta, VHS. MGM/UA ($59.95)

Elvis' grittiest performance and one of the two films noirs that he starred in before entering the military (the other was *King Creole*). Much has been made of the iconic dance sequence in which Elvis sings the immortal "Jailhouse Rock." While the film is not the best Elvis film ever shot, the "Jailhouse Rock" number has placed it indelibly in the minds of an entire generation as *the* Elvis movie. In what is essentially another rags to riches scenario, Elvis plays a young man convicted of manslaughter who learns to sing and play guitar while in prison, thanks to a hardened con, played well by Mickey Shaughnessy. When he gets out, Judy Tyler signs on as his manager, and, together, they make Elvis a multimedia superstar. Trouble comes in the guise of Elvis' ex-con buddy who is paroled and demands a cut of his action. Things end happily when Elvis' character finally comes to terms with the consequences of his meteoric rise to stardom and decides that love is worth more than any amount of money. The accomplishment of this movie, directed by Richard Thorpe, is that it recognizes and exploits the heretofore glossed-over subterranean sensuality of Elvis' image and music. Looking surly and intense, Elvis gets to deliver lines such as "Honey, it's just the beast in me." Songs: "I Want to Be Free," "Baby I Don't Care," "Don't Leave Me Now," "Young and Beautiful," and the title tune. In black and white.

Elvis in *Jailhouse Rock*.

KING CREOLE   ★★♪

ROCK. 1958. Cast: Elvis Presley, Carolyn Jones, Vic Morrow, Dean Jagger, Dolores Hart, and Walter Matthau. 115 min. Beta, VHS. CBS/Fox ($59.95)

Michael Curtiz, who directed the legendary *Casablanca,* took a chance and made *King Creole,* Elvis' fourth and last film before he entered the service, a somber study in film noir technique.

Elvis is a New Orleans native, Danny Fisher, who becomes a local nightclub singer against the wishes of his ineffectual, out-of-work father. Unfortunately, success as a singer in a New Orleans saloon carries with it a price—the attentions of mobster Walter Matthau, who offers Elvis more money to sing at his club. Elvis discovers that the agreement is rather one-sided. Matthau seeks to control Elvis' life, on and off the stage. After a series of brushes with Matthau's underworld organization, Elvis emerges triumphant, killing Matthau in retribution for his father's death at the hands of a young tough (played by the late Vic Morrow) acting on orders from Matthau. Elvis sings thirteen songs: "Crawfish," "You're the Cutest," "Let Me Be Your Lover Boy," "Danny Is My Name," the title tune, and eight others. In black and white.

LISZTOMANIA   ★

ROCK. 1975. Cast: Roger Daltrey, Ringo Starr, Sara Kestelman, Paul Nicholas, Rick Wakeman. 105 min. Beta, VHS. Warner ($59.95)

This ill-conceived film deserves one star for its sumptuous production values. Otherwise, this is just another in Ken Russell's seemingly endless parade of hysterical, semioperatic film curiosities. In *Lisztomania,* Russell wants us to believe the thesis that Franz Liszt, played by Who lead singer Roger Daltrey, was the first musician to be a pop idol, the equivalent of today's rock superstars. The garish, often tasteless, film careens through pointless caricature after caricature of nineteenth-century European society. Ringo Starr has a bit role as a rather decadent Pope who offers counsel to Liszt. The only humorous part of the movie is the scene in which Rick Wakeman, formerly the keyboardist of Yes, portrays Richard Wagner's Frankenstein-like creation, an Aryan superman who has a striking resemblance to the Marvel Comics superhero Thor. Daltrey sings some Wakeman-composed tunes, Ringo doesn't sing, and we wish Russell hadn't directed in the first place. Songs: "Chopsticks Fantasia," "Love's Dream," "Master Race," and "Rape, Pillage, and Burn."

LOVE ME TENDER   ★★

ROCK. 1956. Cast: Elvis Presley, Richard Egan, and Debra Paget. 89 min. Beta, VHS. CBS/Fox ($59.95)

Elvis' film debut was one of the most-celebrated and longest-awaited cinematic events since Al Jolson's *The Jazz Singer*. Whether *Love Me Tender* was any good in reality mattered little since the movie did great at the box office, catapulting Elvis to a stature no pop music artist had ever had or perhaps will ever have again—he was at once a movie star, rock star, and cultural hero. The film itself concerns two brothers who survive the Civil War in quite different fashions. Richard Egan, Elvis' older brother, is a Confederate renegade who tries to rob the U.S. mint just as the war is ending. Elvis, on the other hand, has returned from the war to the family spread and married his older brother's ex-fiancée, played by Debra Paget. This misunderstanding of tragic proportions occurs because Egan is thought to have been killed in the war. When Egan returns home, chased by the authorities no less, things end predictably. Elvis' death scene, in which he warbles the immortal title song, was meant to drive all his female fans to tears—and it did. Beyond its historic significance, it's not a very interesting film. Elvis sings "Poor Boy," "We're Gonna Move," "Let Me," and "Love Me Tender." In black and white.

LOVING YOU   ★★★

ROCK. 1956. Cast: Elvis Presley, Lizabeth Scott, Dolores Hart, and Wendell Corey. 101 min. Beta, VHS. Warner ($59.95)

Elvis' second film and some say it is his best. He plays a simple country boy named Deke Rivers who is discovered by Lizabeth Scott, an aggressive, enterprising manager, who envisions great success for the raw but talented rock singer. Unfortunately, as was the case in real life, Elvis' act is judged indecent by self-appointed regulators of public morality. The quick-thinking Scott vindicates Deke before the leading citizens of the small town in question and America at large by staging a nationally televised debate between the bluenoses and Deke's adoring teenage fans. Paralleling Elvis' real-life climb to overnight success, the movie culminates in a television appearance on an Ed Sullivan-type show where Deke, saving the day and winning the debate, sings "Loving You." Dolores Hart, who plays Elvis' love interest here and in *King Creole,* left show business in the early sixties and entered a nunnery in southern California, where she is to this day. Songs include: "Hot Dog," "We're Gonna Live It Up," "Party,"

"Dancing on a Dare," "Lonesome Cowboy," "Fireworks," "Gotta Lotta Livin' to Do," "Dandy Kisses," "Mean Woman Blues," "Detour," and the big hit, "Teddy Bear."

MAGICAL MYSTERY TOUR ★★

ROCK. 1967. Cast: John Lennon, Paul McCartney, George Harrison, Ringo Starr, and Victor Spinetti. 60 min. Beta, VHS. Media Home Entertainment ($49.95)

The Beatles wrote and directed this hour-long special originally for broadcast over BBC-TV. Done after their epochal album, *Sergeant Pepper,* and after the unfortunate death of their manager, Brian Epstein, *Magical Mystery Tour* is a confusing, extended essay in surreal images and psychedelic music. The best thing that we can say about this effort is that many of the musical sequences, like "I Am the Walrus" and "Your Mother Should Know," are prototypes of today's rock videos, with their cutting between shots of the musicians and provocative images underlining the lyrics. However, much

The Beatles in *Magical Mystery Tour.*

of the show consists of badly done attempts at absurdist British humor, which Monty Python does more convincingly. The Beatles sorely needed a script doctor for this one—and a competent cinematographer and director. Other songs included are: "Fool on the Hill," "Magical Mystery Tour," "Blue Jay Way," "Flying," "All My Loving," and "Hello Goodbye." A wonderful time is *not* guaranteed for all.

THE MAGIC CHRISTIAN   ★★★

ROCK. 1969. Cast: Ringo Starr, Peter Sellers, Yul Brynner, Christopher Lee, Roman Polanski, and Raquel Welch. 95 min. Beta, VHS. NTA ($49.95)

Ringo Starr's extensive career in movies began, of course, with his appearance in *A Hard Day's Night* and *Help!* He virtually stole the show in both features. The comic timing he displayed in those films helped him snare the role of Youngman Grand in *The Magic Christian.* But this film is really a vehicle for Peter Sellers, one of the great comedians of our time, who plays Sir Guy Grand, an eccentric British billionaire whose life is devoted to showing how venal and mercenary people are by devising elaborate hoaxes and perpetrating them on unsuspecting individuals and the public at large. Ringo, a young drifter who sleeps in Hyde Park, is "adopted" by Sir Guy and helps him in his mad schemes. While the film anticipated the outrageous zaniness of Monty Python (John Cleese and Graham Chapman appear briefly in one scene), *Magic Christian,* based on a novel by satirist Terry Southern, is really a late throwback to fifties absurdist humor, exemplified by the British radio series, *The Goon Show,* of which Sellers was a founding member. Badfinger, an Apple band, performs "Come and Get It" and Thunderclap Newman is heard doing their *only* hit, "Something in the Air."

THE MAN WHO FELL TO EARTH   ★★♪

ROCK. 1976. Cast: David Bowie, Candy Clark, Rip Torn, and Buck Henry. 118 min. Beta, VHS. RCA/Columbia ($79.95)

Nicholas Roeg, who had earlier cast Mick Jagger in his ground-breaking rock film, *Performance,* saw Bowie's potential as an actor and gave him his first film role, the alien Thomas Jerome Newton. As Newton, Bowie comes to earth from a drought-stricken planet to seek water for his desperate race. In the process, Bowie makes billions of dollars, is involved with Candy Clark, and ends up as a disillusioned, earth-bound alcoholic. Roeg's sci-fi thriller perfectly suited Bowie, who had, of course, become

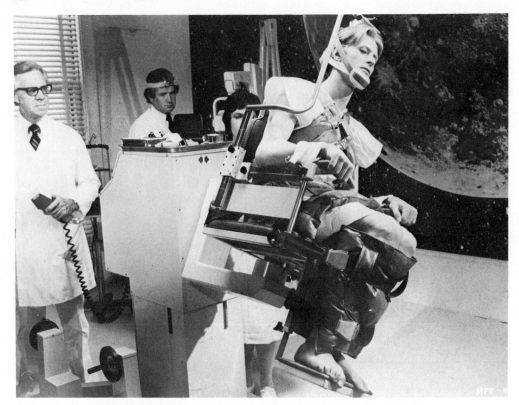

David Bowie, featured in *The Man Who Fell to Earth*.

famous for his Ziggy Stardust character. Drawing on that experience, he was able to convincingly portray the extraterrestrial Newton. In one scene, scientist Rip Torn asks Newton/Bowie if he is an alien. Bowie as Newton responds, with a straight face, "Yes, I'm British." Bowie doesn't sing in this sometimes confusing but unusual film.

MERRY CHRISTMAS MR. LAWRENCE ★★★

ROCK. 1983. Cast: David Bowie, Tom Conti, Ryuichi Sakamoto, Takeshi, and Jack Thompson. 124 min. Beta Hifi, VHS Stereo. MCA ($59.95)

Controversial Japanese film director Nagisa Oshima (*Boy, In the Realm of the Senses*) admired the screen work of English rock star and actor David Bowie and asked him to star in a specially created role in *Merry Christmas Mr. Lawrence.* Bowie, who had worked with a variety of world famous directors over time, jumped at the chance to widen his artistic horizons and play the heroic yet distant character of soldier Jack Celliers, who is captured by the Japanese in 1942 and put in a prisoner-of-war camp. The main story of the film revolves around the relationship of camp commander Captain Yonoi (Ryuichi Sakamoto) and Mister Lawrence (Tom Conti). Yonoi has a command of English. Lawrence has a command of Japanese. Over the course of the film, they try to understand and explain their cultures to each other. Conti's and Sakamoto's Japanese is translated into English with the use of subtitles. But the film cannot provide the Japanese subtexts needed by the American audience if it is going to fully understand and appreciate the myriad Japanese references. Ryuichi Sakamoto, who plays Captain Yonoi, was leader of the Japanese rock phenomenon known as Yellow Magic Orchestra before it broke up. He wrote the film's score. Bowie doesn't sing.

NIGHT SHIFT   ★★★

ROCK. 1982. Cast: Henry Winkler, Michael Keaton, Shelley Long, Richard Belzer, Gina Hecht, and Clint Howard. 106 min. Beta Hifi, VHS Stereo. Warner ($69.95)

Brought to you by many of the people responsible for the TV series *Happy Days, Night Shift* is a pleasant comedy that skirts the outer reaches of wholesome family fare. Though the story involves a scheme to run a prostitution service from a New York City morgue, somehow the salaciousness you might expect never materializes on screen. There is no nudity to speak of, no uncomfortable sex scenes, and very little offensive language. One wonders how Ron Howard, the director, managed it.

Henry Winkler, in one of his few successful movie roles, plays Chuck Lumley, the nebbish of a night supervisor at the morgue. Michael Keaton, in the role that launched his film career, is Bill Blaszjowski, his lovably avaricious assistant. Shelley Long (*Cheers*) is Belinda Keaton, a pleasant, attractive young woman working as a prostitute.

As Chuck and Belinda fall in love, Chuck hatches the plan to run a prostitution service from his office at the morgue. True to his good-hearted nature, Chuck institutes profit sharing, health insurance, and a pension plan. The story is often preposterous but it sails right along on the abundant charm of its three leads. The songs heard on the soundtrack, written by the husband and wife team of Burt Bacharach and Carole Bayer Sager, are "Night Shift" by Quarterflash, Al Jarreau's "Girls Know How," and "That's What Friends Are For" by Rod Stewart.

O LUCKY MAN!   ★★♪

ROCK. 1973. Cast: Malcolm McDowell, Ralph Richardson, Helen Mirren, Rachel Roberts, and Alan Price. 174 min. Beta, VHS. Warner ($59.95)

Malcolm McDowell plays Mick Travis in a quasi sequel to Lindsay Anderson's 1967 film about student rebellion in a British boys' boarding school, *If.* Mick, now a young man in his twenties, is Anderson's Everyman, making his way up the ladder of modern British society. Sort of an updated version of Voltaire's *Candide*, Mick isn't the innocent that Voltaire's protagonist was—he wants to make a lot of money any way he can. Much to his chagrin, it turns out to be a lot more difficult than he thought it would be. Among the uncanny characters he meets on the way to his cash nirvana are: Helen Mirren, playing the bohemian daughter of a billionaire industrialist; Alan Price, as himself; and Ralph Richardson, as a demonic, unethical, and ruthless billionaire whose plan to buy a Caribbean nation includes chemical warfare. Anderson's morality play savages modern society but doesn't offer much hope for a viable alternative. Indeed, after surviving the cumulative insanity of the world, Mick is "discovered" for a role in a movie—*O Lucky Man!* Ultimately, despite some moments of enlightened hilarity, the film is too long and pretty confusing. Alan Price, pianist for the original Animals, offers a running musical commentary on things, singing the title tune, "Poor People," along with "Sell Sell," "Pastoral," "Arrival," "Look over Your Shoulder," "Justice," "My Home Town," and "Changes."

OVER THE EDGE   ★★♪

ROCK. 1979. Cast: Matt Dillon, Michael Kramer, Pamela Ludwig, Ellen Geer, and Vincent Spano. 90 min. Beta, VHS. Warner ($59.95)

Matt Dillon's first screen role was that of a teenager, Richie White, who is stuck in a "planned community" called New Granada, and whose destructive personality is only further inflamed by the sterility and isolation of his surroundings. Jonathan Kaplan, who started out making films for Roger Corman at AIP in the early seventies, directed this early teen flick some years before the trend really caught fire. But this is not a comedy, it's a deadly serious drama. Dillon, Michael Kramer, Pamela Ludwig, and Vincent Spano play bored teenagers who begin committing small crimes and acts of vandalism in order to get attention. The adults in New Granada are incapable of dealing with their children's seemingly random, willful behavior. While intended as a social drama relevant to the plight of today's young generation, this is ultimately a by-now too familiar story of alienated teenagers turning to booze, drugs, violence, and promiscuity. Certainly nothing that hasn't been done before and done better. The music on the soundtrack includes "Speak Now," "Hello There," "Surrender," and "Downed" by Cheap Trick, "Just What I Needed" and "Best Friend's Girl" by The Cars, "All That You Dream" by Little Feat, "Come On" by Jimi Hendrix, "Ooh Child," by Valerie Carter, "Teenage Lobotomy" by The Ramones, and "You Really Got Me" by Van Halen.

PARADISE, HAWAIIAN STYLE   ★ﾉ

ROCK. 1966. Cast: Elvis Presley, Suzanna Leigh, James Shigeta, and Donna Butterworth. 91 min. Beta, VHS. CBS/Fox ($59.95)

For his twentieth foray onto the silver screen, Elvis revisited Hawaii, the setting for at least *four* Elvis films, and played the co-owner of a small island-hopping helicopter service. Struggling to make a go of it, Elvis and James Shigeta, his partner and old buddy, have their ups and downs, scrambling for customers and wrecking their choppers along the way. The end of the film is notable for its attempt, quite unusual for Elvis' low-budget efforts of the sixties, to stage a Hawaiian spectacle—a whole village of Hawaiians form a veritable army of slap-dancers and hula dancers. Songs include: "Drums of the Island," "House of Sand," "Hawaii, U.S.A.," and "Queenie Wahine's Papaya."

PAT GARRETT AND BILLY THE KID   ★ﾉ

ROCK. 1973. Cast: Kris Kristofferson, James Coburn, Bob Dylan, and Jason Robards. 106 min. Beta, VHS. MGM/UA ($59.95)

In this neglected work by the late Sam Peckinpah, James Coburn has the lead role as Pat Garrett, the bandit turned lawman who must apprehend his old friend Billy the Kid, played by Kris Kristofferson. This is really a mood piece rather than a shoot-'em-up western, nor is it the usual hard-bitten statement about aging men who are given few alternatives by a society which is passing them by (as in *The Wild Bunch*). Truth to tell, there's very little going on here of any cinematic interest. While Coburn is restrained and properly weary in his role as the reluctant hunter, Kristofferson is again a wooden actor, bringing nothing to the important part of Billy the Kid. Bob Dylan plays Alias, an odd, silent character who has no particular reason for being in

Bob Dylan as Alias in *Pat Garrett and Billy the Kid*.

the movie. The only song Dylan sings is on the soundtrack, "Knockin' on Heaven's Door." He scored the incidental guitar music heard throughout.

PERFORMANCE ★★

ROCK. 1970. Cast: Mick Jagger, James Fox, Anita Pallenberg, and Michelle Breton. 105 min. Beta, VHS. Warner ($59.95)

Mick Jagger stars in his film debut as Turner, a retired rock star who lives reclusively in a secluded mansion with two beautiful women. James Fox is a criminal on the lam from both the police and the underworld associates whom he has betrayed. He stumbles into Turner's lair and becomes entangled in his rather bizarre life. Director Nicholas Roeg, who later directed David Bowie in *The Man Who Fell to Earth,* used Mick's image as satanic shaman to convey his own ideas about morality, sexuality, and performance. The question that is left to the viewer to answer is: who is more criminal, Turner or the outlaw he harbors from the police? The highlight of the film is the sequence in which Jagger/Turner sings "Memo from Turner," perhaps one of the best, most lyrically powerful tunes ever written by the team of Mick Jagger and Keith Richard. Unfortunately, the rest of the movie is not as exciting, even with Anita Pallenberg and Mick Jagger's obvious sexual chemistry on screen (they were off-screen lovers at the time).

PURPLE RAIN ★★

ROCK. 1984. Cast: Prince, Apollonia Kotero, Morris Day, Olga Karlatos, and Clarence Williams III. 113 min. Beta Hifi, VHS Stereo. Warner ($29.95)

Purple Rain brought in close to $100 million at the box office. *Purple Rain*'s soundtrack album, with a number of hit songs on it, including Prince and the Revolution's "Let's

Prince in *Purple Rain.*

Go Crazy," "Purple Rain," and "When Doves Cry," and The Time's "Jungle Love" and "The Bird," sold over ten million copies. The videocassette *Purple Rain,* priced to sell at a low $29.95, was a guaranteed smash hit in video stores across the country even before it was released. What makes this film so popular? It must be the music. The dark, turgid melodrama borders on the camp. The male characters are misogynistic and completely unappealing. Prince plays The Kid, a musician who sees himself as misunderstood because not everyone loves his techno-rock and kinky stage antics that borrow heavily from the likes of Mick Jagger and James Brown. At home ("at the freak show"), his white mother (Olga Karlatos) and black father (Clarence Williams III) battle it out nightly. The only person who gives him any love or sympathy is Apollonia (Apollonia Kotero). But The Kid takes it upon himself to show his appreciation and affection by beating her. The only characters with any appeal at all are The Kid's rival Morris (Morris Day), the leader of The Time, and Jerome (Jerome Benton), his stooge. They laugh. They sing, run through new versions of ancient Abbot and Costello routines, dress in spiffy forties suits, have fun performing on stage, and reveal the twisted underside of their personalities by throwing an innocent woman into an industrial trash dumpster. If you have to, buy the album. But, if you're one of the few people who haven't seen this extended and boring rock video, spend your time and money elsewhere.

QUADROPHENIA ★ʲ

ROCK. 1979. Cast: Phil Daniels, Sting, Leslie Ash, Garry Cooper. 120 min. Beta, VHS. RCA/Columbia ($59.95)

In Franc Roddam's screen adaptation of The Who's concept album, *Quadrophenia,* Phil Daniels plays an emotionally disturbed teenager in mid-sixties London who becomes embroiled in the running feud between the Mods (of whom he is one) and the Teddys. A climactic riot at Brighton, a resort town, and his rejection by a Mod girl turn our hero's world upside down. When he is disillusioned by Mod leader Ace, played by Sting of The Police, Phil steals Ace's motor scooter and drives off the White Cliffs of Dover. Includes "5:15," "Love Reign over Me," "I Am the Sea," "I Am One," and other songs from the original double album. American audiences will find the crux of this drama, the battle between the Teddys and Mods, and all its social ramifications, almost incomprehensible. Recommended only for Who fans.

The Mods, scooter-riding pill-poppers in *Quadrophenia*.

REPO MAN   ★

ROCK. 1984. Cast: Emilio Estevez, Harry Dean Stanton, Olivia Barash, Vonetta McGee, Jimmy Buffet, The Circle Jerks, and The Untouchables. 93 min. Beta Hifi, VHS Stereo. MCA ($59.95)

Michael Nesmith's Pacific Arts studio attempted to make a cult film which would appeal to young people who dug punk music and sci-fi movies. *Repo Man,* which has

Emilio Estevez and Richard Foronjy in a scene from *Repo Man*.

the music of Iggy Pop and a host of L.A. punk bands as well as a preposterously convoluted plot about alien corpses locked away in a car trunk, failed. It's aggressively unlikeable, thanks in great part to Martin Sheen's son, Emilio Estevez, fast becoming Hollywood's idea of a punk kid, who plays a thoroughly repellent "repo" man. Harry Dean Stanton is the veteran who puts Estevez through the paces of the auto repossession business. Complicating matters further are two alien corpses hidden in a stolen car's trunk, spreading radiation wherever the car goes, Olivia Barash as the repo man's punky girlfriend, and the Rodriguez Brothers, Chicano auto thiefs with a political bent. This is intentionally bad but the cult qualities are nonexistent—it's not stylishly bad enough to elicit more than a yawn. The music is uniformly terrible and indicates why these bands have never gotten out of the L.A. club scene. The Circle Jerks sing "Coup d'Etat" and "When the Shit Hits the Fan"; the Plugz sing "El Caro y la Cruz," "Secret Agent Man," and "Flor de Mal"; the Juicy Bananas play "Lite's Theme," "I Just Want to Satisfy," and "Bad Man"; and Iggy Pop sings "Repo Man."

RISKY BUSINESS   ★★★✦

ROCK. 1983. Cast: Tom Cruise, Rebecca De Mornay, and Richard Masur. 99 min. Beta, VHS. Warner ($39.95)

One of the few contemporary movies about teenagers that has something more to offer than nubile flesh and scatalogical humor, *Risky Business* marked the auspicious directorial debut of Paul Brickman. Well shot, well edited, and very well acted, the movie is a funny *and* thought-provoking examination of the system of values we so blithely hand down to our children. Tom Cruise, as Joel Goodson, a high school senior living in the suburbs of Chicago, is preoccupied with getting into an Ivy League college. His chances aren't good; Joel's nothing more than an average student. When his parents leave for a brief European vacation, Joel is left to care for the house and his father's Porsche. Through a series of comic misunderstandings, he meets Lana (Rebecca De Mornay), a prostitute who is the same age he is—but much more mature and, as he finds out, a great businesswoman. Against his own better judgement, Joel agrees to help Lana use his empty house as a weekend brothel for his high school classmates. Although he makes a lot of cold, hard cash, when Lana's infuriated ex-pimp enters the picture, Joel wishes he had reconsidered his rash move. Basically, Lana, her hooker girlfriends, and her pimp give Joel a lesson in free enterprise he won't likely learn in any Ivy League business class. The score includes some menacing electronic music from Tangerine Dream that seems out of place in this film. Also, we hear The Police ("Every Breath You Take"), Bob Seger ("Old Time Rock and Roll"), Jeff Beck ("Pump (The Pump)"), Bruce Springsteen ("Hungry Heart"), Muddy Waters ("Mannish Boy"), Talking Heads ("Swamp"), Journey ("After the Fall"), Prince ("D.M.S.R."), and Phil Collins ("In the Air Tonight").

ROCK 'N' ROLL HIGH SCHOOL   ★★★

ROCK. 1979. Cast: P. J. Soles, Vincent Van Patten, Clint Howard, Mary Woronov, Paul Bartel, Dey Young, and The Ramones. 94 min. Beta Hifi, VHS Stereo. Warner ($39.95)

This received a lot more critical praise at the time of its initial release than it perhaps truly deserves. Written by Alan Arkush and Joe Dante and directed by Arkush, this rhapsodic epic about rock and roll, high school kids, and the American Way is fitfully successful. As a lampoon of teen flicks, it's a winner, with its archetypal heroine, Riff Randell, played by the very talented P. J. Soles, matching wits with the evil principal (Mary Woronov), but its choice of The Ramones as the focal point of the story casts doubt on its heralded status as a rock and roll film. The Ramones, briefly in the spotlight as a punk rock band, were amateurish noisemakers at best. In the end, Riff Randell's efforts to attend a Ramones concert against the orders of her repressive principal seem unjustified—if The Ramones represent rock and roll, then bring back the big-band sound! But the film should be seen for its satire of suburban teenage existence and the performances of Soles, Woronov, and Bartel. Just cover your ears when The Ramones are on screen.

There's a lot of music in the film: The Ramones perform "Sheena Is a Punk Rocker," "I Wanna Be Sedated," "Teenage Lobotomy," "I Just Wanna Have Something to Do," "I Want You Around," "Blitzkrieg Bop," "California Sun," "DUMB," "I Wanna Be Your Boyfriend," "Do You Wanna Dance?," "Rock 'n' Roll High School," "Questioningly," and "She's the One." We also hear Paul McCartney's "Did We Meet Somewhere Before?," Brownsville Station's "Smoking in the Boys' Room," Lou Reed's "Rock and Roll," Chuck Berry's "School Days," Nick Lowe's "So It Goes," Alice Cooper's "School's Out," Bent Fabric's "Alley Cat," Devo's "Come Back Jonee," Fleetwood Mac's "Albatross" and "Jigsaw Puzzle Blues," MC5's "High School," Paley Brothers' "C'mon Let's Go" and "You're the Best," Eddie and the Hot Rods' "Teenage Depression," Todd Rundgren's "A Dream Goes On Forever," and Brian Eno's "Spirits Drifting," "Alternative 3," and "Energy Fools the Magician."

ROCK, ROCK, ROCK ★★◗

ROCK. 1957. Cast: Alan Freed, Tuesday Weld, Teddy Randazzo, The Moonglows, Chuck Berry, The Flamingos, Jimmy Cavallo and the House Rockers, Johnny Burnette Trio, LaVern Baker, and Frankie Lymon and the Teenagers. 78 min. Beta, VHS. Nostalgia Merchant ($29.95)

This early rock and roll film, in black and white, presents disc jockey Alan Freed and teen starlet Tuesday Weld in a rather curious mix of sitcom-like story and musical performances. The story concerns Tuesday's efforts to get on Alan Freed's television show and win his talent contest. A series of typically teenage mishaps occur and Tuesday's road to TV stardom is blocked. In the meantime, Alan Freed decides to bring his show to Tuesday's high school prom! Quite silly but some of the musical performances are worth seeing. Chuck Berry waxes poetic about his "airmobile" in the classic, "You Can't Catch Me." The Johnny Burnette Trio, one of rockabilly's pioneer groups, sings "Lonesome Train." Frankie Lymon performs "Juvenile Delinquent" and "Baby Baby." Also seen are The Moonglows ("Over and Over Again" and "I Knew from the Start"), The Flamingos ("Would I Be Crying?"), and LaVern

Baker ("Tra La La"). No, Tuesday Weld does not do her own singing. She's dubbed by Connie Francis!

ROUSTABOUT ★★↩

ROCK. 1964. Cast: Elvis Presley, Barbara Stanwyck, Leif Erickson, Joan Freeman, and Jack Albertson. 101 min. Beta, VHS. CBS/Fox ($59.95)

Elvis plays a motorcycle-riding drifter, Charlie Rogers, who hooks up with Barbara Stanwyck's traveling carnival and falls in love with Leif Erickson's daughter (Joan Freeman). With the usual Hal Wallis-produced shenanigans—a song, a fight, a kiss, and another song—*Roustabout* is somewhere squarely in the middle range of Elvis' cinematic output. Stanwyck's presence helps but Elvis was, by now, no longer believable in his umpteenth bad-boy-finds-good-girl-and-flies-straight saga. This was directed by John Rich, better known to television fans as the man who later on directed the majority of the early *All in the Family* episodes. Songs performed are: "Poison Ivy League," "Wheels on My Heels," "It's a Wonderful World," "It's Carnival Time," "Hurry, Hurry, Step This Way," "One Track Heart," "Hard Knocks," "Little Egypt," "Big Love, Big Heartache," "King of the Whole Wide World," and the title tune.

THE RUTLES ★★★

ROCK. 1978. Cast: Eric Idle, Neil Innes, Ricki Fataar, Barry Wom, Mick Jagger, John Belushi, George Harrison, Michael Palin, Gilda Radner, Bill Murray, Dan Aykroyd, Bianca Jagger, Ron Wood, Paul Simon. 90 min. Beta, VHS. Pacific Arts ($59.95)

In this biting satire on the history of The Rutles (a.k.a. The Beatles), Eric Idle, one of the Monty Python troupe, plays the Paul McCartney figure, Dirk McQuigley, and Neil Innes, former leader of the Bonzo Dog Band, plays Ron Nasty, the John Lennon figure. Structurally very similar to *The Compleat Beatles,* the film is anything but reverential. *The Rutles* begins with a look at Rutland, the spawning ground of The Rutles and Rutlemania, in a documentary within a documentary entitled "All You Need Is Cash." This jibe at pop music in general sets the tone for the rest of this hilarious send-up of the Beatles' myth. Other songs heard in the film are: "Get Up and Go," "Piggy in the Middle," "Let It Rot," "Ouch," "I Must Be in Love," "Hold My Hand," "Love Life," "With a Girl Like You," "Never The Less," "Let's Be Natural," "Good Times Roll," "Doubleback Alley," "Cheese and Onions," "Another Day," "Number One," and "Living in Hope."

SERGEANT PEPPER'S LONELY HEARTS CLUB BAND   ★

ROCK. 1978. Cast: The Bee Gees, Peter Frampton, George Burns, Steve Martin, Alice Cooper, Billy Preston, Aerosmith, Earth, Wind, and Fire, Donald Pleasence, and Sandy Farina. 111 min. Beta, VHS. MCA ($39.95)

Robert Stigwood, the man who brought you *Saturday Night Fever,* tried to recapture the success of that opus by dramatizing the Lennon-McCartney songs from the *Sgt. Pepper* and *Abbey Road* albums. Unfortunately, he failed. The idea was to cast The Bee Gees as the Henderson brothers and Peter Frampton as Billy Shears' grandson in a resurrection of the original World War I vintage Sergeant Pepper's Lonely Hearts Club Band. The whole bunch is supposed to hail from Heartland, U.S.A., a place too good to be true. The venerable George Burns plays the town elder, Mr. Kite. Things get

Robin, Barry, and Maurice Gibb—The Bee Gees—in *Sergeant Pepper's Lonely Hearts Club Band.*

complicated when outside forces, in the guise of Mean Mr. Mustard, steal the magic instruments that were willed to the Hendersons and Billy Shears. Without these instruments (and thus the ability to make music), Heartland is unable to defend itself against its evil invaders. While the band is detained in the City of Angels on the pretext that it has been signed to a huge recording contract with Big Disco Records, Billy's girlfriend, Strawberry Fields, played by Sandy Farina, has to devise a plan of attack to help reclaim Heartland and her beloved. Other menaces along the way are Alice Cooper as Father Sun, an evil cult leader, and Steve Martin as Dr. Maxwell Edison, a quack doctor who attempts to turn adults into young children again. Things end up happily in Heartland as the band returns to town, playing at a "benefit for Mr. Kite," where the musical performances of Earth, Wind, and Fire ("Got to Get You out of My Life") and their own tunes rout the evil forces. Billy Preston, as a Gabriel-like figure intended to be a transformation of the original Sgt. Pepper, sings a spirited version of "Get Back." The film gets its one star for this performance. Other songs: "With a Little Help from My Friends," "It's Getting Better," "Fixing a Hole," "Good Morning," "Sgt. Pepper," "Here Comes the Sun," "Nowhere Man," "Polythene Pam," "She Came In through the Bathroom Window," "She's Leaving Home," and many more.

SIXTEEN CANDLES   ★★

ROCK. 1983. Cast: Molly Ringwold, Paul Dooley, Carlin Glynn, Justin Henry, Blanche Baker, Anthony Michael Hall, and Michael Schaeffling. 93 min. Beta Hifi, VHS Stereo. MCA ($79.95)

John Hughes is in a rather lucrative rut. The former *National Lampoon* staff writer is one of the hottest writer-directors in Hollywood, churning out youth pictures aimed at the high school moviegoer (*National Lampoon's Vacation, Breakfast Club,* and this picture). The only distinction they have is that each is told through the sensibility of a typical suburban teenager. However, Hughes' movies do not have the depth of, say, *Risky Business,* which treats the same material with greater style and wisdom. *Sixteen Candles* is Molly Ringwold's movie. As Samantha, a 16-year-old whose older sister is about to be wed, leaving her neglected by the family, Ringwold gives her customary woman-child performance. She's too self-conscious to be believable. Whatever the message (if there is one), the movie is played for laughs of a strictly juvenile kind. In the end, Sam gets that date she wants with the school stud, who also happens to be a millionaire's son. Anthony Michael Hall plays the wimp whom geeks in the audience will identify with. Hughes continues to give signs that he's a 35-year-old geek. The music: "Snowballed" by AC/DC, "Rumours in the Air" by Night Ranger, "True" by

Spandau Ballet, "Wild Sex in the Working Class" by Oingo Boingo, "Little Bitch" by Specials, "Hang Up the Phone" by Annie Golden, "Gloria" by Patti Smith, "Rebel Yell" from Billy Idol, "If You Were Here" by Thompson Twins, and Stray Cats' "Sixteen Candles."

SMITHEREENS ★♪

ROCK. 1982. Cast: Susan Berman, Brad Rinn, and Richard Hell. 90 min. Beta, VHS. Media ($59.95)

The only remarkable thing about *Smithereens* is that its 21-year-old director, Susan Seidelman, shot the picture in color for $100,000. Her director of photography, Chirine El Khadem, raised the hopes of countless independent filmmakers by demonstrating

Susan Berman in a scene from *Smithereens*.

that small film budgets could yield movies with a big-budget look. It's too bad the makers of *Smithereens* didn't pay as much attention to its low-budget story. Wren (Susan Berman), a 19-year-old girl from a working class home in New Jersey, ventures to New York City's Greenwich Village and Lower East Side hoping to make it big in the rock world. It's never clear exactly what she wants to become, but she attacks her ill-defined goal with a great deal of ambition. Shortly after the opening credits, she latches onto Paul (Brad Rinn), an aimless drifter from Montana, and uses his broken-down van as an occasional crash pad. Wren also befriends Eric (Richard Hell), a shiftless, ne'er-do-well would-be punk-rock star and thief, who she believes can set her up as a rock promoter. For the remainder of the film, Wren ping pongs back and forth between Paul and Eric looking for something that she keeps secret from the audience. The character of Wren is never developed. The viewer loses all sympathy for her about halfway through the movie. Maybe Ms. Seidelman should invest *Smithereen's* profits in a screenwriting course. The soundtrack contains a number of New York New Wave and punk club standards: "The Kid with the Replaceable Head," and "Another World" by Richard Hell and the Voidoids, "Guitar Beat" by the Raybeats, "I Never Felt" by The NiteCaps, and "Loveless Love" and "Original Love" by The Feelies.

SPEEDWAY ★♪

ROCK. 1968. Cast: Elvis Presley, Nancy Sinatra, Bill Bixby, Gale Gordon, and Carl Ballantine. 94 min. Beta, VHS. MGM/UA ($39.95)

Norman Taurog strikes again in this strangely appealing but cliché-ridden Elvis opus. For the third or fourth time, Elvis plays a race-car driver. Once again, he's in a lot of hot water because of a crooked buddy, this time his manager, played by television veteran Bill Bixby (*My Favorite Martian, Courtship of Eddie's Father,* and *The Incredible Hulk*). Nancy Sinatra is the Internal Revenue agent sent to collect back taxes from Elvis, whose returns have been mangled by the greedy Bixby. She discovers that Elvis is a humanitarian of sorts who frequently gives away money to people who are in need— a hobbled, down on his luck racer with five little daughters, an impoverished newlywed couple, and others. When Elvis wins the Charlotte 600 stock-car race, his check is divided up, even though Nancy does help him to keep a portion of it—to buy back the gifts that were repossessed by the I.R.S. The film features a rather outlandish disco called The Hangout, where patrons eat in cars and hubcaps are the major feature of the decor. Songs: "Speedway," "Let Yourself," "Your Groovy Self," "Your Time Hasn't Come Yet," "He's Your Uncle Not Your Dad," "Just One Kiss," and "There Ain't Nothing Like a Song."

Elvis in *Speedway.*

STREETS OF FIRE ★

ROCK. 1984. Cast: Michael Paré, Diane Lane, Amy Madigan, Rick Moranis, Deborah Van Valkenberg, Willem Dafoe, Marine Jahan, and The Blasters. 93 min. Beta Hifi, VHS Stereo. MCA ($69.95)

Having ridden the coattails of Eddie Murphy's comic performance in *48 Hours* all the way to the top of the Hollywood heap, director Walter Hill and English graduate student turned screenwriter Larry Gross wanted to make a rock and roll film. In the words of Hill, *Streets of Fire* is a rock and roll fantasy wherein "soldier boy comes home to rescue the queen of the hop from the clutches of the leader of the pack." You can see that Hill's familiarity with rock and roll is outrageously dated—how he expected today's 15-year-olds to groove on a premise based on 25-year-old doo-wop songs is, of course, known only to him and Mr. Gross. On top of that, the film is intentionally structured as a myth set in some indeterminate time period which is neither the past nor the future. That, and the third-rate rock music written by Jim

Steinman (Meatloaf), Tom Petty, Dan Hartman, and Stevie Nicks, and sung by electroni- cally blended voices, make this a hard swallow for Hill's intended audience. Michael Paré is typically stoic as Tom Cody (soldier boy), Diane Lane is unbelievable as Ellen Aim (queen of the hop), and Willem Dafoe is the evil Raven (leader of the pack). Amy Madigan, Rick Moranis, and Deborah Van Valkenberg also appear. The songs are: "Tonight Is What It Means to Be Young," "Nowhere Fast," "Never Be You," "Sorcerer," "Countdown to Love," and "I Can Dream about You," sung by Dan Hart- man; Ry Cooder's "Get Out of Denver," "Hold That Snake," "You Got What You Wanted," "Rumble," and "First Love, First Tears"; and the Fixx's "Deeper and Deeper." The Blasters appear on screen doing "One Bad Stud" and "Blue Shadows."

SURFING BEACH PARTY ★★

ROCK. 1984. Artists: Jan Berry and Dean Torrence. 56 min. Beta, VHS. Media ($29.95)

Dean Torrence, of the early sixties California surf duo, Jan and Dean, hosts this video homage to the music that made west coast beach culture an American myth. Jan and Dean were the stylistic originators of the kind of music that Brian Wilson and The Beach Boys would later make internationally famous. Fusing rockabilly guitars with glee club harmonies and imbuing the combination with a sense of madcap beach bohe- mianism, they gave voice to an emerging mindset—California high times. More than twenty years after the British Invasion and Jan Berry's serious auto accident curtailed their careers, *Surfing Beach Party* is a fond look back at their music. With the aid of a cast of young unknowns clad in bathing suits, seventeen songs are translated into the video medium: "Little Deuce Coupe," "Deadman's Curve," "Drag City," "Little Old Lady from Pasadena," "Fun Fun Fun," "Jenny Lee," "New Girl in School," "Barbara Ann," "Surf City," "Surf with Me," "Surfing Safari," "Ride the Wild Surf," "Baby Talk," "Sidewalk Surfing," "Surfer Girl," "Pipeline," and "Wipe Out." Shot in and around South Padre Beach under the aegis of director Ted Mather.

SYMPATHY FOR THE DEVIL ★↴

ROCK. 1970. Cast: The Rolling Stones (Mick Jagger, Keith Richards, Charlie Watts, Bill Wyman, and Brian Jones), Anne Wiazemsky, and others. 110 min. Beta, VHS. CBS/Fox ($59.95)

Jean-Luc Godard, one of the star directors of the French New Wave, had this great idea. He wanted to star his then wife Anne Wiazemsky in a film about underclass life in London slums. But somehow plans were changed and he came up with a movie called *One Plus One* which intercuts scenes of The Stones in the recording studio against scenes of guerilla street theater and polemical statements. His coproducer added more Stones footage to the final release print without Godard's approval and called it *Sympathy for the Devil.* This is the version available to the video consumer. What the film lacks in narrative unity (and it is, after all, meandering French leftist political claptrap) is made up for by its scenes of The Stones writing and recording their classic, "Sympathy for the Devil," in their London studio.

TAKE IT TO THE LIMIT   ★★

ROCK. 1980. Artists: Foreigner, Jean-Luc Ponty, John McEuen, Tangerine Dream, and Arlo Guthrie. 95 min. Beta Hifi, VHS Stereo. U.S.A. ($39.95)

This high-tech documentary on motorcycle racing, directed by Peter Starr, uses the music of Foreigner and Tangerine Dream, among others, to provide a moody accompaniment to its shots of riders spewing dirt and gravel from their wheels and hurtling through the air. Top racers like Roger De Coster, Barry Sheene, Scott Audrey, and Debbie Evans-Leavitt are interviewed and talk about the hectic schedule and endless risks of being a world-class motorcyclist. In action, these racers are unbelievable for their skill and daring. Some of the in-the-seat camerawork is breathtaking. But, ultimately, you have to be a fan of the sport in order to fully enjoy this look at high-speed thrills. Foreigner plays "Starrider," "Feels Like the First Time," "Double Vision," and "Tramontaine." Jean-Luc Ponty, the French electric violinist, plays "Mirage," "Cosmic Messenger," and "New Country." Tangerine Dream contributes "Stratosphere," John McEuen plays "Miner's Night Out," and Arlo Guthrie sings "The Motorcycle Song" while tooling down the road on his bike.

THAT'LL BE THE DAY   ★★

ROCK. 1973. Cast: David Essex, Billy Fury, Keith Moon, Ringo Starr. 91 min. Beta, VHS. Thorn-EMI ($59.95)

David Essex, whose one American hit was "Rock On," plays a young working class Britisher who leaves his drudge job and his wife to pursue his dream of becoming a rock star. This kitchen-sink drama of early sixties Britain has a smashing soundtrack which includes stuff like Buddy Holly's "That'll Be the Day" and Brian Hyland's

"Sealed with a Kiss." Other early sixties pop hits weave in and out of the narrative. The late Keith Moon, The Who's great drummer, is a costar and credited as a music supervisor. Ringo Starr appears as a coworker in a summer carnival whom Essex befriends and then leaves to be beaten up by a bunch of toughs, demonstrating clearly the protagonist's serious lack of humanity and emotional depth. While the acting from all involved is quite good, the film as a whole is a real downer, much too depressing for the upbeat, very bright soundtrack of golden oldies.

THIS IS SPINAL TAP! ★★★┙

ROCK. 1984. Cast: Michael McKean, Christopher Guest, Harry Shearer, Tony Hendra, June Chadwick, and Ed Begley, Jr. 82 min. Beta Hifi, VHS Stereo. Embassy ($69.95)

A hilarious send-up of the heavy metal phenomenon, *Spinal Tap* was basically a long ad-lib on the part of its director, Rob Reiner, and its stars (many of whom are now regulars on *Saturday Night Live*). Purportedly a "rockumentary" by Martin DiBergi of the rise and fall of the legendary British rock band, Spinal Tap, this film lampoons the often ludicrous world of rock music, hype, and superstardom. Spinal Tap, a group that dates back to the early sixties, has fallen on hard times, with the sales of their newest album, *Smell the Glove,* hitting all-time lows. Despite this, the group is on its first tour of the States in over six years. As canceled concert dates follow one another along the tour, the band decides to ditch their manager, Tony Hendra, and install June Chadwick, who plays Michael McKean's girlfriend, as their new Svengali. This, of course, leads to more dire straits and belly laughs as the group dissolves because of internal bickering and a severe shortage of funds. But what makes this picture so much fun, even beyond the slapstick that fills the screen in scene after scene, is the right-on parodies of heavy metal songs like: "Sex Farm," "Hellhole," "Big Bottom," "Lick My Love Pump," and "Heavy Duty Rock and Roll," this last complete with a Boccherini-inspired guitar solo. The video version also includes the rock video that was made for "Hellhole," another hilarious parody of the genre.

TIMES SQUARE ★┙

ROCK. 1980. Cast: Trini Alvarado, Robin Johnson, and Tim Curry. 111 min. Beta Hifi, VHS Stereo. Thorn-EMI ($59.95)

Robert Stigwood gave up filmmaking after this little opus about decadence, degradation, and mental illness in New York's underground culture. The man who had made millions on *Saturday Night Fever* and *Grease* probably should have read the script more closely this time around. *Times Square* is a big-budget version of Andy Warhol's mid-sixties underground films, films which dealt with every unsavory aspect of human endeavor that Warhol could possibly record. Warhol had the luxury of saying his stuff was art; Stigwood and director Alan Moyle have no such excuse. Trini, a middle class girl, runs away from the hospital where she is being treated for what her parents suspect is an emotional problem. Trini may or may not be crazy, but Robin, the girl she meets in the hospital and escapes with, is a certifiable loony. Together they eke out a living, trying all sorts of hustles and finally settling on becoming a punk-rock duo, the Sleaze Sisters. Tim Curry plays a rock d.j. who rescues Trini for the publicity value of his heroism. Why?! Come to think of it, Warhol's day-long films were more interesting than this piece of cinematic drivel. There's wall to wall music, intended to exploit the then-perceived boom in New Wave punk rock, including "Dangerous Type" by the Cars, "Pretty Boys" by Joe Jackson, "Innocent, Not Guilty" by Garland Jeffreys, "Down in the Park" by Gary Numan, "Talk of the Town" by The Pretenders, "I Wanna Be Sedated" by The Ramones, "Walk on the Wild Side" by Lou Reed, "Same Old Scene" by Roxy Music, "Pissing in the River" by Patti Smith, "Life during Wartime" by Talking Heads, and "Take This Town" by XTC. It boggles the mind that this movie was made.

TOMMY ★★♪

ROCK. 1975. Cast: Roger Daltrey, Ann-Margret, Oliver Reed, Tina Turner, Elton John, Eric Clapton, Keith Moon, Jack Nicholson. 111 min. Beta, VHS. RCA/Columbia ($49.95)

The Who's fabled rock opera was adapted for the screen by the weird but always entertaining Ken Russell, who put his own stamp on this musical story about a "deaf, dumb, and blind kid who plays a mean pinball" and his "rebirth" after a series of attempts to miraculously cure him. Roger Daltrey stars as Tommy in this tour de force that includes Ann-Margret as Tommy's mother, Oliver Reed as Tommy's stepfather, Tina Turner as the Acid Queen, Keith Moon as Uncle Ernie, Eric Clapton as the Preacher, Jack Nicholson as the Doctor, and Elton John as the Pinball Wizard. The musical numbers notwithstanding, and there are several highlights, including Eric Clapton doing the Sonny Boy Williamson blues classic, "Eyesight to the Blind," and Tina Turner giving a scorching rendition of "Acid Queen," Russell's symbolism and generally fatalistic view of humanity tend to make the second half of *Tommy* quite depressing. If you like The Who's music, then you'll want to see this. Some Who fans might claim that *Tommy* is the crowning achievement of Pete Townshend's two decades of songwriting.

TOP SECRET!   ★★↙

ROCK. 1984. Cast: Val Kilmer, Lucy Gutteridge, Peter Cushing, Michael Gough, and Omar Sharif. 90 min. Beta Hifi, VHS Stereo. Paramount ($79.95)

The zany team of Jim Abrahams and David and Jerry Zucker, who hit the jackpot with *Airplane!,* the surprise comedy hit of 1980, have struck again with *Top Secret!* It's a maniacal parody that manages, just for a start, to spoof the Elvis movies of the sixties, James Bond films, and World War II underground films. Val Kilmer is a rock singer on tour in East Germany who gets involved with resistance fighters(?!). Lucy Gutteridge is the daughter of a scientist, Peter Cushing, unjustly imprisoned by East German authorities. When Omar Sharif, as a superspy cast in the Bond mold, fails in his mission to free Cushing, it is up to Kilmer and a band of French freedom fighters to rescue him. There are no sacred cows left unmilked by the writer-directors in this scattershot parade of puns, bad jokes, sight gags, and recycled vaudeville routines, although there is a porcelain sentry who shatters after being thrown off a watchtower and a polka-dotted cow suit used as a decoy. The parody numbers include "Skeet Surfin'," "How Silly Can You Get," "Please Spend This Night with Me," and "Straighten the Rug." Kilmer also does tongue in cheek versions of "Tutti Frutti" and "Are You Lonesome Tonight?"

TO SIR WITH LOVE   ★★★↙

ROCK. 1965. Cast: Sidney Poitier, Christian Roberts, Judy Geeson, Suzy Kendall, Lulu, and The Mindbenders. 105 min. Beta, VHS. RCA/Columbia ($64.95)

This is an excellent film, now neglected, that tries for drama *and* social realism and, for the most part, succeeds. Directed by James Clavell (*Shogun*), it stars Sidney Poitier in one of those dignified-but-quietly-defiant-black-man roles he specialized in—or is it was *allowed* to play. Poitier plays an engineer from British Guyana who finds himself in London without a position and decides to get a job teaching poor whites in the North Quay section of the city. His high school students are a sullen, reflexively racist bunch, accustomed to being taught by condescending, indifferent taskmasters. Through a torturous period of adjustment, Poitier and his students grow to respect each other. He ultimately decides to stay on, overcome by the emotional urgings of his students. Clavell manages to explore many issues (race relations, public education, the British class system, teen identity crises) effectively while still delivering an interesting dramatic story. The Mindbenders play at the graduation party, singing "Off and Running" and "It's Getting Harder All the Time."

UNION CITY ★⤙

ROCK. 1979. Cast: Deborah Harry, Dennis Lipscomb, and Pat Benatar. 87 min. Beta, VHS. RCA/Columbia ($59.95)

Deborah Harry makes her film debut in this low-budget independent art film that, surprisingly, reminds one of a surrealistic version of *The Honeymooners,* the classic fifties sitcom, without the good-natured humor. The muddled plot, based on a Cornell Woolrich short story, concerns the consequences of a murder which involves a missing corpse. Harry's New Jersey schlub of a husband, played by Dennis Lipscomb, gets irate over the theft of bottles of milk from their doorstep, kills the would-be robber, and hides his body in an adjacent, vacant apartment. When Pat Benatar and her newlywed husband move into the empty apartment, Harry's hubby is shocked to discover the corpse missing. All in all, too confusing to be worthy of viewing, unless you must see Deborah Harry and Pat Benatar on the screen together. It also features an electronic music score by Chris Stein, leader of Blondie. Unfortunately, neither Harry nor Benatar gets to sing.

UP THE CREEK ★⤙

ROCK. 1984. Cast: Tim Matheson, Dan Monahan, Steven Furst, Jennifer Runyon, James B. Sikking, and John Hillerman. 95 min. Beta, VHS. Vestron ($79.95)

Tim Matheson, everyone's favorite 35-year-old college student, stars in this formula youth exploitation film about river rafting. John Hillerman, James B. Sikking, and Steven Furst are the other familiar faces who appear in the movie. Newcomer Jennifer Runyon is the comely blonde coed. While the scenario of an intercollegiate river rafting competition is new, the rest of the sophomoric antics involving sex, drugs, and more sex are very stale. The funniest thing in the film is Chuck the wonder dog, who delivers dialogue better than anyone else in the cast. Cheap Trick is heard doing "Up the Creek," Heart performs "The Heat," the Beach Boys sing "Chasin' the Sky," Randy Bishop does "Two Hearts on the Loose Tonight," Ian Hunter sings "Great Expectations," and Danny Spanos contributes "Passion in the Dark," among other tunes.

VIDEODROME ★⤙

ROCK. 1982. Cast: James Woods, Deborah Harry, and Sonja Smit. 87 min. Beta, VHS. MCA ($59.95)

David Cronenberg, the Canadian auteur who hit it big with gory horror films like *Scanners* and *Dead Zone,* tries for a message here. With Deborah Harry as a kinky radio

James Woods and Blondie's Deborah Harry in a scene from *Videodrome*.

talk show host and James Woods as the owner of a local cable-TV network in Toronto, *Videodrome* wanted but failed to deliver a meaningful statement on the effect of television on mass society. The problems begin when Woods stumbles onto a pirate satellite transmission that he imagines is being sent from Malaysia. The "videodrome" programs he receives are actually brainwashing signals that attack the central nervous systems of viewers. Trying to track down their real point of origin, Woods becomes embroiled in an international plot to subliminally manipulate the masses of television viewers. Video fans should be wary of scenes in which the Woods character is forced to perform some repellently gory acts of violence that might attack the central nervous systems of even the most hardy devotees of science fiction and "slasher" films. Harry does not sing. The score is by Howard Shore, one-time musical supervisor of *Saturday Night Live*.

VIVA LAS VEGAS! ★★★

ROCK. 1963. Cast: Elvis Presley and Ann-Margret. 85 min. Beta, VHS. MGM/UA ($59.95)

Elvis' fifteenth film turned out to be his liveliest film of the decade and must be considered his best musical of all time. Teamed with a young Ann-Margret, Elvis is

Elvis with Ann-Margret in *Viva Las Vegas!*

at his exciting best playing a race-car driver who gets waylaid in Sin City, Las Vegas. There he meets and falls in love with the curvaceous Ann-Margret, a dancer and student at U.N.L.V. She and Elvis burn up the screen and define the meaning of rock and roll in their duet of Ray Charles' classic, "What'd I Say." The chemistry between the two carries the otherwise lethargic script. The veteran George Sidney directs in a style that enhances the sheer physical impact of the two leads. When all is said and done, *this* is the one sixties Elvis flick to be placed in a time capsule so that future generations can begin to understand what rock and roll was all about. Other songs include "C'mon Everybody," "If You Think I Need You," and the title tune.

THE WANDERERS ★★★

ROCK. 1980. Cast: Ken Wahl, Karen Allen, Linda Manz, Tony Ganios, and Erland Van Lidth de Jende. 117 min. Beta, VHS. Warner ($59.95)

Veteran maverick director Philip Kaufman (the remake of *Invasion of the Body Snatchers*) followed his pal, George Lucas, and made a film about growing up in the early sixties, this time in the Bronx, in New York City. While not as successful certainly as Lucas' *American Graffiti, The Wanderers* has its moments and is generally a grittier movie. Whereas Lucas' prototypical California valley kids were bellyaching about the emptiness and small town insularity of their lives, Kaufman's manchild gang members were sorting out their feelings about sexual, racial, and familial relations. Ken Wahl stars in an effective portrayal of an Italian kid who can't quite make it out of the neighborhood and the life his parents have planned for him. Not in their plans is Karen Allen as a freethinking college girl whom we last see going to Greenwich Village to hear Bob Dylan. The other supporting actors are all quite good. The number of different gangs and their names—the Del Bombers, the Ducky Boys, the Baldies, the Wanderers, etc.—get confusing after a while. But this is quite a coming of age film, thoughtful, funny, and perceptive. The music includes Dion's "The Wanderer" and "Runaround Sue," the Four Seasons' "Sherry," "Walk Like a Man," and "Big Girls Don't Cry," Lee Dorsey's "Ya Ya," Bob Dylan's "The Times They Are A-Changing," The Shirelles' "Soldier Boy" and "Baby It's You," the Isley Brothers' "Shout," Smokey Robinson's "You've Really Got a Hold on Me," the Angels' "My Boyfriend's Back," and Ben E. King's "Stand By Me."

WHERE THE BUFFALO ROAM   ★↙

ROCK. 1980. Cast: Bill Murray, Peter Boyle, Bruno Kirby, and Rene Auberjenois. 100 min. Beta, VHS. MCA ($59.95)

Bill Murray is one of the top box office names in movies today, trading on his characteristic nonchalance and winking complicity with the audience. Before his run of successes, there were some lowlights in the Murray resume, *Where the Buffalo Roam* being one of them. In a misguided attempt by Art Linson to translate Hunter Thompson's gonzo visions onto the screen, Murray, playing Thompson, is trapped in a meandering scenario which ultimately leaves the viewer baffled as to its original intentions. The screenplay is too episodic to be coherent and some roles are grossly underwritten (Peter Boyle is gallant in a role which would have completely frustrated lesser actors). Even Bill's presence can't save this film. It's safe to say that the definitive movie about Hunter Thompson and his unorthodox vision is yet to be made because this ain't it, friend. The soundtrack does include such sixties memories as "Highway 61 Revisited" by Bob Dylan, "I Can't Help Myself" by The Four Tops, "I Heard It through the Grapevine" by Credence Clearwater Revival, "Chooglin'," also by Credence, "Purple Haze" by Jimi Hendrix, "Heat Wave" by Martha and the Vandellas, "How Long" by The Pointer Sisters, "All along the Watchtower" by Hendrix, and "Papa Was a Rolling Stone"

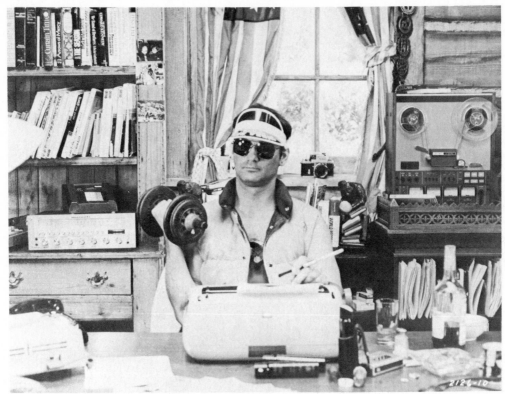

Bill Murray as gonzo journalist Hunter Thompson in *Where the Buffalo Roam.*

by The Temptations. Bill sings "Lucy in the Sky with Diamonds," and Neil Young contributes an electric guitar version of "Home on the Range."

WILD IN THE COUNTRY ★ɬ

ROCK. 1961. Cast: Elvis Presley, Hope Lange, Tuesday Weld, and Millie Perkins. 114 min. Beta, VHS. CBS/Fox ($59.95)

In the seventh Elvis film, our hero gets to deliver dialogue written by the famed American playwright Clifford Odets. While this whole project might have started out as an attempt to place Elvis in a top-drawer, socially meaningful movie, it ended up being just another run-through of the soon to be institutionalized Elvis-as-hillbilly scenario. Elvis must have thoroughly enjoyed making this film. After all, he gets three— count 'em, three—love interests to smooch: Hope Lange, a social worker, Tuesday

Weld, a sex kitten, and Millie Perkins, the wholesome girl next door. In this predictable "serious" drama, Elvis is a juvenile delinquent with a sensitive side who gets on the right track through the efforts of Hope Lange, his caseworker. Not the worst sixties Elvis flick by a long stretch but not much better than some of the worst ones. Songs added to make the whole thing more palatable include "I Slipped, Stumbled, and Fell," "Lonely Man," "In My Way," the title tune, and others.

YOU'RE A BIG BOY NOW   ★★↲

ROCK. 1966. Cast: Peter Kastner, Elizabeth Hartman, Geraldine Page, Rip Torn, Michael Dunn, Tony Bill, Karen Black, and Julie Harris. 96 min. Beta, VHS. Warner ($59.95)

The most interesting thing about *You're a Big Boy Now* is the novelty of its being Francis Ford Coppola's second film. The Lovin' Spoonful, New York's premier electric jug band, scored the film with a number of compositions, including "Hey, Beautiful Girl, Can I Look at Your Insides," "Darlin' Be Home Soon," and the title tune "You're a Big Boy Now." Peter Kastner plays Bernard, a 21-year-old boy who moves from Great Neck, Long Island, to New York City to gain his independence, learn about sex, and become a man. He gets a job working for his demanding father (Rip Torn) at the New York Public Library and tries to avoid the meddling of his overprotective mother (Geraldine Page), his spinster landlady (Julie Harris), and the attentive Amy (Karen Black), a girl who works with him at the library. He pursues Barbara (Elizabeth Hartman), an actress who toys with his affection throughout most of the film. In the end, he settles down with Amy and the promise of a secure relationship.

ZABRISKIE POINT   ★↲

ROCK. 1970. Cast: Mark Frenchette and Daria Halprin. 110 min. Beta, VHS. MGM/ UA ($79.95)

Michaelangelo Antonioni's second film made in English was considered to be a master-piece of existentialist drama when it was released during the days of campus unrest in 1970. Since then, *Zabriskie Point,* which was scripted by Antonioni, Fred Gardner, Sam Shepard, Tonio Guera, and Clare Peploe, has grown old and today is completely dated. Antonioni, the Italian director who clearly described the alienation of dying

Mark Frenchette and Daria Halprin in
Zabriskie Point.

European civilization, was overpowered by his subject when he tried to find out what made young America tick. Mark, a Los Angeles student radical, is falsely accused of shooting a policeman. He escapes a police dragnet, steals a small plane, and flies to Death Valley where he meets Daria, an aimless girl who befriends him. The famous, seemingly endless, scene from which the film takes its title takes place at California's Zabriskie Point. Mark returns to Los Angeles in the stolen plane. Daria drives in her car to the desert home of her land-developer boss. Mark is ambushed by waiting police when he lands at a Los Angeles County airport and is killed in their crossfire. Daria hears of Mark's death over the radio. She plants a bomb in the home of her employer. She walks back to her car. As an acid-drenched guitar drones on Pink Floyd's "Careful with That Axe, Eugene," the house blows up in an anarchic explosion that is repeated at the end of the film over and over again. Pink Floyd composed a number of tunes in addition to "Careful," including "Heart Beat Pig Meat" and "Crumbling Land." The Band plays "Kaleidoscope." "Dark Star" is provided by the Greatful Dead.

ZACHARIAH ★★

ROCK. 1971. Cast: John Rubenstein, Pat Quinn, Country Joe and the Fish, Doug Kershaw, The James Gang, New York Rock and Roll Ensemble, Elvin Jones, and Dick Van Patten. 93 min. Beta, VHS. CBS/FOX ($79.95)

In this melange of Biblical parable, morality play, old west shoot-out, rock opera, and satire scripted by the Firesign Theater, Zachariah (John Rubenstein) buys a six-shooter through a mail-order catalogue and convinces his friend, Matthew, the village blacksmith, to leave their one-horse town with him to become a trigger-happy hired gun and search for truth in the old west. They join up with a rock group that does double duty as a bunch of ne'er-do-well hold-up men, The Crackers (Country Joe and the Fish). While the band performs "We're Poor and Lonely Crackers" at one end of a clapboard town, attracting the town's populace, Matt and Zack sneak into town from the other side and quietly rob the town's only bank. But soon they grow tired of the lazy Crackers and venture to Apache Wells, an outpost run by Job Cain, "the fastest gun in the west." Cain (Elvin Jones) and Zack have a showdown and pull their guns in a dead even draw. Zachariah realizes the answers to his quest are not in the world of the gunfighter. He leaves Matthew with Cain and his men and travels to El Camino, a town dedicated to the pursuit of carnal pleasures, where he falls in love with the notorious Belle Starr (Pat Quinn). Meanwhile, Matt calls out Job Cain, shoots him, and becomes the "fastest draw in town." But he is bothered by the thought that Zachariah might be faster. Meanwhile, Zack has put down his guns to learn how to respect life and appreciate nature; he has been listening to the teachings of the Old Man, a peace-loving naturalist. Matt finds Zack tending his vegetable garden; he calls Zack out and demands that he draw. Zachariah refuses and convinces Matthew that the taking of human life is wrong. They throw down their guns and ride off into the sunset. Cajun fiddle player Doug Kershaw plays "Zachariah." Jazz drummer Elvin Jones plays a powerful solo in his saloon in Apache Wells. Country Joe and the Fish sing "One More Mount," "We're the Crackers," and "I Want to Wash in a Bathtub of Gold." The New York Rock and Roll Ensemble performs "I Really Had to Set Her Free" in the nude in Belle Starr's boudoir.

MOVIE MUSICALS

ALL THAT JAZZ ★★★

MUSICAL. 1979. Cast: Roy Scheider, Jessica Lange, Ann Reinking, Ben Vereen, Cliff Gorman, John Lithgow, and Leland Palmer. 119 min. Beta, VHS. CBS/Fox ($69.95)

This Oscar-winning homage to himself was Bob Fosse's gift to the movies in 1979. Roy Scheider, in a silly-looking goatee, plays Joe Gideon, a thinly veiled alter ego for Fosse himself, who directed and cowrote the opus. Gideon's the most successful Broadway director alive, although it doesn't seem he's going to be alive for long, the way he's going through women, cigarettes, and pills. His trip downward through the real and the surreal is chronicled in loving detail by Fosse's obsessed camera. As a straight narrative, this movie would be worse than intolerable but, to Fosse's credit, he throws in a lot of extravagant, Felliniesque production numbers which the audience can take as seriously as they want. Fosse couldn't have been serious. Right? The finale, "Bye-bye Life," is the production number Gideon imagines while he's undergoing open heart surgery. It features Ben Vereen, Ann Reinking, Leland Palmer, Jessica Lange, and all the other denizens of his fevered life and mind. Other songs include "On Broadway" (George Benson), "A Perfect Day" (Harry Nilsson), "Everything Old Is New Again" (Peter Allen), "There's No Business Like Show Business" (Ethel Merman), and "Take Off with Us." Stylish, imaginative, incredibly indulgent, and often simply repellent.

AN AMERICAN IN PARIS ★★★★

MUSICAL. 1951. Cast: Gene Kelly, Leslie Caron, Oscar Levant, Georges Guetary, and Nina Foch. 102 min. Beta, VHS. MGM/UA ($59.95)

Under the brilliant direction of Vincente Minnelli (*Meet Me in St. Louis, Gigi*), Gene Kelly won an Oscar for his role in *An American in Paris,* the film that won the Oscar for best picture in 1951. In this movie with an all-Gershwin score, Gene stars as an American bohemian painter, Jerry Mulligan, who lives a carefree life in Paris. His equally bohemian friend Adam Cooke (Oscar Levant) lives in a nearby garret and dreams of performing his as yet unpublished piano concertos in front of admiring audiences. In a wonderful dream sequence, Oscar Levant, dressed in tails, plays his concerto at the piano in a concert hall. He also conducts the orchestra. A number of Levants fill the string section. Of course, the audience is filled with a myriad of applauding Levants too. Jerry is pursued by a rich, beautiful American suntan-oil heiress who wants to set him up as an established painter in his own studio. But Jerry's heart belongs to Lisa (Leslie Caron), a French shop clerk who Jerry learns is engaged to his friend Henri Barrel, a famous French pop singer. The plot comes to its resolution at the famed Beaux Arts Ball. Not wanting to be a kept man, Jerry rejects the offer of the suntan-oil heiress. He pines for Lisa, who leaves the festivities to marry Henri. But Lisa returns to Jerry. True love triumphs. The movie is a cornucopia of Gershwin standards. Gene dances with some French children and sings in the delightful "I Got Rhythm" number. Kelly and Caron dance a subdued, yet beautiful, pas de deux by the Seine to the melody of "Love Is Here to Stay." The famous finale is the 17-minute "An American in Paris" ballet set to Gershwin's tone poem. MGM studio executives thought it was quite daring to replace the usual tap routines found in movie musicals with an extended ballet number. They took a chance. You'll be glad they did. Other songs include Gershwin's "Stairway to Paradise," "S'Wonderful," "Strike Up the Band," and "Not for Me."

Harpo and Chico creating zaniness in *Animal Crackers.*

ANIMAL CRACKERS ★★★★

MUSICAL. 1930. Cast: The Marx Brothers (Groucho, Chico, Harpo, and Zeppo), Marga-ret Dumont, Lillian Roth. 98 min. Beta, VHS. MCA ($59.95)

This is the quartet's second movie (*Coconuts* was the first). The Marx Brothers' antics in *Animal Crackers* were thought to be lost for many years. Prints of this black and white comic masterpiece were uncovered in the mid-seventies and were re-released to theaters, generally shown to SRO audiences. Groucho gets to sing the classic "Hooray for Captain Spaulding," which contains the lyric, "Hello, I must be going." Written by Morrie Ryskind, based on the play by Ryskind and George S. Kaufman, and directed by Victor Heerman, this movie about the brothers' invasion of a Long Island high society weekend affair, hosted, of course, by Margaret Dumont, is a continual string of puns, sight gags, and double-talk. Highly recommended.

THE BANDWAGON ★★★↓

MUSICAL. 1953. Cast: Fred Astaire, Cyd Charisse, Oscar Levant, Jack Buchanan, and Nanette Fabray. 112 min. Beta, VHS. MGM/UA ($69.95)

In *The Bandwagon,* Hollywood takes a lighthearted look at the damage movies did to the American stage. When the parvenus took over "entertainment," American theater was left to survive on a staple of "serious" subjects: Shakespeare, the Greek classics, Odets, etc. In the end, *The Bandwagon* ironically seems to suggest Broadway return to the musicals that Hollywood has already appropriated and use them as a means to a stage renaissance. Musical comedy writers Lily and Lester Marton (Nanette Fabray and Oscar Levant) convince has-been hoofer Tony Hunter (Fred Astaire) to star in a joke-filled vaudeville revue that they want directed by a celebrated serious English stage genius played by Jack Buchanan. They all seem to be in accord as to how the show should be presented when they perform the memorable "That's Entertainment" number, but in the hands of Buchanan's mad genius their fun musical revue turns into a ponderous musical reworking of Faust. Needless to say, it lays an egg in Hartford on the way to New York. Tony, who has been a sport up to this point and has gone along with Buchanan's "modern" vision, takes matters in hand and produces a show that is all soft-shoe and singing, *The Bandwagon.* In the show that becomes *the* hit on Broadway, Fred, Nanette, and Oscar perform the very funny "Triplets" number. Fred dances in the Mickey Spillane take-off, "Girl Hunt." Other Howard Dietz-Arthur Schwartz songs include "You, the Night and the Moonlight," "Dancing in the Dark," "I Love Louisa," "Louisiana Hayride," and "I Lost the One Girl I Found."

BELLS ARE RINGING ★★★

MUSICAL. 1960. Cast: Dean Martin, Judy Holliday, Fred Clark, Eddie Foy, Jr., Jean Stapleton, and Frank Gorshin. 120 min. Beta, VHS. MGM/UA ($69.95)

Vincente Minnelli could always be counted on to take some unpromising material and make a good movie musical out of it, usually by choosing to present it from a unique angle. *Bells Are Ringing* was not Betty Comden and Adolph Green's best Broadway show, although it does include two particularly well known songs, "Just in Time" and "The Party's Over" (Don Meredith's favorite song, it seems). The plot is meager: a plain Jane (Judy Holliday) who works as an operator at an answering service becomes the muse of a Broadway writer with a mental block (Dean Martin). Comic complications of course ensue but this musical relies heavily on the charm and ebullience of its two stars. Only Judy Holliday's bravura performance as the goody-two-shoes operator and Dean's nonchalance make the film worth seeing. Reservations aside, though, when the film is on target, it's funny and entertaining. Eddie Foy, Jr., who plays a con artist, sings cleverly amidst other cons in the number, "Simple Little System." Dean and Judy put on a show for spectators in a public park, singing and dancing to "Just in Time." But it is Judy's turn to shine in two wonderfully realized numbers, "The Party's Over" and "I'm Going Back to the Bonjour Tristesse Brassiere Company." Other songs are "PLO-4433," "You're on Your Own," "Better Than a Dream," "I Met a Girl," "The Midas Touch," and the title tune.

THE BELLS OF ST. MARY'S ★★★

MUSICAL. 1945. Cast: Bing Crosby, Ingrid Bergman, Henry Travers, William Gargan, Ruth Donnelly, Joan Carrol, and Una O'Connor. 126 min. Beta, VHS. Republic ($49.95)

Bing Crosby recreates his role of Father O'Malley, the gentle but resourceful young pastor of *Going My Way* (for which Crosby received a best actor Oscar), and finds himself in a difficult new job, the new parish pastor of St. Mary's parochial school. Ingrid Bergman plays Sister Benedict, with whom Father O'Malley spars on the correct way to instruct students. The story concerns their efforts to regain some adjoining land that they had sold to a crusty old millionaire realtor, Mr. Bogardus. Bogardus gives up the exclusive pursuit of wealth when he's "born again" and generously returns the land, with its already erected office building, to the school for its use in expanding the campus. Bergman and Crosby have a great chemistry on screen—this in a movie about a nun and a priest, no less. The movie's wholesome charms are aided and abetted by its light tone; it mixes moral lessons with gentle humor. Bing sings "Aren't You Glad You're You?," "Bells of St. Mary's," "Adeste Fideles," "O Sanctissima," and "In the Land of Beginning Again." Directed by Leo McCarey.

BRIGADOON ★★★

MUSICAL. 1954. Cast: Gene Kelly, Van Johnson, Cyd Charisse, and Elaine Stewart. 108 min. Beta Hifi, VHS Stereo. MGM/UA ($69.95)

This could have been a great musical, given the magnitude of the talent involved in it. Vincente Minnelli directed, Frederick Loewe and Alan Jay Lerner wrote the songs, and Gene Kelly, Van Johnson, and Cyd Charisse were the performers. Two Americans on a hunting trip in Scotland discover a magical village, Brigadoon, that materializes for only one day each century. Kelly and Johnson find the charms of the village lifestyle and its women, especially Cyd Charisse, too much to resist. In the end, they leave the outside world and enter the phantom world of Brigadoon forever. Along the way there are some fine songs and lots of energetic dancing: "Brigadoon," "Come Ye to the Fair," "Waiting for His Dearie Me," "I'll Go Home with Bonnie Jean," "Heather on the Hill," and "Almost Like Being in Love." What is lacking finally is a compelling reason for the Gene Kelly character to leave the real world—no matter the charms of Cyd Charisse. The premise is way ahead of the drama.

BYE BYE BIRDIE ★★◗

MUSICAL. 1963. Cast: Dick Van Dyke, Janet Leigh, Ann-Margret, Paul Lynde, Maureen Stapleton, Ed Sullivan, and Bobby Rydell. 111 min. Beta, VHS. RCA/Columbia ($59.95)

For several reasons, this film has not aged well. It, in fact, is quite a curiosity now. The premise, used successfully in the opportunistic Broadway hit musical upon which the film is based, is simple: Conrad Birdie, an Elvis clone, is about to enter the Army and has decided to make a final appearance before induction on *The Ed Sullivan Show*. The race is on for Dick Van Dyke, a songwriter in New York City, to get Birdie to sing his "One Last Kiss" on television. Janet Leigh, Van Dyke's long-suffering girlfriend, hatches a scheme to do it. The Birdie appearance will be moved to Columbus, Ohio, and he will have the chance to give his "one last kiss" to some lucky middle-American teenage girl, chosen at random. Sullivan buys the idea and the wheels are set in motion. Ann-Margret, who defined the term "sex kitten," is the lucky girl and this causes major problems for her boyfriend, Hugo (Bobby Rydell), and her socially prominent father (Paul Lynde). Problems also crop up that deter Van Dyke and Leigh from marrying as they had planned. All of these problems are happily solved by the time we get to the finale. The more memorable songs are "Bye Bye Birdie," "Ed Sullivan," "Kids" (featuring Lynde's bravura mugging and vocal), and the ensemble dance number, "Got a Lot of Living to Do," which features Ann-Margret's eye-opening terpsichoreal splendor. It's all too obviously a cynical adult's swipe at teenage idol worship. Rather than being light and breezy, it's infused with a lot of needless hypocrisy.

CABARET ★★★★

MUSICAL. 1972. Cast: Liza Minnelli, Michael York, Helmut Griem, Marisa Berenson, and Joel Grey. 119 min. Beta, VHS. MGM/UA ($69.95)

Cabaret, the winner of eight Academy Awards, fuses the singing of English actor Michael York, the sardonic clowning of Joel Grey (who had been in the original Broadway production), and the obsession with the tawdry and decadent of director Bob Fosse. The most recent recycling of Christopher Isherwood's Berlin stories, *Cabaret* tells the bittersweet tale of the love affairs of Sally Bowles, an American singer who performs at a sleazy Berlin night club, The Kit Kat Klub, and dreams of becoming a film star in Germany just before Hitler's rise to power. On stage at the club, Sally and the Kit Kat's emcee (Joel Grey) perform the John Kander-Fred Ebb songs that made the musical such a hit: "Mein Herr," "Wilkommen," "If You Could See Her through My Eyes," "Come to the Cabaret," and the hit tune written for the movie version, "Money, Money, Money." Off stage, Fosse capably directs the raunch and raucous mayhem of the Kit Kat Klub and the story of Sally, Brian Roberts (Michael York), Natalia (Marisa Berenson), and Fritz (Fritz Wepper) and how they and their lives are changed by the Nazi quest for political power.

CAN-CAN ★★♪

MUSICAL. 1960. Cast: Frank Sinatra, Shirley MacLaine, Juliet Prowse, Maurice Chevalier, Louis Jourdan. 113 min. Beta, VHS. CBS/Fox ($59.95)

Shirley MacLaine, doing what she loves—singing and dancing—plays a nightclub owner in 1890s Paris whose can-can revue scandalizes the French bourgeoisie. The high-kicking antics of Shirley and her chorines get her arrested and the nightclub closed. Frank Sinatra, playing a young barrister smitten with Shirley, fights to clear her of all charges and reopen the club. In this colorful, though slow-paced, musical, one is treated to Frank's authoritative presence, Juliet Prowse's leggy dancing, Shirley's histrionics, and a good score by Cole Porter, upon whose Broadway musical the film is based. There's plenty of dazzle and big names on the screen in this one. The highlight is undoubtedly the big production number where Shirley *and* Juliet do the can-can. Recommended for those who like flash, but those who prefer a stronger story line and witty dialogue should look elsewhere.

CAN'T STOP THE MUSIC ★★♪

MUSICAL. 1980. Cast: Village People, Valerie Perrine, Bruce Jenner, Steve Guttenberg, Paul Sand, Tammy Grimes, June Havoc, Barbara Rush, and The Ritchie Family. 117 min. Beta, VHS. Thorn-EMI ($59.95)

It started as an in joke among the gay community in New York City: six young men dressed as the stereotypes of the gay subculture (a biker, a cop, a hardhat, an Indian,

Bruce Jenner, Valerie Perrine, and the Village People in *Can't Stop the Music.*

a cowboy, and a G.I.) singing disco songs filled with double entendres like "Y.M.C.A." and "In the Navy." The brainchild of Jacques Morali and Henri Belolo, the Village People surprised everyone with a string of dance floor hits in 1978 and 1979, the height of the disco craze. By the time this film biography of sorts was shot, their popularity had already seriously declined. Nancy Walker(!) directed this Allan Carr-produced farrago of ambiguous sexuality and slapstick. It's not as bad as its initial reviews suggested although it's not that good either. Valerie Perrine and Bruce Jenner (quite funny actually) are the "normal" people who help Steve Guttenberg, as Jacky Morell, and his group, the Village People, obtain a record contract from recording executive Paul Sand. There's a scene in a Y.M.C.A., of course. The Village People are heard doing "Can't Stop the Music," "Liberation," "I Love You to Death,"

"Y.M.C.A.," "Magic Night," "Milkshake," "Samantha," and "Sophistication." The Ritchie Family, another Morali-Belolo creation, sing "Give Me a Break" and "The Sound of the City."

COPACABANA ★★♪

MUSICAL. 1947. Cast: Groucho Marx, Carmen Miranda, Andy Russell, Steve Cochran, and Gloria Jean. 91 min. Beta, VHS. Republic ($49.95)

This passably entertaining movie musical boasts the rather eccentric combination of Groucho Marx and Carmen Miranda. Groucho, here without his comedic brothers, plays the agent and lover of Carmen Miranda in a ridiculously clichéd plot about their efforts to get booked at the Copacabana Club, an exclusive night spot in New York City. It seems Groucho's efforts are too successful—Carmen gets booked twice! She's hired once as the Brazilian Bombshell, again as Mademoiselle Fifi. Thus, Carmen spends the entire movie shuttling back and forth between two personae, trying to keep the wool over the eyes of the club manager (Steve Cochran). Groucho is around to provide the laughs between production numbers featuring Miranda's dual chanteuses. This is your chance to see Carmen as a blonde. As the Brazilian Bombshell, Carmen sings "Tico Tico" and "Copacabana." As Mademoiselle Fifi, she sings "Je Vous Aime" and "If You Want to Make a Hit with Fifi." Groucho is featured in a western parody number called "Go West Young Man," written by Bert Kalmer and Harry Ruby. Other songs are "Hollywood Bound," "The Bolero in Rio de Janeiro," "He Hasn't Got a Thing to Sell," "Stranger Things Have Happened," and others. In black and white.

THE COURT JESTER ★★♪

MUSICAL. 1956. Cast: Danny Kaye, Glynis Johns, Angela Lansbury, Basil Rathbone, and John Carradine. 101 min. Beta, VHS. Paramount ($49.95)

Danny Kaye's special comic talents, a rare combination of physical and verbal humor, make this rather lifeless musical comedy worth seeing. In yet another version of Kaye's favorite story line, an ineffectual buffoon gains a position of authority and leadership through a series of misunderstandings and, to his and everyone else's surprise, becomes a true hero. Danny plays the nebbish who must masquerade as a court jester in order to overthrow a pretender to the crown. The movie is also brightened by the presence of two beautiful costars, Glynis Johns and Angela Lansbury. The songs, written by Kaye's wife, Sylvia Fine, and Sammy Cahn, are "Life Couldn't Possibly Better Be,"

"They'll Never Outfox the Fox," "I'm Giacomo," "The Maladjusted Jester," and others. Directed by two noted Hollywood veterans, Norman Panama and Melvin Frank.

DAMES ★★★

MUSICAL. 1934. Cast: Joan Blondell, Dick Powell, Ruby Keeler, Zasu Pitts, Guy Kibbee, and Hugh Herbert. 90 min. Beta, VHS. Key ($59.95)

A wonderful Warner Bros. musical which is worth seeing both as a singing and dancing extravaganza and as a comic tale. One of the black and white musicals choreographed by Busby Berkeley in the early thirties that established his legend in the annals of Hollywood. Marked by a wild imagination, wicked humor, and an astute sense of the camera, Berkeley's production numbers have often been imitated but never equaled. He was one of filmdom's eccentric, one of a kind visionaries. *Dames* is about the efforts of Dick Powell, a young writer of show tunes, to put on a Broadway revue and win over the snobbish father of his beloved, played by Ruby Keeler. Guy Kibbee, a great character actor, plays the father, who is struggling to be worthy of his millionaire cousin's esteem and money and wants his daughter to have nothing at all to do with Powell. Joan Blondell is a showgirl who embroils Kibbee in a comic dilemma. The songs performed in the production numbers are: "When You Were a Smile on Your Mother's Lips and a Twinkle in Your Father's Eye," the classic "I Only Have Eyes for You," "A Girl Who Works in the Laundry," "Dames," and "Try to See It My Way." Not the best Berkeley but still vastly entertaining.

DUCK SOUP ★★★★

MUSICAL. 1933. Cast: Groucho Marx, Chico Marx, Harpo Marx, Zeppo Marx, Margaret Dumont, Raquel Torres, and Louis Calhern. 70 min. Beta, VHS. MCA ($39.95)

Rufus T. Firefly (Groucho) becomes the new leader of Freedonia, a small democracy on the brink of bankruptcy and threatened with war by neighboring Sylvania. He has to win over two spies in his midst, Chico and Harpo, and woo the wealthy Margaret Dumont. In the end, Firefly proves to be a great military leader, winning the war against Sylvania. The story is told with the usual Marx Brothers freneticism. *Duck Soup,* directed by Leo McCarey, is considered by many to be the brothers' finest comedy. The madness is end to end with nary a letdown as Groucho and his brothers make a mockery of modern diplomacy. There are two musical numbers: "When the Clock on the Wall Strikes Ten," introducing Groucho, and "We're Going to War," a hilarious

Chico and Groucho Marx in *Duck Soup.*

mélange of visual and verbal puns, using everything from American folksongs to Broadway hits to a howling parody of Cab Calloway's "Minnie the Moocher." In black and white.

EASTER PARADE ★★★★

MUSICAL. 1948. Cast: Fred Astaire, Judy Garland, Peter Lawford, Ann Miller, and Jules Munshin. 103 min. Beta, VHS. MGM/UA ($59.95)

In Irving Berlin's *Easter Parade,* successful vaudeville dancer Don Hewes (Fred Astaire) is jilted by his girlfriend and celebrated dance partner Nadine (Ann Miller), who decides to strike out on her own as a solo act. In a moment of desperation, the great Don Hewes pulls chorus-line hoofer Hannah Brown (Judy Garland) out of the ranks of a saloon show and, determined to get back at Nadine, decides to make her his new dance partner. At first Hannah has two left feet and the duo fail miserably. But, after months of practice, they are the toast of Broadway, the stars of the Easter Parade,

Judy Garland and Fred Astaire in *Easter Parade.*

and in love. In a beautiful marriage of stage and film special effects, Fred Astaire dances in slow motion in the foreground to Irving Berlin's "Stepping Out with My Baby" while the chorus and dancers in the background sing and dance at normal speed. Hannah and Hewes join the Ziegfeld Follies and perform the memorable "A Couple of Swells" while dressed as hobos. Other Berlin songs include the wonderful "I Love the Piano," "Snooky-ukums," "I'm Just a Fellah with an Umbrella," and the Easter favorite, "On the Avenue."

EUBIE!   ★★✦

MUSICAL. 1981. Cast: Gregory Hines, Maurice Hines, Terry Burrell, Leslie Dockery, Lynne Godfrey, Donna Ingram, David Jackson, Mel Johnson, Jr., Bernard J. Marsh, Alaina Reed, and Jeffrey V. Thompson. 85 min. Beta Hifi, VHS. Warner ($59.95)

In the tradition of *Sophisticated Ladies, Ain't Misbehaving,* and *My One and Only, Eubie!* is a Broadway musical stage revival built on the songbook of a great American composer.

Eubie Blake, the creator of these classic tunes, was fortunate enough to see his lifework recognized in such a popular salute before his death at 100. These numbers, some of which were first performed 75 years earlier, are given new life by a cast of singers and dancers that includes in its ranks Gregory and Maurice Hines, who later starred in Francis Ford Coppola's *Cotton Club*. Like the other shows mentioned above, *Eubie!* tries to maintain the integrity of each song but does not burden each number with period costumes that immediately date the production. *Eubie!* is performed on a stage without any referential sets. Blake's good-time music and moving blues are timeless and this tribute to his work presents them in a way that's timeless. The show starts with a production number based on Eubie's composition, "Souls of Africa." The company then kicks into a spirited rendition of Blake's most famous tune, "I'm Just Wild about Harry." "In Honeysuckle Time," "Those High Steppin' Days," "You Get the Getting While the Getting Is Good," and "I'm Weary of the Pain" are all performed by the cast. "Memories of You," a song cowritten by Blake's longtime collaborator Noble Sissle, is performed before Gregory Hines dances in "Hot Feet."

FIDDLER ON THE ROOF   ★★★♪

MUSICAL. 1971. Cast: Topol, Molly Picon, Leonard Frey, Paul Michael Glaser, Rosalind Harris, and Michele Marsh. 150 min. Beta, VHS. CBS/Fox ($79.95)

In this energetic film adaptation of the Sheldon Harnick-Jerry Brock Broadway musical, Teve (Topol), the milkman of the early twentieth century Ukrainian village of Anatekva, tries to uphold the traditions of his Jewish faith against the winds of change. His eldest daughter, Tzeitel (Rosalind Harris), breaks the marriage arrangement made by Yente (Molly Picon), the village matchmaker. Tzeitel is promised to the rich butcher Lazar Wolf (Paul Mann), but insists on marrying Motel (Leonard Frey), a poor tailor. Teve's second daughter, Hodel (Michelle Marsh), marries Perchik (Paul Michael Glaser), a student radical from Kiev, and leaves town to join him in the city. The Jews are ordered to leave Anatekva by the government as Teve's third daughter, Havel, marries Fetka, a Christian. Teve, his wife Golda (Norma Crane), and his two youngest daughters, along with Tzeitel and Havel and their husbands, leave Anatekva for a new life in America. *Fiddler on the Roof* includes such Broadway favorites as "Matchmaker, Matchmaker," "If I Were a Rich Man," "To Life," "Sunrise, Sunset," and "Anatekva, Anatekva."

FINIAN'S RAINBOW ★★

MUSICAL. 1968. Cast: Fred Astaire, Petula Clark, Tommy Steele, Al Freeman, Jr., Keenan Wynn, and Don Francks. 141 min. Beta, VHS. Warner ($59.95)

Francis Ford Coppola tackled this Broadway musical about an eccentric Irishman (Fred Astaire) with a belief in leprechauns who finds himself in the American deep south. Filmed some years before Coppola's masterpiece, *The Godfather, Finian's Rainbow* was a first foray into a genre he would try to master in *One from the Heart* and *The Cotton Club.* Not surprisingly, each movie has been both a critical and a commercial failure. Coppola simply doesn't understand how a musical film should be paced. He insists on the elegiac length that has marked all of his films with the singular exception of *The Conversation.* Given some wonderful songs by E. Y. Harburg and Burton Lane, a fine cast including Astaire, Clark, and Tommy Steele, and choreography by Hermes

Fred Astaire in *Finian's Rainbow.*

Pan, Coppola has fashioned an amorphous, aimless 2-hour-plus yawner. Even some ill-advised laughs caused by Keenan Wynn in the role of a bigoted southern Senator who turns into a black man for a few days cannot save this vague mélange of current events and Irish lore. Astaire is wasted and Clark's role is underwritten—sadly, since she's in fine form vocally. Some of the songs featured are "Look to the Rainbow," "This Time of the Year," "How Are Things in Gloccamorra?," "That Old Devil Moon," "If This Isn't Love," "C'mon and Get It Day," "When the Idle Poor Become the Idle Rich," "Begin the Begat," and "When I'm Not Near the Girl I Love, I Love the Girl I'm Near."

THE FIRST NUDIE MUSICAL   ★

MUSICAL. 1976. Cast: Cindy Williams, Bruce Kimmel, Leslie Ackerman, Diana Canova, Alexandra Morgan, and Ron Howard. 94 min. Beta, VHS. Media ($49.95)

On the road to success, which led from their film debut in George Lucas' *American Graffiti* to their hit television comedy series, *Happy Days* and *Laverne and Shirley*, Ron Howard and Cindy Williams somehow took a wrong turn and accidentally appeared in *The First Nudie Musical*. Lucky Ron had only a cameo role, but poor Cindy costarred as the secretary of a young Hollywood studio head who, hounded by creditors and faced with certain financial ruin, brainstorms a solution to his financial problems. He produces the first pornographic musical in a record 14 days. The cast of harried but bored porno stars and lackluster dancers go through their paces in production numbers that are intended to be sexy and clever, but are anatomical and silly at best. Musical numbers like "Dancing Dildos," "Come, Come Now," and "Let 'em Eat Cake" rely on their prurience instead of their musical content to evoke excitement from the viewer. The whole show is a dud.

FOOTLIGHT PARADE   ★★★★

MUSICAL. 1933. Cast: James Cagney, Joan Blondell, Ruby Keeler, Dick Powell, Guy Kibbee, Hugh Herbert, and Claire Dodd. 105 min. Beta, VHS. Key ($59.95)

This Busby Berkeley-choreographed musical gets a boost from the forceful performance of Jimmy Cagney in the leading role. Jimmy plays a stage director who comes up with a great idea. In the face of the movies' domination of live theater, he wants to put on brief revues before the evening shows at large movie houses in Chicago. The "prologues," as he calls them, catch on and make him a wealthy but extremely busy man. The story, of course, only serves as a dramatic breather between those dizzily imaginative Busby Berkeley production numbers. "Sitting on a Backyard Fence" and "Cats on Parade" feature dancers in cat costumes. (They're forerunners of the antics in Broadway's current cat-fetish smash hit, *Cats.*) Dick Powell sings "I've Got a Feeling It's Love." In "Honeymoon Hotel," Powell and Ruby Keeler play newlyweds in a production extravaganza topped by the next number, "By a Waterfall," which features a water ballet sequence only equaled in the later Esther Williams films. But the finale, "Shanghai Lil," with Jimmy Cagney as an American soldier in China and Ruby Keeler as his beloved, Shanghai Lil, tops them all, ending in a tableau of infantrymen forming a human American flag.

42nd STREET ★★★★

MUSICAL. 1933. Cast: Warner Baxter, Dick Powell, Ruby Keeler, Ginger Rogers, Bebe Daniels, and Guy Kibbee. 89 min. Beta, VHS. CBS/Fox ($59.95)

The legendary movie musical on which the current Broadway smash hit is based. The apotheosis of the backstage drama, with its understudy-becomes-the-star plot, *42nd Street* benefits from Busby Berkeley's production numbers and the hoofing of such perennial stars as Dick Powell, Ruby Keeler, and Ginger Rogers. Warner Baxter is both suave and harried, if that's possible, as Julian Marsh, the "greatest musical-comedy director in America," trying to put on a Broadway revue called *Pretty Lady* with limited time and resources. Ruby Keeler taps her way into movie folklore as she joins Dick Powell in Busby Berkeley's *first* screen choreographic work. The big dance numbers, "42nd Street," "You're Getting to Be a Habit with Me," "Shuffle Off to Buffalo" (which has become part of the American language), and "Young and Healthy," are all winning examples of Berkeley's outrageous vision. In black and white.

FUNNY GIRL ★★★♪

MUSICAL. 1968. Cast: Barbra Streisand, Omar Sharif, Walter Pidgeon, Kay Medford, and Anne Francis. 155 min. Beta Hifi, VHS Stereo. RCA/Columbia ($79.95)

Barbra Streisand made a spectacular film debut in this musical based on the Broadway show that had launched her career. She plays Fanny Brice, the Ziegfeld Follies performer who went on to Broadway stardom on her own, with verve and depth. And, of course, there are her wonderful pipes. The songs by Jule Styne and Bob Merrill seem to have been written especially for Streisand, they suit her brassy, expressive voice so well.

And make no mistake about it, Barbra is what makes this motion picture watchable. Aside from Omar Sharif's portrayal of Nicky Arnstein, Fanny's playboy husband, who gambles away more money than he's got, there are no other interesting characters in this vehicle for Barbra's talents. As drama, this is little more than glossy soap opera, but as a musical entertainment, it provides the viewer an occasion to enjoy lots of twenties pageantry and several sprightly songs. William Wyler, one of Hollywood's legendary directors, helmed this successful screen adaptation of a Broadway show— of which there are very, very few. Streisand won the Oscar for best actress her first time out of the box. The songs: "If a Girl Isn't Pretty," "I Am the Greatest Star," "I'd Rather Be Blue over You," "Second Hand Rose," "People," "Don't Rain on My Parade," "Sadie," "Funny Girl," and "My Man."

A FUNNY THING HAPPENED ON THE WAY TO THE FORUM   ★★★♩

MUSICAL. 1966. Cast: Zero Mostel, Phil Silvers, Jack Gilford, Michael Crawford, Michael Hordern, and Buster Keaton. 99 min. Beta, VHS. CBS/Fox ($59.95)

Imagine the declining days of the Roman Empire as a burlesque laugh-fest starring Zero Mostel and Phil Silvers. *A Funny Thing* is precisely that. Richard Lester, who was hot off his two Beatles smashes, *Hard Day's Night* and *Help!*, improved on the Broadway musical by Stephen Sondheim by loading up on the sight gags, vaudeville patter, and music hall antics. Zero Mostel, in his usual overbearing performance, comes off well as the ambitious slave, Pseudolus, who wants his freedom at any cost. When Michael Crawford falls for a virgin about to be initiated into a life of prostitution, Pseudolus agrees to help him rescue the girl in return for his freedom. Phil Silvers, as the owner of the brothel, Jack Gilford, as Hysterium, Pseudolus' wimpy fellow slave, and Buster Keaton, as Erroneus, a nearsighted nobleman, add to the hilarity with their assured comic performances. Some of the Sondheim songs are "Comedy Tonight," "Lovely," "Everybody Ought to Have a Maid," and "Miles Gloriosus."

GIGI   ★★★

MUSICAL. 1958. Cast: Leslie Caron, Louis Jourdan, Hermione Gingold, Maurice Chevalier, Eva Gabor, and Jacques Bergerac. 115 min. Beta, VHS. MGM/UA ($69.95)

Lerner and Loewe's *Gigi* stars the nucleus of Hollywood's French community in the fifties. Based on the story by Colette and set in the Paris of the early twentieth century, *Gigi* tells the story of a rich Parisian industrialist, Gaston (Louis Jourdan), who is so bored with life that his only pleasure is visiting his friend Mamita (Hermione Gingold) and her teenage granddaughter, Gigi (Leslie Caron). As Gigi grows into a young woman, Gaston becomes attracted to her, and in a supposedly typical French way, wants to set her up in an apartment of her own as his mistress. He makes the proper arrangements with her family. Gigi refuses, thinking the practice unsavory. Realizing that his attraction is more than a passing fancy, Gaston swears his undying love and asks Gigi to marry him. Maurice Chevalier plays Gaston's Uncle Honore, and has the pleasure of singing "Thank Heaven for Little Girls" and "I Remember It Well" in a charming duet with Hermione Gingold. Louis Jourdan in the role of Gaston sings "It's a Bore." Leslie Caron in the title role performs "I Don't Understand the Parisians," "The Night They Invented Champagne," and "Say a Prayer for Me Tonight."

GILDA LIVE ★★♪

MUSICAL. 1980. Cast: Gilda Radner, Don Novello, Paul Shaffer, and Rouge. 90 min. Beta, VHS. Warner ($39.95)

Strictly for fans of Gilda Radner and her assortment of funny characters. In between Saturday Night Live seasons, she headlined a limited-run musical comedy revue on Broadway. This is a filmed record of one performance during that run, directed by SNL producer Lorne Michaels. Gilda comes on stage to sing "Let's Talk Dirty to the Animals," and that segues into the first skit, Gilda as a young, extremely nervous chorine auditioning for her first stage production. She sings "I Love to be Unhappy." Don Novello, as Father Guido Sarducci, appears now and then to deliver his fractured Italian/English observations on life, love, and the Church. Among the other highlights are: "The Judy Miller Show"; Gilda as Candy Slice, a send-up of punk rocker Patti Smith, hairy underarms and all, singing "Gimme Mick"; the comeback performance of the little-known Rhonda Weiss and the Rhondettes, singing "Goodbye Saccharine"; Lisa Loopner (of the Nerds) playing "The Way We Were" at a piano recital; and Roseanne Roseannadanna giving the commencement speech to the graduating class of the Columbia School of Journalism. In the finale, Gilda sings a nostalgic salute to the early sixties called "Honey." Nothing you haven't seen her do on Saturday Night Live.

GLORIFYING THE AMERICAN GIRL ★★

MUSICAL. 1929. Cast: Mary Eaton, Eddie Cantor, Rudy Vallee, and Helen Morgan. 95 min. Beta, VHS. Video Yesteryear ($49.95)

This is an early talkie musical, shot in Astoria, New York, that attempts to give its audience a little bit of everything. The story involves a showgirl (Mary Eaton) who has to choose between a Broadway career and true love, but the entire second half of the movie is given over to a recreation of Flo Ziegfeld's vaunted musical revues, hence the title *Glorifying the American Girl,* taken from an actual Ziegfeld production. Historically intriguing but quite schizoid. You may want to fast forward your VCR to the finale, which features Rudy Vallee singing "Vagabond Lover," Helen Morgan performing "Can't Help Loving That Man," from the hit show of the time, *Showboat,* and Eddie Cantor in a skit about two haberdashers who won't take no for an answer from their customer. In the strange prologue to the film, a series of musical vignettes is presented: "A Pretty Girl Is Like a Melody," "No Fooling," and "Baby Face."

GOLD DIGGERS OF 1933 ★★★★

MUSICAL. 1933. Cast: Warren Williams, Joan Blondell, Aline MacMahon, Ruby Keeler, Dick Powell, and Ginger Rogers. 97 min. Beta, VHS. Key ($59.95)

Another black and white Warner Bros. musical classic from the thirties, this Busby Berkeley-choreographed marvel is only a notch short of the brilliance of *Gold Diggers of 1935,* which featured the iconic "Lullabye of Broadway" production number. In this one, Dick Powell, as yet another "juvenile," and Ruby Keeler are lovers and costars of a Broadway revue once again. Blondell and MacMahon play two showgirls who take a Boston blueblood (Warren Williams) and his attorney (Guy Kibbee) on quite a comic adventure of misunderstanding. Ginger Rogers appears as a showgirl, doing a pig latin version of "We're in the Money" while wearing a cardboard silver-dollar headpiece. It is to laugh! The finale, featuring Blondell, is a stunning stage montage of scenes from the depression entitled "Remember My Forgotten Man." Other songs are "In the Shadows," "Torch Song," and the charming "Petting in the Park."

THE GONDOLIERS ★★★

MUSICAL. 1982. Cast: Keith Mitchell, Christopher Booth-Jones, Francis Egerton, Eric Shilling, Nan Christie, and Fiona Kimm. 96 min. Beta, VHS. CBS/Fox ($49.95)

Sir William Schwenck Gilbert and Sir Arthur Sullivan wrote operettas that were parodies of the bombastic grand operas written and performed in Europe at the end of the nineteenth century. *The Gondoliers* is a fine example of Gilbert and Sullivan at their humorous best. The plot is so completely confusing that it is almost impossible to unravel. The gist of the story is that two gondoliers in Venice, who are filled with the republican idealism of the time, are informed that one of them is actually the current king of Barataria. It seems that the father of one of them, the former prince of Barataria, had handed his son over to a Venetian gondolier for safekeeping during a period of political strife and had never returned. The gondolier raised the prince's son as his own, teaching the boy his trade. Upon hearing the news, the two young gondoliers leave their jobs and their fiancées to take up their duties as corulers of Barataria. The co-princes learn that whichever one of them is the real prince has been engaged since birth to Casilda, who is in love with Luiz, a young man in the Baratarian court. So now one of the gondoliers is engaged to two women. But which one is he? Luiz' mother, who had been foster mother to the infant prince (and can therefore tell them apart), saves the day. She declares that her own son Luiz is the missing king of Barataria, allowing Casilda to marry him and the two gondoliers to return to Venice to marry their fiancées. The Gilbert and Sullivan score includes "Take Life as It Comes," "Bridegroom and Bride," and "We Act in Perfect Unity."

GREASE ★★★

MUSICAL. 1978. Cast: John Travolta, Olivia Newton-John, Stockard Channing, Jeff Conaway, Eve Arden, Sid Caesar, Didi Conn, and Sha Na Na. 110 min. Beta Hifi, VHS Stereo. Paramount ($29.95)

Based on the long-running Broadway musical, *Grease* had the biggest box office gross of any musical movie of all time with domestic rentals approaching $150 million. This shot of grease and poodle skirts from the past had the right ingredients: two attractive leads, some interesting if not spectacular music, and Randall Kleiser's vaseline-smeared vision of teen anxieties. It's as if every shot in the picture were planned according to a chart of pastel colors. Because it came first, before the spate of teen pictures, *Grease*'s calculated nostalgia isn't too offensive. There's plenty of good-natured humor to go around, especially with comic veterans like Sid Caesar and Eve Arden in the cast. Stockard Channing is appropriately bizarre as Rizzo, the leader of the Pink Ladies. Jeff Conaway (*Taxi*) is also fine as one of Travolta's buddies. But in the final analysis, it was the presence of John Travolta, as Danny Zucco (lots of Italians in this here Rydell High School back in 1959, eh?), which carried this film to box office heights. Olivia, as Sandy, an exchange student from Australia(?!), is pretty enough to be Travolta's romantic foil. The music includes Frankie Valli's "Grease," "Summer Nights," "I'm Sandra Dee," "Hopelessly Devoted to You," "You're the One That I Want," and "We Go Together." Sha Na Na appears and sings "Those Magic Changes,"

Olivia Newton-John and John Travolta in *Grease*.

"Born to Hand Jive," "Rock and Roll Is Here to Stay," "Tears on My Pillow," "Hound Dog," and "Blue Moon." Cindy Bullens and Frankie Avalon also contribute songs.

GREASE II ★⌐

MUSICAL. 1982. Cast: Maxwell Caufield, Michelle Pfeiffer, Adrian Zmed, Lorna Luft, Didi Conn, Eve Arden, Connie Stevens, Sid Caesar, Tab Hunter, Dody Goodman, and Liz and Jean Sagal. 115 min. Beta Hifi, VHS Stereo. Paramount ($62.95)

Patricia Birch, who had choreographed *Grease* among other movie musicals, received her first directorial assignment courtesy of producer Allan Carr in *Grease 2*, the ill-fated semisequel to the smash hit original. It is 1961 at Rydell High and the lead roles have been reversed—here, Maxwell Caufield plays an exchange student from England and Michelle Pfeiffer is the local girl who wants a "with it" boy, not some geek from overseas. Adrian Zmed, Romano on *T. J. Hooker,* plays Johnny Nogarelli,

Grease II.

the school hood, continually embattled by the principal, Eve Arden. In the end, which takes a long time to get to, Caufield and Pfeiffer get together. But by then, you'll probably be asleep. Birch seems a competent director. Let's hope she gets better material to work with next time. The cast sings "Charades," "Score Tonight," "Girl for All Seasons," "Rock-A-Hula Luau," "Prowlin'," "Brad," "Reproduction," "Cool Rider," "We'll Be Together," and "Do It for Our Country." The Four Tops can be heard singing "Back to School Again."

I DO! I DO! ★★

MUSICAL. 1983. Cast: Lee Remick and Hal Linden. 116 min. Beta, VHS. RKO ($39.95)

Videotaped at the Wilshire Theater in Beverly Hills, California, *I Do! I Do!*, the Harvey Schmidt-Tom Jones musical, covers 50 years of the marriage of Michael (Hal Linden), a writer, and Agnes (Lee Remick), his wife. The story begins just before the turn of the century and takes place within the confines of their bedroom. In this sometimes tedious celebration of a life together, Michael and Agnes sing songs that mark the different stages of their marriage. They get married and sing "I Do! I Do!" and "Together, Forever, Forever, Together." They mark the occasion of their wedding night with the songs "Goodnight, Goodnight" and "I Love My Wife." Agnes performs "My Cup Runneth Over with Love" when she finds out that she's pregnant. After their second child, Michael has an affair and sings "Nobody's Perfect." Agnes wants to sue for divorce and tells Michael so in "The Honeymoon Is Over." Some years later, their children get married. Michael pulls his hair out over the fact in "My Daughter's Marrying an Idiot." Agnes sings "Roll Up the Ribbons" as the two of them grow old together.

JESUS CHRIST, SUPERSTAR ★★✦

MUSICAL. 1973. Cast: Ted Neeley, Carl Anderson, Yvonne Elliman, Barry Dennen, and Joshua Mostel. 108 min. Beta Hifi, VHS Stereo. MCA ($59.95)

Jesus Christ, Superstar is the Andrew Lloyd Weber-Tim Rice rock opera version of the story of the Passion of Christ. Filmed on location in Israel, this mixture of scripture, minimalist sets, and rock music stars Ted Neeley as Jesus, Carl Anderson as Judas

Ted Neeley as Christ in *Jesus Christ, Superstar.*

Iscariot, Yvonne Elliman as Mary Magdalene, and Barry Dennen as Pontius Pilate. Although it tells the story of Jesus in a very innovative way, it might not be in keeping with everyone's religious beliefs. The music includes "I Don't Know How to Love Him," "Will You Mend Me Christ," "My Time Is Almost Through," and "The Great Jesus Christ."

KISMET ★★★

MUSICAL. 1956. Cast: Howard Keel, Vic Damone, Ann Blyth, Sebastian Cabot, Monty Wooley, and Dolores Gray. 111 min. Beta, VHS. MGM/UA ($69.95)

Vincente Minnelli directed this colorful musical fashioned from the folk imagery in *A Thousand and One Nights.* Based on the Broadway show by Charles Lederer and Luther Davis with music by Richard Wright and George Forrest, using the themes of romantic composer Alexander Borodin, this is a delightful mixed bag of pageantry and song. Howard Keel, as a clever con man in ancient Baghdad, and Ann Blyth, as his beautiful and loyal daughter, give excellent performances. Vic Damone makes a handsome vizir and Sebastian Cabot is appropriately conniving as the corrupt caliph who is plotting behind the vizir's back. Some of the production numbers include: Ann Blyth singing the standard "Baubles, Bangles, and Beads," Vic Damone singing "Stranger in Paradise" (Brian Aherne has informed a generation of TV watchers that the song is based on a theme by Borodin), Howard Keel singing "This Is My Beloved" and "Kismet," and Dolores Gray, as the caliph's wife, singing "Not Since Nineveh." A fail-safe entertainment that trades successfully on its use of color, delightful music, and charming performances.

LE BAL ★★↓

MUSICAL. 1982. Cast: Christophe Allwright, Aziz Arbia, Marc Berman, Regis Bouquet, Chantal Capron, and Martine Chauvin. 112 min. Beta, VHS. Warner ($59.95)

This musical without dialogue directed by Ettore Scola (*La Nuit de Varennes, A Special Day*) won the French equivalent of the Academy Award for best movie of the year, the Cesar. To American audiences it will seem little more than a cinematic curiosity since its treatment of modern French history in the setting of a dance hall will seem irrelevant. But to the French, Scola's vignettes about French society from 1936 to the present as told through the activities of dance hall patrons of each era were as affecting

Scene from *Le Bal*.

as Lucas' *American Graffitti* was to us. In succession, Scola shows us the dance hall: in the thirties; being used as a bomb shelter in the war; on liberation day in 1944; as a ballroom for big bands in the late forties; as a sock hop site for fifties rock and roll; used by protesters during the 1968 student revolt; and, finally, as a disco frequented by some typical singles. Music is played throughout and nary a word of dialogue is uttered. Among the tunes heard are "In the Mood," "Top Hat," "Harlem Nocturne," "La Vie en Rose," "Hernando's Hideaway," "Tutti Frutti" (sung by Cliff Richard), and the Beatles' "Michelle."

LILI ★★★

MUSICAL. 1953. Cast: Leslie Caron, Mel Ferrer, Jean Pierre Aumont, Zsa Zsa Gabor, and Kurt Kasznar. 81 min. Beta, VHS. MGM/UA

This dark and heavy postwar musical drama stars Leslie Caron in the title role as a naive French teenage orphan who latches onto a traveling Parisian carnival as the

Leslie Caron in the title role of *Lili*.

assistant of angry puppeteer Paul Berthalet (Mel Ferrer). Paul had been a great professional dancer before the war, but permanently injured his leg in battle. Lili falls in
love with Marc, the carnival's magician (Jean Pierre Aumont). Paul is secretly in love
with Lili and will declare his love only through his puppets during his performances.
At all other times, he treats her roughly. Lili discovers his true feelings for her only
after she finds that Marc is married to Rosalie (Zsa Zsa Gabor). Lili runs to Paul's
arms. They live happily ever after. The film's song, "Hi Lili, Hi Lo," by Bronislau
Kaper, won an Oscar.

MAME ★↲

*MUSICAL. 1974. Cast: Lucille Ball, Beatrice Arthur, Robert Preston, and Bruce Davidson.
131 min. Beta Hifi, VHS. Warner ($59.95)*

Director Gene Saks takes us on the episodic adventures of Mame Dennis (Lucille
Ball), known to everyone simply as Mame, a woman in love with life and always

ready to throw a party. Although the film remake of the Lawrence-Lee-Herman Broad-way smash is thin on plot, it does provide plenty of opportunity to showcase a number of memorable hit songs. The movie begins at the height of the roaring twenties. Mame's brother dies and leaves her custody of his 9-year-old boy, Patrick, who arrives at his Aunt Mame's house in New York City during one of her wild parties. Mame and her guests sing "It's Today" to welcome Patrick to his new home. Mame and Patrick visit restaurants, go to plays, and sample the variety that New York has to offer while performing "Open a New Window." The depression hits Mame with a wallop as she loses all of her money in the stock market crash. Not one to allow her spirits to be let down by a minor setback, she takes a variety of odd jobs and fails at each one, yet attracts the attention of Beauregard (Robert Preston), a rich southern gentleman who wants to marry Mame. She and Patrick celebrate their change of fortune with "We Need a Little Christmas." Mame and company travel south to meet Beauregard's family. At first, the family greet the northern intruder with icy glares, but Mame wows them with her fox-hunting abilities and is welcomed into the clan. Mame is celebrated in high southern style in the title tune, "Mame." Soon after their marriage, Beauregard dies in an avalanche. Patrick gets married, and has a son. Auntie Mame takes it upon herself to show him the world as she had shown the world to his father. "My Best Girl," "The Man in the Moon Is a Lady," and "If He Walked into My Life" are also included in the film.

MAN OF LA MANCHA   ★ᴶ

MUSICAL. 1972. Cast: Peter O'Toole, Sophia Loren, and James Coco. 130 min. Beta, VHS. CBS/Fox ($59.95)

Man of la Mancha is an adaptation of an actual event in the life of Miguel de Cervantes and chapters from his book *Don Quixote de la Mancha,* the masterpiece of the golden age of Spanish literature. Director Arthur Hiller and screenwriter Dale Wasserman take the musical far too seriously and fail to translate the slapstick buffoonery, wicked satire, and clever dialogue that has entertained the readers of Cervantes for four centuries. Taking their courage from the old Don Quixote himself, actors Peter O'Toole, as Cervantes and Don Quixote, Sophia Loren, as Dulcinea del Toboso, and James Coco, as Sancho, venture through the script, fighting plodding dialogue and singing lackluster songs. In the movie, Cervantes and his traveling troupe of players are thrown into a dark, dank dungeon by the Inquisition for presenting offensive plays and entertainments. Although we live under a system of government that guarantees us the right of free speech under the Constitution, perhaps we should revive some of the practices of the Inquisition for offensive artists such as the director and writer of *Man of la Mancha.* The musical gave birth to "The Impossible Dream," the hit song that launched the careers of a thousand lounge lizards. Unfortunately, the other songs in the musical's litter were stillborn. Worth passing up.

MY FAIR LADY ★★★★

MUSICAL. 1964. Cast: Rex Harrison, Audrey Hepburn, Stanley Holloway, and Theodore Bikel. 170 min. Beta, VHS. CBS/Fox ($89.95)

Film director George Cukor artfully brings the smash Broadway musical to the screen with Rex Harrison in his Oscar-winning role of Professor Henry Higgins and Audrey Hepburn as Eliza Doolittle. In Lerner and Loewe's careful adaptation of George Bernard Shaw's play *Pygmalion,* Professor Higgins, who is certain that the way a person speaks in England defines that person's class, bets his associate Colonel Pickering that he can transform a flower peddler, Eliza Doolittle, into a lady, complete with proper diction and manners, and can present her formally at a royal reception at the end of that time. So begins a rigorous 3 months of linguistic training. At the reception, Eliza is a hit. She convinces everyone that she is a Hungarian of royal extraction. Once the wager is won, Eliza becomes a girl with perfect diction but no skills. She opts to become Professor Higgins' assistant and to teach others how to speak properly. With set and costume design by photographer Cecil Beaton and choreography by Hermes Pan, *My Fair Lady* presents one of the best collections of melodies of any Broadway show from the sixties: "Why Can't the English?," "Wouldn't It Be Lovely," "A Little Bit of Luck," "Just You Wait Henry Higgins," "Poor Professor Higgins," "The Rain in Spain," "I Could Have Danced All Night," "On the Street Where You Live," "Get Me to the Church on Time," and "I've Grown Accustomed to Her Face."

NAUGHTY MARIETTA ★★★

MUSICAL. 1935. Cast: Jeanette MacDonald, Nelson Eddy, Frank Morgan, Elsa Lanchester, and Cecilia Parker. 106 min. Beta, VHS. MGM/UA ($59.95)

Seeing Jeanette MacDonald and Nelson Eddy in their first film together, *Naughty Marietta,* one gets a good idea of why they were such a popular box office duo. MacDonald's clear soprano and Eddy's bel canto tenor aside, it was their fabulous screen chemistry that endeared them to millions of moviegoers during the thirties and early forties. As in this film, Eddy's brash but charming personality was a perfect foil for MacDonald's coquettish appeal. Here, Nelson essays the role of a French army captain in Louisiana (before it was sold to the U.S.) who falls for a runaway princess named Marietta (Jeanette). Try to guess the way in which the two finally get together, overcoming

Nelson Eddy and Jeanette MacDonald in *Naughty Marietta*.

such obstacles as Marietta's intended, an ugly nobleman, and the captain's commanding officer, who wants Marietta for himself. The songs are based on Victor Herbert's music for the original operetta and include "Italian Street Song," "Ah, Sweet Mystery of Life," "Tramp, Tramp, Tramp," "Beneath the Southern Moon," and "I'm Falling in Love with Someone."

ON A CLEAR DAY YOU CAN SEE FOREVER ★★⌥

MUSICAL. 1970. Cast: Barbra Streisand, Yves Montand, Bob Newhart, Jack Nicholson, and Larry Blyden. 130 min. Beta, VHS. Paramount ($39.95)

This is an overlong musical from the camera of Vincente Minnelli, one of the last movies that he directed in an illustrious career. In the final analysis, this is the type

Yves Montand and Barbra Streisand in *On a Clear Day You Can See Forever.*

of movie musical that spelled the death of this subgenre. As production costs have spiraled upwards, the feasibility of making musical extravaganzas of this kind has plummeted. The music and lyrics by Alan Jay Lerner and Burton Lane, from their hit Broadway show, are pleasant enough but irrelevant to the tastes of today's audiences. As Minnelli well knew, a certain suspension of disbelief is required of the audience of any traditional musical. It wasn't until Hollywood came up with movies like *Fame, Flashdance,* and *Saturday Night Fever* that a viable and realistic form of the movie musical could be recovered. The story here is simple: Barbra is a college girl who goes to psychiatrist Yves Montand to stop smoking. Under hypnosis, she reveals a past life— that of Lady Melinda Tentrees in the England of the early nineteenth century. Montand believes he can make a case for reincarnation with Barbra as the proof positive but doesn't anticipate Barbra's falling in love with him. Jack Nicholson has a small role as a childhood sweetheart of Barbra's. The songs are: "On a Clear Day," "He Wasn't You," "There Once Was You," "Go to Sleep," "What Did I Have," and "Come Back to Me."

ONE FROM THE HEART ★★

MUSICAL. 1982. Cast: Teri Garr, Raul Julia, Nastassia Kinski, Frederic Forrest, Lainie Kazan, and Harry Dean Stanton. 100 min. Beta Hifi, VHS Stereo. RCA/Columbia ($79.95)

It's puzzling to see a man who could be so right, so on target, in *The Godfather* be so wrong on *One from the Heart.* This lavish musical romance set in a surreal, fantasy Las Vegas is visually striking but dramatically pointless. Technically, the production made some news; it was the first in which video hardware was used extensively to complement the shooting of a major studio feature film. Many of the chromatic and special effects (making the back-lot Las Vegas look even more unreal than it is) would not have been possible without video technology. That aside, there is a gaping void in this film—there's no story! Garr, Forrest, Kinski, and Julia are mired in a farrago of misunder-

Dream sequence from Francis Ford Coppola's *One from the Heart.*

standings and unrequited love. The viewer could care less. The music, provided by Tom Waits and Crystal Gayle, is supposed to be boozy and worldly; it's barely intelligible and not helped by the fact that Coppola buries it deep in the soundtrack (perhaps he was disappointed in the songs that Waits came up with after thinking it would be such a great idea to have him score it). Just another piece in the growing puzzle that is Francis Ford Coppola.

ON THE TOWN   ★★★

MUSICAL. 1949. Cast: Gene Kelly, Frank Sinatra, Betty Garrett, Ann Miller, Jules Munshin, and Vera-Ellen. 98 min. Beta, VHS. MGM/UA ($59.95)

Three sailors, Gene Kelly, Jules Munshin, and Frank Sinatra, are given 24 hours shore leave in New York City, where they expect to see the sights and get some kicks,

Alice Pearce, Sinatra, Garrett, Kelly, Miller, and Munshin in *On the Town*.

FRANK SINATRA

Born on December 12, 1915, in Hoboken, New Jersey, Frank Sinatra is perhaps the greatest male pop singer who ever lived. He has crossed over into every entertainment field that exists and been successful. Sinatra gained his earliest fame as a teen idol band singer in the early forties, making girls swoon in the aisles of theaters like New York's Paramount. "All or Nothing at All" was Frank's first big seller, totaling over a million copies upon its re-release in 1943. Throughout the forties, while working as front man for the Harry James and then the Tommy Dorsey band, Sinatra scored Top 10 hits and developed his unique vocal phrasing, basing it on Dorsey's trombone style.

In the fifties, Sinatra branched out into films, starring in *From Here to Eternity, Guys and Dolls,* and *The Man with the Golden Arm.* The classic Sinatra, boozy saloon songs about adult relationships and life's hard knocks, can be found on his sides recorded for Capitol Records starting in 1953. The image of Frank with his raincoat draped over one shoulder and a fedora cocked rakishly to one side of his head dates from this period of collaboration with big-band arranger Nelson Riddle.

The sixties saw Frank spending time with a group of buddies affectionately called The Rat Pack (including Dean Martin, Sammy Davis, Jr., and Joey Bishop) in Las Vegas and making a comeback of sorts on the pop charts with "Strangers in the Night," "That's Life," and "My Way." After retiring and unretiring several times during the seventies, "Ol' Blue Eyes" is back to stay, busier now than ever before. His problems with the press aside, he is the most respected international pop music performer of our time.

Video Resume

Can-Can, (1960), CBS/Fox.

Guys and Dolls, (1955), CBS/Fox.

Higher and Higher, (1943), Blackhawk.

On the Town, (1949), MGM/UA.

Step Lively, (1944), Blackhawk.

That's Entertainment, I and II, (1974, 1976), MGM/UA.

Till the Clouds Roll By, (1946), MGM/UA.

Young at Heart, (1954), Republic.

and hope to find true love. They do all three when they meet up with model Vera-Ellen, cab driver Betty Garrett, and scientist and tap dancer extraordinaire Ann Miller. Directors Kelly and Stanley Donen filmed part of the musical on location in New York, shooting such wonderful Leonard Bernstein, Adolf Green, and Betty Comden tunes as "New York, New York" at the base of the Statue of Liberty. Also included in the score were "Come Up to My Place," "You Can Count on Me," and the title tune, "On the Town." A real treat!

PAINT YOUR WAGON   ★★✦

MUSICAL. 1970. Cast: Lee Marvin, Clint Eastwood, Jean Seberg, Ray Walston, Harve Presnell, and The Nitty Gritty Dirt Band. 164 min. Beta, VHS Stereo. Paramount ($72.95)

The star of *Dirty Harry,* Clint Eastwood, and the star of *The Dirty Dozen,* Lee Marvin, team up to star in the muddy movie musical about the old west, *Paint Your Wagon.* In an extreme version of the Lerner and Loewe plot formula in which a beautiful woman is torn between the loves of two men (see *Camelot* and *My Fair Lady*), Elizabeth (Jean Seberg), the only woman for miles around, is bought at auction and "shared"

Clint Eastwood and Lee Marvin in *Paint Your Wagon.*

by two gold prospectors, Ben (Lee Marvin) and Pardner (Clint Eastwood), in the frontier town of No Name City, California. Lee, Clint, and Jean do their best to sing "The First Thing You Know," "When I Think of Love," and "I Still See Elisa," but their real talents are for acting, and they give firm dramatic support to the comedy of the film. Ben decides to make the camp of No Name City a respectable boom town by hijacking a stagecoach full of prostitutes and bringing them to camp to set up business. The prospectors in the region follow with their bags of gold dust to spend; they find what is soon a town crammed with hotels, saloons, gambling halls, and bordellos. Ben then hatches a plan to recover the gold dust that has fallen between the floor boards of all the buildings in town. Ben, Pardner, and their associates dig tunnels under the town's structures. After they have collected all the spare gold dust, the ground under No Name City is honeycombed. In the film's climactic finish, No Name City and its brand of frontier civilization literally collapse. The Nitty Gritty Dirt Band performs "Good Times Are Here." Harve Presnell and chorus sing "They Call the Wind Mariah."

PERILS OF PAULINE ★★★

MUSICAL. 1947. Cast: Betty Hutton, John Lund, Billy De Wolfe, and William Demarest. 96 min. Beta, VHS. Media ($29.95)

With Betty Hutton in the leading role of Pearl White, the silent film actress who starred in the *Perils of Pauline* serials, this musical is full of pep and quite entertaining. It takes a lot of liberties with the facts, but, in the end, director George Marshall is justified in his revisionism. John Lund, as Michael Farrington, Pearl's true love, cuts quite a dashing figure as the "serious" actor who lowers himself to appear in films. And Billy De Wolfe and William Demarest are very funny in supporting roles. The songs by Frank Loesser include "The Sewing Machine," "Rumble," "As Long as This," and "Papa, Don't Preach to Me." Hutton's later personal life was rather tragic, but in her musicals of the forties, she was an infectiously sunny performer.

PIAF ★★

MUSICAL. 1981. Cast: Jane Lapotaire, Zoe Wanamaker, Peter Friedman, and Nicholas Woodeson. 114 min. Beta, VHS. CBS/Fox ($69.95)

Pam Gems' episodic play portrays the difficult life of internationally famous French pop singer Edith Piaf in a series of vignettes that depicts Piaf's miserable childhood as a street urchin in Paris, her rise to fame, her failed love affairs, her numerous self-destructive car accidents, and her bouts with alcoholism and drug addiction. Jane

Lapotaire, in a performance that won her a Tony Award in 1981, portrays Piaf as a streetwise yet sensitive chanteuse who could move an audience to tears with her bitter-sweet ballads. Lapotaire translates Piaf's lower class French accent into a Cockney one, giving an excellent portrayal of Piaf's sometimes coarse personality. Lapotaire's imitation of Piaf's singing can at best only be an approximation. Piaf's ability to touch an audience regardless of its nationality only can be grasped by listening to records of the late singing star. Lapotaire sings eleven Piaf songs including "L'Accordioniste," "La Belle Histoire d'Amour," "Deep in the Heart of Texas," "La Ville Inconnue Mon Dieu," "Les Trois Cloches," "Non, Je Ne Regrette Rien," "Bravo Pour le Clown," "La Goulante du Pauvre Jean," "La Vie en Rose," "Hymne a l'Amour," and "A Quoi Ça Cert l'Amour."

PIPPIN ★★

MUSICAL. 1981. Cast: William Katt, Ben Vereen, Chita Rivera, and Martha Raye. 120 min. Beta, VHS. FHE ($69.95)

Taped at the Hamilton Palace Theater in Hamilton, Ontario, *Pippin,* the musical that was one of director and choreographer Bob Fosse's first hits on Broadway in the early seventies, tells the story of the son and heir apparent of Charlemagne, the ninth-century Carolingian king and Holy Roman Emperor. Pippin, a student at the University of Padua (played by William Katt (*The Greatest American Hero*)), is not unlike the disillu-sioned youth who occupied campuses across America during the period of the musical's creation. He hasn't "found himself," yet has decided he wants to change the world for the better. For lack of anything to do, he becomes involved in court intrigue, then becomes tired of politics and rejects his royal inheritance. After more aimless drifting, Pippin reluctantly settles down and gets married. The character's innocence, mixed with what would become Fosse's well-worn trademark, tawdry stage sensuality and self-conscious cynicism, make *Pippin* a thought-provoking night of theater. One must ask oneself: why would anyone shell out $35 for a ticket to such a depressing musical? Fosse regular Ben Vereen stars as the Leading Player. Benjamin Rayson plays Charlemagne. Chita Rivera stars as Charlemagne's wife, Fastrada. Martha Raye makes a special appearance as Berthe.

THE PIRATE ★★★♪

MUSICAL. 1948. Cast: Judy Garland, Gene Kelly, Walter Slezak, and the Nicholas Brothers. 102 min. Beta, VHS. MGM/UA ($69.95)

Critical concensus on this Vincente Minnelli musical gives it the nod as best movie musical ever made. Most of those critics are undoubtedly Judy Garland fans. While this film has its charms—an exotic setting (the Caribbean), the song "Be a Clown," and the dancing prowess of Gene Kelly and the amazing Nicholas Brothers—the intentionally artificial look given to it by Minnelli continues to erode its effectiveness as the years pass. Despite the surreal, bathed-in-red ballet sequence featuring Gene as the pirate, the Black Macoco, most of this film is too obviously soundstage-bound. This lack of production values really foils Minnelli, whose intent was to make a fantasy escape with campy aspects. The plot, involving Gene Kelly's attempt to masquerade as the dreaded Mack the Black in order to win the love of Judy Garland, is played for laughs by the cast, with winks at the audience. Judy Garland, as usual, is a spunky young woman with a romantic dream. The realization of her dream takes up the bulk of the movie as Gene and Judy overcome obstacles to their union. The songs, not the best Cole Porter had ever written (see his *Silk Stockings*), include "Be a Clown," "Niña," "Mack the Black," "You Can Do No Wrong," "Love of My Life," and others.

THE PIRATE MOVIE ★♪

MUSICAL. 1982. Cast: Kristy McNichol, Christopher Atkins, and Ted Hamilton. 98 min. Beta Hifi, VHS Stereo. CBS/Fox ($59.95)

Sir William Schwenck Gilbert and Sir Arthur Sullivan would most certainly turn over in their graves if they could somehow be told of the existence of this "tribute" to their masterwork, *The Pirates of Penzance.* A mixture of six songs from the original operetta and a number of silly, sugary tunes written with today's bubblegum-music audience in mind, this film fails as a musical, as a love story, as a "sexy" farce filled with bad double entendres, as an adventure film, as a comedy, etc., etc. Filmed entirely in Australia, *The Pirate Movie,* which is set in what looks like a contemporary California suburb, tells the tale of Mabel, played by American Kristy McNichol (*Family*), a girl too shy to participate in the "grown-up" activities of her girlfriends. As her friends sail away in a Puffin sailboat with their heartthrob, Frederick, who is played by American Christopher Atkins (*Blue Lagoon*), Mabel pursues them in a dinghy, is washed up on the shore of an uncharted isle, falls asleep, and dreams that she and Frederick have been transported back to the time of sea piracy. They become *the* Mabel and *the* Frederick of the Gilbert and Sullivan operetta and are soon in a rather warped version of *The Pirates of Penzance.* Mabel is captured by the pirates. She is rescued by Frederick. She's recaptured. She's rescued. She's recaptured. The audience falls asleep and dreams it is somewhere else. Songs include "I'm the Very Model of a Modern Major-General," "The Policeman's Lot," "With Cat-Like Tread," all from the operetta, and "Happy Ending" and "Stand Up and Sing," performed by Kool and the Gang. Ted Hamilton plays the Pirate King.

THE PIRATES OF PENZANCE ★★★

MUSICAL. 1983. Cast: Linda Ronstadt, Angela Lansbury, Kevin Kline, George Rose, Rex Smith, and Tony Azito. 112 min. Beta Hifi, VHS. MCA ($69.95)

Linda Ronstadt, who could easily be dubbed the queen of seventies pop rock, ventured out of the contemporary pop field in the eighties to record a Number 1 album of forties standards with veteran arranger-conductor Nelson Riddle. The album, *What's New?*, which sold over two million copies, led Linda to star as Mimi in Joseph Papp's English-language version of Giacomo Puccini's *La Bohème.* Although she received only a "nice try award" for each of the former ventures, she was greeted with applause for her portrayal of Mabel in Joseph Papp's stage and film productions of Gilbert and Sullivan's *The Pirates of Penzance.* Ronstadt brought a certain amount of sweetness to the role of Mabel, bringing the character to life with the voice that had skillfully handled so many changes in the past. She plays opposite Rex Smith's self-conscious portrayal of the innocent Frederick and Kevin Kline's Pirate King, played for laughs with campy dastardliness. Angela Lansbury takes the part of Frederick's not so innocent nursemaid, Ruth. Kline really carries the show and creates a *Pirates of Penzance* that is far better than the run of the mill production. Linda Ronstadt sings Mabel's solo, "Poor Wanderin' One." The rest of the cast performs "I'm the Very Model of a Modern Major-General," "With Cat-Like Tread," "The Policeman's Lot," and "The Pirate King."

THE PRODUCERS ★★★♪

MUSICAL. 1968. Cast: Zero Mostel, Gene Wilder, Kenneth Mars, Dick Shawn, Lee Meredith, and Estelle Winwood. 88 min. Beta, VHS. Embassy ($79.95)

The man who would come to stand for a school of comic cinema made his feature film directorial debut with *The Producers,* a brilliant, wacky satire on show business greed that verges on the tasteless. Mel Brooks perfected his eclectic, hellzapoppin' style in *Blazing Saddles* some years later, but this first effort, which garnered a best screenplay Oscar for Brooks, is already full of the absurdity—born of a thousand old vaudeville and burlesque routines—that would continue to mark his work. With Zero Mostel in the lead role of Max Bialystock, a conniving Broadway producer, and Gene Wilder as Leo Bloom, the trusting simp who falls in with Max's plan to bilk backers of a bogus production, *Springtime for Hitler,* to the tune of a million dollars, *The Producers* is a riotous, if very cynical, look at basic human nature. Some hilarious performances are contributed by Kenneth Mars, as the ex-Nazi playwright whose work Max and Leo are sure will offend theatergoers, Dick Shawn, as LSD, who is so incongruous as Hitler in the play that audiences make the show a hit, and Lee Meredith, as Max's bosomy Swedish secretary. Mel Brooks also wrote the songs: "Love Power," sung by LSD in Dick Shawn's outrageous parody of Jim Morrison, "We're Prisoners of Love," and "Springtime for Hitler." This is a comic trip!

THE ROAD TO BALI ★★♪

MUSICAL. 1952. Cast: Bob Hope, Bing Crosby, and Dorothy Lamour. 90 min. Beta, VHS. Unicorn ($49.95)

The next to last Road picture for Hope and Crosby, this pale little entertainment relies heavily on the duo's vaunted vaudeville banter. Dorothy Lamour is also along for the ride, playing a Polynesian princess. What else? There are seven songs in all, written by Johnny Burke and James Van Heusen, including "To See You Is to Love You," "Merry Go Runaround," and "Moonflowers." As for the plot, it is a farrago about two vaudevillians (Hope and Crosby) stranded in Australia who get mixed up with a south seas princess and her sunken treasure. Misunderstandings with rival island tribes place Hope and Crosby squarely in the middle of a power struggle. Both vie for the hand of the princess and almost get thrown into a live volcano for their troubles. Hope is very funny, as usual, and his repartee with Crosby is still delightful to hear. However, viewers will have to wait until the other Road pictures are released on home video to see the duo at their hilarious best.

THE ROAD TO LEBANON ★

MUSICAL. 1964. Cast: Danny Thomas, Bing Crosby, Claudine Auger, Hugh Downs, and Sheldon Leonard. 50 min. Beta, VHS. Video Yesteryear ($39.95)

Originally broadcast on NBC-TV in April of 1964, this Danny Thomas special falls flat on its face trying to do a send-up of the old Hope-Crosby pictures. Danny plays himself and receives an offer from Bing to replace Bob Hope in a Road picture entitled *The Road to Lebanon.* Complications occur when a distant Arab relative of Danny's, a tribal chieftain, decides to exact revenge against him for some supposed transgression against his own people (a nose job). The chieftain's daughter, played by Claudine Auger, is given the task of bringing Danny to her father's tent for appropriate retribution. Bing sings "The Road to Lebanon," Danny sings "O Moon," Bing and Claudine duet on "I Enjoy Being a Girl," and Danny and Bing sing "Together." Terrible stuff!

ROYAL WEDDING ★★★

MUSICAL. 1951. Cast: Fred Astaire, Jane Powell, Peter Lawford, Sarah Churchill, and Keenan Wynn. 93 min. Beta, VHS. MGM/UA ($59.95)

In *Royal Wedding*, Fred Astaire and Jane Powell star as a Broadway brother and sister dance team, Tom and Ellen Bowen. They travel to London to play the Mayfair Theatre. On their arrival in England, they both fall in love. Tom falls for Anne Ashmond (Sarah Churchill). Ellen falls for Lord John Brindale (Peter Lawford). The four of them decide to get married in a dual ceremony on the day of the royal wedding. Although *Royal Wedding* might not feature Fred Astaire's most technically brilliant dancing, it does display his most imaginative. Astaire always brought the best out in his dance partners. In one well-known scene, while making the Atlantic Ocean crossing on ship, Fred dances with a coatrack during a dance rehearsal and makes the coatrack look good. Fred and Jane dance for an audience of passengers on a floor that pitches and yaws as the ocean liner hits rough seas. In the best scene in the movie, some of the most famous feet of celluloid in movie history, Fred sings "You're All the World to Me" and dances on the walls, the ceiling, and the floor! Amazing.

SCRAMBLED FEET ★♪

MUSICAL. 1982. Cast: Madeline Kahn, John Driver, Jeffery Haddow, and Roger Neil. 100 min. Beta, VHS. RKO ($39.95)

There are two popular theories about the current demise of Broadway: (1) that the talent reserve that, in the past, was tapped by Broadway has gone to the more lucrative fields of pop recording, television, and movies, or (2) that the audience's tastes have been so transformed by TV that it won't sit still through the average stage show, nonstop, without commercials and familiar faces. Whatever the reasons, it's clear that the concerns of most Broadway and off-Broadway productions are not shared by a mass audience, the kind that could reduce the alarming number of darkened houses on Broadway. *Scrambled Feet* is a taping of the successful off-Broadway revue that lampoons current stage hits and the theater in general, with songs written by its costars, John Driver and Jeffery Haddow. Madeline Kahn, though not given much to do, is the best thing about this snore-fest about life on the boards. There are skits on curtain-call milking, Carol Channing sing-a-likes, and avant-garde plays. Also a musical based on Attila the Hun's life, a possessive answering machine, the art of sham dancing, and Elizabethan dinner theater. Songs, basically in the Manilow/Sager/Allen mold, include "Making the Rounds," "Brittania Rules the Boards," "Love in the Wings," "Good Connections," "Child Star," and "Theater Party Ladies."

SEVEN BRIDES FOR SEVEN BROTHERS   ★★★

MUSICAL. 1954. Cast: Jane Powell, Howard Keel, Russ Tamblyn, Julie Newmar, and Jacques D'Amboise. 103 min. Beta, VHS. MGM/UA ($59.95)

Another of those eccentric movie musicals churned out by Hollywood in the forties and early fifties, this Stanley Donen film has lots of dancing and lots of clapboard sets. It has no story to speak of, and the central relationship between Howard Keel, as Adam Pontipée, a trapper with six younger brothers, and Jane Powell as Millie, the woman who agrees to marry him for no apparent reason, is beyond belief in its inanity. The plot line is based on Stephen Vincent Benét's reworking of the rape of the Sabine women, "Sobbing Women," and there's a lot more satire going on here than Donen and his cast will let on. After all, what would possess six young women to marry the Pontipee brothers after they've been kidnapped from their homes? Things are tough in the great northwest but not that tough. This film certainly adheres to the theory that love is strange. The songs by Johnny Mercer and Gene De Paul are largely undistinguished ("She's the Gal for Me," "Wonderful Day," "When You're in Love," "Goin' Courtin'," "Lonesome Polecat," "Sobbin' Women," "June Bride," and "Spring, Spring, Spring"), but the acrobatic ensemble dancing, choreographed by Michael Kidd, does feature Russ Tamblyn and Jacques D'Amboise. A fun curiosity for those who don't take their musicals seriously.

1776   ★★♪

MUSICAL. 1972. Cast: William Daniels, Howard Da Silva, Ken Howard, Donald Madden, John Cullum, Roy Poole, David Ford, Ron Holgate, Ray Middleton, William Hansen, Blythe Danner, and Virginia Vestoff. 141 min. Beta, VHS Stereo. RCA/Columbia ($59.95)

Most of the original Broadway cast can be found in this film version of the award-winning Sherman Adams-Peter Stone musical about the Continental Congress and the other events leading up to the Declaration of Independence and America's break with the British crown. All of the legendary historical figures are brought to life as legal technicalities and the logistical problems of waging war against England are discussed, and the political infighting between the individual colonies portrayed. William Daniels creates the role of the tough puritan from New England, John Adams. Howard Da Silva conjures up the witty and practical Benjamin Franklin. Ken Howard plays the young and brilliant Thomas Jefferson, who pines for his young bride (Blythe Danner). The suspense builds as the delegates to the congress revise each draft of the declaration until the climactic and historic signing of the document. Songs include "Sit Down, John," "The Lees of Virginia," "He Plays the Violin," and "Molasses to Rum."

SHOWBIZ BALLYHOO ★★✦

MUSICAL. 1982. Cast: David Steinberg, Milton Berle, Humphrey Bogart, James Cagney, Gary Cooper, Bing Crosby, Bette Davis, Errol Flynn, and others. 78 min. Beta, VHS. U.S.A. ($59.95)

David Steinberg hosts this cable-TV special examining the Hollywood publicity machinery of the golden age of movies, with glimpses of two dozen or more stars in everything from public service spots, bloopers, home movies, and film interviews to early commercials. Shirley Temple in a Red Cross pitch, Judy Garland and Mickey Rooney in a March of Dimes PSA, the premieres of *Hell's Angels* and *Gone with the Wind,* Dick Powell stumping for the New Deal, and bloopers from Bogie, Errol Flynn, Bette Davis, Cagney, and Ronald Reagan. Some of the musical numbers heard are "Love Me Tonight" (Jeanette MacDonald), "I Got Rhythm" (George Gershwin), "Falling in Love Again" (Marlene Dietrich), "Louise" (Maurice Chevalier), and "Here's Looking at You" (Milton Berle). Directed and produced by Norman Sedawie and Gayle Gibson Sedawie.

SHOW BOAT ★★✦

MUSICAL. 1951. Cast: Kathryn Grayson, Howard Keel, Ava Gardner, Joe E. Brown, Agnes Moorehead, Marge and Gower Champion, and William Warfield. 115 min. Beta, VHS. MGM/UA ($59.95)

For those of you who have heard the original Broadway cast recording of *Show Boat* with Paul Robeson in the role of Joe and Helen Morgan as Julie, or have seen the James Whale film version from 1936, this version, directed by George Sidney, will be very disappointing. Jerome Kern's classic of the American stage receives a rather uninspired mounting, hampered by the strangest choice of actors you'll see for a musical of this magnitude. Howard Keel does well enough in the role of Gaylord Ravenal, the riverboat gambler who has to change his ways to win the heart of Magnolia Hawks (Kathryn Grayson), the daughter of a show boat captain. But Ava Gardner as the sultry but world-weary Julie is bad casting. And the film is almost a crawl at the 115-minute length. There are still the great Jerome Kern songs, though: "Make Believe," "Can't Help Loving Dat Man," "Ol' Man River," "You Are Love," "My Man Bill," "Life upon the Wicked Stage," and "After the Ball."

SILK STOCKINGS   ★★★✦

MUSICAL. 1957. Cast: Fred Astaire, Cyd Charisse, Janis Paige, George Tobias, Peter Lorre, Jules Munshin, Joseph Buloff, and Wim Sonneveld. 117 min. Beta, VHS. MGM/ UA ($69.95)

Ernst Lubitsch's 1939 light comedy film classic, *Ninotchka,* was made into a Cole Porter Broadway musical that itself was made into a movie. The wonderful 1957 remake, *Silk Stockings,* stars Fred Astaire in the male lead, this time as an American film producer by the name of Steve Canfield, and Cyd Charisse as the dour representative of the Soviet government, Ninotchka Yashenko, who is sent to Paris to retrieve Vasiliev Markovitch (George Tobias), a Russian composer, contracted by Canfield to score his next picture. Steve has already bought off three commissars sent earlier from Moscow, Ivanov (Joseph Buloff), Boroff (Wim Sonneveld), and Bibinski (Peter Lorre), with wine, women, and song. Steve falls in love with Ninotchka. Ninotchka warms to Steve's advances, but breaks up with him and leaves Paris with Markovitch, Ivanov, Boroff, and Bibinski when she learns that the music Markovitch had written to celebrate the accomplishments of the proletariat and the Soviet farmer is now being used in a leggy production number, "Josephine," starring film idol Peggy Dayton (Janis Paige). After returning to Moscow, Ninotchka realises that she is in love with Steve regardless of his politics. Luckily, the Politburo again sends her back to Paris to repatriate Ivanov, Boroff, and Bibinski, who have opened a restaurant, "La Vielle Russie," in town. Ninotchka is shocked to see Steve in top hat and tails on stage singing Cole Porter's answer to Elvis Presley, "The Ritz Rock and Roll." Ninotchka falls into Steve's arms and the world is a little better off for it. Cole Porter also wrote "Siberia," "Silk Stock-ings," "The Red Blues," "Fated to Be Mated," "Stereophonic Sound," "All of You," "Satin and Silk," and "Hail Bibinski."

SINGIN' IN THE RAIN   ★★★★

MUSICAL. 1952. Cast: Gene Kelly, Debbie Reynolds, Donald O'Connor, Jean Hagen, Cyd Charisse, and Rita Moreno. 103 min. Beta, VHS. MGM/UA ($59.95)

One of the best musicals ever made in Hollywood. In this delightful mix of satire and nostalgia, Gene Kelly and Debbie Reynolds play lovers and dance partners in the early days of the talkies. When Kelly gets Debbie, an unknown chorine, to overdub silent starlet Jean Hagen's Brooklynese honk of a voice, the audience at the movie's premiere discovers this, makes Debbie the silver screen's new shooting star, and dumps poor Jean. A comic treatment of what, unfortunately, really did happen to many silent stars whose voices were their downfall when the era of talkies arrived. A lot of fun along the way, as songs written originally for classic thirties musicals by Herb Nacio Brown and Arthur Freed weave in and out of the narrative. Some highlights are: Gene Kelly's inspired production number, "Singing in the Rain," in which he cavorts in the pouring rain on a sidewalk set; the 17-minute "Make 'em Laugh"; and Kelly and Debbie together on an empty soundstage in "You Were Meant for Me." Simply superior entertainment. Directed by Kelly and Stanley Donen.

SOUTH PACIFIC   ★★★♪

MUSICAL. 1958. Cast: Mitzi Gaynor, Rossano Brazzi, Ray Walston, John Kerr, Juanita Hall, France Nyen, and Ken Clark. 150 min. Beta, VHS. CBS/Fox ($69.95)

Filmed on location in Hawaii, Rodgers and Hammerstein's *South Pacific* tells the story of two pairs of lovers caught in the midst of the strife of the Pacific theater during World War II. American nurse Nellie Forbush (Mitzi Gaynor) is in love with French plantation owner Emile DeBeque (Rossano Brazzi), but breaks off their engagement when she discovers he has two children from a previous marriage to a Polynesian woman. Lt. Cable (John Kerr) falls in love with a Tokinese girl, Liat (France Nyen), but refuses to marry her because she's not white. DeBeque and Cable volunteer for a suicide reconnaissance mission on a nearby Japanese-held island. Their mission is a success, changing the tide of the war in that section of the Pacific, but Lt. Cable dies in action. Upon Emile's return, nurse Forbush realizes her love for him is stronger than her devotion to her parents' social mores and marries the French planter to live happily ever after in the south Pacific. The film contains a number of wonderful songs including "Some Enchanted Evening," "Younger Than Springtime," "Bali H'Ai," "There Is Nothing Like a Dame," "Honey Bun," and "Happy Talk."

A STAR IS BORN, 1954 (Original) ★★★↓

MUSICAL. 1954. Cast: Judy Garland, James Mason, Jack Carson, Charles Bickford, and Tommy Noonan. 150 min. Beta, VHS. Warner ($59.95)

After a 4-year absence from the screen, Judy Garland returned to star as Esther Blodgette, an unknown big-band singer who makes it to the top in this realistic musical drama. James Mason rewards the audience with a portrait of a complex, generous, but alcoholic and self-destructive Hollywood movie star, Norman Maine. A very drunk yet very perceptive Maine notices Esther performing at a charity show. He tracks her down at a closed after-hours club, and his hunch that she is extremely talented is confirmed when he hears her sing the heart-stopping "The Man That Got Away." Maine is convinced she must be put in the movies. In his excitement, he offers her a screen test, completely forgetting that he will leave at dawn for 6 weeks of on-location shooting at sea. Eager to succeed, Esther quits her job with the band and the next day finds herself stranded in Los Angeles for the 6 weeks of shooting. However, Maine returns, tracks Esther down again, and gets her the screen test he promised. Her star begins to rise. Esther, now known to film audiences as Vicki Lester, carves her place

James Mason and Judy Garland in *A Star Is Born.*

in the firmament in her first film in a production number tracing her rise to stardom. In a beautifully staged medley, Esther sings "Swanee," "Born in a Trunk," the Academy Award-nominated Arlen-Gershwin tune written for the movie, "You Took Advantage of Me" "Black Bottom," "The Peanut Vendor," and "It's a New World." Vicki is a hit! She and Norman get married and buy a beach house as their new love nest. As Vicki's star rises, Norman's is on the decline. He loses his contract and is forced to sit at home while Vicki goes to work at the studio. The former movie idol starts drinking heavily. Vicki tries to comfort him by recreating her newest studio number, "Somewhere There Is a Someone" in their living room. Norman's condition becomes worse. He embarrasses his wife during the Academy Awards ceremony by walking on stage during her acceptance speech. He is arrested for driving while intoxicated. In his last act of desperation, he swims out into the Pacific to commit suicide. A sobering look at Hollywood Babylon.

A STAR IS BORN, 1954 (Restored)   ★★★

MUSICAL. 1954. Cast: Judy Garland, James Mason, Jack Carson, Charles Bickford, and Tommy Noonan. 176 min. Beta Hifi, VHS Stereo. Warner ($69.95)

When *A Star Is Born* premiered at Hollywood's Pantages Theater on September 29, 1954, it ran 181 minutes, and was considered to be too long by exhibitors. Warner Brothers cut out 27 minutes of the film. It was assumed for years that this footage was lost until Ronald Haver, the head of the film department of the Los Angeles County Museum, and his staff painstakingly searched for the missing sections of film and replaced them to recreate the original premiere version. Some scenes are lost forever; sepia-tone publicity stills that were taken on the set of *A Star Is Born* during production have been substituted. These still images, when placed between two pieces of live-action color film, jolt the audience and ultimately do not advance the story at all. The benefit of the restoration is the inclusion of two "lost" production numbers starring Judy Garland, "Here's What I'm Here For" and "Lose That Long Face." As the original version tells the story, the restored version emphasizes the music.

STAYING ALIVE   ★★♪

MUSICAL. 1983. Cast: John Travolta, Cynthia Rhodes, and Finola Hughes. 110 min. Beta Hifi, VHS Stereo. Paramount ($39.95)

It is 6 years later and Tony Manero, the Brooklyn boy who can disco dance with the best of them in *Saturday Night Fever,* is trying to make it on Broadway. John Travolta,

John Travolta in *Staying Alive*.

so electric in the original, returns to recreate his role, but this time, under the direction of Sylvester Stallone, the excitement is gone. The Bee Gees also scored this film, although the only hit record to come out of the movie was Frank Stallone's "Far from Over." With a story that smacks of *Fame* and *Flashdance* (another account of an ambitious dancer's rise to the top), Travolta has little to do except strut around in leotards and try to make time with both Cynthia Rhodes and Finola Hughes. The finale is a production number from *Satan's Alley,* the Broadway show that Tony wins a leading role in. It looks like a Bob Fosse extravaganza from *All That Jazz.* The Bee Gees sing "The Woman in You," "I Love You Too Much," "Breakout," "Someone Belonging to Someone," "Life Goes On," and "Staying Alive." Frank Stallone sings "Far from Over," "Hope We Never Change" (with Cynthia Rhodes), "Waking Up" (again with Rhodes), and "Moody Girl."

TAKE IT BIG   ★★

MUSICAL. 1943. Cast: Jack Haley, Harriet Hilliard, Mary Beth Hughes, Ozzie Nelson and his Orchestra. 75 min. Beta, VHS. Video Yesteryear ($49.95)

A black and white musical from the war years that stars Jack Haley, the Tin Woodsman in *Wizard of Oz,* and Ozzie and Harriet, of television sitcom fame. The movie is divided roughly into two halves, the first half dealing with Haley's attempts to cure his insomnia by consulting a psychiatrist, the second half dealing with his problems in trying to rehabilitate a dude ranch in Nevada that his late uncle bequeaths to him. The musical numbers, some written by Lester Lee and Jerry Seelen and some by Johnny Burke and Jimmy Van Heusen, are a pedestrian lot. "Life Can Be a Beautiful Thing," "Love and Learn," "Uncle Willy Was a Dilly," "I'm a Big Success with You," and "Sunday, Monday, and Always" feature the singing of Haley and Harriet Hilliard Nelson and are backed by Ozzie Nelson's big band. Could be fairly entertaining, wholly depending on how much you like Haley's nonchalant charm.

THAT'S ENTERTAINMENT   ★★★★

MUSICAL. 1974. Cast: Fred Astaire, Bing Crosby, Gene Kelly, Peter Lawford, Liza Minnelli, Donald O'Connor, Debbie Reynolds, Mickey Rooney, Frank Sinatra, James Stewart, Elizabeth Taylor, and over one hundred and twenty other stars. 121 min. Beta, VHS. MGM/UA ($59.95)

On the fiftieth anniversary of the founding of Metro-Goldwyn-Mayer, during the closings of the production facilities and soundstages of the major Hollywood studios, the executives at MGM decided to search their vaults for film clips and put together a salute to the studio's golden age, a film that would celebrate MGM's contribution to America—the movie musical. The resulting compilation is a selection of excerpts from over a hundred musicals, some of the finest and most memorable moments ever put on celluloid. From the first "all singing, all dancing, all talking" musical *Hollywood Revue* of 1929, featuring the first appearance of the song "Singin' in the Rain," to the finale, the ballet from Gene Kelly and Vincente Minnelli's *An American in Paris, That's*

Entertainment packs the best of 35 years of Hollywood musicals into 2 hours. The home video audience is treated to Judy Garland singing "On the Atchison, Topeka and the Santa Fe" in *The Harvey Girls*; to Fred Astaire doing his fancy footwork in a variety of films from the last black and white musical, *Broadway Melody of 1940*, with Eleanor Powell, to his movies with Ginger Rogers; to Astaire's unforgettable dance with a coatrack in *Royal Wedding*; and to Gene Kelly, Donald O'Connor, and Debbie Reynolds in what has been called "the best musical of all time," *Singin' in the Rain*. The list of highlights seems almost endless. A wonderful movie worth watching over and over again.

THAT'S ENTERTAINMENT, PART II ★★★↓

MUSICAL. 1976. Cast: Gene Kelly, Fred Astaire, and over one hundred other stars. 126 min. Beta, VHS. MGM/UA ($69.95)

That's Entertainment, Part II picks up where *That's Entertainment* left off. Hosts Gene Kelly and Fred Astaire lead us through more MGM back-lot memories in a film that ultimately is not as cohesive as its predecessor. Still, *That's Entertainment, Part II* has it's moments! In addition to musical highlights, Fred and Gene take a look at great moments in MGM comedy including the classic stateroom scene from *A Night at the Opera* with the Marx Brothers. Other musical highlights include Fred, Nanette Fabray, and Oscar Levant singing "That's Entertainment" in *The Bandwagon*. A young Bing Crosby croons "Temptation" in the black and white film *Goin' Hollywood*. Fred Astaire and Gene Kelly dance together for the only time in their careers in "The Babbitt and the Bromide" to music written by the Gershwin brothers in a scene from *The Zeigfeld Follies*. Judy Garland sings "The Trolley Song" from *Meet Me in Saint Louis*. Judy and Mickey Rooney sing "I Got Rhythm" to the musical accompaniment of Tommy Dorsey and his Orchestra in Busby Berkeley's "Girl Crazy." Ethel Waters sings "Taking a Chance on Love" from *Cabin in the Sky*.

THE THREEPENNY OPERA ★★↓

MUSICAL. 1931. Cast: Rudolph Forster, Lotte Lenya, Vladimir Sokoloff, Valeska Gert, and Reinhold Schunzel. 113 min. Beta, VHS. Embassy ($59.95)

One of the landmarks of twentieth-century theater is Kurt Weill and Bertolt Brecht's *The Threepenny Opera*, a musical fantasy based on John Gay's Restoration drama, *The*

Beggar's Opera. Shortly after its premiere, plans were afoot to prepare a screen adaptation of it to be directed by German auteur G. W. Pabst. But by the time the film was completed, Brecht had disavowed any connection to it—it was not politically sharp enough for his approval. The black and white film, here with English subtitles, is presented as a fantasy about the Soho criminal underworld in 1890s London. Divergent from Brecht's original notion of an overtly theatrical "guerilla" staging that puts the audience intentionally at a distance from the proceedings, Pabst's treatment is expressionistic—a sort of belated expressionism—with the actors trying to construct a dramatic context. The stark photography by Fritz Arno Wagner makes Mack the Knife sinister rather than opportunistic, an antihero rather than a businessman with a switchblade. Modern-day audiences may find *The Threepenny Opera* a bit too abstract for their liking, but one does get to hear "Mack the Knife" sung in its original German.

THE UMBRELLAS OF CHERBOURG ★★★♪

MUSICAL. 1963. Cast: Catherine Deneuve and Nino Castelnuovo. 90 min. Beta, VHS. U.S.A.

Sung entirely in French, this Michel Legrand pop opera tells the story of 17-year-old Genevieve (Catherine Deneuve), who works in her mother's umbrella shop in her native Cherbourg, and her 18-year-old boyfriend, Guy, a local mechanic. They fall in love. She becomes pregnant just before he leaves to serve in the French army in Algeria. When he doesn't send word, she has no alternative but to marry a wealthy businessman. When Guy returns to Cherbourg, he learns that Genevieve has married and left town, marries a local girl, and opens a service station. Years later, Genevieve and Guy accidentally meet with children in tow, and notice how life has changed their plans. Director Jacques Demy tried to capitalize on this success with a sequel, *The Young Girls of Rochefort,* using a Michel Legrand score again as a basis for his story.

VICTOR/VICTORIA ★★★

MUSICAL. 1982. Cast: Julie Andrews, James Garner, Robert Preston, Lesley Ann Warren, and Alex Karras. 133 min. Beta Hifi, VHS Stereo. MGM/UA ($69.95)

Blake Edwards manages to make two kinds of films—funny or tasteless. Make that three kinds of films. *Victor/Victoria* is both funny *and* tasteless! With his wife, Julie Andrews, in the lead role of a singer in depression-era Paris who is convinced by

Julie Andrews masquerading as a male transvestite in
Victor/Victoria.

Robert Preston, her gay friend, that she can make a lot of money by masquerading as a male transvestite in cabarets, Edwards has fashioned the most troubling of his recent farces (*10, S.O.B.*). Anticipating *Tootsie* by several months, this film alternately repels and charms the viewer. Andrews and Garner—he plays the Chicago nightclub owner who falls for Victor/Victoria—give excellent comedic performances in the middle of this rather smarmy drama of gender confusion. The fact that the movie is based on a German film of the thirties, *Viktor/Viktoria*, indicates the potential for tastelessness in Edwards' chosen material. Enjoy the movie for Andrews, Garner, and the performance of Lesley Ann Warren as Garner's brassy, jealous showgirl companion. The musical numbers range from the sensational (Warren's "Chicago, Illinois," and Andrews' "Le Jazz Hot") to the embarrassing (Preston in drag singing "Shady Dame from Seville"). The music was by Henry Mancini, the lyrics by Leslie Bricuse. Not Blake's best work but it has a certain outré charm.

WEST SIDE STORY   ★★★★

MUSICAL. 1961. Cast: Natalie Wood, Richard Beymer, George Chakiris, Rita Moreno, Russ Tamblyn, and Jose De Vega. 155 min. Beta, VHS. CBS/Fox ($79.95,)

This classic musical, based on Shakespeare's *Romeo and Juliet,* sets the love story of Tony (Richard Beymer) and Maria (Natalie Wood) against the violence of rival street gangs on the old West Side of New York City. Tony, a cofounder of the Jets gang, has decided to go straight. He meets Maria, the sister of Bernardo, leader of the Puerto Rican gang, the Sharks. At a local dance, they are split apart by the Jets' challenge of the Sharks to a rumble. Despite Tony's efforts to make peace, the rumble ends in the stabbing death of Riff, Tony's best friend. To avenge Riff, Tony kills Bernardo. Believing the Sharks have killed Maria in retribution, Tony is surprised to find Maria alive and well. Chino, a Shark, ambushes Tony and shoots him. Tony dies in Maria's arms. This film, winner of ten Academy Awards, features the music of Leonard Bernstein, the lyrics of Stephen Sondheim, and the choreography of Jerome Robbins. *West Side Story* brings to the screen such favorites as "Something's Coming," "Maria," "America," "Tonight," "Gee, Officer Krupke!," "I Feel Pretty," and many others. One of the most influential cultural events in postwar American history.

WHERE THE BOYS ARE (Original)   ★★★

MUSICAL. 1960. Cast: Dolores Hart, George Hamilton, Yvette Mimieux, Jim Hutton, Paula Prentiss, Barbara Nichols, and Connie Francis. 99 min. Beta, VHS. MGM/UA ($59.95)

After the spate of rock and roll movies that emphasized the delinquency of their youthful subjects and before the arrival of the irreverent Beatles, Hollywood devised a species of teenage entertainment which was inaugurated with *Where the Boys Are* and continued through such cinematic gems as *Beach Party, Ski Party,* and the innumerable Elvis pictures. The concept was simple: depict a group of wholesome college students on spring break; show them struggling with temptation (in the form of sex, drugs, and rock and roll), and ultimately learning from their mistakes and returning to the accepted norms of mainstream society. Throw in a little music and you've got a box office winner. *Where the Boys Are* is a good movie, much more serious in tone than its spiritual descendents. Four students from a midwestern women's college (Hart, Mimieux, Prentiss, and Francis) decide to spend their spring break in Ft. Lauderdale, Fla., where they eventually pair up with George Hamilton, a millionaire's son, Jim Hutton, a brainy but ineffectual kook, Frank Gorshin, the leader of a cool jazz band,

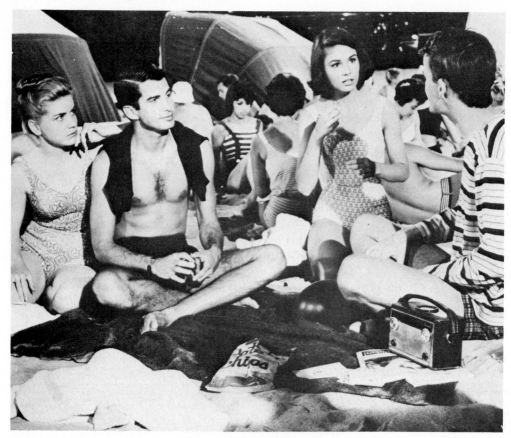

Fun on the beach in *Where the Boys Are*.

and, in Yvette's case, an entire Ivy League fraternity. Connie Francis, in her movie debut, sings "Turn On the Sunshine" and the title tune. Frank Gorshin's parody of a post-bebop, academic jazz band plays "Nuclear Love Song," "A Meeting between Shakespeare and Satchel Paige on Hempstead Heath," and "Don't Litter the Streets of Philadelphia." Barbara Nichols sings "Have You Met Miss Fandango?"

WHERE THE BOYS ARE (Remake) ★↗

MUSICAL. 1984. Cast: Lorna Luft, Lisa Hartman, Russell Todd, Wendy Schaal, Lyn-Holly Johnson and The Rockats. 95 min. Beta Hifi, VHS Stereo. Key ($59.95)

Allan Carr, who produced the *Grease* series of films and whose Broadway shows including *La Cage aux Folles* have had long runs, is responsible for this terrible remake of the 1960 Connie Francis movie, *Where the Boys Are.* Whereas the first version was halfway serious in tone, this version is unintentionally funny from the first scene onward. Luft, Hartman, Schaal, and Johnson play the four college girls headed for Ft. Lauderdale this time out. Somewhere along the line, the bottom fell out of this picture. It is confusing—not a good trait for a film aimed at the lowest teenage denominator. The Rockats, a poor substitute for The Stray Cats, sing "Slow Down," "Rip It Up," "Woman's Wise," and "Show No Fear." Rick Derringer, on the soundtrack, sings "All Fired Up" and "Shake Me." Sparks contributes "Mini-Skirted." Lisa Hartman sings the title tune.

XANADU ★

MUSICAL. 1980. Cast: Olivia Newton-John, Gene Kelly, Michael Beck, and The Tubes. 96 min. Beta Hifi, VHS Stereo. MCA ($69.95)

The people who thought this one up must have been smoking something illegal. Unfortunately, they didn't bother to share any of it with the audience. A bomb from the word go, *Xanadu* doesn't even have enough plot to fill a 4-minute rock video. Olivia, Gene Kelly, and The Tubes should have added up to passable entertainment but they were sabotaged by inept scriptwriters and Lawrence Gordon, the director, who I'm sure won't soon list this among his greatest achievements. Olivia plays a Muse (one of the Greek goddesses of the arts) who comes to earth to inspire Michael Beck, a painter working for the art department of a record company, and Gene Kelly, a retired big-band clarinetist. The movie is an improbable mix of roller disco, the music of Electric Light Orchestra, and art deco architecture and design. What is Gene Kelly doing in this film? For the record, Olivia sings "Xanadu," "Magic," "You Made Me Love You," "Whenever You're Away from Me" (with Gene), "Suddenly," and "Suspended in Time," ELO performs "I'm Alive," "Don't Walk Away," "All over the World," and "The Fall," and The Tubes are seen doing "Dancin'."

YOU'LL NEVER GET RICH ★★★

MUSICAL. 1941. Cast: Fred Astaire, Rita Hayworth, and Robert Benchley. 88 min. Beta, VHS. RCA/Columbia ($59.95)

Fred Astaire and Rita Hayworth are enlisted to whip up a little patriotic pride and entertain the civilians at home in *You'll Never Get Rich,* a black and white wartime musical that surrounds Cole Porter's songs and lyrics and Fred and Rita's dancing with a plot that is as enjoyable as it is unbelievably contrived. Robert Benchley plays a married, skirt-chasing stage-show producer, Martin Courtland, who buys a bracelet for the new chorus girl in his show, Sheila Winthrop (Rita Hayworth), who catches his attention. Sheila is shocked and dismayed to hear that Robert Curtis (Fred Astaire), Courtland's assistant producer, reluctantly backed up the lie that Courtland had told to his wife: that Courtland had bought the bracelet for Robert to give to Sheila. As a joke, Sheila approves a mean way to pay Robert back for his insincerity. Sheila asks her boyfriend to "threaten" Robert with a pistol loaded with blanks. Much to Sheila's bewilderment, Robert flees, leaves town, and joins the army at a nearby boot camp. After committing a variety of minor infractions, Private Curtis is left to do a little tap dancing in the stockade only to learn Courtland is bringing his show to the military base to put Robert in the show to entertain the troops and get out of the watchful glare of Mrs. Courtland. Robert tries everything he can to attract Sheila, who has captured his heart. Nothing works. As a last ditch effort, he writes "The Wedding Cake Walk" into the show in which he tricks her into marrying him. When she learns the truth, she's the happiest girl in the world. *You'll Never Get Rich* has a whole company of Cole Porter tunes including "I'm Shooting the Works on Uncle Sam," "Since I Kissed My Baby Goodbye," and "You're So Near, Yet So Far."

YOUNG AT HEART ★★★

MUSICAL. 1954. Cast: Frank Sinatra, Doris Day, Gig Young, Ethel Barrymore, Dorothy Malone, Robert Keith, Elizabeth Fraser, and Alan Hale, Jr. 117 min. Beta, VHS. Republic ($49.95)

A classy soap opera based on a Fannie Hurst (*Back Street*) short story, "Four Daughters," which explores our society's notions of success and failure. The songs, sung by Sinatra and Day, are appropriately integrated into the action, detracting not at all from the drama of the movie. Sinatra gives one of his better performances as Barney Sloan, a ne'er-do-well arranger and piano player asked by successful Broadway writer Gig Young to collaborate with him on his next production. Through Gig, Barney makes the acquaintance of Laurie (Doris Day), one of three daughters in a middle class Connecticut family (Dorothy Malone and Elizabeth Fraser play the other daughters). Laurie finds herself drawn to Barney even though he thinks of himself as an utter failure in life. They marry and, only through a series of near-tragic events, Barney realizes that his concept of success was all wrong. With the love of a good woman, and the birth of their first child, he recommits himself to life and the pursuit of his dreams. The acting of the principals makes this potentially sentimental story palatable. The music is superb!

Doris sings "Til My Love Comes," "Ready, Willing and Able," "Tonight Was Meant to Be," and "There's a Rising Moon for Every Falling Star." Frank sings "Young at Heart," "Someone to Watch over Me," "Just One of Those Things," "One More for the Road," and "My Love."

ZIEGFELD FOLLIES ★★★

MUSICAL. 1946. Cast: Fred Astaire, Lucille Ball, Fanny Brice, Judy Garland, Kathryn Grayson, Lena Horne, Gene Kelly, James Melton, Victor Moore, Red Skelton, Esther Williams, and William Powell. 109 min. Beta, VHS. MGM/UA ($29.95)

What would have happened had the great Broadway producer Flo Ziegfeld, who created and managed the spectacular Ziegfeld Follies from their start in 1907 to his death in 1932, been able to produce a brand new Follies from his cloud in heaven in 1946? Film producer Arthur Freed thought he would have to go no further than the MGM back lot to find the best stage talent in America. In this updating of the famous Ziegfeld review, Gene Kelly and Fred Astaire dance together for the *only* time in their film careers in "The Babbitt and the Bromide," with music by George and Ira Gershwin. Another highlight of this varied sampling of MGM talent is Judy Garland in "The Interview." The beautiful Lena Horne sings the sultry "Love." Original Ziegfeld Follies star Fanny Brice appears in "A Sweepstakes Ticket" with Hume Cronyn and William Frawley. Comic Red Skelton acts as a network pitchman for "Guzzler's Gin" in his solo piece, "When Television Comes." A number of rewards for the patient.

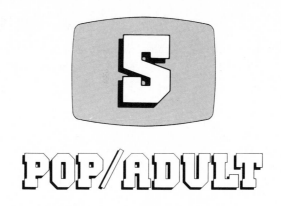

POP/ADULT

ABBA ★★♪

POP/ADULT. 1980. Artists: ABBA (Agnetha, Bjorn, Benny, and Frida). 60 min. Beta Hifi, VHS Stereo. Monterey ($39.95)

Arguably the most popular musical group of the seventies, ABBA claims to have sold 100 million LPs worldwide. They are so successful, in fact, that shares of common stock in ABBA, Inc. are traded on the Swedish stock exchange. Their achievements can be attributed to two things: a knack for hook-filled pop songs that are about nothing in particular and an aggressive campaign to put across their visual attractiveness. In this collection of promo films, ABBA hearkens back to the origins of the rock video. In the late sixties, groups often made promo films in order to introduce the public to what they looked like and make it possible for them to appear on as many TV shows as they could, without actually being there live. This was before groups got increasingly conceptual with their videos. Function over form, as it were. And these clips certainly show off ABBA at their most attractive. "Gimme! Gimme! Gimme!," "Knowing Me, Knowing You," "Take a Chance on Me," "Money, Money, Money," "The Name of the Game," "Eagle," "Voulez-Vous," "On and On and On," "One

Man, One Woman," "Summernight City," "Dancing Queen," "Does Your Mother Know," and "The Winner Takes It All" fill out this 60-minute program.

AIR SUPPLY LIVE IN HAWAII ★★↙

POP/ADULT. 1983. Artists: Air Supply (Graham Russell and Russell Hitchcock). 73 min. Beta Hifi, VHS Stereo. RCA/Columbia ($59.95)

Yet another of the Australian Invasion bands that hit the pop chart jackpot in the early eighties, Air Supply, a Mutt and Jeff duo from Down Under (Graham's the tall one, Russell's the short one), specializes in melodic, slow-dance ballads. They heartily subscribe to the early Lennon-McCartney theory of using plenty of personal pronouns in their song lyrics. Despite the fact that neither of them is exactly exciting as a performer, this video concert, shot at the Neil Blaisdell Arena in Honolulu, Hawaii, is actually quite a stage show, filled with special laser effects and well-choreographed lighting. The motif is borrowed from Superman II (obviously it made more of an impression in Australia than it did here). Including seven of their Top 10 singles,

Air Supply.

they perform: "I Can't Get Excited," "Chances," "Lost in Love," "Every Woman in the World," "Don't Turn Me Away," "Now and Forever," "Here I Am," "Sweet Dreams," "I Want to Give It All," "All Out of Love," "I've Got Your Love," "The One That You Love," "This Heart Belongs to Me," "Even The Nights Are Better," "One Step Closer," and "Late Again." Air Supply also can boast of being one of the few rock groups to be profiled on *Lifestyles of the Rich and Famous*.

BETTE MIDLER SHOW ★★♪

POP/ADULT. 1976. Artist: Bette Midler. 84 min. Beta Hifi, VHS Stereo. Embassy ($39.95)

In this HBO special, filmed in Cleveland, Ohio, at the height of Bette Midler's career in 1976, the stage antics and charming vulgarity that uncovered a surprisingly large audience for the diva of depravity are on full view. She arrives on stage in a hospital bed to sing the Buzzy Linhart tune she made popular, "Friends." Joined by the Harlettes, her trio of female singers, Bette embarks on a show that involves several scene changes, the use of outrageous props, and some incredibly garish costumes. A veritable compendium of recherché music, Bette mounts production numbers for such old favorites as "I Sold My Heart to the Junk Man," "Salt Peanuts," "In the Mood," "Flat Foot Floogie," "Come-On-A-My-House," "Lullaby of Broadway," and "Boogie Woogie Bugle Boy." Also included are her characters, Vicki Eydie, the ultimate lounge singer, doing "Fiesta in Rio," and the bag lady, singing "Hello in There," as well as her notoriously filthy Sophie Tucker jokes. Other songs heard are "O My My," "Hurry On Down," "Delta Dawn," "Dr. Long John," and "Up the Ladder to the Roof." Directed by Tom Trbovich.

BODY MUSIC ★★

POP/ADULT. 1984. Cast: Leslie-Ann, Angie-Layne, Sheree, Jilly, Sally, and Amanda. 30 min. Beta Hifi, VHS Stereo. Sony ($19.95)

Body Music combines the talents of photographer Brian Aris, composer Chris Rainbow, who is also lead singer for the Alan Parsons Project, video director and video graphics designer Peter Conn, and six seminude models. Brian Aris' photographs of six partially-clad women, shot on the islands of Ibiza and Jamaica, are animated and computer enhanced to change their color and set to the music of Chris Rainbow's jazz fusion compositions, "Looking at You," "Red Light," "Girls in Collision," "Can't Let Go," "Body Music," and "Sheree." The effect is like slightly erotic wallpaper, a continuous chain of changing images that really don't affect the viewer at all.

CAROLE KING: ONE TO ONE ★★★

POP/ADULT. 1982. Artist: Carole King. 60 min. Beta Hifi, VHS Stereo. MGM/UA ($59.95)

An engrossing documentary look at Carole King's life, times, and career. King, one of the pillars of the Brill Building songwriting operation during the era of New York pop music songwriters, has had a dichotomous career. For the first half of her foray into the music world, Carole, by herself and with ex-husband Gerry Goffin, was strictly a songwriter, coming up with hits for dozens of pop artists ranging from The Shirelles

Singer/songwriter Carole King.

to The Byrds to Little Eva to James Taylor to The Monkees. But she, along with the times, was going through a lot of changes in the late sixties. Divorced from Goffin, having moved to the west coast, Carole began to launch a singing career. Her smash album, *Tapestry,* broke all sales records in 1971 and ushered in the short reign of the singer-songwriter in pop circles. Personal problems and vast changes in the record business have since blunted her performing career. Here, shown in concert and at home near Austin, Texas, Carole reminisces about the highlights of her life and sings "Jazz Man," "Tapestry," "Locomotion," "Looking Out for Number One," "Take Good Care of My Baby," "It Might as Well Rain until September," "Smackwater Jack," "Hey Girl," "One Fine Day," "Chains," "Up on the Roof," "I Feel the Earth Move," "You've Got a Friend," "War," "One to One," "A Natural Woman," and more.

CHERYL LADD: FASCINATED ★★

POP/ADULT. 1982. Artist: Cheryl Ladd. 50 min. Beta, VHS. Thorn-EMI ($49.95)

The ex-Charlie's Angel is seen here to good advantage singing a collection of soft pop-rock tunes. Depending on your opinion of Ms. Ladd's blonde charms, this program should prove more or less satisfying. Cheryl plays a professional photographer whose musical fantasies are spurred by her snapshots. Slightly more plausible than the gimmicks other artists have used to string their music videos together. The music, by the way, is basically L.A. studio pop; competent, derivative, and forgettable. She sings "Fascinated," "Think It Over," "Just Like Old Times," "Lesson from the Leavin'," "Lady Gray," "Just Another Lover Tonight," "Sakura, Sakura," "The Rose Nobody Knows," "I Love How You Love Me," "It's Only Love" (not the Lennon song), "Try a Smile," "Cold as Ice," and "Victim of Circumstance."

DREAMS OF GOLD ★★★

POP/ADULT. 1984. Artist: Ken Nordine. 55 min. Beta, VHS. Pacific Arts ($29.95)

Best known for his Levi jeans television commercials and his "Word Jazz" albums, Ken Nordine is a television and radio writer, a musician, a recording engineer—in short, a master of the audio track. In *Dreams of Gold,* Ken turns his attention to the individual sporting events of the National Sports Festival, the warm-ups for the 1984 Los Angeles Olympics. In the tradition of his Grammy-nominated *Stare with Your Ears* album, he combines beautiful video footage with an unexpected soundtrack. For example, in the sequence titled "Women's Tennis," Ken cuts the slow-motion film of the two women playing tennis to sounds of the forest (birds chirping, a babbling brook, etc.). The effect is startling. Not only does he capture the viewer's attention, but by disassociating the viewer's aural expectations from the image, Nordine makes you notice the visual beauty inherent in athletic competition. A fascinating experiment in video.

THE FIRST BARRY MANILOW SPECIAL   ★★★

POP/ADULT. 1977. Artist: Barry Manilow. 52 min. Beta Hifi, VHS Stereo. MGM/UA ($59.95)

This ABC-TV special won an Emmy Award in 1977 in the category of outstanding music special. Produced by Steve Binder, with Alan Thicke, who failed to buck Johnny Carson on the late night tube, as one of the writers, Manilow's showcase does exactly that—it showcases the talents and charms of the gifted songwriter-arranger whose career has adapted to several changes in the pop climate in a production that is part live concert performance and part TV-studio spectacle. Barry also calls upon the help of his trio of female singers, Lady Flash, and guest star Penny Marshall. In the opening segment, we hear "It's a Miracle," "This One's for You," "Could It Be Magic?," and "Mandy." The scene shifts to a soundstage where Penny Marshall and Lady Flash join Barry in a salute to forties big-band tunes: "Jump Shout Boogie," "Avenue C," "Jumpin' at the Woodside," "Cloudburst," and "Bandstand Boogie." A medley of his commercial jingles brings smiles of recognition from the audience—they include jingles for Kentucky Fried Chicken, State Farm Insurance, Stridex Pads, Dr. Pepper, and McDonald's. The climactic production number does homage to life in the big city with "New York City Rhythm," "Sandra," and "Early Morning Stranger." Finally, Barry sings "I Write the Songs," his signature song. Ironically, he didn't "write *that* song." Bruce Johnston of The Beach Boys inked it.

FRANKIE VALLI IN CONCERT   ★★✦

POP/ADULT. 1982. Artists: Frankie Valli and the Four Seasons. 60 min. Beta, VHS. Prism ($29.95)

Another in the *Music America Live* series of concerts originally broadcast over PBS affiliate WTTW in Chicago, this program features Frankie Valli and the Four Seasons celebrating

BARRY MANILOW

Born June 17, 1946, in Brooklyn, New York, Barry Manilow first came to prominence as the pianist-arranger for Bette Midler's traveling road show, after the two had met while working together at New York's Continental Baths. At the same time, he wrote numerous TV-commercial jingles for Dr. Pepper, Band-Aids, State Farm Insurance, and others.

When Manilow finally embarked on a solo career, he hit almost immediately with songs like "Mandy," "Could It Be Magic," "It's a Miracle," and "I Write the Songs."

Since his breakthrough in 1975, Barry has become a leading figure on the pop music scene, as a writer, singer, and record producer (for Dionne Warwick, among others). His latest effort, an album that tries to recapture the ambience of "saloon singing," *2:00 AM—Paradise Café,* shows that Manilow is still growing as an artist, exploring new types of music.

Video Resume

Barry Manilow: The Making of 2:00 AM— Paradise Cafe, (1984), RCA/Columbia Musicvision.

The First Barry Manilow Special, (1977), MGM/UA.

their twentieth anniversary together. Truthfully, the only original members of the Four Seasons still with the group are Valli and Bob Gaudio, the man whose songwriting and arranging formed the basis of their distinctive sound in the early sixties. This gathering at Chicago's Park West Club is not going to remind you too much of the Four Seasons' original years. Valli's signature falsetto isn't the bubblegum delight it was in songs like "Dawn (Go Away)," "Sherry," and "Rag Doll." The show and the band arrangements are too "Vegas" to envelop one in nostalgia; it's more like listening to an anonymous lounge group cover the Four Seasons' material. But, for those who must indulge, there are a few good moments when the performance and the memory coincide. The long list of golden oldies includes "Dawn," "Who Loves You," "Grease," "Our Day Will Come," "My Eyes Adored You," "Working My Way Back to You," "Will You Still Love Me Tomorrow," "Opus 17," "I've Got You Under My Skin," "Sunday Kind of Love," "Can't Take My Eyes Off of You," "Sherry," "Walk Like a Man," "Bye-bye Baby," "Save It for Me," "Candy Girl," "Big Man in Town," "Rag Doll," "Silence Is Golden," "Tell It to the Rain," "Beggin'," "Stay," and "Let's Hang On."

Many viewers will probably feel left out in this all-out nostalgia attack. After all, the Four Seasons who hail from New Jersey were basically a local attraction in New York.

GINO VANELLI ★★

POP/ADULT. 1981. Artist: Gino Vanelli. 56 min. Beta, VHS. Warner ($39.95)

A lion-maned power pop singer from Canada, Gino Vanelli appeals to an audience that is predominantly young and female. His stage show is a sedate version of Rod Stewart's bump and grind spectacle—Gino's approach is more soulful and less salacious. His ballads, "Living inside Myself" and "I Just Wanna Stop," were his only chart singles in the United States. In Canada, of course, Gino is a recording artist of some magnitude. This video program offers in-concert footage shot in New Orleans, Detroit, Chicago, and Toronto, along with views of Vanelli relaxing in myriad motel rooms and doing auditorium sound checks. Also, there are music videos shot in Los Angeles for "Living inside Myself" and "Nightwalker." The songs performed in concert are "Powerful People," "The Evil Eye," "Appaloosa," "Omens of Love," "I Just Wanna Stop," "Brother to Brother," "People Gotta Move," "Where Am I Going," "One Night with You," and "Wheels of Life."

HARD TO HOLD ★

POP/ADULT. 1984. Cast: Rick Springfield, Janet Eilber, Patti Hansen, and Albert Salmi. 93 min. Beta Hifi, VHS Stereo. MCA ($69.95)

Another testament to the simple truth that you can take a boy out of a soap opera but you can't take the soap opera out of the boy. Rick Springfield's feature film debut is hard to take. In addition to lacking a story, woefully miscasting Janet Eilber in the costarring role of a counselor for emotionally troubled children who, herself, acts like a child, and forgetting to put in any hit songs (like "Jessie's Girl"), *Hard to Hold* is directed by Larry Peerce with blissful incompetence. Even Patti Hansen, Keith Richard's wife, in an unintentionally hilarious portrayal of Rick's ex-girlfriend can't enliven this story of a tortured and confusing love affair. The songs are: "Stand Up," "Don't Walk Away," "Love Somebody," "Great Lost Art of Conversation," "Bop Til You

Rick Springfield as rock star Jamie Roberts in *Hard to Hold*.

Drop," and "S.F.O." Nona Hendryx, Graham Parker, and Peter Gabriel also contribute songs to the soundtrack.

HARRY CHAPIN: THE FINAL CONCERT   ★★★

POP/ADULT. 1981. Artist: Harry Chapin. 89 min. Beta, VHS. CBS/Fox ($49.95)

Before his tragic death in a car accident on his native Long Island, New York, in 1981, Harry Chapin was the standard bearer of a fading folk troubadour tradition. He wrote and sang narrative tunes, filled with humor and wry observations on everyday life. He was active in several charities including the World Hunger benefits that he tirelessly organized and performed in. What marked his music was his humanity. He was not a superstar by any means, although his "Taxi" sold millions of copies and became an FM-radio classic, but Chapin's concert tours inevitably were greeted by packed houses and a fervently loyal following. This concert video is not actually his final concert (just as there is no complete footage of Elvis' last concert although often an earlier concert is claimed to be his last), but it's certainly a good concert. The audience at the Hamilton Place in Hamilton, Ontario, is quite enthusiastic and seems to have memorized all their favorite Chapin songs, especially "30,000 Pounds of Bananas." Harry's brothers, Tom and Stephen, join him on "Story of a Life," "Shooting Star," "Taxi," "Mr. Tanner," "WOLD," "Better Place to Be," "Cat's in the Cradle," "Flowers Are Red," "Dreams Go By," "Mail Order Annie," "30,000 Pounds of Bananas," "Sequel," "You are the Only Song," and "Circle."

THE JACK BENNY PROGRAM   ★★★♪

POP/ADULT. 1958. Cast: Jack Benny, Eddie Anderson, Mel Blanc, Don Wilson, Dennis Day, and Richard Deacon. 50 min. Beta Hifi, VHS Stereo. MCA ($29.95)

Two episodes from the classic television comedy series, *The Jack Benny Program,* are a cornucopia of laughs for the viewer. They really don't make them like this anymore. The master of timing and the small, meaningful comic gesture, Benny leads his repertory company through material verging on the surreal yet entirely accessible. In "The Christmas Show," Jack and Rochester (Eddie Anderson) go Christmas shopping in a large department store. The torture that Jack puts store clerk Mel Blanc through over a simple gift card is hilarious in its unfolding. Dennis Day sings "Rudolph the Red-Nosed Reindeer." In "The Railroad Station," Mel Blanc is an irritating plumber who crosses paths with Jack at the railroad station where he is getting ready to board the Super Chief to New York City. Recommended viewing. In black and white.

THE JAZZ SINGER ★★

POP/ADULT. 1980. Cast: Neil Diamond, Lucie Arnaz, Laurence Olivier, Catlin Adams, and Franklyn Ajaye. 115 min. Beta Hifi, VHS Stereo. Paramount ($29.95)

At last report, Neil Diamond was still trying to get a major studio to back a feature film version of his *Beautiful Noise* album from 1976. Hopefully, he isn't showing them a print of *The Jazz Singer* as an entrée. It fits very nicely into the long history of Hollywood's vanity productions—movies made solely and expressly for a non-actor with lots of money or pull. Diamond, who has developed an amazing reputation as a pop artist with an over-thirty audience, plays Jess Robinovich, a cantor's son bent on being a pop star. The cantor (Laurence Olivier) is not happy with this and threatens to disown his son if he persists. Eventually, Jess leaves his wife in New York and arrives in L.A. to start a musical career under his new name, Jess Robin. There, he finds

Laurence Olivier and Neil Diamond in *The Jazz Singer.*

success and his second wife, Lucie Arnaz. Of course, once he's made it, there are still so many unresolved personal issues. Not a very serious remake of the Al Jolson *Jazz Singer*. The score is a curious mixture of traditional Hebrew songs and liturgical compositions and Diamond's own bathetic compositions: "America," "You, Baby," "Havah Nagilah," "Love on the Rocks," "Robert E. Lee," "Songs of Life," "Acapulco," "Jerusalem," "Hello Again," "Hime Man Tove," "Summer Love," "My Name Is Yussel," "Adon Olom," "Hey Louise," "Amazed and Confused," and the "Kol Nidre."

JINXED ★★

POP/ADULT. 1982. Cast: Bette Midler, Ken Wahl, Rip Torn, Jack Elam, Benson Fong, and Val Avery. 104 min. Beta, VHS. MGM/UA ($69.95)

Bette Midler in a film about Las Vegas losers trying to find some kind of supernatural edge against the overwhelming odds at the gaming tables and in life sounds like a

Bette Midler in *Jinxed.*

perfect combination. Right? Don Siegel (*Dirty Harry, Invasion of the Body Snatchers*) didn't get it right in this potentially special movie. Bette gives a good performance as the lounge singer who is caught between her live-in lover, Rip Torn, a professional gambler, and new love, Ken Wahl, a blackjack dealer who believes Torn has put a jinx on him. She finally decides that the constant abuse she gets from Torn is too much and schemes with Wahl to kill Torn for his insurance money. But in a kind of Hitchcockian twist, Bette discovers that Torn's jinx on Wahl won't go away, even in death. The film switches moods so often that it is difficult to receive it as a comedy, murder thriller, or comedy-thriller. It just never makes up its mind. Bette sings two songs: "Cowgirl's Dreams" and "No Jinx." Sam Peckinpah is listed in the credits as the second-unit director.

KENNY LOGGINS ALIVE! ★★★

POP/ADULT. 1981. Artist: Kenny Loggins. 60 min. Beta Hifi, VHS Stereo. CBS/Fox ($29.95)

Compiled from tape of two different concerts played at the Santa Barbara County Bowl, one during the afternoon, the other at night, this performance tape shows Kenny at his ebullient best. Loggins, whose work with Jim Messina sold millions of albums in the early seventies, has been making the same kind of music for 15 years. "Danny's Song" and "House at Pooh Corner" perfectly encapsulate his blend of folk, country, and pop idioms—his songs are best-suited to the kind of acoustic guitar troubadours who came to the fore in the L.A. of the early seventies. Even in his latest work ("Footloose"), the basics of his sound have changed little. In this tape, shot in 1981, Loggins epitomizes an optimistic west coast outlook with his music, his dress, and his demeanor. One of the extra touches in the program is the precise cutting between the day and night concerts in mid-song, right on the beat! Kenny sings "I Believe in Love," "Love Has Come of Age," "Kiss Your Lucky Lady Goodbye," "Angry Eyes," "Roll Over Beethoven," "I'm Alright," "House at Pooh Corner," "Danny's Song," "Fall in the Fire," "Celebrate Me Home," "Do It Tonight," "This Is It," and "Keep the Fire."

THE KIDS FROM FAME! LIVE AT THE ROYAL ALBERT HALL, LONDON ★★↓

POP/ADULT. 1983. Cast: Debbie Allen, Lee Curreri, Erica Gimpel, Carlo Imperato, Gene Anthony Ray, and Lori Singer. 75 min. Beta Hifi, VHS Stereo. MGM/UA ($39.95)

Alan Parker's film about New York City's Performing Arts High School, *Fame*, was *the* sleeper hit of 1980 and created a virtual *Fame* industry. *Fame* gave birth to the

Cast of *Fame*.

movie, the hit record, Irene Cara's film and recording career, and the syndicated television show. Now the television show, *Fame,* has given birth to a marketing grandchild, *The Kids from Fame,* a tape that spotlights the individual talents of the stars of the TV show. Live from the Royal Albert Hall in London, Lori Singer, Gene Anthony Ray, Debbie Allen, Lee Curreri, Erica Gimpel, and Carlo Imperato dance, sing, and play instruments for an appreciative crowd. Highlights include the ensemble's singing of "Body Language," Gene Anthony Ray's dance piece entitled "Mannequin," Erica Gimpel's song, "Be Your Own Hero," and Lori Singer's cello version of Michael Jackson's electric "Don't Stop 'Til You Get Enough."

KIM CARNES   ★★

POP/ADULT. 1983. Artist: Kim Carnes. 15 min. Beta Hifi, VHS Stereo. Sony ($16.95)

Having spent almost a decade as a studio backup vocalist in Los Angeles, Kim Carnes burst onto the music scene with her 1981 blockbuster hit, "Bette Davis Eyes," originally recorded and cowritten by Jackie DeShannon. Her first real break had come in 1978 when Kenny Rogers, then beginning his move into country pop, used a few of her compositions on his *Gideon* album. That led to her duet hit with Rogers, "Don't Fall in Love with a Dreamer." MTV, in its earliest days, placed Kim Carnes' videos on heavy rotation, realizing that her music was pleasing to the eyes as well as to the ears. There are four videos in this package: "Invisible Hands," directed by Jim Yukich, which quite possibly inspired Herbie Hancock's "Rockit" video, "Voyeur," directed by Russell Mulcahy, "Draw of the Cards," which explored the color and pageantry of Carnival in Rio de Janeiro before Lionel Richie's much better known "All Night Long," and "Bette Davis Eyes," which became Carnes' ticket to stardom. The last two are also directed by Russell Mulcahy.

LINDA RONSTADT: WHAT'S NEW?　★★

POP/ADULT. 1984. Artist: Linda Ronstadt with the Nelson Riddle Orchestra. 60 min. Beta Hifi, VHS Stereo. Vestron ($29.95)

Linda Ronstadt, who had smash hits in the mid-seventies singing everything from country to soft rock to New Wave and back, decided to try her hand at big-band

Linda Ronstadt in vintage 1940s gown for *What's New?*

LINDA RONSTADT

Linda Ronstadt was born in Tucson, Arizona, on July 15, 1946. Of Mexican and German ancestry, Linda grew up in Arizona listening to such diverse music as Hank Williams, Elvis Presley, and mariachi singers like Lola Beltran. In fact, her earliest recordings were in a country-rock vein, including her first hit single, "Different Drum," written by ex-Monkee Michael Nesmith. But success was fleeting and her country-rock stance proved uncommercial.

Then, with the help of Peter Asher, formerly of Peter and Gordon, as her record producer, Ronstadt set about redefining pop music in the mid-seventies. The neo-

classic pop sound displayed in albums like *Simple Dreams, Heart Like a Wheel,* and *Living in the U.S.A.* (1974–1978), was a crystallization of Los Angeles session musicianship, providing a real boon to crack players like David Sanborn, Russ Kunkel, and Andrew Gold. Her interpretations of songs by Smokey Robinson, Chuck Berry, Warren Zevon, Elvis Costello, and Jackson Browne made the concept of "cover artist" a dominant new category in pop music.

As Ronstadt's career has progressed, she has ventured into other musical forms, singing in the operetta *Pirates of Penzance* and the opera *La Bohème,* as well as other subgenres within pop music itself. Most recently, Linda's gained critical and commercial kudos for her renditions of big-band favorites like "Keepin' Out of Mischief Now," "Someone to Watch over Me," and "Lover Man" on her platinum albums, *What's New?* and *Lush Life.* She continues to gauge her core audience—young, but over twenty-one, educated, and upwardly mobile—correctly in its meandering shifts from sixties idealism to seventies nostalgia to eighties romance and class.

Video Resume

A Flower Out of Place, (1974), Media.

Linda Ronstadt: What's New?, (1984), Vestron.

Pirates of Penzance, (1983), MCA.

standards from the forties, the age of the female singer. To help her, she recruited Nelson Riddle, whose charts stand as some of the best big-band arrangements ever put on wax and who has worked with Sinatra, Bennett, Sarah Vaughan, you name it. The result of their collaboration, *What's New?*, was one of the best-selling LPs of 1984. In this video version of the album, shot before a live audience at the Arlington Theater in Santa Barbara, California, Linda dresses up in gala forties fashion, swings on a giant crescent moon, joins in on an Andrews Sisters take-off, and tries desperately to match the authenticity of Riddle's charts with a voice lacking in subtlety and power. While it may all be an act (after all, those forties singers were rather air-headed), Linda walks around like she doesn't have a clue as to what these standards are all about. Some of the classics Linda sings are "I've Got a Crush on You," "What's New?," "Keepin' Out of Mischief Now," "Hang My Tears Out to Dry," "Falling in Love Again," "Someone to Watch over Me," "Mr. Sandman," "Kalamazoo," "Choo-Choo Boogie," "Ghost of a Chance with You," and "Lover Man." Way off target.

Although this is really the culmination of Ronstadt's career as a "cover" artist, younger fans would be better advised to listen to some of the original recordings of these classics.

LITTLE RIVER BAND: LIVE EXPOSURE ★★★

POP/ADULT. 1981. Artists: Little River Band (Glen Shorrock, Graham Goble, Beeb Birtles, Wayne Nelson, Derek Pellicci, Malcolm Logan, and Steven Housden). 60 min. Beta Hifi, VHS Stereo. Thorn-EMI ($49.95)

One of the bands that triggered the Australian Invasion of the early eighties, Little River Band's music is somewhere between the sentimental ballads of Air Supply and the reggae-tinged hard rock of Men At Work. And ultimately, their popularity has outlasted that of the other two bands as they continue to have chart singles on American soil. In this concert recorded at The Summit in Houston, Texas, on October 7, 1981, the band plays a surprisingly hard-rocking set, spotlighting the guitar playing of Steve Housden. Glen Shorrock, with his bushy blond hair and surfer's physique, is the lead singer, the stereotype of an Australian man. "It's a Long Way There," their first U.S. hit in 1976, "Man on Your Mind," "Mistress of Mine," "Happy Anniversary," "Don't Let the Needle Win," "Reminiscing," "Ballerina," "Cool Change," "The Night Owls," "Help Is on Its Way," "Lonesome Loser," "It's Not a Wonder," "Lady," and "Just Say That You Love Me" sound more convincing in concert than on vinyl. Directed by Derek Burbidge. Glen Shorrock, incidentally, left the group for a solo career in 1982.

MELLOW MEMORIES   ★★♪

POP/ADULT. 1984. Artists: Neil Diamond, John Denver, Helen Reddy, The Association, Bobby Sherman, Jerry Reed, Tommy James and the Shondells, Diana Ross and the Supremes, Nitty Gritty Dirt Band, Wayne Newton, Shirley Bassey, Billy Joe Royal, The Osmonds, Brian Hyland, Loggins and Messina, Harpers Bizarre, David Cassidy, Dionne Warwick, Sonny and Cher, and Mickey Newbury. 60 min. Beta Hifi, VHS Stereo. U.S.A. ($29.95)

Basically a compilation of performances on various TV programs from the sixties and early seventies, *Mellow Memories* has enough bizarre and/or nostalgic moments to be worth seeing. You'll soon guess that all the songs are lip-synced, but if you're a person with a soft spot in your heart for all those regional music shows that were epidemic before the age of rock videos made personal appearances obsolete, you won't mind at all. Exactly as advertised, there are no intros, no narrators, no nothing. Just appearance after appearance assemble-edited together. Some of the highlights are: Neil Diamond, as a belated rockabilly act, singing "Cherry Cherry"; The Association, lounging around a motel pool, singing "Never My Love"; Wayne Newton, with lots of baby fat, singing "Daddy Don't You Walk So Fast"; The Osmonds doing their Jackson 5 impression on "One Bad Apple"; Sonny and Cher, looking like refugees from Sunset Strip circa 1966, singing "Beautiful Story"; Mickey Newbury singing the number he wrote for Elvis, "An American Trilogy"; and teen idols Bobby Sherman and David Cassidy, showing us all why fame can be fleeting.

MENUDO EN UNA AVENTURA LLAMADA MENUDO   ★★

POP/ADULT. 1982. Cast: Menudo (Ricky, Charlie, Xavier, Johnny, and Miguel). 86 min. Beta, VHS. Embassy ($59.95)

The international teeny-bopper sensation, Menudo, the group that has sold three platinum and four gold albums, stars in its first movie, the Spanish-language *Una Aventura Llamada Menudo,* presented here without subtitles. In a featherweight plot, the boys in the group have to leave their base in San Juan, Puerto Rico, to play a concert date on the other side of the island in Ponce. They decide to make the journey in a balloon, but the balloon crashes midway and they meet up with Clara, an attractive girl about their age, and her mysterious aunt. Since they have no other place to stay, Clara's aunt allows the group to spend the night in her well-appointed hacienda. Strange things start happening to the boys and they soon realize that Clara's aunt wants to hold them locked up in her house against their will. Why? She's secretly Menudo's biggest fan. The boys sing for her. As a token of gratitude, Clara's aunt whisks them off in a helicopter so that they can arrive in Ponce in time to entertain thousands of screaming "puertorriqueñas" at the outdoor concert. Big fun for the Menudo fan. The boys sing their Europop hits "A Volar," "Lluvia," "Clara dame un beso," "Sube a mi moto," "Estrella polar," "La Banda toca rock," and "Quiero rock."

THE MUSIC OF MELISSA MANCHESTER   ★★✦

POP/ADULT. 1981. Artist: Melissa Manchester. 60 min. Beta, VHS. Warner ($29.98)

As we entered the seventies, traditional musical categories that had organized radio programming for two decades or more were undergoing a critical transformation. The great distinctions between "youth" music and "adult" music no longer were valid as an entire generation had grown up on rock and roll. Middle of the road, or MOR, became the term used to describe the music which appealed to the older fringes of the rock generation, music that unmistakably bore the mark of a rock and roll pedigree, only softened and more worldly. Melissa Manchester, a graduate of Julliard, was discovered by Bette Midler and her arranger, Barry Manilow. They hired her as one of the Harlettes, Bette's backing vocalists. Soon, writing songs by herself and with Carole Bayer Sager, Manchester developed a solo career. She has always worked in the MOR vein, writing and singing music that can stand side by side with the songs of Peter Allen, Barry Manilow, and Elton John. In this concert, directed by veteran Marty Callner, Melissa sings "Help Is on the Way," "Midnight Blue," "O Heaven," "Whenever I Call You Friend" (written with Kenny Loggins), "Working Girl," "As Time Goes By," "It's All in the Sky Above," "Home to Myself," "This Lady's Not Home Today," "Peace in My Heart," "Good News for the Lady," "We've Got Time," "Easy," "Talkin' to Myself," "Don't Cry Out Loud," "Boy Next Door," and "Come In from the Rain."

NEIL DIAMOND LIVE AT THE GREEK   ★★★

POP/ADULT. 1976. Artist: Neil Diamond. 52 min. Beta Hifi, VHS Stereo. Vestron ($29.95)

The Greek Theater in Los Angeles was the site of this televised concert, originally broadcast over NBC-TV on February 24, 1977. Neil Diamond, by the mid-seventies, had established himself as a premier MOR recording artist, whose music, a mixture of soft rock, doo-wop, and show tune rhythms, appealed to the older fringes of the rock generation. He had been a songwriter in New York's Tin Pan Alley in the early sixties who adapted quickly to become one of the rising class of singer-songwriters filling record company rosters in the late sixties and early seventies. After some early rockabilly-tinged singles, he hit his stride with melodic songs bespeaking the concerns

NEIL DIAMOND

Born January 24, 1941, in Brooklyn, New York, Neil Diamond was a songwriter in the famous Brill Building tune factories of the late fifties and early sixties. After writing The Monkees' hit single, "I'm A Believer," Neil's solo career began to take off, as he scored his own hits, "Cherry, Cherry," "Girl, You'll Be a Woman Soon," "Kentucky Woman," and others during 1966 and 1967.

It wasn't until Diamond moved to Los Angeles in the late sixties that he developed a distinctive, now easily identifiable "Neil Diamond" sound, eschewing the pseudo-rockabilly of his earliest recordings. He established MOR (middle of the road) music as a viable radio format along with artists like Barry Manilow, Carole King, James Taylor, and Melissa Manchester. Among his audience's concert favorites are "Sweet Caroline," "Beautiful Noise," "Song Sung Blue," "Cracklin' Rosie," "Holly Holy," "I Am . . . I Said," and "America." He starred in a remake of *The Jazz Singer* in 1980.

Neil commands a legion of adoring fans who pack his sold-out concert appearances all over the world. While recent recording successes have been few and far between, Diamond's authoritative position as a major pop star has not been challenged. He continues to tour and is trying to bring his 1976 album, *Beautiful Noise,* an intimate look backward at his Brill Building days, to the silver screen.

Video Resume

The Jazz Singer, (1980), Paramount.

Jonathan Livingston Seagull, (1973), Paramount.

Mellow Memories, (1983), U.S.A.

Neil Diamond Live at the Greek, (1977), Vestron.

of a maturer audience. Strangely enough, Diamond has always insisted upon the "significance" of his works—even as he walks onto the stage in clothes that seem hand-me-downs and rejects from the wardrobes of Elvis Presley and Wayne Newton. Ultimately, the only things that separate him from the bathos of someone like Bobby Vinton are a dark baritone voice and his not inconsiderable writing skills. The songs are: "Cherry Cherry," "Sweet Caroline," "Play Me," "Beautiful Noise," "Street Life," "Lady Oh," "If You Know What I Mean," "Song Sung Blue," "Cracklin' Rosie," "Holly Holy," "I Am . . . I Said," "Brother Love's Traveling Salvation Show," and "I've Been This Way Before." Robbie Robertson, of The Band, was the sound supervisor.

NEIL SEDAKA IN CONCERT (1981) ★★★

POP/ADULT. 1981. Artist: Neil Sedaka. 54 min. Beta, VHS. MCA ($39.95)

Don Kirshner, who later created *The Monkees* and the landmark late night TV series, *Rock Concert,* employed a legion of soon to be famous songwriters at his offices in Manhattan's Brill Building during the early sixties. Writers like Neil Diamond, Carole King and Gerry Goffin, Randy Newman, Doc Pomus and Mort Shulman, and Barry Mann and Cynthia Weil worked alongside each other in tiny cubicles. Also in one of those cubicles were Howard Greenfield and Neil Sedaka. Neil, of course, made it as a performer with hits like "Oh Carol," "Stairway to Heaven," "Calendar Girl," and "Breaking Up Is Hard to Do." Absent from the pop scene during the late sixties and early seventies, Sedaka returned with a vengeance in 1975, as a songwriter, with The Captain and Tenille's "Love Will Keep Us Together," and as a performer, with the gold singles "Laughter in the Rain" and "Breaking Up Is Hard to Do" (the slow version). His benefactor during his comeback was Elton John, and in this concert video, you'll see why the two have a mutual admiration. Other songs heard in this concert taped at the Jubilee Auditorium in Edmonton, Canada, are: "Sing Me," "Love in the Shadows," "Hey, Little Devil," "Happy Birthday Sweet Sixteen," "New York City Blues," "Solitaire," "Bad Blood," "Immigrant," "Stormy Weather," and "That's When the Music Takes Me."

NEIL SEDAKA IN CONCERT (1982) ★★꜀

POP/ADULT. 1982. Artist: Neil Sedaka. 60 min. Beta Hifi, VHS Stereo. RKO ($39.95)

Not to be confused with the MCA video which featured Sedaka in concert in Edmonton's Jubilee Auditorium a year or so earlier, the RKO *In Concert* is Neil in a more sedate and restrained performance. Looking much thinner and rather tired, Neil plays in front of a packed house at the Forum, Ontario Place, Toronto. By 1982, his comeback was already beginning to flag and the pressures of a year of touring show in Sedaka's lethargic concert. Because of the size of the Forum, the intimacy which was part of the MCA concert can't be found here. Songs: "Keep On Dancing," "Laughter in the Rain," "Love Will Keep Us Together," "Solitaire," "Oh Carol," "Stairway to Heaven," "Where the Boys Are," "Happy Birthday Sweet Sixteen," "Living Right Next Door to An Angel," "Calendar Girl," "I Should Have Never Let You Go," "Superbird," "Immigrant," "Love in the Shadows," "Breaking Up Is Hard to Do," and "That's When the Music Takes Me."

RICK SPRINGFIELD PLATINUM VIDEOS ★★↓

POP/ADULT. 1984. Artist: Rick Springfield. 24 min. Beta Hifi, VHS Stereo. RCA/Columbia ($19.95)

Rick Springfield first showed up on our shores in the early seventies as a teen idol singing bubblegum music. The response to him was lukewarm, but instead of returning

Rick Springfield.

to his native Australia, Springfield stayed in California to pursue both his musical and acting careers. For a number of years he was virtually invisible. Then he landed the role of Dr. Noah Drake on the daytime soap opera *General Hospital.* With the help of his familiarity to TV fans, *Working Class Dog* and its platinum single, "Jessie's Girl," put him back in the pop music limelight as a serious recording artist in 1981. He followed that up with two more platinum albums, *Success Hasn't Spoiled Me Yet* and *Living in Oz.* In this compilation of his videos, Springfield shows us he's a smooth performer, aware of the camera and at ease with the visual side of today's music. Though most of his music falls into the category of pop fluff, calculated stuff, "Jessie's Girl," which he wrote, is a clever, melodic reworking of familiar material. The videos directed by Doug Dowdle, "Affair of the Heart" and "Human Touch," are the most elaborate and entertaining ("Human Touch" is set in a futuristic spaceship where crew members have been placed in suspended animation). The other videos are "Don't Talk to Strangers," "What Kind of Fool Am I," and "Souls."

SATURDAY NIGHT LIVE: ELLIOTT GOULD   ★★◢

POP/ADULT. 1976. Cast: Elliott Gould, Chevy Chase, John Belushi, Dan Aykroyd, Jane Curtin, Gilda Radner, Garrett Morris, Laraine Newman, Leon Redbone, and Harlan Collins and Joyce Everson. 67 min. Beta, VHS. Warner ($39.95)

An early SNL episode featuring Elliott Gould (*E/R*) as the guest host and the eccentric Leon Redbone as the musical guest. While, on the whole, this show isn't particularly funny (Gould's lack of comedy timing in a live setting is a major reason), there are three skits that stand out. In one, Dan Aykroyd plays a buffoonish southern gentleman who gets involved in a strange poker game with two con men, Gould and Chase, posing as European nobility. Another is a *Star Trek* parody in which NBC programming executives appear on the bridge of the *Enterprise* to notify Captain Kirk (Belushi) and Spock (Chase) that their series has been canceled. And Belushi, Aykroyd, and Radner do a Bees version of *The Honeymooners.* Musically, Gould sings "Anything Goes," Leon Redbone does his rather sedate versions of the standards, "Shine On, Harvest Moon" and "Without My Cane," and Harlan Collins and Joyce Everson, a folk duo, sing "Heaven Only Knows."

SATURDAY NIGHT LIVE: MADELINE KAHN   ★★★

POP/ADULT. 1976. Cast: Madeline Kahn, John Belushi, Chevy Chase, Dan Aykroyd, Jane Curtin, Gilda Radner, Laraine Newman, Garrett Morris, and Carly Simon. 68 min. Beta, VHS. Warner ($39.95)

One of the better episodes of SNL available on home video. Madeline Kahn, easily one of the best comediennes in films and on stage today, is the guest host and Carly

Simon appears (on tape!) as the musical guest. Some of the skits are: Chevy Chase, as Ronald Reagan, getting down with some "hep organ playing"; Madeline singing "M-O-T-H-E-R-P" to celebrate Mother's Day; John Belushi as the wilderness comedian; Baba Wawa (Radner) interviewing Marlene Dietrich (Kahn) as they exchange lisps; an appeal for fondue sets to be sent to Namibia; Madeline, as the Bride of Frankenstein, singing "I Feel Pretty"; and Belushi and Kahn in a wicked parody of *Chinatown*. Carly Simon, exhibiting her notorious case of stage fright, appears on tape performing "Give Half a Chance" and "You're So Vain." As a finale, Madeline sings "Lost out Here in the Stars."

SATURDAY NIGHT LIVE: PETER COOK AND DUDLEY MOORE   ★★★

POP/ADULT. 1975. Cast: Peter Cook, Dudley Moore, Chevy Chase, John Belushi, Dan Aykroyd, Jane Curtin, Garrett Morris, Laraine Newman, Gilda Radner, and Neil Sedaka. 67 min. Beta, VHS. Warner ($39.95)

Another case of the regular SNL cast getting a shot of comedy vitamins from visiting Britons. Peter Cook and Dudley Moore were appearing on Broadway in a two-man show at the time. This was before they unofficially split up to pursue solo careers and Moore found fame and fortune with his performance in *10*. Cook, whose comic talent shines through here, is the guiding spirit of a series of absurdist sketches: Cook as a stage director who has volunteered his services to direct a prison revue (the inmates who audition for him include Belushi as a maniacal Elvis imitator); Don Pardo's holiday in an elevator; Emily Litella is puzzled by all the fuss about "Soviet jewelry"; Cook and Moore's Scottish version of Sonny and Cher, singing "I Got You, McBabe"; and Cook and Moore's classic dialogue concerning the notorious restaurant called The Frog and Peach. Neil Sedaka, in the midst of his celebrated comeback, performs "Breaking Up Is Hard to Do" and "Lonely Night" ("Angel Face"), which later became a hit for the Captain and Tenille. Considering Dudley Moore's declining fortunes on the silver screen lately, this is a useful reminder that Peter Cook was as funny as Moore, if not funnier.

SATURDAY NIGHT LIVE: SISSY SPACEK   ★★↓

POP/ADULT. 1977. Cast: Sissy Spacek, John Belushi, Dan Aykroyd, Bill Murray, Jane Curtin, Gilda Radner, Laraine Newman, Garrett Morris, Franken and Davis, and Richard Baskin. 68 min. Beta, VHS. Warner ($39.95)

Before Sissy Spacek became a well-known mainstream actress in the class of a Jane Fonda or Meryl Streep, she was noted for her portrayal of kooks in *Carrie, Three Women,* and *Welcome to L.A.* As a cult actress, she was able to fit in quite nicely with the cast of SNL. Spacek is in practically every skit, many more than most guest hosts. As Amy Carter, Sissy is told an eye-opening bedtime story by her black nanny, played by Garrett Morris. Sissy joins Gilda and Laraine in a skit about "Gidget's Disease." In a serious slice of life playlet, Sissy and John Belushi play a rural couple. A Gary Weis film short has Sissy displaying her baton-twirling talents to the accompaniment of David Bowie's "Fame." Other highlights of the show include Emily Litella's musings on "endangered feces," the Bad Playhouse production of an existentialist Dutch drama, *The Millkeeper,* and Bill Murray's deadpan portrayal of a man who can only say five words, "That's true, you're absolutely right." Richard Baskin sings "One, I Love You" and "City of One-Night Stands."

SHEENA EASTON: ACT ONE ★★✦

POP/ADULT. 1983. Artists: Sheena Easton, Al Jarreau, and Kenny Rogers. 60 min. Beta Hifi, VHS Stereo. Prism ($39.95)

Dwight Hemion, one of the veterans of TV variety shows still active today, directed this television special starring Sheena Easton. It suffers from the use of a tired device—

Sheena Easton.

the star, about to tape her special, wanders off and narrates her inner thoughts, as if extemporaneously. This time, Sheena leaves her studio and wanders onto the set of *The Tonight Show.* She interviews herself from behind Johnny Carson's desk. In this way, footage from a BBC documentary on her meteoric rise to fame is introduced. We see Sheena auditioning for EMI records in 1979. Quite interesting, really, and we're surprised she'd want her fans to see it. Musically, there is a smorgasbord of songs: "A Song for You," "Feelings," "For Your Eyes Only," "He's a Rebel," "The Entertainer," "On My Own," "Madness, Money, and Music," and "Wind beneath My Wings." Al Jarreau sings "Boogie Down" and duets with Sheena on "Danceland" and "Waltzing in the Garden." Surprisingly, Kenny Rogers appears only to sing "We've Got Tonight" with Sheena. Johnny Carson makes a brief appearance at the end.

SHEENA EASTON: LIVE AT THE PALACE   ★★

POP/ADULT. 1982. Artist: Sheena Easton. 60 min. Beta Hifi, VHS Stereo. Thorn-EMI ($49.95)

This is a video record of Sheena Easton's first concert performance in the United States, taped at the Hollywood Palace in 1982. One gathers as the concert progresses that Sheena is not the most self-assured performer in the world, especially in front of an American audience. Part of the reason for her lack of confidence is the fact that she's masquerading as a pop-rock singer when, in essence, she is really a cabaret performer. She is Helen Reddy or Jane Olivor, not Pat Benatar or Cyndi Lauper. Her selection of material ranges all over the place, with the only distinctive songs being her three Top 10 hits, "Modern Girl," "Morning Train," and "For Your Eyes Only." To fill out the concert she sings cover versions of Little River Band's "Help Is on the Way," Elvin Bishop's "Fooled Around and Fell in Love," and Joni Mitchell's "Raised on Robbery." It sounds like a set you might hear from a pub band or a lounge band in a casino. She has since defined her image more sharply and, recently, moved toward a harder-rocking sound. This early concert, though, exposes the weaknesses in her musical foundation. Other songs heard are "Prisoner," "I Wouldn't Beg for Water," "Are You Man Enough," "When He Shines," "Money, Madness, and Music," "In the Winter," "Weekend in Paris," "You Could Have Been with Me," and "Wind beneath My Wings."

A STAR IS BORN (1976)   ★

POP/ADULT. 1976. Cast: Barbra Streisand, Kris Kristofferson, and Gary Busey. 140 min. Beta, VHS. Warner ($39.98)

Screenwriters Joan Didion, John Gregory Dunne, and Frank Pierson tried to write a thought-provoking, contemporary adaptation of the 1954 classic musical drama, trans-

Kris Kristofferson and Barbra Streisand, featured in the 1976 remake of *A Star Is Born*.

ferring its setting from the movie industry to the record business. In contrast to the entertaining and moving performances of the captivating Judy Garland and the suave James Mason, Barbra Streisand as L.A. club singer Esther Hoffmann, and Kris Kristofferson as the over the hill, strung-out rock star on the decline, John Howard Norman, deliver performances that are boorish and completely unlikeable. The Didion, Dunne, and Pierson screenplay is laden with painfully ingenuous, plodding dialogue. The physical scale of the movie, with its enormous mansions, blocklong limousines, and gigantic rock concerts, completely dwarfs the main story—the love affair between Norman and Esther. As Esther becomes a star and Norman loses his record audience, the viewer loses any sympathy he or she might have for the two leads. The score includes the Oscar winner for best song in 1976, "Evergreen," Leon Russell and Barbra Streisand's "Lost Inside of You," Rupert Holmes' "Queen Bee," and "I Believe in Love" by Kenny Loggins and Marylyn and Alan Bergman.

STEVE ALLEN'S MUSIC ROOM, VOLUME I ★★⌐

POP/ADULT. 1983. Artists: Steve Allen, Rosemary Clooney, Lou Rawls, James Raphael, Red Holloway, Doc Severinson and Zebron, Patti Page, Ann Jillian, and Terry Gibbs and his Orchestra. 116 min. Beta Hifi, VHS Stereo. Buena Vista ($49.95)

Two episodes from the Disney Cable Channel series *Music Room* form Steve Allen's tribute to the music that is closest to his own heart, the sounds of the late forties and early fifties. With guest stars like Rosemary Clooney and Patti Page, Allen's penchant for indulging his, by now, peripheral tastes is given full rein. There is very little Allenesque humor here, just a somber, almost dirgelike observance of a bygone era. But there's lots of music in that early modern pop vein (post-World War II and pre-rock and roll) for those of that inclination. Rosemary Clooney sings "You're Gonna Hear from Me Now" and "Hey There." There's a clip from a 1957 Bing Crosby TV show which has Bing, Frank Sinatra, and Rosemary doing a medley of "I Got Rhythm" and "Mama Done Told Me." Lou Rawls, always a smooth song stylist, sings "You're Gonna Miss My Loving" and joins Rosemary on "I Cried over You," "Who's Sorry Now?," and "Goody Goody." James Raphael plays piano on a recital of Gershwin's *Rhapsody in Blue.* Lou Rawls solos on "Wind beneath My Wings." In episode two, Doc Severinson and his group of young jazz musicians, Zebron, play an instrumental jazz-fusion number. Patti Page sings "Release Me" and "Old Cape Cod" and Ann Jillian sings "Let the Good Times Roll" and "Second Time Around." Finally, the ensemble sings "You Go To My Head." Nostalgic but rather slow-moving.

TOM JONES LIVE IN LAS VEGAS ★★★

POP/ADULT. 1981. Artist: Tom Jones. 60 min. Beta Hifi, VHS Stereo. U.S.A. ($59.95)

Shown here in a typical performance at Caesar's Palace in Las Vegas, Tom Jones, pushing fifty, is still a dynamic, hip-swiveling, husky-voiced sex symbol. His adaptation to the Vegas mode of entertainment has not diminished Jones' musical ardor one bit. In a suit that must have been painted on (it seems too tight to be believed), Tom's raucous moves thrill his Vegas audience and hint at the power of another noted Vegas performer of the recent past, Elvis Presley. While not approaching Elvis as a singer, nevertheless Tom Jones is as intense and hot a performer as Vegas can come up with today. Fans who recall Jones' earlier days as an R&B crooner will have to bear with the first half of the concert before Tom reaches into his bag of greatest hits from the past. "Till," "We Don't Talk Anymore," "She Believes in Me," "Ladies Night," "Do That to Me One More Time," "I'll Never Love This Way Again," "I Don't Know

Why I Love You But I Do," and "Working My Way Back to You" fulfill his requirements for the role of human adult contemporary radio station. Then, as a fitting climax, Jones rips off eleven hit songs from his 15-year repertory: "Delilah," "She's a Lady," "I'm Never Gonna Fall in Love Again," "Green Green Grass of Home," "Stay until Tomorrow," "What's New Pussycat?," "Woman," "Daughter of Darkness," "I Who Have Nothing," "Love Me Tonight," and "It's Not Unusual." As an encore, he does a scorching version of Isaac Hayes' soulful disco hit "Don't Let Go."

TONY POWERS: DON'T NOBODY MOVE ★★★

POP/ADULT. 1983. Cast: Tony Powers, Peter Riegert, Marcia Strassman, Treat Williams, Lois Chiles, and Corine Lorain. 24 min. Beta Hifi, VHS Stereo. Sony ($19.95)

Winner of the 1983 Silver Award at the twenty-sixth annual International Film and Video Festival of New York, this long-form video is diverting but ultimately quite confusing. The music, by Powers, a songwriter from the Brill Building era of hitmakers like Neil Sedaka, Carole King, and Ellie Greenwich, is not exceptional either in the rock or pop categories. What makes this program noteworthy is that it attempts, however tentatively, to establish an autonomous genre, the music video, which is totally independent of records. "Don't Nobody Move (This Is a Heist)" is a hood movie done by a beatnik rapper (Powers) whose unintelligible verses militate against viewer involvement. After all, how does Powers expect anyone born after, say, 1955 to know what a hipster is? "Odyssey" is more successful if only because Lois Chiles appears in it, playing a mystery woman whom Powers follows about the misty, fog-laced piers of Manhattan after dark. Finally, "Midnite Trampoline" is Powers' attempt to parody Italian cinema of the sixties. He plays a Marcello Mastroianni-type gigolo who seduces beautiful heiresses, billing himself as a "professor of love." Replete with English subtitles and grainy film stock. The music was produced by Powers and Gene Cornish, guitarist of the sixties group the Rascals. Directed by Tony Powers and Brian Owens.

WAYNE NEWTON AT THE LONDON PALLADIUM ★★♪

POP/ADULT. 1983. Artist: Wayne Newton. 63 min. Beta Hifi, VHS Stereo. MGM/UA ($59.95)

The ultimate Vegas entertainer, Wayne Newton has shaped a very prosperous career out of bits and pieces picked up from other popular singers—Elvis Presley, Frank

Vegas entertainer Wayne Newton.

Sinatra, and Dean Martin, to name just three. With his Errol Flynn moustache, Elvis belt, and formfitting tuxedo jumpsuit, Newton's appeal to adult audiences is undeniable. Exhibiting the chameleonlike approach to popular tastes that is the foundation of his success as a Vegas attraction, he sings lounge music, country and western, pop ballads, soft rock, and cabaret standards. He's not much of a singer and he's got to make up for it with loads of enthusiasm and self-confidence. Considering his core audience, Newton does a creditable job of satisfying their entertainment needs. This video program was recorded live at London's Palladium Theater, where Newton, in a rare concert appearance outside of Las Vegas and Reno, is backed up by a forty-two piece orchestra directed by Don Vincent. The songs are: "C.C. Rider" (Elvis' old opening number), "Georgia," "Red Roses for a Blue Lady," "Danke Schoen," "The Hungry Years," "Daddy Don't You Walk So Fast," "Jambalaya," "Lonesome Me," "Goodhearted Woman," "The Impossible Dream," "New York, New York," "I Am . . . I Said," "Baby Face," "Robert E. Lee," "Orange Blossom Special," "The Saints Go Marching In," and "I Made It through the Rain." Directed by Scott Sternberg.

WELCOME TO L.A.   ★♪

POP/ADULT. 1976. Cast: Keith Carradine, Geraldine Chaplin, Sissy Spacek, Lauren Hutton, Sally Kellerman, Harvey Keitel, Richard Baskin, and Denver Pyle. 106 min. Beta Hifi, VHS Stereo. CBS/Fox ($59.95)

Using a sexual metaphor, "the city of one-night stands," director Alan Rudolph, a protegé of Robert Altman, has attempted a cinematic essay on what makes Los Angeles tick. Nothing really dramatic happens as Rudolph hammers home his point that L.A. is a city of emotional transients, going from one business deal to another, one bedmate to another, and one dream to another—all of which we already knew quite well. Just as his characters, led by Keith Carradine as a songwriter caught between the greed of his multimillionaire father and the emptiness of show business, keep searching unsuccessfully for meaning, so Rudolph's movie is a quest for something profound to say about west coast culture. Unhappily, everyone comes up empty. There are some quirky performances to look for: Sissy Spacek's spaced-out maid who likes to do her dusting topless, Harvey Keitel's sexually ambivalent dairy-company executive, and Geraldine Chaplin as Keitel's wife, a woman on the edge of sanity. There are songs written by Richard Baskin, sung by Baskin and Keith Carradine, which are intended to serve as musical commentary on the goings-on. They include "Where the Arrow Flies," "The Best Temptation of All," and "After the End."

BLACK ARTISTS

ALWAYS FOR PLEASURE ★★★

BLACK POPULAR. 1978. Artists: Professor Longhair, The Wild Tchoupitoulas, Kid Thomas Valentine, and the Olympia Brass Band. 58 min. Beta, VHS. Rhapsody ($70.00)

Independent filmmaker and gourmet Les Blank traveled from his home in San Francisco to record the events of Mardi Gras in New Orleans. He first presents the viewer with a picture of a traditional New Orleans funeral procession. The world famous Olympia Brass Band plays a dirge on the way to the cemetery, and on the way back, the band plays an up-tempo dance number that moves mourners to kick up their heels and dance, or "cut up," on the way home. The director then takes his camera into two Creole restaurants to show his audience how the Cajuns prepare red beans and rice and the local delicacy, crawfish. After the culinary diversion, Blank examines the history of the New Orleans ritual of dressing in feathery, colorful Indian costumes for the Mardi Gras parade, a tradition that has continued since the time of slavery. Each participant belongs to one of several neighborhood "tribes." These "tribes" compete with one another in wild dances along the parade route. Blank and his camera catch up with the members of the Wild Tchoupitoulas tribe in rehearsal for the parade as they practice the jumpy Mardi Gras tune "Handa Wanda." The late New Orleans pianist Professor Longhair adds to the festivities by singing his tribute to the parade tribes, "Big Chief." If you can't get to New Orleans on Mardi Gras, *Always for Pleasure* is the next best thing to being there.

AMERICA'S MUSIC: RHYTHM & BLUES I ★◡

BLACK POPULAR. 1983. Artists: Billy Eckstine, Ruth Brown, Billy Preston, Gloria Lynn, and Sheer Delight. 57 min. Beta, VHS. Genesis ($39.95)

Part of a continuing series that examines different types of indigenous American music, this low-budget 57-minute overview (it was made for television) lacks the depth and resources to explore and present a complete and accurate history of rhythm and blues. In front of a studio audience of people strangely dressed in costumes from the thirties and the forties, Billy Eckstine sings a song he recorded more than forty years ago with the Count Basie Orchestra, "Little Mama." He then briefly traces the history of early rhythm and blues by showing short film clips of Louis Jordan and his Tympany Five playing their 1946 hit, "Let the Good Times Roll," and Amos Milburn and his Chickenshackers playing their chart-topping R&B hit from 1950, "Bad, Bad Whiskey," before introducing Ruth Brown. Ruth, who had a monster R&B hit with "Mama, He Treats Your Daughter Mean," walks out on stage to blast out versions of "Baby, Baby, Baby (I've Got to Have You for My Own)" and "Everytime It Rains I Think of You." This examination of R&B continues into the soul years with the introduction of keyboard wizard Billy Preston, who plays an unintentionally campy version of Gershwin's "Summertime," with passages rendered in the piano styles of J. S. Bach and Ray Charles. Billy Preston then launches into his 1972 hit single, "Will It Go Round in Circles." Sheer Delight, an all-female vocal group, takes to the stage to show the audience the future of the rhythm and blues tradition, ironically, by singing a medley of old standards. They race through "The Man That Got Away," "The Man I Love," and Duke Ellington's "Don't Get Around Much Anymore" and "I'm Beginning to See the Light" without any apparent feeling for the lyrics. Rhythm and blues deserves a better tribute than this.

ASHFORD AND SIMPSON ★★★◡

BLACK POPULAR. 1984. Artists: Nicholas Ashford and Valerie Simpson. 21 min. Beta Hifi, VHS Stereo. Sony ($16.95)

One of the better short-form videos to be released in 1984, *Ashford and Simpson* contains three videos, one of them the really successful narrative video "High Rise." Made for the title track of their album, "High Rise" is a beautifully directed visual companion piece to the song. In a contemporary tale of love and ambition, Valerie, a piano player and singer at a dive, dreams she leaves her job and her bartender boyfriend, Nick, to seek her fortune in the record business. As she gets her act together, composing music, taking dancing lessons, and recording songs, Nick, her ex-boyfriend, stands secretly in the wings silently helping her career by making contacts and paying off company bigwigs. She reaches the top of the charts and makes an appointment to see the record company president who turns out to be Nick, her former bartending boyfriend. Valerie snaps out of her daydream to find herself still playing piano at the same old dive. The narrative form of video is the most satisfying and entertaining of all the forms available for promotional use. Such videos as "High Rise" and David Bowie's "Blue Jean" capture the viewer's attention as the riot of jumbled images seen in the mainstream of broadcast videos do not. Also included on this tape is the "Street Opera Medley," a video that features Ashford and Simpson on a city street set singing "It Takes Mighty, Mighty Strong Love," "Woman Here I Stand," "On Any Street Corner," and "Times Will Be Good Again." Nick and Valerie can be seen in "It's Much Deeper," an unorganized patchwork of images.

THE ASHFORD AND SIMPSON VIDEO   ★★

BLACK POPULAR. 1984. Artists: Nicholas Ashford and Valerie Simpson. 56 min. Beta Hifi, VHS Stereo. Thorn-EMI ($29.95)

Longtime pop and soul songwriters Nick Ashford and Valerie Simpson decided to form a singing duet and perform the hits that they had written for other artists. Backed by a solid band on this tape, they appear on stage in their trademark frilly costumes in front of a flashing neon backdrop and play before a packed house singing a number of the hits they penned including "If We Let Nothing Get in Our Way (We Can Make It to a Brighter Day)," "Nobody Knows the Inside," and a song they wrote for Chaka Khan, "It's Gonna Rain." Nick and Valerie sing each song with so much passion that they look like they are in the throes of ecstasy on stage. The highlight of this tape is the "Street Opera Medley" in which Ashford and Simpson sing a string of their songs on a city street set. As they pass street people they gyrate, dance, and sing such songs as "It Takes Mighty, Mighty Strong Love," "Woman Here I Stand," "On Any Street Corner," and "Times Will Be Good Again." The tape returns to an earlier concert performance in which they sing "Gonna Love It Away," "Found a Cure," and "I'll Take the Whole World Over for You." Nick and Valerie then launch into a series of songs they wrote for Motown including Diana Ross' monster hit "Ain't No Mountain High Enough," Marvin Gaye and Tammi Terrell's famous "Ain't Nothing Like the Real Thing, Baby," and Gaye and Terrell's "You're All I Need to Get By."

Ashford and Simpson.

BALLAD IN BLUE   ★★★

BLACK POPULAR. 1965. Cast: Ray Charles, Tom Bell, Mary Peach, Dawn Addams, and Joe Adams. 88 min. Beta, VHS. U.S.A. ($39.95)

This British film, shot in black and white, was produced by Alexander Salkind (the *Superman* series) and directed by Paul Henreid (*Now Voyager* with Bette Davis). It's really an excuse to film the great Ray Charles in concert, singing the songs which made him an international sensation in the late fifties and early sixties. The action, which takes place in London's Mayfair district, the bohemian enclave of artists and musicians, and Paris, concerns Ray's involvement with a blind boy and the boy's overprotective mother. When the mother's boyfriend, Tom Bell, a jazz composer, is hired by Charles to arrange for his orchestra, the action shifts to Paris and Ray convinces the boy's mother to allow a French eye surgeon to treat her son. The story is there to bide the time between Ray's dynamic performance segments. Backed by his orchestra and the Raelettes, Ray sings "Let the Good Times Roll," "Careless Love," "Hit the Road, Jack," "Lucky Old Sun," "Unchain My Heart," "Hallelujah, I Just Love Her So," "Don't Tell Me Your Troubles," "I Got a Woman," "Busted," "Talkin' about You," "Light Out of Darkness," and "What'd I Say." If only they had just given us a full-length concert film. Recommended as a record of what the great Ray Charles sounded like a little closer to his prime.

BEAT STREET   ★★♪

BLACK POPULAR. 1984. Cast: Rae Dawn Chong, Guy Davis, Leon W. Grant, Saundra Santiango, Robert Taylor, New York City Breakers, Rock Steady Crew, and Grandmaster Melle Mel and the Furious Five. 106 min. Beta Hifi, VHS Stereo. Vestron ($29.95)

It seems that every producer of a dramatic breakdancing film to come down the pike in the last 3 years has bought the same worn out Hollywood plot from the same ancient scriptwriter: "By sheer nerve, kids with raw talent get the attention from the world that they deserve. Love interest optional." In *Beat Street*, a high-gloss look at the ghetto culture of the South Bronx, master d.j. Kenny (Guy Davis) struggles to leave his uptown home to become a "record scratcher" at the Roxy, a club devoted to breakdancing. Kenny falls in love with Tracy (Rae Dawn Chong) a dancer at City College who is choreographing her first ballet. The two of them look more like well-heeled preppies than members of the underclass. Ramón, Kenny's best friend, is a "bomber," a graffiti artist who covers subway trains with his spray-can paintings. By the end of the film, Ramón gets in a fist fight with another bomber in a subway tunnel. They both are accidentally electrocuted when they careen into the power rail on the tracks. In the finale, the saving grace of the film, Kenny, Tracy, and the kids put on a multimedia "celebration" in memory of Ramón. Grandmaster Melle Mel and the Furious Five perform the powerful "Beat Street Breakdown," a tough, sinewy rap tune that decries the current state of the world.

THE BLUES ACCORDIN' TO LIGHTNIN' HOPKINS/ THE SUN'S GONNA SHINE   ★★

BLACK POPULAR. 1967. Artists: Lightnin' Hopkins, Mance Lipscomb, and Billy Bizor. 42 min. Beta, VHS. Rhapsody ($60.00)

This rambling portrait of country bluesman Lightnin' Hopkins by Les Blank follows the singer as he visits his birthplace and boyhood home, Centerville, Texas. In between shots of Lightnin' meeting old friends, walking around town, seeing a rodeo, and going to a barbeque, he ponders the meaning of the blues in various interviews. Lightnin' provides some fine numbers on guitar and sings "Good Morning Little Schoolgirl," "I Get Up in the Morning" (with Billy Bizor on harmonica), "Meet Me in the Bottom," and "How Long Have It Been Since You Been Home." Also included on this tape is Les Blank's *The Sun's Gonna Shine,* a short made in which leftover footage from *The Blues Accordin' to Lightnin' Hopkins* is set to Hopkins' composition, "The Sun's Gonna Shine."

BLUES ALIVE ★★★

BLACK POPULAR. 1982. Artists: John Mayall's Original Blues Breakers (John Mayall, Colin Allen, John McVie, and Mick Taylor), Etta James, Albert King, Sippie Wallace, Buddy Guy, and Junior Wells. 92 min. Beta Hifi, VHS Stereo. RCA/Columbia ($29.95)

John Mayall's Original Blues Breakers reunited in 1982 for a tour across America. In this concert at the Capitol Theater in Passaic, New Jersey, drummer Colin Allen, who left the Blues Breakers to join Rod Stewart's group, bassist John McVie, who left the band to become one of the founding members of Fleetwood Mac, guitarist Mick Taylor, who left the group to spend 6 years with the Rolling Stones, and Blues Breakers leader John Mayall are joined on stage by R&B singer Etta James, blues guitarist Albert King, one of the original blues shouters, 83-year-old Sippie Wallace, and the great harmonica and guitar duo, Buddy Guy and Junior Wells. Mayall and the band open the show with "Hard Times Again," on which John plays harp and piano and Mick Taylor plays a very sleepy slide guitar. John brings Etta James out to sing a few gritty barrelhouse numbers: "Let it Roll," "You Got Me Where You Want Me," and "You Don't Treat Me Like You Used to Do." Chicago's own Buddy Guy and Junior Wells take the stage to deliver unspirited versions of their rockers "Messin' with the Kid," and "Single File Has Got to Go." For some unfathomable reason Mayall and the Blues Breakers play Buddy Guy's "My Time after Awhile" after Buddy and Junior have left the stage. Living legend Sippie Wallace is greeted on stage by a rousing round of applause and she musters enough energy to shout out the "Shorty Doll Blues." The Blues Breakers play "The Dark Side of Midnight" before inviting Albert King to join them on stage to sing his famous "Born under a Bad Sign" and "Stormy Monday." Mick Taylor's listless guitar playing is overshadowed by the powerful, dynamic whine of King's guitar. As the finale of the set, Mayall brings everyone back on stage to sing a disorganized and aimless version of the Ma Rainey classic, "See See Rider Blues" before the Blues Breakers perform their biggest hit, "Room to Move."

Mick Taylor, Albert King, John Mayall, and Buddy Guy performing in *Blues Alive*.

BREAKIN'   ★★★

BLACK POPULAR. 1984. Cast: Lucinda Dickey, Adolfo "Shabba-Doo" Quinones, and Michael "Boogaloo Shrimp" Chambers. 87 min. Beta Hifi, VHS Stereo. MGM/UA ($79.95)

Of the flurry of breakdancing and hip-hop movies that were produced in fiscal 1983–1984, *Breakin'* is by far the best. Famous low-budget Hollywood film producers Menahem Golan and Yoram Globus threw the social statements found in the other films out the proverbial window and made a high-gloss movie with a paper-thin plot, a dynamic, chartbusting soundtrack, and an almost solid 87 minutes of L.A.-style breakdancing. Their simple formula worked. *Breakin'* grossed over $30 million in its first month in release, putting it on *Variety*'s list of the top fifty grossing films of the week. Its soundtrack produced an album featuring the smash title tune, "Breakin' . . . There's No Stoppin' Us," as well as "99½" and "Freak Show on the Dancefloor," making it worthy of platinum sales. In the movie, reserved Los Angeles jazz dancer Lucinda

Featured dancers from *Breakin'*.

Dickey leaves her dance class and the attentive glances of its teacher to learn how to breakdance on Venice's boardwalk. Her instructors, Aldolfo "Shabba-Doo" Quinones and Michael "Boogaloo Shrimp" Chambers, not only teach her their fancy footwork, but decide to join her at the tryouts for a "big professional show." The trial judges are miffed that Shabba-Doo and Boogaloo Shrimp do not have formal training, but of course are duly impressed when the three pull out all the stops during the "Breakin' " ballet that forms the film's finale. A good, big dose of mindless entertainment.

BREAKIN' IN THE USA ★★★

BLACK POPULAR. 1984. 50 min. Beta Hifi, VHS Stereo. Sony ($29.95)

Breakin' in the USA is an adequate breakdancing instructional tape that covers all the basic moves used in breakdance including "Electric Boogie," "Breaking," and "Freestyle." More specifically, this tape delivers detailed instructions on how to "Warm Up," to do the "Moon Walk," the "Glide," the "Jump Rope," the "Tut," the "Robot," the "Wall," the "Rope," the "Scarecrow," "Locking," the "Masterswipe," the "Handglide," and the "Back Spin."

BREAKIN' NEW YORK STYLE ★⌐

BLACK POPULAR. 1983. 60 min. Beta, VHS. Continental ($19.95)

Breakin' New York Style is a poorly produced instructional tape that appears to have been made quickly to cash in on the national breakdancing craze. Host Lori Eastside is supposedly an authentic breakdancer from New York's Lower East Side. She raps the instructions for each dance step so that her directions become almost impossible to understand. In addition, she raps with such a complete lack of rhythm that she sounds more like a California Valley Girl than a kid from Orchard Street. Her rap instructions are too general and the camerawork too cursory to provide effective instruction for the beginner or the advanced dancer. This tape was poorly planned and poorly executed, and is a complete waste of time.

BREAKING WITH THE MIGHTY POPPALOTS ★★★

BLACK POPULAR. 1984. Artists: The Mighty Poppalots. 60 min. Beta, VHS. Vestron ($39.95)

Breaking with the Mighty Poppalots is a breakdancing instructional tape that spotlights the technique and teaching method of Washington, D.C.'s own breakdancing troupe, The Mighty Poppalots. The Poppalots, who can still be seen performing their breathtaking routines on Washington street corners from Anacostia to Georgetown on weekends, run through demonstrations of the proper method for performing a variety of breakdancing steps. The treatment given to basic steps is good, but not as thorough as the coverage found on Warner's *Let's Break*. The real advantage to viewing *Breaking with the Mighty Poppalots* is the instruction the dance team gives in advanced team, or group, breakdancing and performing. They demonstrate the "Windmill," the "One Arm Spin," and "Routines" that include the "Up-Rock," "Locking," the "Pyramid," the "Helicopter," and the "King Tut." *Breaking with the Mighty Poppalots* is recommended for the serious and advanced breakdancer.

BUSTIN' LOOSE ★★♪

BLACK POPULAR. 1981. Cast: Richard Pryor, Cicely Tyson, Robert Christian, and George Coe. 94 min. Beta Hifi, VHS Stereo. MCA ($39.95)

Richard Pryor's attempt to make a family picture is inconsistently funny and ultimately disappointing. He is successful for the most part at avoiding mushy sentimentality but is not successful at keeping any sort of plausible story line going. Joe Braxton (Pryor) is a third-rate ex-con who is given an assignment by his parole officer: driving a busload of orphaned problem kids cross-country from Philadelphia to Seattle. With them is Vivian Perry (Cicely Tyson), a crusading TV reporter who makes the plight of these children her own personal obsession. Much of the humor comes from Pryor's attempts to cope with the filthy mouths and dubious behavior of his charges—among them are a pyromaniac, a former child prostitute, and a girl who has an invisible companion. The love story between Pryor and Tyson is only palatable given the innate charm of the two actors. Otherwise, there are great holes in the plot and characterization in this film. The music was composed and performed by Roberta Flack, who sings the title tune.

Comedian Richard Pryor in *Car Wash*.

CAR WASH ★★↵

BLACK POPULAR. 1976. Cast: Franklyn Ajaye, George Carlin, Professor Irwin Corey, Ivan Dixon, Bill Duke, Antonio Fargas, Melanie Mayron, Garrett Morris, Leon Pinkney, The Pointer Sisters, Richard Pryor, and James Spinks. 97 mins. Beta Hifi, VHS Stereo. MCA ($59.95)

The comedy *Car Wash* takes a look at a day in the life of the men and machines of a commercial car wash in downtown Los Angeles. Using an ensemble cast and a large number of characters whose stories are told in an interwoven network of episodic vignettes, a method used in countless disaster films of the same period, writer Joel Schumscher (*D.C. Cab, Sparkle*) and director Michael Schultz (*Sergeant Pepper's Lonely Hearts Club Band*) construct a series of sight gags and comic bits of business that usually exceed the bounds of good taste and usually get a laugh. Highlights include Richard Pryor's appearance as Daddy Rich, a fast-talking charlatan posing as a preacher. The Pointer Sisters appear as his backup singers and chorus. George Carlin makes a cameo appearance as a cab driver. Rose Royce provides the songs on the soundtrack. The title tune, "Car Wash," hit high numbers on the soul chart upon its release.

DANIEL ★★↵

BLACK POPULAR. 1983. Cast: Timothy Hutton, Mandy Patinkin, Lindsay Crouse, Ed Asner, Ellen Barkin, Amanda Plummer, and Tovah Feldsuh. 129 min. Beta, VHS. Paramount ($59.95)

Paul Robeson's recordings of several folk and gospel standards, including "This Little Light of Mine," "Peat Bog Soldiers," and "Witness for the Lord," can be heard on the soundtrack of this Sidney Lumet film which fictionally recounts the lives of Julius and Ethel Rosenberg, who went to the electric chair for high treason. The atmosphere of the McCarthy era of anticommunist paranoia is captured in the story of the Isaacsons, a New York Jewish couple active in radical causes who are arrested, convicted, and executed for allegedly funneling U.S. military secrets to the Russians. Twenty years later, after the suicide of his emotionally distraught sister (Amanda Plummer), Daniel Isaacson (Timothy Hutton) decides to find out, once and for all, whether his parents were framed or really guilty. Based on E. L. Doctorow's novel of the same name. While the performances are all excellent and Lumet's mounting of the story thought-provoking, the fact that it's doubly nostalgic—the Isaacsons' story takes place in the forties and early fifties, Daniel's in the late sixties—makes it all the more remote to the audience.

D.C. CAB ★★★

BLACK POPULAR. 1982. Cast: Mr. T, Adam Baldwin, Charlie Barnett, Irene Cara, Anne De Salvo, Max Gail, Gloria Gifford, and Gary Busey. 100 min. Beta Hifi, VHS Stereo. MCA ($69.95)

There are two kinds of people in Washington, D.C., those who live there and those who work there. The people who work there pack up and leave at the end of each administration. The people who live there pick up the pieces and try to carry on. In this very funny and sometimes very accurate portrait of unofficial Washington, a company of misfit cab drivers wreak havoc on the Nation's Capital, alienate everyone, and restore their self-respect and public image by movie's end. Mr. T (*Rocky III, A-Team*) delivers a one-two punch to a couple of meanies and his best performance ever in *D.C. Cab* in another manifestation of his tough-guy-with-a-heart-of-gold image. Former New York City street comic Charlie Barnett gives a memorable performance as a real looney tune. Let's hope he's cast in another movie soon. Gary Busey (*The*

Mr. T in *D.C. Cab.*

Buddy Holly Story) stars as another real looney tune. The whole movie is lots of fun. Irene Cara makes a brief appearance on screen and is featured on the soundtrack singing "The Dream." The soundtrack also contains Stephanie Mills' "Party Me Tonight," DeBarge's "Single Heart," Gary U.S. Bonds' "One More Time around the Block, Ophelia," Jimmy Cliff's "Vietnam," and Gary Busey's "Whv Baby, Why."

DIANA ROSS IN CONCERT ★★★

BLACK POPULAR. 1979. Artist: Diana Ross. 80 min. Beta Hifi, VHS Stereo. RCA/Columbia ($29.95)

In the seventies, black musical performers who had earlier never dreamed of appearing in Las Vegas became ubiquitous on the stages of the never-never land of the high

Diana Ross.

DIANA ROSS

Did Our Love Go?," "Baby Love," "Come See about Me," "Stop! In the Name of Love," "Back in My Arms Again," "I Hear a Symphony," "You Can't Hurry Love," "Someday We'll Be Together," and "Ain't No Mountain High Enough."

Going solo in 1970 with the Ashford and Simpson songs "Reach Out and Touch (Somebody's Hand)" and "Ain't No Mountain High Enough," Diana continued to chalk up a number of hit records: "Touch Me in the Morning," "Last Time I Saw Him," "Theme from Mahogany," and "Love Hangover." Diana paralleled her success in the recording field with a string of acting roles in hit movies: *Lady Sings the Blues, Mahogany,* and *The Wiz,* all of which are available on tape for the home video enthusiast.

Video Resume

Diana Ross in Concert, (1979), RCA/Columbia.

Lady Sings the Blues, (1972), Paramount.

Mahogany, (1975), Paramount.

The Wiz, (1978), MCA.

The Girl Groups: The Story of a Sound, (1983), MGM/UA.

Mellow Memories, (1984), U.S.A.

Diana Ross was born March 26, 1944, in Detroit, Michigan. Diana, Mary Wilson, and Florence Ballard started singing together in Detroit's Brewster housing project in 1960 and under the tutelage of Motown Records' founder Berry Gordy took the world by storm as the Supremes, pocketing a number of gold records including "Where rollers and one-armed bandits. Acts like The Four Tops, The Miracles, and The Temptations regularly worked the casino circuit, playing in front of nostalgia-minded vacationers who had left the sixties behind and were attracted by the bright neon lights of the Strip. So it was that Diana Ross, once the lead singer of the Supremes, the girl group of all girl groups, had come to Caesar's Palace in Vegas to entertain that same dinner crowd of upwardly mobile couples. In the tradition of the city's tawdry but dazzling stage revues, Diana manages to make several costume changes, dance with a few chorus boys in tights, and walk into the audience, mingling with the tourists from Oshkosh and other distant burgs. In the audience are Marvin Gaye, Diana's mother, and her children. The show they see is quite a recapitulation of Diana's career, with and without the Supremes. She performs "Ain't No Mountain High Enough," "Too Shy to Say," "Touch Me in the Morning," "I Wanna Be Bad," "I Ain't Been Licked," "Home," "It's My House," "No One Gets the Prize," "Love Hangover," "Reach Out and Touch," "Baby Love," "Remember Me," "Lady Sings the Blues," "Ain't Nobody's Business," "God Bless the Child," "My Man," "The Boss," "Do You Know Where You're Going To," and "All for One."

DIONNE WARWICK IN CONCERT   ★★★

BLACK POPULAR. 1983. Artist: Dionne Warwick. 60 min. Beta Hifi, VHS Stereo. Prism ($29.95)

This episode of the *Music America Live* concert series originally televised over WTTW in Chicago features Dionne Warwick at the Rialto Square Theater in Joliet, Illinois. Warwick first came onto the scene as a soul singer often touring with Dick Clark's traveling rock and roll show, but she gained lasting fame as the foremost interpreter of Hal David and Bert Bacharach's sixties pop ballads, like "Walk On By," "I Say a Little Prayer," "Alfie," "Do You Know the Way to San José?," and "I'll Never Fall in Love Again." Dionne offers the audience a lot of glib chatter between songs, treating the concert as if it were an evening in a cabaret. The full orchestra backing Dionne gives her songs a fullness of sound perhaps only to be found on her records and that is always a plus in such live concerts. The songs are: "What You Won't Do for Love," "Friends in Love," "Will You Still Love Me Tomorrow?," "Walk On By," "I Say a Little Prayer," "Do You Know the Way to San José?," "What's It All About, Alfie?," "Take the Short Way Home," "Yours," "Heartbreaker," "Déja Vu," and "I'll Never Love This Way Again."

EARTH, WIND, AND FIRE IN CONCERT   ★★★

BLACK POPULAR. 1982. Artists: Earth, Wind, and Fire with the Phoenix Horns. 58 min. Beta Hifi, VHS Stereo. Vestron ($29.95)

Maurice White's excursion into sophisticated funk, the obverse side of George Clinton's Parliament/Funkadelic project during the same time period, Earth, Wind, and Fire has recorded some of the finest dance-based rhythm and blues music in the past decade. In the same neighborhood with Lionel Richie, before and after his split with The Commodores, White's group is funkier if not nastier (pace George Clinton). In this concert performance shot at the Oakland Coliseum, the group is augmented, as usual, by the Phoenix Horns, whose precise yet swinging horn arrangements Maurice has always utilized well. The stage show is all flash and fantasy with laser effects and everyone decked out in space-age costumes. Maurice shares the singing chores with Philip Bailey, who has since gone on to a very successful solo career (including a smash duet with Phil Collins on "Easy Lover"). Together, they take the audience through a brief history of the group's biggest hits: "Let Your Feelings Show," "In the Stove," "Fantasy," "Sing a Song," "Reasons," "Remember the Children," "Where Have All the Flowers Gone?," "Shining Star," "Keep Your Head to the Sky," "Gratitude," "That's the Way of the World," "I've Had Enough," "Jupiter" ("The Battle"), and "Let's Groove." Highly polished intergalactic R&B funk.

AN EVENING WITH RAY CHARLES   ★★★✦

BLACK POPULAR. 1981. Artist: Ray Charles. 50 min. Beta, VHS. MCA ($39.95)

There have been several phases in the long and illustrious career of Ray Charles. He has stretched out in many musical directions, moving from rhythm and blues to jazz to soul to pop to country and western and back. Currently, Charles has decided to concentrate on country and country gospel, having recorded several duets with country giants like Willie Nelson, Ricky Scaggs, and George Jones. This, of course, is a return to the material that brought him his greatest commercial success. But, in true perspective, Ray's big achievement was his pioneering work in soul music, that dynamic blend of R&B, gospel, and Latin dance music that made Motown and its successors possible. It is not often that Ray cuts loose to shout and moan the way he did in those epochal late fifties and early sixties sides. For the most part, he spent the seventies taking a pop music show on the road. Of course, Ray Charles singing pop is decidedly better than Wayne Newton or Bobby Vinton singing pop. In this concert shot for British TV at the Jubilee Auditorium in Edmonton, Canada, Ray appears in his signature

An Evening with Ray Charles.

powder-blue suit and bow tie, backed by the ITV Concert Orchestra with conductor Sid Feller and the Raylettes. In between Ray's characteristic hip patter and the inventive rap introductions to his classic songs, he delivers fine, if somewhat restrained, renditions of "Riding Thumb," "Busted," "Georgia on My Mind," "Oh, What a Beautiful Morning," "Some Enchanted Evening," "Hit the Road, Jack," "I Can't Stop Loving You," "Take These Chains from My Heart," "I Can See Clearly Now," "What'd I Say," and "America the Beautiful." An American musical legend!

FOUR TOPS LIVE AT PARK WEST, CHICAGO, ILL.   ★★↲

BLACK POPULAR. 1982. Artists: The Four Tops (Levi Stubbs, Renaldo "Obie" Benson, Abdul "Duke" Fakir, and Lawrence Dayton). 60 min. Beta, VHS. JLT ($59.95)

Four Tops Live at Park West balances a night club performance of a medley of their Motown hits with a recording session of their newest songs taped in a professional sound studio. The set at the Park West is a golden oldies show for an enthusiastic dance floor crowd that seems to be composed of slightly older American Bandstand regulars who do dances that were popular 20 years ago. This nostalgic trip down memory lane is very pleasant. The Four Tops recreate the powerful vocals that have made such hits as "Baby, I Need Your Loving," "Ain't No Woman Like the One I Got," "Bernadette," and "The Same Old Song" timeless classics. When we follow the group into the recording studio we can appreciate the group's wonderful ability to interpret songs and create nuances of meaning when they sing their new, unfamiliar material. The Four Tops lay down the tracks on their hit, "When She Was My Girl," "Tonight I'll Love You All Over," and "Baby, I'll Set You Free." The tape cuts back to the set at the Park West where the group sings "Keeper of the Castle," "Still Waters Run Deep," "Walk Away, Renee," "Reach Out, I'll Be There," and "Standing in the Shadows of Love."

GOSPEL   ★★★

POPULAR BLACK. 1982. Artists: Mighty Clouds of Joy, Shirley Caesar, Walter Hawkins and the Family, The Clark Sisters, and Reverend James Cleveland. 92 min. Beta Hifi, VHS Stereo. Monterey ($49.95)

Satisfying concert film spotlighting some of the best and most popular gospel music acts of today. Shot at the Paramount Theater in Oakland, California, where five big acts perform many favorites and best-sellers of the gospel genre. Reminding us all of the roots of today's rock, R&B, and pop music, highly entertaining yet devotional groups like the Clark Sisters, with Twinkie Clark playing some Memphis-like organ, and The Mighty Clouds of Joy could easily find an audience in the secular world of pop music. The Clouds sing "Mighty High," "Walk around Heaven," and "I Came to Jesus." The Clark Sisters perform "Name It and Claim It," "Is My Living in Vain?," and "Hallelujah," outdoing Bette Midler and The Pointer Sisters at their own game. Walter Hawkins and the Hawkins Family present a rousing quartet of hymns, "Goin' to a Place," "He Brought Me," "Until I Found the Lord," and "Right On." Edwin Hawkins, Walter's brother, who had a hit many years ago with "O Happy Day," is part of the Family. The two performers who headline the occasion are the legendary Shirley Caesar and the Rev. James Cleveland, perhaps the greatest female and male gospel singers of our time. Shirley sings "He's Got It All in Control," "No Charge," and "(This Joy) The World Didn't Give It to Me," and Cleveland sings "Waiting on You," "I Don't Feel Noways Tired," "Can't Nobody Do Me Like Jesus," and "I Have a Determination." After viewing this, you'll come to agree with Walter Hawkins that these gospel greats have "come to let you know that Jesus is the *baddest* man in town." A must-see video.

THE HARDER THEY COME ★★★

BLACK POPULAR. 1972. Cast: Jimmy Cliff. 93 min. Beta, VHS. Thorn-EMI ($59.95)

Perry Henzell's *The Harder They Come* brought reggae to American shores, launched Jimmy Cliff's career in the States, and soon became a staple of weekend midnight shows at art houses across the country. Ivan (Jimmy Cliff) leaves his inland country home to arrive in the Jamaican capital of Kingston to seek his fortune. He is first exploited by his boss, an unscrupulous preacher who resents Ivan for trying to win the heart of Elsa, the preacher's young ward and intended bride. The preacher accuses Ivan of stealing and has him taken to jail, where he is beaten. Upon release, Ivan convinces Sir Hilton, Jamaica's largest record producer, to allow him to cut a single. Hilton takes Ivan into the studio where he records the film's theme song, "The Harder They Come." Ivan is paid a total of $20 for his trouble. Filled with hope that he is going to become the island's newest singing sensation, Ivan steals Elsa away in the night and is soon forced to become a dope runner in order to support her. He gets caught in a police crackdown, escapes, and soon is the target of a national police dragnet. Sir Hilton releases his record. Ivan is the folk hero he dreamed of becoming. But he is shot down in cold blood in a police ambush. Not only did *The Harder They Come* introduce American audiences, mostly young white college students, to reggae, but it also revealed the importance of marijuana in the religious practices of reggae music's creators, the Rastafarians, endearing the music to millions. In addition to "The Harder They Come," Jimmy Cliff sings "Many Rivers to Cross," "You Can Get It If You Really Want It," and "Sitting in Limbo." The soundtrack also features Scotty's "Draw Your Brakes," The Melodians' "Rivers of Babylon," Toots and the Maytals' "Sweet and Dandy" and "Pressure Drop," The Slickers' "Johnny Too Bad," and Desmond Dekker's "Shanty Town."

HEARTLAND REGGAE ★★✦

BLACK POPULAR. 1978. Artists: Bob Marley and the Wailers, The I-Threes, Peter Tosh, Jacob Miller and the Inner Circle, Judy Mowatt and the Light of Love, Dennis Brown, U-Roy, Althea and Donna, Lloyd Parkes, and We The People. 90 min. Beta, VHS. Continental ($29.95)

Heartland Reggae, a compilation of filmed performances by a variety of reggae musicians, includes the *only* filmed concert footage of the late Bob Marley. Marley sang at the One Love Peace Concert in Kingston, Jamaica, on April 22, 1978, demonstrating that not only was he at the height of his artistic powers, but also, as the unofficial leader

Bob Marley, featured in *Heartland Reggae*.

of reggae and the Rastafarian movement, a potent force in Jamaican politics; he brought about a truce between the rivals Prime Minister Michael Manley and opposition leader Edward Seega on stage during the concert, ending months of political violence that had plagued the country. Bob Marley and the Wailers perform "Trenchtown Rock," "War," "Jamming," "Natty Dread," and "Jah Live." The late Jacob Miller can be seen performing with the Inner Circle before a small concert crowd. He sings "Peace Treaty" and "I'm a Natty." Peter Tosh plays a set in what looks like a night club, backed up by the most influential studio musicians in reggae today including Robbie Shakespeare on bass, "Sly" Dunbar on drums, "Mao" Chung on guitar, and "Sticky" Thompson on percussion. Peter plays his hit song, "Legalize It," "400 Years," "African," and the third world anthem he cowrote with Bob Marley, "Get Up, Stand Up." In addition, Althea and Donna perform "Uptown Top Rankin'." Dennis Brown plays "Whip Them Jah." Judy Mowatt and the Light of Love sing "Black Woman."

HERBIE HANCOCK AND THE ROCKIT BAND ★★♪

BLACK POPULAR. 1984. Artist: Herbie Hancock. 75 min. Beta Hifi, VHS Stereo. CBS/ Fox ($29.95)

Veteran jazz pianist Herbie Hancock, who has played with such greats as trumpeter Miles Davis and the new musical wunderkind Wynton Marsalis, decided to bring his talent and experience to the composition of breakdancing music. His creations, "Autodrive" and "Rockit," hit the charts in 1984 as some of the most danceable music of the year. Herbie's videos of "Autodrive" and "Rockit," considered by many to be the most intriguing and imaginative around, filled with images of the robot machines created by Jim Whiting, captivated viewers on both cable and broadcast television. These videos along with a full-length concert of Herbie and his Rockit Band live at the Hammersmith Odeon in London are included in this tape. Herbie brought together three synthesizer players, two drummers, a bassist, and a hip-hop record scratcher/d.j. to help him create the propulsive, punctuated, and percussive beat that made the "Rockit" sound so popular. The band not only plays "Rockit" and "Autodrive," but slams into the funky "Future Shock," the ballad "You've Got Stars in Your Eyes," and a new version of the 1973 Hancock hit from his *Headhunters* album, "Chameleon."

HOT PEPPER ★★♪

BLACK POPULAR. 1972. Artist: Clifton Chenier. 56 min. Beta, VHS. Rhapsody ($70.00)

This 1972 portrait of the King of Zydeco finds accordion player Clifton Chenier at home in Cajun country, Layfette, Louisiana, before his move to Houston, Texas, and international cult stardom. In his native surroundings, Clifton introduces us to the culture of the Cajuns, patois-speaking Franco-Americans who can trace their ancestry to French-Canadians who moved to Louisiana in the eighteenth century. The black and white inhabitants of the region share the same francophone roots and get along without the racial animosity that plagues their English-speaking counterparts in the rest of the United States. Clifton celebrates this confluence of cultures in his zydeco music, a healthy mixture of rock, rhythm and blues, and French accordion music. In various zydeco clubs around Louisiana, filmmaker Les Blank captures Clifton singing "Don't You Lie to Me," "I'm a Hog for You," "Please Little Girl," and "I'm Coming Back Home."

KOOL STREET VIDEOS   ★★

BLACK POPULAR. 1983. Artists: Earth, Wind, and Fire, Kool and the Gang, Rick James, Midnight Star, Shalamar, Stephanie Mills, and The Whispers. 60 min. Beta, VHS Stereo. Continental ($29.95)

Kool Street Videos is a collection of the good, the bad, and the ugly of early commercial soul, R&B, and funk videos. At the top of the list is Kool and the Gang. They open and close the show, doing "Oo, La, La" ("Let's Go Dancing"), which they perform in front of an enthusiastic crowd at a block party in New York City, "Hi De Hi, Hi De Ho (This Is How the Story Goes)," which is a tribute to Cab Calloway and his timeless classic, "Minnie the Moocher," sung by the band in forties zoot suits in a New York subway station, and "Get Down on It," which ends the tape. The rhythmic, pulsating video effects that are added to each performance mirror the senuous, romantic mood of the group's songs. Next in line is Midnight Star, a group out of Cincinnati that went double platinum with their first album, *No Parking on the Dancefloor.* The Star explodes onto your TV set with the dynamic "Freakazoid," in which the band and a number of dancers in strange, extraterrestrial costumes strut and dance for the camera. They put so much excitement into their performance that the home video audience just has to stand up and dance. This tape also delves into the bizarre. Shalamar's song, "Dead Giveaway," is portrayed on video as a surreal detective story in which a lone gumshoe pursues a mysterious woman who disappears just as he is about to apprehend her. Stephanie Mills' "Pilot Error" was intended to be either humorous, or strange, or both, but comes across as embarrassingly weird. In her video, she starts as a flight attendant who works on an airplane piloted by a crazed World War II Japanese Imperial Air Force pilot whose copilot is a chimpanzee in flight togs. Rick James appears in two performance videos, "Sixty-Nine Times" and "Throwdown," in his trademark braided wig that is so distracting that the viewer misses the point of his songs. The videos presented by San Francisco's The Whispers and supergroup Earth, Wind, and Fire suffer from bad production values.

LET'S BREAK: A VISUAL GUIDE TO BREAKDANCING   ★★★♪

BLACK POPULAR. 1984. 59 min. Beta Hifi, VHS Stereo. Warner ($39.95)

Let's Break is the best basic breakdancing instructional tape available to the home video viewer. Narrator Marvin D. Moore and three teenage dancers, Suzie, Frank, and Tony, lead the home video audience through the basic breakdancing steps with emphasis on repetition and practice. Starting with the most basic move, the wave, the dancers break each step or move into its component parts and demonstrate them at normal speed and in slow motion. They repeat them and urge the viewer to rewind the tape and practice each step over and over again until he or she feels comfortable performing the move. During the course of the 59-minute tape, the dancers demonstrate the body wave, popping, guiding, breaking, foot work, back spin, the worm, and the break jam. A great tape for the beginner.

MAHALIA JACKSON   ★★✦

BLACK POPULAR. 1974. Artists: Mahalia Jackson and Elizabeth Cotten. 60 min. Beta, VHS. Mastervision ($50.00)

Mahalia Jackson is actually an abbreviated title for the two biographies on this tape. The first is indeed a CBS News Report on the life of gospel great Mahalia Jackson. The second is a short film on the life of folk singer Elizabeth Cotten. It is commonly said that Mahalia Jackson was the greatest gospel singer who ever lived. This short biography covers the events in her life, often in her own words, and presents Mahalia singing a number of spirituals including "Down by the Riverside," "When the Saints Go Marching In," and "Jesus, Draw Nearer to Me." Elizabeth Cotten, the folk singer, learned to play the guitar at a very early age. She composed the classic, "Freight Train," at the age of twelve. Elizabeth Cotten put down her guitar, left her native North Carolina, and moved to Washington, D.C. to work as a domestic—by chance in the home of folklorists Charles and Ruth Seeger. They "discovered" her talent and helped her become one of the voices in the folk music revival of the sixties. In addition to "Freight Train," Elizabeth Cotten sings "I'm Going Away," "Oh Babe, It Ain't No Lie," and "Going down the Road Feeling Sad."

MAKING MICHAEL JACKSON'S THRILLER   ★★★✦

BLACK. 1983. Artists: Michael Jackson, the Jacksons, Michael Peters, and Ola Ray. 60 min. Beta Hifi, VHS Stereo. Vestron ($29.95)

The first 14 minutes of this tape present the complete "Thriller" music video as directed by John Landis, who helmed such movie hits as *The Blues Brothers* and *Trading Places* as well as one of the segments in the film *Twilight Zone.* Besides the obvious danceability of the song itself, another example of Michael's distinctive pop style, "Thriller" is also an innovative video. Unlike the disjointed visuals of most rock videos, "Thriller" successfully tells a story. Michael plays a high school romantic who turns into a werewolf after viewing a late night horror movie. The images, alternately comic and scary, and the music perfectly reflect each other. Vincent Price's rap bit in the middle of the song is a treat to listen to. The video was so striking that Michael tried unsuccessfully to get it nominated for an Oscar as best short film of the year. But then again, Michael is not at a loss for awards, is he? The rest of the tape is a documentary on the making of "Thriller" and the history of Michael's meteoric career. We see John Landis directing Michael before the cameras, Michael Peters choreographing Michael and his costar Ola Ray, how the masks were created, the "Billie Jean" and "Beat It" videos, a home movie of the young Michael, the Jackson 5 on *Ed Sullivan* in 1970, and more. A very special look into the world of a musical dynamo.

MAZE ★★★

BLACK POPULAR. 1984. Artists: Maze. 20 min. Beta Hifi, VHS Stereo. Sony ($16.95)

The popularity of the group Maze can be attributed to the many talents of its nucleus, Frankie Beverly. As producer, arranger, writer, and lead vocalist, Beverly creates tunes

Maze, featuring singer/songwriter/producer Frankie Beverly (wearing hat).

that are mellow and at the same time very danceable. In the video of the title tune from their audio album, "We Are One," the camera leisurely cuts back and forth between shots of the band in a television studio and shots of different kinds of people in and around the Los Angeles area as the band cruises through the laid-back and jazzy composition. The band performs in tuxedos in "Never Let You Down" while an elegant man and woman act out a pantomime on a north African set reminiscent of the one in *Casablanca.* The funky and rocking "Southern Girl" and the mellow "Happy Feelin's" are performed in concert before a capacity crowd.

MIDNIGHT STAR IN CONCERT   ★★★

BLACK POPULAR. 1984. Artists: Midnight Star (Reggie Calloway, Belinda Lipscomb, Vincent Calloway, Bo Watson, Melvin Gentry, Kenneth Gant, Jeff Cooper, Bill Simmons, and Bobby Lovelace). 48 min. Beta, VHS. U.S.A. ($39.95)

Cincinnati's own nine-piece wonder, Midnight Star, burns through seven songs from their amazing first album, *No Parking on the Dancefloor,* which shipped double platinum in a matter of months. The Star rocks things off for this SRO L.A. concert crowd with "Electricity," a song that has them dancing in the aisles. Belinda Lipscomb, the group's lead singer, performs "Playmates," "Slow Jam," and "Wet My Whistle," before

Midnight Star.

the band really lays down a groove on the extremely danceable "Night Rider," the title tune of their album, "No Parking on the Dancefloor," and their smash single, "Freakazoid."

SAN FRANCISCO BLUES FESTIVAL   ★★♪

BLACK POPULAR. 1983. Artists: Clifton Chenier, Clarence "Gatemouth" Brown, Albert Collins, Johnny Littlejohn, Robert Cray, and the Clifton Ford Band. 60 min. Beta Hifi, VHS Stereo. Sony ($29.95)

This recording of the tenth annual San Francisco Blues Festival presents a rather uneven look at the contemporary blues scene. Included in this tape are parts of some wonderful performances, perforated by interviews with the musicians and members of the audience. The end result is a collection of too many short musical excerpts and too few extended numbers. If the producers had removed the footage of a few of the lesser musicians and devoted the extra time to the fine bluesmen who do appear on the tape, then *San Francisco Blues Festival* would be an extraordinary video. Clifton Chenier, the King of Zydeco, the Louisiana Cajun dance music, leads off the festival on accordion, with his brother Cleveland on washboard, and the rest of his Red Hot Louisiana Band. They tear into the funky "Louisana Two Step" and Ray Charles' classic "What'd I Say." Clifton then sings his "Calinda" in his native French patois. New York blues scholar John Hammond, Jr., successfully reproduces the sound of the Delta blues on "Look on Yonder Wall" and "Drifting Blues." Albert Collins, the Master of the Telecaster, shows off his blistering guitar playing on "Frosty." Newcomer Robert Cray sings a very soulful version of Willie Dixon's "Too Many Cooks" and demonstrates his talents on guitar on Albert King's "Let's Have a Natural Ball." The tape ends with the great Clarence "Gatemouth" Brown, who performs "Sometimes I Slip" and "Six Levels below Plant Life."

SATURDAY NIGHT LIVE: CARRIE FISHER   ★★

BLACK POPULAR. 1978. Cast: Carrie Fisher, Dan Aykroyd, John Belushi, Bill Murray, Gilda Radner, Garrett Morris, Laraine Newman, Tom Scott, Matt "Guitar" Murphy, Paul Shaffer, Steve Cropper, and Donald "Duck" Dunn. 67 min. Beta, VHS. Warner ($39.95)

What happens when two garage-band musicians who happen to be stars on America's favorite comedy show decide they want to sing rhythm and blues standards profession-

Dan Aykroyd and John Belushi perform as The Blues Brothers.

ally? They hire the musicians who played on the original classic recordings of those songs, put on dark suits, think up some funny stage business, and premiere their band, The Blues Brothers, on national television. Dan Aykroyd and John Belushi as Jake and Elwood Blues jump and roll around on stage and bleat out a very funny version of Sam and Dave's "Soul Man." This is followed later in the show by the band's return and a version of "B Movie Box Car Blues." Both performances are very amusing and entertaining. Later the executives took all this foolishness very seriously and decided to sink more than $20 million into a movie version of the skit, *The Blues Brothers.*

SATURDAY NIGHT LIVE: GARY BUSEY ★★★

BLACK POPULAR. 1979. Cast: Gary Busey, John Belushi, Dan Aykroyd, Bill Murray, Jane Curtin, Gilda Radner, Laraine Newman, Garrett Morris, Eubie Blake, and Gregory Hines. 69 min. Beta, VHS. Warner ($39.95)

The late Eubie Blake, justly celebrated for his ragtime jazz compositions, made a rare television appearance in this SNL episode from 1979. Gary Busey, nominated that year for an Oscar for his performance in *The Buddy Holly Story*, is the guest host and is quite funny in several skits. The put-on opening has Busey and Belushi feuding because Belushi didn't get nominated for his role in *Animal House.* Then, in another Jimmy Carter lampoon, Busey plays the president's embarrassing brother, Billy. Bill Murray, Garrett Morris, and Dan Aykroyd join Gary on a panel show called "Women's Problems," a forum for men to discuss the foibles of women. In a rather strange skit, Busey plays a depression-era "slopjockey," a man who dives into cesspools for tips from onlookers—then charges a stiffer fee for leaving the premises. Gregory Hines (*Cotton Club*) is accompanied by Eubie Blake on piano as he sings three of Eubie's most famous tunes, "Low Down Blues," "Simply Full of Jazz," and "I'm Just Wild about Harry." Gary Busey sings "Stay a Little Longer" and "Nadine."

SATURDAY NIGHT LIVE: RAY CHARLES ★★★♪

BLACK POPULAR. 1977. Cast: Ray Charles, John Belushi, Dan Aykroyd, Bill Murray, Gilda Radner, Laraine Newman, Jane Curtin, Garrett Morris, and Franklyn Ajaye. 62 min. Beta, VHS. Warner ($39.95)

From a musical point of view, at least, this is the best of the SNL episodes available on home video. It features a healthy helping of Ray Charles, the man who virtually invented soul music by combining blues, jazz, gospel, and Afro-Cuban dance rhythms into an infectious, passionate American art form. The funniest skit features the cast posing as the Young Caucasians, a choral group from the early sixties, singing Ray's "What'd I Say" but in a cleaned-up, grammatically correct version, "What Did I Say?" Also, Laraine Newman and Gilda Radner play the Doody Girls, the widow and sister of the late Howdy Doody, and Dan Aykroyd, as Tom Snyder, interviews Ray. But the real highlight is the extended session in which Ray cuts loose with his band and the Raylettes, his group of female backup singers, on "I Can See Clearly Now," "Georgia on My Mind," "What'd I Say," "I Got a Woman," "I Believe to My Soul," "Hit the Road, Jack," "I Ain't Got Nothing Yet," and "I Can't Stop Loving You."

SAY AMEN SOMEBODY ★★★♪

BLACK POPULAR. 1983. Artists: Willie Mae Ford Smith, Thomas A. Dorsey, The Barrett Sisters, The O'Neal Twins, and Zella Jackson Price. 100 min. Beta Hifi, VHS Stereo. Pacific Arts ($59.95)

This exuberant and thoughtful documentary looks at the world of gospel music through the lives and trials of such major gospel artists as Mother Smith, Thomas A. Dorsey,

the Barrett Sisters, and The O'Neal Twins. The footage dealing with Mother Smith
and her extended family as they make preparations for both a tribute to her in her
native St. Louis and the National Convention of Gospel Choirs and Choruses in Houston, Texas, is especially insightful and touching. Willie Mae Ford Smith is the leading
female figure in gospel music and her struggle to establish the position of women in
the black church is heroic and inspiring. But, even more than her efforts to gain equal
participation for women in church music, she is noted for her great singing, filled
with passion and conviction. "It's a feeling within . . . it goes between the marrow
and the bones . . . I feel like I can fly away. I forget I'm in the world sometimes,"
Mother Smith tells the camera. The other highlight is time spent with Thomas A.
Dorsey, generally thought to be the man responsible for creating gospel music as it
is performed today. Now in his eighties, Dorsey is revered by the gospel community
for his innovative restructuring of traditional spirituals. The music includes performances by The O'Neal Twins ("He Chose Me" and "Jesus Dropped the Charges"),
the Barrett Sisters ("The Storm Is Passing Over," "No Ways Tired," and "He Brought
Us"), Mother Smith ("What Manner of Man," "Singing in My Soul," "Never Turn
Back," "Is Your All on the Altar," and "Canaan"), and Thomas Dorsey ("When I've
Done My Best," "Take My Hand, Precious Lord," "If You See My Savior," and "How
about You").

SPARKLE ★★

*BLACK POPULAR. 1976. Cast: Irene Cara, Philip M. Thomas, Lonette McKee, Dawn
Smith, Mary Alice, Dorian Harewood, and Tony King. 98 min. Beta, VHS. Warner
($39.98)*

Academy Award-winning singer Irene Cara (*Fame, Flashdance, D.C. Cab, City Heat*) stars
as Sparkle Williams, the youngest of three sisters in the Harlem of 1958 who form a
singing group, not unlike the Supremes, and become a stage act in a local nightclub.
In the formulaic story written by Joel Schumacher (*Car Wash, D.C. Cab*), every character
with the exception of Sparkle falls victim to one vice or another in the show biz
milieu. Sparkle's eldest sister falls in love with Satin, the neighborhood hood, he beats
her up and introduces her to heroin. She soon dies of an overdose. Sticks, Sparkle's
boyfriend, played by Philip M. Thomas (*Miami Vice*), convinces Sparkle to strike out
on a solo career. He gets mixed up with the mob to borrow the $10,000 to pay for
the recording of Sparkle's first two hit singles, "Look into Your Heart" and "Loving
You Baby." He almost gets his head blown off. In the end, Sparkle beat the odds,
avoided disaster, and became a smash hit. *Sparkle* was a good place for Schumacher,
Cara, and Thomas to hone their film talents, but their best work appeared in later

Dawn Smith, Lonette McKee, and Irene Cara as the Glitter Girls in *Sparkle*.

films and on television. Curtis Mayfield, formerly of the vocal group the Impressions, and the composer of the music for *Superfly,* wrote the score. His songs include "Now You Jump," "This Love Is Real," "Givin' Up Is So Hard to Do," "Sparkle," "Hooked on Your Love," "Look into Your Heart," and "Rock with Me."

SECOND CITY INSANITY ★★↓

BLACK POPULAR. 1978. Cast: Gloria Gaynor, John Candy, Tim Caserinsky, Fred Willard, and Audrey Neenan. 60 min. Beta, VHS. Karl ($39.95)

Gloria Gaynor, the Queen of the Discos, appears as the musical guest on this show from the original *Second City* television series which was broadcast from Chicago before the Second City company moved to Canada. Gloria sings her seventies megahit, "I Will Survive." The rest of the show, hosted by John Candy (*SCTV Network 90, Stripes*), is a comic free-for-all that includes Candy's hilarious Mr. Mambo and his appearance on "Uncle Silvio's Kid Show."

TEDDY PENDERGRASS LIVE IN LONDON ★★★

POPULAR BLACK. 1982. Artist: Teddy Pendergrass. 75 min. Beta Hifi, VHS Stereo. CBS/Fox ($39.95)

Known as Teddy Bear to his vast following of female fans, Teddy Pendergrass left Harold Melvin and the Bluenotes in 1976 to embark upon a highly successful solo career. Although Pendergrass' crooning soul ballads, invariably narrating some aspect of romantic activity, never made much of a dent in the pop charts, he was a consistent R&B Top 10 artist. Exploiting his suave good looks, dapper male model figure, and intensely seductive but well-crafted lyrics, Pendergrass was riding high when the fates did him in. Since 1982, he has been paralyzed from the neck down as the result of a serious automobile accident in Philadelphia. Although Pendergrass has courageously continued to record, this concert video is valuable, first and foremost, as a lasting testament to his incredible charisma on stage. Always the showman, and of course, above all, a ladies' man. In concert at London's Hammersmith Odeon shortly before his car crash, Teddy sings "Just Can't Get Enough," "I Can't Live without Your Love,"

Teddy Pendergrass.

"Love T.K.O.," "Lady," "My Latest, Greatest Inspiration," "Keep On Lifting Me Higher," "Where Did All the Loving Go?," "The Whole Town's Laughing at Me," "Come On Over to My Place," "Close the Door," "Turn Off the Lights," "Tell Me What You Want to Do," "You Got What I Want," and "Reach Out" (joined by a children's choir).

THANK GOD IT'S FRIDAY ★★♪

BLACK POPULAR. 1978. Cast: Jeff Goldblum, Valerie Landsburg, Terri Nunn, Andrea Howard, Paul Jabara, Dewayne Jessie, Donna Summer, The Commodores, Ray Witte, and Debra Winger. 90 min. Beta Hifi, VHS Stereo. RCA/Columbia ($59.95)

A whole host of young actors and performers got some early exposure in this disco film for black music audiences. As a rejoinder to the box office success of *Saturday Night Fever,* Casablanca Records head Neil Bogart, whom most people believe was the executive in the industry most responsible for bringing disco music to its dominant position in the charts, masterminded this epic about a disco called The Zoo, located in L.A. Jeff Goldblum, Valerie Landsburg (*Fame*), Terri Nunn (the rock group Berlin),

Donna Summer in *Thank God It's Friday.*

and Debra Winger are some of the dreamers, schemers, and screamers who've congregated in the place on a particular summer evening. The music is provided by Casablanca and Motown acts, including The Commodores (featuring lead singer Lionel Richie) singing "Brickhouse," "Easy," and "Too Hot to Trot," and Donna Summer, then the uncrowned queen of disco, singing "Love to Love You Baby," "Try with Your Love," "Last Dance," and "Je T'Aime." On the soundtrack, one can hear "Find My Way" and "It's Serious" by Cameo, "You're the Person I Feel Like Dancing With" by the Fifth Dimension, "Love Masterpiece" and "I'm Here Again" by Thelma Houston, "Disco Queen" and "Trapped in a Stairway" by Paul Jabara, and the title tune by Love and Kisses.

TINA TURNER LIVE: NICE 'N' ROUGH ★★♪

BLACK POPULAR. 1982. Artist: Tina Turner. 60 min. Beta Hifi, VHS Stereo. Thorn-EMI ($49.95)

One of the musical events of 1984 was Tina Turner's unexpected return to prominence in the pop music world. A top-flight R&B performer from the early sixties, first with

Tina Turner.

ex-husband Ike Turner and then by herself, Tina had seemingly dropped out of sight with the arrival of disco in the mid-seventies. It's conjecture as to whether Tina has adjusted to the changes in musical tastes or whether we've all caught up to her. It was back in 1969 and Ike and Tina were the opening act for The Rolling Stones on their American tour. Who can forget Tina's outrageously sexual performance of "I've Been Loving You Too Long" in *Gimme Shelter?*

The "new" Tina Turner sports a blond Rod Stewart wig, but her style hasn't changed much since those days—direct, aggressive, and knowing. In this video concert, shot by David Mallet in some unknown European venue, Tina's soul revue delivers a testament to her command of the R&B idiom. Songs include "Kill His Wife" ("Foolish Behavior"), "Tonight's the Night," "Honky Tonk Woman," "Crazy in the Night," "River Deep, Mountain High," "Nutbush City Limits," "Giving It Up for Your Love," "Jumping Jack Flash," "It's Only Rock and Roll," "Acid Queen," "Proud Mary," and "Hollywood Nights."

TONIGHT: KOOL AND THE GANG   ★★★

BLACK POPULAR. 1984. Artists: Kool and the Gang. 84 min. Beta Hifi, VHS Stereo. RCA/Columbia ($29.95)

After years as a fine, funky, mainly instrumental band that stayed either on top of or near the summit of the soul chart with dance tunes that were built around Kool's muscular bass lines, the Gang invited suave vocalist James "J. T." Taylor into their ranks. Revamping their sound, they surrounded James' liquid voice with laid-back, yet funky melodies that are soothing, sensuous, and at the same time, definitely danceable. Soon they began to command their place on the Top 40 pop chart with sixteen monster hits. In their long-form performance video *Tonight,* they demonstrate before an audience at the New Orleans' Louisiana World Exhibition Quality Seal Amphitheater why they have sold out concerts the world over. After a slow start, the Gang gets in the groove and delivers an exciting show of their back-to-back superhits. They begin with the disco anthem "Celebration," and the equally popular "Ladies Night." Going back a few years to their *Wild and Peaceful* album, the band plays a spirited version of "Hollywood Swinging" with a new twist. The band members are joined on stage by teenage breakdancers, who although they seem oblivious to the music, nevertheless have a good time. The concert really picks up steam with the up-tempo dance favorites "Tonight" and "Get Down on It." Kool then changes the tempo of the show. J. T. sings a romantic trilogy of "Too Hot," "No Show," and "Jones vs. Jones," before moving into "Love Somebody" and the catchy and effervescent "Take My Heart." To emphasize the song's lyric, J. T., the stage performer, hands a heart-shaped pillow to a swooning girl in the front row. The Gang, who early in their career played jazz in and around their native New Jersey, pay tribute in "Summer Madness" to their idols in the pantheon of American jazz. As they play, photos of Wes Montgomery, Charlie Parker, Sarah Vaughan, Count Basie, and Dizzy Gillespie are superimposed on the tape for the benefit of the home video audience. Kool and the Gang then kick off their finale. Starting with their smash single "Joanna," they lead into the reggae-influenced "Oo, La, La (Let's Go Dancing)." As fireworks burst above the open air amphitheater, they close by returning to their up-tempo "Celebration." A wonderful concert that displays the imimitable style, multifarious influences, and wide-ranging talents of one of America's leading pop music groups.

WILD STYLE   ★★

BLACK POPULAR. 1982. Cast: George "Lee" Quinones, Sandra "Pink" Fabara, Frederick Brathwaite, Patti Astor, DST, Grand Master Flash, The Rock Steady Crew, and Double Trouble. 83 min. Beta, VHS. Program ($59.95)

Independent filmmaker Charlie Ahearn seems to have added a dramatic plot at the last minute to what would have been an interesting documentary about the hip-hop culture of the South Bronx and Lower East Side that gave birth to breakdancing, "record scratching," custom mixing of big-beat breakdancing music, and graffiti "bombing," the spray-can painting of large, colorful murals on subway trains and walls in New York City. In *Wild Style,* Zoro, a graffiti "bomber," played by real-life graffiti artist "Lee" Quinones, who pulls down top dollar for his graffiti-covered canvases at one of New York's finest Soho galleries, leads Virginia (Patti Astor), a *Village Voice* reporter who is in the South Bronx to investigate the action, on a journey through the breakdancing clubs, subway trainyards, and dark, depressing squalor of the ghetto before she takes him to a midtown party to make connections with rich art dealers. The closest thing this movie has to a dramatic climax is the breakdancing festival at the end of the film held on the Lower East Side, for which Zoro paints an enormous mural and where the rapping duet Double Trouble, Grand Master Flash, and the breakdancers The Rock Steady Crew perform before a large audience. Disc jockey/rapper Fab 5 Freddy and pop group Blondie's mastermind Chris Stein wrote the music for the soundtrack.

THE WIZ ★★

BLACK POPULAR. 1978. Cast: Diana Ross, Michael Jackson, Richard Pryor, Lena Horne, Nipsey Russell, Ted Ross, Mabel King, and Theresa Merritt. 133 min. Beta, VHS Stereo. MCA ($39.95)

Diana Ross plays a very tired Dorothy in the filmed version of the William F. Brown-Charlie Smalls Broadway smash musical, *The Wiz*, the all-black reworking of Frank L. Baum's classic *The Wizard of Oz*. She looks so tired in fact that she seems to sleepwalk through the whole picture. A homebody at heart, Dorothy is swept away from her native Harlem by a local blizzard and is taken to the magic Land of Oz, which seems to be located somewhere near Wall Street. She meets a rusted tin man (Nipsey Russell), whose performance is as rusty as his clothes, the Cowardly Lion (Ted Ross), and the Scarecrow (Michael Jackson). Jackson seems to be saving up his energy for the *Thriller* album that he was to release 5 years after the opening of this film. After the four sing the rousing "Ease On down the Road," they find Richard Pryor, whose performance as The Wiz is one of the most reserved in his movie career. Tony Walton's production

Ted Ross, Michael Jackson, Diana Ross, and Nipsey Russell in *The Wiz*.

and costume design are supposed to be a free interpretation of the vitality of New York City street life, but actually run the range from the very scary (as in the design of what were the "flying monkeys" in the 1939 MGM version and have been transformed in *The Wiz* into half-monkey, half-motorcycle creatures that look like the creation of a child's nightmare) to an overall costume design conception that, to quote the Wicked Witch of the West, "puts the 'ug' back in 'ugly'." The only character to shine is Gilda, the Good Witch of the North, played by Lena Horne. It seems that the two stumbling blocks that get in the way of all these superstars are the direction of Sidney Lumet and the screenwriting of Joel Schumacher. Songs include "Is This What Feeling Gets?," "Can I Go On Not Knowing?," "He's the Wiz," "You Can't Win," "I'm a Mean Ol' Lion," and "Can't You Feel a Brand New Day."

THE WOMAN IN RED   ★★⸴

BLACK POPULAR. 1984. Cast: Gene Wilder, Kelly Le Brock, Charles Grodin, Joseph Bologna, Judith Ivey, and Gilda Radner. 87 min. Beta Hifi, VHS Stereo. Vestron ($79.95)

Gene Wilder's attempt to make a sophisticated sex comedy for adults has its moments but not enough of them to make it a success. The best thing about it really is Stevie Wonder's hit score. It includes his Number 1 single and an Oscar-winning song, "I Just Called to Say I Love You." The story itself, borrowed from the French film *Pardon Mon Affair,* concerns a middle-aged advertising executive whose seemingly drab, predictable life is momentarily interrupted by Kelly Le Brock, the "woman in red." Wilder, as the exec, goes to great and farcical lengths to have a rendezvous with this woman, in the process confusing his wife (Judith Ivey), his amorous secretary (Gilda Radner), and his group of friends (Joe Bologna and Charles Grodin). Le Brock is quite attractive in her role as the Circean advertising model who causes Wilder to turn his life topsy-turvy. The other songs include Dionne Warwick's interpretations of Wonder originals, "Moments Aren't Moments," "It's You" (with Stevie), and "Weakness" (also with Stevie). Stevie sings "The Woman in Red," "Don't Drive Drunk," and "Love Light in Flight," and other vocalists sing "Let's Just" and "It's More Than You."

COUNTRY/FOLK

ALL-STAR COUNTRY MUSIC FAIR ★★✦

COUNTRY/FOLK. 1982. Artists: Razzy Bailey, Sylvia, Earl Thomas Conley, and Charlie Pride. 60 min. Beta, VHS. RCA/Columbia ($29.95)

The Nashville Fan Fair takes place annually, and is always a rousing success, but the 1982 fair was certainly one of the best in memory. RCA Records presents a quartet of its hottest country artists to an enthusiastic, sold-out grandstand full of music lovers. Razzy Bailey sings "She Left Love All over Me," "Loving Up a Storm," "Friends," "Nightlife," and "Midnight Hauler." Sylvia, who has parlayed good looks and a cross-over voice into instant country music stardom, sings "Drifter," "Sweet Yesterday," "Not Tonight," "Nobody," and "Matador." Earl Thomas Conley, who became a big, big star right after this program was taped, performs "Silent Treatment," "Tell Me Why," "After the Love Slips Away," "Heavenly Bodies," and "Fire and Smoke." The climax of the show is, of course, Charlie Pride's set. "A Whole Lotta Love," "Kiss an Angel Good Morning," "I Ain't All Bad," "Never Been So Loved," "Oklahoma Morning," "Someone Loves You, Honey," "Crystal Chandeliers," "I Don't Think She's in Love Anymore," "Mountain of Love," and "When I Stop Loving You (I'll Be Gone)" bring repeated ovations from the enraptured audience.

BARBAROSA ★★★

COUNTRY/FOLK. 1982. Cast: Willie Nelson, Gary Busey, and Gilbert Roland. 90 min. Beta, VHS. CBS/Fox ($59.95)

In the title role, Willie plays an outlaw caught between two families who have bones to pick with Willie and his sidekick (Gary Busey). The Mexican Zavallas family, into which Willie married many years ago, wants revenge on him for shooting off the leg of the elder Zavallas at his own wedding feast. A German immigrant family is after Gary Busey for shooting one of their sons. Together, the two survive by outwitting their pursuers. Willie doesn't sing in this western epic, but it benefits greatly from the credibility Willie lends to the lead role, since he's the man who basically reintroduced the outlaw/cowboy motif into country music in the seventies. Three stars for Willie's convincing acting job.

THE BEST LITTLE WHOREHOUSE IN TEXAS ★

COUNTRY/FOLK. 1982. Cast: Dolly Parton, Burt Reynolds, Charles Durning, Dom De-Luise, and Jim Nabors. 111 min. Beta, VHS. MCA ($79.95)

When it came time to adapt the hit Broadway musical *Best Little Whorehouse* for the silver screen, the producers thought a potentially dynamite box office duo in the lead roles would be Burt Reynolds and Dolly Parton. They were proven wrong. Although Burt and Dolly, as well as Charles Durning and Dom DeLuise, turned in good performances, *Best Little Whorehouse* did not have the benefit of a good screenplay and was not able to convey the fun-loving quality of the stage production. Colin Higgins, who had directed Dolly in *Nine to Five*, misses the mark here by a wide margin. Dolly plays Miss Mona, the proprietress of the Chicken Ranch, Texas' leading bordello and an institution unto itself in the history of the region. When Charles Durning, a seemingly moralistic governor, and Dom DeLuise, a television crusader against obscenity and immorality, start a campaign to oust Miss Mona from the borders of the state, Burt Reynolds, as Ed Earl Dodd, the local sheriff, is hard pressed to stop them. Songs include: "Sneakin' Around," "I Will Always Love You" (words and music by Dolly Parton), "Twenty Fans," "Little Old Bitty Pissant Country Place," "Hard Candy Christ-

Dolly Parton and Burt Reynolds in *The Best Little Whorehouse in Texas.*

mas," "The Watchdog Theme," "Sidestep," and "The Aggie Song" (words and lyrics by Carol Hall).

BOB & RAY, JANE, LARAINE & GILDA ★★★♪

COUNTRY/FOLK. 1979. Cast: Willie Nelson, Leon Russell, Bob Elliott, Ray Goulding, Jane Curtin, Laraine Newman, and Gilda Radner. 75 min. Beta, VHS. Pacific Arts ($59.95)

Legendary radio humorists Bob Elliott and Ray Goulding bring their wonderfully zany sense of humor to this television special. With a fine supporting cast, Bob and Ray act as two identical twins, Clyde and Claude, who say the same thing at the same time. They double date two women named Patty, one of whom Clyde and Claude had met at a "two for one" sale. In another skit, the audience is introduced to two of Bob and Ray's businesses, their shoelace cleaning service and the House of Toast. In a musical number, Bob and Ray, dressed in business suits, sitting in armchairs, and backed by a rocking band, mumble Rod Stewart's sultry "Do You Think I'm Sexy?" The real musical treat is Willie Nelson's appearance with Leon Russell playing piano. Willie croons stirring versions of the classics, "Georgia On My Mind," "Heartbreak Hotel," and "One More for the Road."

A CELEBRATION   ★★✚

COUNTRY/FOLK. 1980. Artists: Gary Busey, Tanya Tucker, Kris Kristofferson, Delaney and Bonnie, Duane Eddy, Rocky Burnette, Billy Burnette, Maureen McGovern, Roger Miller, and Glen Campbell. 68 min. Beta, VHS. Monterey Home ($39.95)

Dorsey Burnette, brother of the great rockabilly pioneer Johnny Burnette and writer of some of the best country hit songs to ever come down the pike, died in 1979. Glen Campbell, who had recorded Dorsey's "Hey, Little One," put together a memorial concert at the Forum in Los Angeles, enlisting the help of many of his friends in the country music world. Gary Busey is the first performer in the show. The actor who has starred in *The Buddy Holly Story* and *Barbarosa* (with Willie Nelson) sings a rockabilly version of Chuck Berry's classic "Rock and Roll Music." Tanya Tucker, who at that time was involved with Campbell, sings up a storm with "Crossfire" and "Lay Back in the Arms of Someone You Love." Kris Kristofferson, songwriter, movie star, and legend, enters unassumingly to a rousing ovation and then quietly sets about singing two of his most powerfully eloquent compositions, "The Truth Will Set You Free" and "Me and Bobbie McGee." Delaney and Bonnie Bramlett reunite after almost seven years apart to perform "Only You Know and I Know," the Dave Mason song that was their biggest hit. Duane Eddy, the man with the twangy guitar style, does his anthem, "Rebelrouser." Rocky Burnette, Johnny's son, sings a Dorsey Burnette classic, "Tear It Up." His cousin, Dorsey's son Billy Burnette, sings a song his dad wrote for Ricky Nelson and which became a big hit, "I Believe What You Say." Maureen McGovern makes an inexplicable appearance before Roger Miller takes the stage to perform "You Don't Want My Love" and "Dang Me," two of his funnier tunes. Finally, Glen Campbell performs "Rhinestone Cowboy," "Hey, Little One," and "Southern Nights." As the credits roll, the assembled performers and their families sing "Will the Circle Be Unbroken."

CHARLIE DANIELS BAND: THE SARATOGA CONCERT ★★★

COUNTRY/FOLK. 1981. Artists: Charlie Daniels Band. 75 min. Beta Hifi, VHS Stereo. MGM/UA ($49.95)

Originally produced as a music special for Home Box Office, Charlie Daniels' concert at the Saratoga Performing Arts Center in upstate New York is both visually satisfying and musically rewarding. The band is in fine form and the setting, an amphitheater with classic dimensions carved into the Saratoga countryside, is perfect for Charlie's special brand of southern rock and country lyrics. With the American flag projected onto the backdrop of the stage, Charlie opens the concert with "God Bless America Again," "Ain't No Ramblers No More," and "Lonesome Boy from Dixie." "The Legend of Woody Swamp" is presented with an accompanying video that seeks to illustrate the Tom T. Hall-like narrative about three scalawags who kill a miser for his stash of money. With confederate flags raised up high in the audience, Charlie performs the title tune from his 1979 hit album, *Million Mile Reflections,* a song that pays homage to the pioneers of southern rock from Elvis to Duane Allman to Ronnie Van Zant, all of whom died tragically and all too young. "The Lady in Red" is an excellent honky-tonk blues number sung by pianist Dave Gregorio, who along with Charlie and guitarist James Thomas Brown handle all the lead vocals. The concert is brought to a close with some more crowd-pleasing tunes like "Sweet Home Alabama," "Carolina, I Remember You," "The Devil Went Down to Georgia," "The South's Gonna Do It Again," "The Orange Blossom Special," "Amazing Grace," and "Will the Circle Be Unbroken?"

COALMINER'S DAUGHTER ★★★⁄

COUNTRY/FOLK. 1980. Cast: Sissy Spacek, Tommy Lee Jones, Levon Helm, Beverly D'Angelo, and Phyllis Boyens. 124 min. Beta, VHS. MCA ($59.95)

In this sensitively crafted telling of Loretta Lynn's life story, British director Michael Apted was able to draw fine performances from his principal actors and remain true to the spirit of this quintessential country music tale. It begins, as Loretta's life began, in the coal mining area around Butcher Hollow, Kentucky. Her father, played by Levon Helm of The Band, is a coal miner whose sensitivity and wisdom belie his dirt-poor environment. With his love, Loretta, played winningly by Sissy Spacek (who won an Oscar for her performance), is able to have a richer childhood than people more materially fortunate often enjoy. At the age of fourteen, she marries Doolittle Lynn, played by Tommy Lee Jones, a brash young man fresh out of the army whose ambition is to escape the coal mines. With his help, Loretta embarks on a singing career which would later bring her great wealth as well as personal anguish over her divided loyalties

Sissy Spacek in her Oscar-winning performance as singer Loretta Lynn in *Coalminer's Daughter.*

to show biz and her family. Songs included in the film are: Ernest Tubb's "Walking the Floor over You," Bill Monroe's "Blue Moon of Kentucky," Kitty Wells' "It Wasn't God Who Made Honky Tonk Angels," and Red Foley's "Satisfied Mind." Sissy Spacek does her own singing in a voice that reminds one hauntingly of the real Loretta Lynn. Loretta Lynn songs performed include "Honky Tonk Girl," "You Ain't Woman Enough," "You're Looking at Country," "Don't Come Home A-Drinkin'," "Coalminer's Daughter," "We've Come a Long Way," and many more.

CONVOY ★♪

COUNTRY/FOLK. 1978. Cast: Kris Kristofferson, Ali McGraw, Burt Young, Madge Sinclair, Franklin Ajaye, and Ernest Borgnine. 110 min. Beta, VHS. Thorn-EMI ($79.95)

During the Ford administration in the mid-seventies, the oil crisis necessitated a mandatory 55 mile-per-hour speed limit on the nation's highways and freeways. This was, to say the least, unpopular with independent truckers who made their livings through being able to cut down on the amount of time it took them to carry a load from one city to another. Relations between the truckers and the state police (called "bears" in CB lingo) approached a state quite close to all-out war. In this film, based on country d.j. C. W. McCall's hit single, "Convoy," Rubber Ducky, the hero trucker, is played by Kris Kristofferson. R. D. sets off a small scale revolution of sorts when he beats up the overly aggressive Ernest Borgnine, a "bear," and leads a convoy of truckers to the state line to avoid arrest. This simple act of self-preservation on R. D.'s part is misunderstood by other truckers as a protest against the double nickel. Complications ensue when the state police take justice into their own hands. The country soundtrack includes: C. W. McCall's "Convoy," Crystal Gayle's "Don't It Make My Brown Eyes Blue," Doc Watson's "Keep on the Sunny Side," Billy Joe Spear's "Blanket on the Ground," Merle Haggard's "Okie from Muskogee," Kenny Rogers' "Lucille," Glen Campbell's "Southern Nights," Anne Murray's "Walk Right Back," and Billy Crash Craddock's "I Cheated on a Good Woman's Love."

CRYSTAL GAYLE IN CONCERT ★★♪

COUNTRY/FOLK. 1982. Artist: Crystal Gayle. 56 min. Beta, VHS. Prism Entertainment ($39.95)

Crystal Gayle burst onto the music scene with her hit single "Don't It Make My Brown Eyes Blue," which knocked the country music establishment for a loop. Not many fans would have thought that a southern girl with beautiful, knee-length hair and classic, down-home looks would choose to sing in a jazzy, California-mellow style. Since she was Loretta Lynn's kid sister, everyone assumed she would imitate the honky-tonk brassiness of her famous older sister. But Crystal grew up in Indiana listening to Theresa Brewer, not Patsy Cline, and her music is accordingly in the crossover mode. Here we have straightforward concert footage of Crystal shot on video at the Hamilton Place in Hamilton, Ontario, Canada. To a packed crowd, Crystal enters in a white, tassled, sequined knee-length gown. Immediately, she breaks into song with a rendition of the gospel standard "Gone at Last." This is followed by "It's Been a Long Time Since You Went Away" and "You Left the One You Left Me For." Then Crystal does a number of forties pop and jazz standards: "Someday Your Wish Will Come True," "What a Little Moonlight Can Do," "You Never Gave Up on Me," and others. Her phrasing is suited to the vocal tasks these swing-inflected numbers require, and her features, in close-up, echo the classic forties siren look. "Same Old Story, Same Old Song," "True Love," "Our Love Is on the Fault Line," "Brown Eyes Blue," "You Fill Me Up," and "Rocky Top" complete the concert.

THE DIRT BAND TONITE   ★★★

COUNTRY/FOLK. 1981. Artists: Dirt Band (Jeff Hanna, Jimmie Fadden, John McEuen, Bob Carpenter, Richard Hathaway, Vic Mastrianni, Rosemary Butler, and Bryan Savage). 58 min. Beta Hifi, VHS Stereo. Thorn-EMI ($49.95)

Originally known as the Nitty Gritty Dirt Band, the Dirt Band has always played an amalgam of country, bluegrass, and other authentic American musical styles. Their *Will the Circle Be Unbroken?* album of a decade ago was a document of country and western classic songs and performers (like the Carter Family). Critically praised to the skies, it didn't sell as well as many expected. For many years afterward, the Dirt Band couldn't find the sound that would take them out of the bar circuit, playing to folkies and country rock fans. Then, after the surprising success of Jimmy Buffet's boozy Tex-Mex song cycles, including the hit "Margaritaville," the Dirt Band returned to the charts with their own paean to piña coladas and beach life, "An American Dream." So when this concert took place on a fall evening in 1981 at Denver's Rainbow Music Hall, the Dirt Band had been reborn as a good-times country rock group. Derek Burbridge, the director, has interspliced some silent film clips along with footage from an early Max Fleischer cartoon throughout the proceedings. The energetic set includes "Too Close for Comfort," "Fire in the Sky," "An American Dream," "Harmony," "Fish Song," "Randy Lynn Rag," "Rocky Top," "Make a Little Magic," "Some of Shelly's Blues," "Mr. Bojangles," "Badlands," "Bayou Jubilee," "Battle of New Orleans," "Jealousy," and "Will the Circle Be Unbroken."

DOLLY IN LONDON   ★★★

COUNTRY/FOLK. 1983. Artist: Dolly Parton. 90 min. Beta, VHS. RCA/Columbia ($29.95)

Originally shown as an HBO special in 1983, Dolly's concert in the Dominion Theater in London is a rollicking good time, filled with music and humorous patter. The tape begins with Dolly's arrival at Heathrow Airport in London. A customs official asks Dolly what her business in Britain is. She answers simply, "I sing." At a press conference held at her hotel, Dolly remarks that "if I'd been born a man, I probably would have been a drag queen." The scene outside the Dominion Theater on her opening night reveals her tremendous following among young punk rockers, out in force in shocking pink hair and leather studs, as well as the more conservative factions of English society. When Dolly arrives in a chartered double-decker bus, she is led through the throngs of adoring fans into the theater, where a group of beefeaters (traditional English royal guardsmen) form a cordon for her entrance. Once on stage, Dolly immediately goes

Dolly Parton in *Dolly in London*.

into a rendition of "Baby, I'm Burning" which segues into the first of her many favorites, "Jolene." "Two Doors Down," "Coat of Many Colors," "Appalachian Memories," and "Apple Jack" follow in succession, wowing the captivated English crowd, which shows its enthusiasm for Dolly's songs throughout. The other songs: "Did I Ever Cross Your Mind?," "Brother Love's Traveling Salvation Show," "Rhumba Girl," "All Shook Up" (including a very funny impression of Elvis Presley), "Me and Little Andy," "Down from Dover," "Here You Come Again," "Nine to Five," "Great Balls of Fire," and "I Will Always Love You."

THE ELECTRIC HORSEMAN   ★★★

COUNTRY/FOLK. 1979. Cast: Robert Redford, Jane Fonda, Willie Nelson, and Valerie Perrine. 120 min. Beta, VHS. MCA ($69.95)

In this film, directed by Sidney Pollack, Robert Redford plays Sonny Steele, a washed-up former rodeo champion who earns a very good living making personal appearances

DOLLY PARTON

Born on January 19, 1946, in Sevierville, Tennessee, Dolly Parton grew up in a musical family of twelve children, six of whom later became professional musicians. Starting at the age of 10 Dolly became a regular on Cas Walker's Knoxville radio show and after 8 years moved to Nashville and signed with the Monument Record Company.

In 1967, she signed with RCA Records and became a regular on the nationally syndicated *Porter Wagoner Show* on television and soon was known to countless fans as "Miss Dolly." Duets with Wagoner, "Just Someone I Used to Know" and "Daddy Was an Old Time Preacher Man"

became country hits in 1969 and 1970 respectively. She had a number of country and western hits including "Coat of Many Colors," which Emmylou Harris later covered, while with the Wagoner show, before striking out on her own as a solo artist and moving into the pop charts with "Here You Come Again" in 1978. Then came a stack of gold and platinum albums, including *Here You Come Again, Heartbreaker, Great Balls of Fire, Best of Dolly Parton, Dolly Parton's Greatest Hits,* and *Burlap and Satin.*

Dolly's success as a recording artist brought her a chance to act in the smash comedy *Nine to Five* with Lily Tomlin and Jane Fonda. She also wrote the Oscar-nominated title tune, which hit the top of the pop and country charts. In 1982, she costarred with Burt Reynolds in one of the year's top-grossing films, *The Best Little Whorehouse in Texas,* writing additional songs for the film version of the Broadway hit musical, including the Grammy-nominated "I Will Always Love You." Her latest film venture was "Rhinestone," an ill-conceived comedy in which she starred with Sylvester Stallone.

Video Resume

Best Little Whorehouse in Texas, (1982), MCA.
Dolly in London, (1983), RCA/Columbia.
Nine to Five, (1981), CBS/Fox.
Rhinestone, (1984), CBS/Fox.

Jane Fonda and Robert Redford clinch in *The Electric Horseman.*

and endorsing a breakfast cereal marketed by a huge conglomerate, Ampco. The plot turns when Sonny discovers that the $12 million racehorse, Rising Star, bought by the company to serve as its corporate symbol, is doped up on steroids and tranquilizers in order to keep it under control during public appearances. Sonny escapes with the horse into the open range of Utah, where they are pursued by agents of Ampco, federal authorities, state troopers, local police, and a national television correspondent, played by Jane Fonda. Willie Nelson, in his cinematic debut, plays Sonny Steele's manager, Wendell Hickson. He also sings the songs on the soundtrack, including "Midnight Rider," "My Heroes Have Always Been Cowboys," "Mammas Don't Let Your Babies Grow Up to Be Cowboys," "So You Think You're a Cowboy," and "Hands on the Wheel."

EVERY WHICH WAY BUT LOOSE ★★★

COUNTRY/FOLK. 1978. Cast: Clint Eastwood, Sondra Locke, Geoffrey Lewis, Beverly D'Angelo, Ruth Gordon, Mel Tillis, Phil Everly, Charlie Rich, and Manis the Orangutan. 105 min. Beta, VHS. Warner ($59.95)

In the age-old tradition of "give the people what they want," Clint Eastwood fashions yet another popular character for box office consumption. As Philo Beddoe, a slightly dim but morally upstanding strong man, Eastwood has tapped into the lifestyle and values of the new southwest, the fastest growing region in our nation. As *Every Which Way But Loose* pointedly shows, it's a land of individualistic dreamers held back by their all too obvious limitations. Amidst an arid landscape sprinkled with recreational vans, eighteen-wheelers, and roadside bars playing country music, the distinctions between law and anarchy, love and libido, and home and the road receive comic but enlightening treatment from Eastwood's underrated sensibility. As Philo fights his way to extra money (in "tough man" bouts), he involves himself with Sondra Locke, playing an ex-prostitute without a heart of gold, and places his friend (Geoffrey Lewis), his mother (a cantankerous Ruth Gordon), and his pet orangutan, Clyde, in danger from a pair of off-duty cops, a bike gang, and Locke's former pimp. Eastwood's portrait of the big, dumb sucker Beddoe is laced with dignity and humor. Lots of music, on camera ("Coca Cola Cowboy" and "Send Me Down to Tucson" by Mel Tillis, "I'll Wake You Up When I Get Home" and "Behind Closed Doors" by Charlie Rich, and "Don't Say You Don't Love Me No More" by Phil Everly and Sondra Locke) and on the soundtrack ("Every Which Way But Loose" by Eddie Rabbitt, "Ain't Love Good Tonight" by Wayne Parker, "Honky Tonk Fever" by Cliff Clifford, "I Seek the Night" by Sondra Locke, and "Six Pack to Go" by Hank Thompson).

HELL'S ANGELS FOREVER ★★♪

COUNTRY/FOLK. 1983. Artists: Willie Nelson, Johnny Paycheck, Jerry Garcia, and Bo Diddley. 93 min. Beta, VHS. Media ($59.95)

This is a documentary on the Hell's Angels motorcycle gang commissioned by the gang itself and, as such, shouldn't be received as an objective look at their lifestyle, beliefs, and activities. Done over a period of 10 years, with three different directors (Richard Chase, Kevin Keating, and Leon Gost), this film makes a case for the Angels as a harassed, misunderstood, and politically oppressed group of social outcasts who just happen to like dressing like vagrants, riding noisy machines, and picking fights at the drop of a Harley chain. You can believe whatever you wish but an hour and a half of their antics on screen made this viewer extremely squeamish. Fortunately, the torture of watching these neanderthals cavort is interrupted here and there by some fine country music including Willie Nelson performing in concert, "I Can Get Off on You" and "Angel Flying Too Close to the Ground." Bo Diddley is seen singing "Do Your Thing" and "Nasty Man." Jerry Garcia performs "That's All Right" and Elephant's Memory plays "The Pirates' Ball" and "Angels Forever." On the soundtrack, one can hear Johnny Paycheck's "Too Bent to Boogie," "Angel of the Highway," and "Ride On, Sonny," Jerry Garcia's "It Takes a Lot to Laugh, It Takes a Train to

Cry," Mission Mountain Wood Band's "Take a Whiff on Me," and Bob Van Dyke's "Give Me a Harley."

HONEYSUCKLE ROSE ★★★

COUNTRY/FOLK. 1980. Cast: Willie Nelson, Dyan Cannon, Amy Irving, and Slim Pickens. 120 min. Beta, VHS. Warner ($59.95)

Willie plays a Texas country singer named Buck Bonham whose life is a continual tour of one-night stands. His road life comes into conflict with his home life when his wife, played by Dyan Cannon, refuses to go on the road again with him. On tour without his wife, Willie begins a relationship with best friend Slim Pickens' daughter (Amy Irving), who is a guitarist with his band. When his wife discovers this, she threatens to divorce him. Through the intervention of Slim Pickens, Willie is reunited with Dyan in a joyful, musical ending. The film is chock-a-block with fine songs and cameo musical appearances by Emmylou Harris and others. Willie's sensitive country music style shows in such songs as "On the Road Again," "Loving Her Was Easier," "You Show Me Yours," "A Song for You," "Whiskey River," "Yesterday's Wine," "Angel Eyes," "If You Could Touch Her at All," and others. A quiet winner of a movie.

HONKYTONK MAN ★★

COUNTRY/FOLK. 1982. Cast: Clint Eastwood, Kyle Eastwood, Linda Hopkins, Ray Price, Marty Robbins, and Porter Wagoner. 122 min. Beta, VHS. Warner ($69.95)

In a change of pace, Clint Eastwood passes over his regular role as a hard-as-nails contemporary policeman to play a hard-drinking depression-era country singer named Red Stovall. His lifelong ambition is to audition for the Grand Ole Opry in Nashville. Trouble presents itself when Red realizes he has tuberculosis. But, he is determined to fulfill his dream. Red and his 11-year-old nephew, Whit, played by Kyle Eastwood, Clint's son, set out from the family farm in California for the Opry in Tennessee. On the way, they play in honkytonks, get in trouble with the law, and have other supposedly comic misadventures that along with Red's illness drag the picture to a near crawl instead of the fast pace that this father and son film was intended to have. Clint does a credible job of singing and receives firm support from country greats Ray Price, Marty Robbins, and Porter Wagoner, and blues singer Linda Hopkins. But in the end, having failed his Opry audition because his honkytonk repertoire was too coarse for the radio audience of the Grand Ole Opry, Red is forced to muster all of his strength to record a few 78s for a small record label before he finally dies. *Honkytonk Man* is a little too elegiac to properly celebrate a past era in country music and too slow and heavy to hold the viewer's interest.

LIVE AT THE LONE STAR CAFE   ★★★

COUNTRY/FOLK. 1981. Artists: Johnny Paycheck, Bo Diddley, and Levon Helm. 59 min. Beta, VHS. Vestron ($39.95)

It was one of the most eclectic bills ever to play the Lone Star: Johnny Paycheck, Bo Diddley, and Levon Helm. In the hot night spot located in the heart of New York City, the Lone Star Cafe, also known as "the unofficial embassy of Texas," urban cowboys and cowgirls gathered together for a rollicking evening of country, rock and roll, and blues. Johnny Paycheck, who first struck gold with his blue-collar anthem, "Take This Job and Shove It," written by outlaw David Allan Coe, hits the stage first to do "Ragged But Right" and "The I.R.S." Bo Diddley follows with gut-bucket renditions of his standards, "Accuse Me Jam," featuring the gyrating dancing of some lovely cowgirls in attendance, and "I'm a Man," delivered with the growl only Bo can wrench from his innards. Levon Helm, backed by the Cates Brothers Band, gives a short rendition of the rhythm and blues classic, "Milk Cow Blues." This is followed by a song that Levon made famous when he was the drummer for the original Band, "Rag Mama Rag." In the concluding segment, Johnny Paycheck returns to close out with "Rambling Fever," "Drinking and Driving That Woman Right off My Mind," "She's a Friend, She's a Lover, She's My Wife," "Don't Take Her, She's All I've Got," "New York Town," and "Take This Job and Shove It."

LORETTA LYNN   ★★★

COUNTRY/FOLK. 1980. Artist: Loretta Lynn. 61 min. Beta, VHS. MCA ($39.95)

Recorded at Harrah's in Reno, Nevada, this concert film shows Loretta doing her captivating act for an appreciative country music crowd. Those in the audience who want traditional good-time country honky-tonk music will find satisfaction in this performance by the one and only coalminer's daughter. "Hey Loretta" opens the show, followed by "You're Looking at Country," "Country Roads," "I Want You Out of My Bed," and "I'm Pregnant Again." While Loretta goes backstage to change, her band plays a diverting gospel medley including "Papa Sang Bass," "Will the Circle Be Unbroken?," "Operator," and "Gone at Last." Loretta returns to sing "Don't Come Home A-Drinkin'," "Rain, Rain," and "Coalminer's Daughter." Here, she treats the audience to a slide show depicting her family origins in Kentucky and a film clip from *Coalminer's Daughter,* the 1980 movie based on her life. The show comes to a rousing climax with "They Don't Make 'em Like My Daddy Anymore," "We've Come a Long Way," and "I Saw the Light."

Paul Le Mat as Melvin Dummar, claimant to the fortune of billionaire Howard Hughes, in *Melvin and Howard.*

MELVIN AND HOWARD ★★♪

COUNTRY/FOLK. 1981. Cast: Paul Le Mat, Jason Robards, Mary Steenburgen, Pamela Reed, Dabney Coleman, and Michael J. Pollard. 95 min. Beta, VHS. MCA ($69.95)

Jonathan Demme directed this whimsical slice of life comedy based on the real life exploits of Melvin Dummar, who claimed to be an heir of billionaire Howard Hughes, producing a handwritten will allegedly signed by Hughes. According to Dummar, who, at the time, owned a gas station in Willard, Utah, Hughes hitched a ride with him one evening after a motorcycle accident in the desert. While much of this film is fictional (a lot of it is too slapstick to have actually occurred to any one man), the real focus of this film is the American Dream of instant gratification, set against the mundane lives of blue-collar working people in today's west. Demme wants to put across the point that our values, as a society, are completely corrupted by our need to have instant wealth. Melvin's very human failing was that he didn't have the perseverance to make money the old-fashioned way, earn it. It is no coincidence that much of the action in this fairy tale of the new west takes place in Las Vegas and Anaheim, California (the home of Disneyland). The soundtrack includes The Amazing Rhythm Aces performing "Amazing Grace Used to Be Her Favorite Song," Credence Clearwater Revival's "Fortunate Son," Ray Conniff's "It Came Upon a Midnight Clear," Bob Wills and The Texas Playboys' "San Antonio Rose," Eddy Arnold's "Tennessee Stud," and Faron Young's classic singing of "Hello Walls."

NINE TO FIVE ★★★

COUNTRY/FOLK. 1981. Cast: Dolly Parton, Jane Fonda, Lily Tomlin, Dabney Coleman, Elizabeth Wilson, and Sterling Hayden. 110 min. Beta, VHS. CBS/Fox ($69.95)

In her movie debut, Dolly plays Dora Lee, a secretary who works for Consolidated Companies, a conglomerate which serves as a symbol of corporate America. Dora Lee's major problem in life, other than trying to make ends meet as a typical working woman, is her boss, Mr. Hart, played by Dabney Coleman in yet another of his classic portrayals of a bumbling curmudgeon. Along with her coworkers Jane Fonda and Lily Tomlin, Dolly hatches a plan to pay their boss back for his sexual harassment and chauvinistic behavior. Comic complications ensue as the three women kidnap and hold their much-hated boss. Dolly's "Nine to Five" serves as the theme song for the film. It was a big hit movie and a big hit single for Dolly. Her great reviews in her role as Dora Lee got her film career off to a sensational start. However, Parton hasn't really capitalized on it, considering her recent string of box office flops.

THE OTHER SIDE OF NASHVILLE ★★★

COUNTRY/FOLK. 1984. Artists: Kenny Rogers, Owen Davis, Bobby Bare, Porter Wagoner, Billy Strange, Rattlesnake Annie, Willie Nelson, Gail Davies, Terri Gibbs, Barbara Mandrell, Emmylou Harris, Chet Atkins, Charlie Daniels, Hank Williams, Hank Williams, Jr., Carl Perkins, Bob Dylan, Johnny Cash, Kris Kristofferson. 118 min. Beta Hifi, VHS Stereo. MGM/UA ($59.95)

In this low-key, informative, yet entertaining documentary on the history and development of Nashville, the creative crucible of the country music industry, fans will discover, much to their delight, a multitude of their favorite stars speaking freely about the industry that has fulfilled their dream of musical success. The technical superiority of the video enhances one's enjoyment of this journey through the history of country music. Important background material is dealt with, including the origins of WSM, the legendary radio station that broadcast the new sounds of "hillbilly" music from Texas to Canada, and the mecca of country music, the Grand Ole Opry, in Nashville. From these humble beginnings, a billion-dollar country music industry emerged. But with its growth as a business have come adaptations to the more mainstream tastes of a national and international audience. Figures such as Chet Atkins, Willie Nelson, and Kris Kristofferson discuss the influences of other types of music and how they have changed "pure" country into "crossover" music. Both for its music and its wealth of information, this video is an excellent choice for country fanatics and the general viewer alike. Songs include: Kenny Rogers' "The Gambler," Porter Wagoner's "Y'All Come," Bobby Bare's "They Call Me the Breeze," Ricky Scaggs' "Get Above Your Raisin'," Emmylou Harris' "Two More Bottles of Wine" and her version of Bruce Springsteen's "Racing in the Streets," Hank Williams' "Hey, Good Lookin'," Hank Williams, Jr.'s "Jesus Just Left Chicago," Carl Perkins' "Matchbox," "Honey Don't," and "Blue Suede Shoes," and Bob Dylan and Johnny Cash's "Girl from the North Country" and "One Too Many Mornings." As a topper to the whole video, we see Willie Nelson in concert, performing "Whiskey River" and "Always on My Mind."

PLAYBOY VIDEO MAGAZINE, VOLUME IV ★⌐

COUNTRY/FOLK. Artist: Willie Nelson. Beta Hifi, VHS Stereo. CBS/Fox ($59.95)

Volume IV of the *Playboy Video Magazine* features a short interview with country great Willie Nelson. Willie talks about his dreams, his heroes, his first good song, his many marriages, why he became a musician, and his life on the road. For the hard core Nelson fan only.

Willie Nelson, featured on *Playboy Video Magazine, Volume IV.*

SEMI-TOUGH   ★★★

COUNTRY/FOLK. 1977. Cast: Burt Reynolds, Kris Kristofferson, Jill Clayburgh, Roger E. Moseley, Bert Convy, Lotte Lenya, Carl Weathers, and Robert Preston. 99 min. Beta, VHS. CBS/Fox ($69.98)

Michael Ritchie (*Smile, The Candidate*) took Dan Jenkins' novel about professional football, *Semi-Tough,* and made a film about American pop psychology in the "me decade." Forget about seeing stirring football footage in this one. Ritchie focuses on the friendship of two pro football players, Billy Clyde Puckett (Reynolds) and Shake Tiller (Kristofferson), and their relationship with Barbara Jane Bookman (Clayburgh), daughter of their team's owner, as the three attempt to find a suitable approach to life's pressures, whether

WILLIE NELSON

Willie left Nashville after his house burned down in 1970 to record the milestone concept album, *The Red-Headed Stranger,* in Texas in 1975. This was followed by the million-seller *Wanted: The Outlaws,* a compilation album with Waylon Jennings, Tompall Galser, and Jessi Colter; *Stardust,* in which Willie covers a number of pop standards; and his triple platinum *Always on My Mind.*

Willie launched his film career as his popularity as a recording artist began to grow. After a supporting role as Robert Redford's right-hand man in *Electric Horseman,* Willie starred in *Honeysuckle Rose* and *Songwriter.*

Willie Hugh Nelson was born in Abbot, Texas, on April 30, 1933. He learned to play music from his grandfather and by listening to the Grand Ole Opry and to jazz and blues stations on the radio. In the late fifties, he returned to Texas after a gig as a disc jockey in Vancouver, Washington.

Willie sold his famous "Night Life" for $150, before moving to Nashville where, in 1961, Patsy Cline recorded Willie's "Crazy," which hit Number 1 as did Faron Young's rendition of Willie's "Hello Walls." Willie and his second wife, Shirley Collie, hit the Top 10 with "Willingly" and "Touch Me" in 1962.

Video Resume

Barbarosa, (1982), CBS/Fox.

Bob & Ray, Jane, Laraine & Gilda, (1979), Pacific Arts.

Hell's Angels Forever, (1983), Media.

Honeysuckle Rose, (1980), Warner.

The Other Side of Nashville, (1984), MGM/UA.

Playboy Video Magazine, Volume IV, (1983), CBS/Fox.

Songwriter, (1985), RCA/Columbia.

Thief, (1981), CBS/Fox.

Willie Nelson and Family in Concert, (1983), CBS/Fox.

it's "pelfing," "pyramid power," or "beat." "Beat," Ritchie's version of the then hugely popular est, turns out to be the philosophy that brings Billy Clyde and Barbara Jean together, sort of. Bert Convy, as beat's version of Werner Erhard, is perfect as the charlatan who won't allow people to leave the room, even to go to the bathroom. The soundtrack is filled with the songs of Gene Autry, Billy Clyde's favorite singer. It includes "Back in the Saddle Again," "Gold Mine in the Sky," "Silver Haired Daddy of Mine," "The Last Round-Up," "Have I Told You Lately That I Love You?," and "Don't Fence Me In."

SIX-PACK ★★

COUNTRY/FOLK. 1982. Cast: Kenny Rogers, Erin Gray, Diane Lane, Justin Henry, and Molly Ringwald. 108 min. Beta, VHS. CBS/Fox ($59.95)

Kenny Rogers fans who liked the hit single he had with this film's theme song, "Love Will Turn You Around," will do better by going out and buying Rogers' greatest hits album than viewing this adorable and inane piece of fluff. Rogers is cast in the role of a stock-car racer (the thousandth appearance of a country singer on screen as a professional race-car driver, à la Elvis) who "adopts" and tries to reform a family of six cute orphans turned auto strippers. Predictably, the urchins become Kenny's expert pit crew and help him win the race which puts his life back on the right track. Along with his new family, Kenny develops a meaningful relationship with TV's *Silver Spoons* star, Erin Gray. This film is reserved only for the diehard Rogers fan.

SONGWRITER ★★★♪

COUNTRY/FOLK. 1984. Cast: Willie Nelson, Kris Kristofferson, Lesley Ann Warren, Rip Torn, and Melinda Dillon. 94 min. Beta, VHS. RCA/Columbia ($79.95)

This charming and underrated movie about a musician and his struggle to survive in the Nashville music business suffered from a limited releasing schedule during first-run theatrical distribution. Willie Nelson plays Doc Jenkins, a good-natured guitarplayer who, unlike his singing-partner Blackie (Kris Kristofferson), naively believes that he can make money as easily as he can make music in the Nashville music scene. After a number of bad business investments, Doc's wife Honey (Melinda Dillon) gives him an ultimatum—either clear out of the music business or clear out of the house. Doc leaves and decides he can make a great deal of money by becoming a songwriter. Contracted to an unscrupulous record producer by the name of Rocky Rodeo, Doc soon finds himself bound and gagged by miles of red tape. Although Doc and Rocky shook hands on a deal that evenly split the royalties of Doc's songs, Doc failed to read the fine print on their written contract that stated Rocky owns 100% of the rights to Doc's material. But Doc moves to Austin and, with the help of his life-long friend Blackie and an unknown singer named Gilda (Lesley Ann Warren), has the last laugh on Rocky, is able to leave the music business, and reunite with his wife. *Songwriter* covers most of the topics in the average movie about the country music business—less-than-honest practices, adultery, sex, drugs, and alcohol, etc.; but it never loses its sense of humor and avoids the mawkish sentimentality and melodrama that taint most films about country music. Willie and Kris reinforce the overall solidity of the film's story and Alan Rudolph's direction. With fine renditions of songs this duo wrote for the film, they sing "How Do You Feel About Fooling Around," "Forever in Your Love," "Night to Remember," "Who Am I?," "Under the Gun," "Cajun Hide Away," and "Nobody Said It Was Going to Be Easy."

SOUTHERN COMFORT ★★★

COUNTRY/FOLK. 1981. Cast: Keith Carradine, Powers Boothe, Franklyn Seales, Peter Coyote. 106 min. Beta, VHS. Embassy ($79.95)

This suspenseful chase film set in the Bayou country of Louisiana boasts a soundtrack of authentic Cajun folk music supervised, arranged, and performed by talented guitarist-musicologist Ry Cooder. Walter Hill (*48 Hrs., Streets of Fire*) has always been at his best as an action film director, the disciple of Sam Peckinpah. A platoon of National Guardsmen on maneuvers in the Bayou are thrown into a frightening, disorienting situation when their commander Peter Coyote (*E.T.*) is killed by Cajun poachers who don't take kindly to strangers in their territory. Tracked through the thick swamps by seemingly invisible pursuers, the members of the platoon slowly but surely lose their wits—and their lives. Finally, only Keith Carradine and Powers Boothe survive. But for how long against the hostility and uncertainty of the Bayou and its inhabitants? The last 45 minutes of this film are breathtakingly exciting.

THIEF ★★

COUNTRY/FOLK. 1981. Cast: James Caan, Tuesday Weld, Jim Belushi, and Willie Nelson. 123 min. Beta, VHS. CBS/Fox ($69.95)

Willie Nelson, in a purely dramatic, non-singing role, plays a master thief and prison inmate who taught James Caan everything he knows about safecracking and sophisticated burglary. He lies dying in a prison hospital when James Caan realizes that he can't give him the one thing he wanted most—freedom. Willie shows us that, in a role which has nothing to do with music or the west, he is a more than capable actor. As for the rest of the film, it's a somber, slow-moving study of a man on the edge. Caan, the thief of the title, has to decide the future bent of his life when he meets Tuesday Weld and marries her. Unfortunately, he finds it almost impossible to sever his working relationship with the mob boss who has been assigning burglaries to him for a number of years. How he wriggles free from the mob's grasp is the core of this film.

URBAN COWBOY ★★★✔

COUNTRY/FOLK. 1980. Cast: John Travolta, Debra Winger, Scott Glenn, Madolyn Smith, Mickey Gilley, Johnny Lee, and Charlie Daniels. 132 min. Beta, VHS. Paramount ($39.95)

This film was one of the movie events of 1980. A bold idea that was inspired by the success of *Saturday Night Fever,* which also starred John Travolta and was a salute to

Smith and Travolta in *Urban Cowboy.*

the music and culture of the disco phenomenon, *Urban Cowboy* is a gritty, realistic portrayal of the blue-collar workers who, when the whistle blows, put on cowboy duds, go to Gilley's (the largest honky-tonk in the world), look at women, dance the two-step, and ride the mechanical bull. John Travolta plays Bud Davis, a young man who moves from his rural Texas home to the big city, Houston, to make his way in life. At Gilley's, Bud meets Sissy (Debra Winger) and despite their tempestuous relationship, they get married within two weeks. Trouble starts when Sissy decides to take lessons in riding the bull, her teacher being villain Scott Glenn. The plot concerns Bud and Sissy's breakup and eventual reconciliation. In this allegory of the shifting values of the new, industrial southwest culture, where real cowboys have been replaced by "urban cowboys," the tensions between home and work, work and play, and men and women are effectively dramatized. This film's soundtrack is awesome! Besides the screen appearances of Mickey Gilley, Johnny Lee, Bonnie Raitt, and Charlie Daniels, we hear such country gems as "Texas," "Rode Hard and Put Up Wet," "Looking for Love," "Lyin' Eyes," "Orange Blossom Special," "Rockin' My Life Away," "Stand by Me," "Here You Come Again," and "The Devil Went Down to Georgia."

WASN'T THAT A TIME!   ★★★

COUNTRY/FOLK. 1980. Artists: The Weavers (Pete Seeger, Lee Hays, Ronnie Gilbert, and Fred Hellerman), Arlo Guthrie, Don McLean, Holly Near, and Peter, Paul, and Mary. 78 min. Beta, VHS. MGM/UA ($29.95)

The folk group The Weavers was plucked out of obscurity in the early fifties by Gordon Jenkins, who heard them in a Greenwich Village night club and signed them to a record contract. Their first single for Decca Records, "Goodnight Irene," sold a million copies. Other smash hits followed. They were soon known throughout America as good-natured, well-groomed performers of family entertainment. Then they were rumored to be politically active, left-leaning unionists and were blacklisted. The Weavers didn't work for years until they themselves rented and sold out Carnegie Hall in New York for one night in 1955. In the audience were many of the young performers who would become the leaders of the folk movement in the sixties. Twenty-five years after that historic concert, Pete Seeger, Lee Hays, Ronnie Gilbert, and Fred Hellerman decided to revive The Weavers for one more concert at Carnegie Hall. This tape traces the group's history and records this special revival. *Wasn't That a Time!* is a cornucopia of Weavers songs, including "On Top of Old Smokey," "When the Saints Go Marching In," "Tzena, Tzena, Tzena," "Goodnight, Irene," "Wasn't That a Time," "Wimoweh" ("Mbube"), "Nobody Knows You When You're Down and Out," "Venga Jaleo," "If I Had a Hammer," "Banjo Breakdown," "Kisses Sweeter Than Wine," "Darling Corey,"

The Weavers, then and now, in *Wasn't That a Time!*

"Allelujah," "Tomorrow Lies in the Cradle," "Woody's Rag," "Miner's Life," and "We Wish You a Merry Christmas."

WILLIE NELSON AND FAMILY IN CONCERT ★★★♪

COUNTRY/FOLK. 1983. Artist: Willie Nelson. 90 min. Beta Hifi, VHS Stereo. CBS/ Fox ($59.95)

In 1983, Willie Nelson played the Opry House in Austin, Texas, to a sellout crowd of Texas partisans of all ages. On stage, with his longtime extended family of musicians, Willie opens with "Tougher Than Leather" and "Good Old-Fashioned Karma." A whole host of other shorter songs and country standards are intertwined in these two memorable Nelson compositions so that it all sounds like a long medley of tunes. The most striking aspect of the early moments of the concert is Willie's splendid work on acoustic guitar. Willie makes allusions to the guitar styles that have influenced his work as a whole: Tex-Mex, western swing, bluegrass, and the playing of the Gypsy jazz guitarist, Django Reinhardt! "Nobody Slides" ends this segment, and after a short intermission, Willie and family return with jazz guitarist Jackie King, whose work Willie deeply admires. King does an instrumental version of "Tenderly" and accompanies Willie on "There Will Never Be Another You." After the second short intermission, Willie performs "Nightlife," "Blue Eyes Crying in the Rain," "Blue Skies," "Georgia on My Mind," "All of Me," and "Stardust." Finally, closing the concert with a rush, Willie sings "Mamas, Don't Let Your Babies Grow Up to Be Cowboys," "Angel Flying Too Close to the Ground," "On the Road Again," "Always on My Mind," and a last country gospel hymn.

JAZZ

AFTER HOURS ★★★✦

JAZZ. 1961. Artists: Coleman Hawkins, Roy Eldridge, Milt Hinton, Johnny Guarnieri, Cozy Cole, and Carol Stevens. 27 min. Beta, VHS. Rhapsody ($50.00)

New York disc jockey William B. Williams hosts this black and white film intended to be the pilot for a television series that was never made. Too bad. In what would have been the opening episode, Willy B. and his cameraperson just happen to be in the After Hours Club on New York's "Swing Street" at four o'clock in the morning to catch an "impromptu" jam session by some of the finest jazz musicians who ever lived. Roy Eldridge picks up his trumpet. Coleman Hawkins saunters up to the band-stand with his sax. Milt Hinton and his bass, Johnny Guarnieri and his piano, and Cozy Cole and his drum kit form the rhythm section for a wonderful jam. After a breathy "Lover Man" and Roy Eldridge's rendition of "Sunday," singer Carol Stevens joins the group to sing "Just You, Just Me." The Band begins to jam on an untitled selection that is the highlight of this film. "Bean" and "Little Jazz" and the other guys in the group take off, go into orbit, and wail! It will take some doing to obtain a copy of *After Hours,* but the finale is well worth the trouble.

347

BILL EVANS ON THE CREATIVE PROCESS ★★ɟ

JAZZ. 1966. Artist: Bill Evans. 20 min. Beta, VHS. Rhapsody ($50.00)

Bill Evans discusses jazz piano improvisation with his brother, music educator Harry Evans, and elaborates on his theories while playing "Star Eyes," "Time Remembered," and "My Belle."

THE BILL WATROUS REFUGE WEST BAND ★★ɟ

JAZZ. 1983. Artist: Bill Watrous. 25 min. Beta Hifi, VHS Stereo. Sony ($19.95)

Bill Watrous, the jazz trombonist who led the *Downbeat* reader's poll for 7 consecutive years, leads an eighteen-piece big band at Howard Rumsey's Concerts-By-The-Sea in Redondo Beach, California. The band starts off with "Space Available," a dynamic tune that features solo work by Watrous on trombone, Chad Wackerman on drums, and Gordon Goodwin on tenor saxophone. Watrous then leads the band through the lyrical ballad written by Sam Nestico, "Samantha." Watrous features his trombone wizardry on "The Slauson Cutoff" and "Birdland," the tune penned by Joe Zawinul, the pianist for Weather Report. This short set was recorded digitally and the audio on *The Bill Watrous Refuge West Band* is superlative.

BORN TO SWING ★★★

JAZZ. 1973. Artists: Gene Krupa, Andy Kirk, John Hammond, Dicky Wells, Buddy Tate, Buck Clayton, Earle Warren, Jo Jones, Eddie Durham, Snub Mosley, Gene Ramey, Tommy Flanagan, and Joe Newman. 50 min. Beta, VHS. Rhapsody ($70.00)

Born to Swing is a documentary that examines the history and high points of America's fabulous golden age of jazz, the swing era. From Andy Kirk's recollections of the midwestern "territory" bands of the thirties to Gene Krupa's memories of the radio broadcasts of the great dance hall bands of the forties, *Born to Swing* paints a detailed picture of the music, the musicians, and the era of their heyday. Director John Jeremy tracked down some of the great soloists from the memorable Count Basie band of the late thirties and brought them together for an impromptu recording session. Joining trumpeter Buck Clayton, drummer Jo Jones, tenor saxophonist Buddy Tate, alto sax player Earle Warren, and trombonist Dicky Wells are some other fine practitioners of the swing era style. Guitar and trombone player Eddie Durham, pianist Tommy Flanagan, trombonist Snub Mosley, trumpet player Joe Newman, and bassist Gene Ramey sit in with the Count's players for a recreation of the sound that they helped foster 40 years beforehand.

THE COTTON CLUB   ★★

JAZZ. 1984. Cast: Richard Gere, Gregory Hines, Diane Lane, Lonette Mc Kee, Nicolas Cage, Allen Garfield, and Fred Gwynne. 128 min. Beta, VHS. Embassy ($79.95)

It is said that out in Hollywood, big-time producers "do power lunches" and spend large amounts of money to turn notions into concepts and then into ideas which later become stories, and after another large infusion of cash, become scripts and then movies. Millions of dollars and the talents of William Kennedy, Mario Puzo, and Francis Ford Coppola could not turn producer Robert Evans' notion about the famed Harlem night club of the twenties into a story. They attempted to set the story of two white lovers, cornet player Dixie (Richard Gere) and professional gun moll Vera (Diane Lane), who get mixed up with mobster Dutch Schultz and his attempt to take over the Harlem numbers racket against the backdrop of the high-steppin' musical numbers of the Cotton Club review. *Cotton Club* suffers from a lack of focus. Although the writers made a weak attempt to tell the story of the black musicians and performers, they failed to see that that was the real story, and that an additional gangster plot was superfluous and made the film confusing. The dance numbers in the film are worth seeing. Bob Wilber did a fine job recreating the "jungle" sound of Duke Ellington's 1920s band on "East St. Louis Toodle-O," "Ring Dem Bells," "Creole Love Call," and "Mood Indigo."

COUNT BASIE LIVE AT THE HOLLYWOOD PALLADIUM   ★★♪

JAZZ. 1974. Artists: Count Basie and his Orchestra, featuring Eddie "Lockjaw" Davis, Al Grey, and Fran Jeffries. 42 min. Beta, VHS. VCL ($29.95)

This 1974 television special features the Basie Band as they play a dance set at Hollywood's Palladium. Tenor sax player Eddie "Lockjaw" Davis takes a solo on "The Spirit Is Willing." Fran Jeffries sings "I Like It" and "Still Swinging." The band plays slow tempo versions of "All of Me," legendary rhythm guitarist Freddie Green's "Corner

Count Basie.

Pocket," Jim Croce's pop hit "Leroy Brown," "Splanky," and Frank Foster's "Shiny Stockings."

DIFFERENT DRUMMER: ELVIN JONES ★★★♪

JAZZ. 1979. Artists: Elvin Jones and Ron Carter. 30 min. Beta, VHS. Rhapsody ($50.00)

Drummer Elvin Jones and his music are beautifully portrayed in this short but well-made documentary. The film is structured around the composition, explanation, and

Different Drummer **Elvin Jones.**

performance of Elvin's "Three Card Molly," which he plays with his quartet. In the pause after each segment, director Edward Gray explores a different facet of Jones' professional career and his personal life. Elvin talks about his years with Bud Powell and John Coltrane and his polyrhythmic drumming style that became so influential. Elvin also takes us to his home in Flint, Michigan, where he and his brothers, pianist Hank and trumpet player Thad, grew up and formed their own combo. A very interesting examination of an artist and his life.

DIZZY GILLESPIE'S DREAM BAND ★★★★

JAZZ. 1981. Artists: Dizzy Gillespie, Max Roach, Gerry Mulligan, Pepper Adams, Candido, Paquito d'Rivera, George Duvivier, George Davis, John Faddis, Frank Foster, Curtis Fuller, Slide Hampton, Sir Roland Hanna, Jimmy Heath, Milt Jackson, Melba Liston, John Lewis, Benny Powell, Victor Paz, Marvin Stamm, Grady Tate, Frank Wess, and Joe Wilder. 16 min. Beta Hifi, VHS Stereo. Sony ($19.95)

Excerpted from a concert given at Avery Fisher Hall in New York City on Washington's Birthday, 1981 (which can be seen in its entirety on Embassy Home Entertainment's

Jazz in America) *Dizzy Gillespie's Dream Band* features master trumpeter Dizzy Gillespie playing two bebop standards he made famous, "Groovin' High" and "Hot House." He is aided by one of the most impressive gatherings of jazz talent to play together in one place in the last 10 years. Diz and Gerry Mulligan trade solos on "Groovin' High." Milt Jackson, John Lewis, and Max Roach join them and the twenty-piece band to burn up the stage on "Hot House." Not to be missed.

EVOLUTIONARY SPIRAL ★★★

JAZZ. 1984. Artists: Weather Report. 15 min. Beta Hifi, VHS Stereo. Sony ($16.95)

In one of the most innovative video programs yet released, Joe Zawinul and Wayne Shorter of the electronic jazz ensemble Weather Report provide music to accompany some rather spectacular computer graphic effects. Written and directed by Larry Lachman, with the help of Joni Carter and Helen Davis in the area of computer animation, *Evolutionary Spiral* attempts an encapsulated video history of life on earth and the universe. It opens with clouds of gas condensing to form the solar system: the sun, the planets, and the earth. It then moves through the ages of different animal species, through the human species' brief reign, past the nuclear explosion that heralds our demise, into the future of space exploration, the stars, the galaxies, the void. One is reminded of Chuck Braverman's 2-minute film capsules which shot images at the viewer in a veritable machine-gun burst. Three compositions are used for the soundtrack: Joe Zawinul's "Procession" and "Two Lines" and Wayne Shorter's "Plaza Real."

THE FABULOUS DORSEYS ★★♪

JAZZ. 1947. Cast: Jimmy Dorsey, Tommy Dorsey, Paul Whiteman, Art Tatum, Charlie Barnet, Ziggy Elman, Ray Banduc, and Janet Blair. 91 min. Beta, VHS. NTA ($39.95)

Jimmy and Tommy Dorsey play themselves in their own life story! After learning to play their instruments in their hometown of Shenandoah, Pennsylvania, the boys played over Baltimore's first radio station as the Dorsey Novelty Band before joining the Paul Whiteman Orchestra in the mid-twenties. They soon set out with their own band with Jimmy on alto saxophone and Tommy on trombone, but tempers flared and Tommy left to form his own group. Bob Eberly and Helen O'Connell and the Jimmy Dorsey Orchestra scored a hit with "Green Eyes," while Tommy and his band hit the charts with "Marie." The brothers refused to speak to each other or to play together with Whiteman's Orchestra for a special performance of the Dorsey Concerto. They were brought together only at their father's deathbed. After the release of the film in 1947, the Dorseys formed a united band and had an NBC network television program, *Stage Show. The Fabulous Dorseys* features a jam session with the Dorseys, pianist Art Tatum, saxophonist Charlie Barnet, and trumpeter Ziggy Elman.

FREDDIE HUBBARD STUDIO LIVE ★★★

JAZZ. 1981. Artists: Freddie Hubbard, Bud Shank, Bill Perkins, Bob Tricario, Chuck Findley, Gary Grant, Bill Watrous, Frank Foster, Bill Mays, Dan Ferguson, Abe Laboriel, Bill Maxwell, and Joe Porcaro. 59 min. Beta Hifi, VHS Stereo. Sony ($29.95)

Not only does this tape give you an hour of Freddie Hubbard's clear, clean, muscular trumpet playing, but it takes you into the recording studio and lets the home video viewer examine the anatomy of a professional recording session first hand. Backed up by a group of first-rate L.A. studio musicians, Bud Shank on flute, Chuck Findley on French horn, Bill Watrous and Frank Foster on trombone, and Bill Maxwell on drums to name a few, Freddie cuts a digitally recorded album covering some of 1981's top pop and jazz fusion hits. After laying down the tracks for "Hubbard's Cupboard"

Freddie Hubbard Studio Live.

and "Two Moods for Freddie," Freddie and the band record Weather Report's "Bird-land," Christopher Cross' "Ride Like the Wind," "Bridgette," "Condition Alpha," and "This Is It."

GERRY MULLIGAN ★★★

JAZZ. 1981. Artists: Gerry Mulligan, Billy Hart, Frank Luther, and Harold Danko. 18 min. Beta Hifi, VHS Stereo. Sony ($19.95)

Baritone sax master Gerry Mulligan fronts a quartet filled out by Billy Hart on drums, Frank Luther on bass, and Harold Danko on piano. In two numbers on this 18-minute excerpt from a set recorded at Eric's on New York's Upper East Side (a complete

Sax artist Gerry Mulligan.

version of the performance is available as *Jazz in America Starring Gerry Mulligan* on Embassy), Mulligan concentrates on rendering the sensation of the movement of travel. "North Atlantic Run," a tune dedicated to 747 pilots, depicts a flight across the North Atlantic. A tune titled "K4 Pacific" (the name of the type of steam locomotive that made the New York to Chicago run in the forties) captures Gerry's memories of the trip in a variety of tempos that mimic the various speeds traveled along the rails between the two cities.

I LOVE YOU (EU TE AMO) ★★✈

JAZZ. 1983. Cast: Sonia Braga and Paulo C. Pereio. 105 min. Beta, VHS. MGM/UA ($59.95)

Brazilian Antonio Carlos Jobim, who along with guitarist Joǎo Gilberto created the bossa nova sound in the late fifties and early sixties, cowrote the title tune of *"Eu Te*

Sonia Braga in *I Love You.*

Amo'' ("I Love You") with Chico Buarque, the composer of the memorable music for the film *Dona Flor and Her Two Husbands*. Jobim also wrote "Spanish Veranda," which is included on the soundtrack. In *I Love You,* a Brazilian version of Bernando Bertolucci's *Last Tango in Paris,* a bankrupt industrialist, Paulo (Paulo C. Pereio), is jilted by his wife at the same time that Maria's boyfriend leaves her. They meet accidentally. Although penniless he shows off his luxurious apartment as just one of his many possessions to impress her. Maria (Sonia Braga) pretends to be a tough, highly paid prostitute. They spend the remainder of the film maintaining their charade and soothing their emotional pain with sexual pleasure. By the end of the film, they have fallen in love.

JAZZ HOOFER: BABY LAURENCE ★★

JAZZ. 1981. Artists: Baby Laurence, Bill Robinson, and John Bubbles. 30 min. Beta, VHS. Rhapsody ($50.00)

Laurence Donald Jackson, a.k.a. Baby Laurence, was one of the last of a dying breed of jazz tap dancers who combined the movements of tap dancing with the rhythms and signatures of jazz drumming. In two rare film clips, one shot at Fells Point in Baltimore, the other at the Jazz Museum in New York, Baby Laurence demonstrates the complexity and artistry of jazz tap. He breaks down each step and explains its origin and significance for the camera. In the process, Baby covers the history of jazz tap and examines the contributions of such great practitioners as Bill Robinson and John Bubbles. Although this low-budget film suffers from a number of technical deficiencies, it is an excellent record of an American original and his art form.

JAZZ IN AMERICA ★★★★

JAZZ. 1981. Artists: Dizzy Gillespie, Max Roach, Gerry Mulligan, Pepper Adams, Candido, Paquito d'Rivera, George Duvivier, George Davis, John Faddis, Frank Foster, Curtis Fuller, Slide Hampton, Sir Roland Hanna, Jimmy Heath, Milt Jackson, Melba Liston, John Lewis, Benny Powell, Victor Paz, Marvin Stamm, Grady Tate, Frank Wess, and Joe Wilder. 90 min. Beta Hifi, VHS Stereo. Embassy ($39.95)

In 1981, trumpeter Dizzy Gillespie brought together more than twenty first-rate jazz musicians to form his Dream Band for two Washington's Birthday concerts at Avery Fisher Hall in New York City. Dizzy and the other headliners hoped to recreate the excitement and energy that had created the original sound of bebop almost forty years before. Using the original charts, the musicians who had played on the original dates of such classics as "Things to Come" join together again, along with such talented newcomers as saxophonist Paquito d'Rivera and trumpeter John Faddis, to play powerful versions of Gillespie's "Manteca" and "Night in Tunisia." Gerry Mulligan joins Dizzy on stage with his baritone sax to assume Charlie Parker's role on the famous "Groovin' High." Mulligan is interviewed during the tape and he talks about his times with Parker and how Parker forced him to practice and play on stage. Max Roach plays a tribute to Basie drummer Jo Jones called "Mr. Hi-Hat" on a single hi-hat. Dizzy then brings out vibraphonist Milt Jackson and pianist John Lewis, both of the Modern Jazz Quartet, and bassist Paul West to run through the Parker and Gillespie standard, "Hot House." As an introduction to the number, the home video audience is shown a rare kinescope of a television show from the early fifties showing Parker and Gillespie playing an original version of the tune. The spotlight falls on Milt Jackson, who plays a very smooth "Lover Man." The band is joined by vocalist Jon Hendricks of Lambert, Hendricks, and Ross fame, who sets the words of Gillespie's presidential campaign song, "Vote Dizzy," to the music of the bop anthem, "Salt Peanuts." A wonderful concert that should not be missed.

JAZZ IN AMERICA STARRING GERRY MULLIGAN ★★★♩

JAZZ. 1981. Artists: Gerry Mulligan, Harold Danko, Billy Hart, and Frank Luther. 60 min. Beta Hifi, VHS Stereo. Embassy ($29.95)

Gerry Mulligan is best known to jazz fans as an accomplished saxophone player, concentrating on the baritone, and accompanying such diverse musicians as Miles Davis, who nicknamed him "Jeru," the players of the New York Philharmonic, for which he played solo soprano saxophone in Ravel's "Bolero," and Argentine bandoneón player Astor Piazzolla. Mulligan is also a very well known composer and arranger. From his pianoless quartet, with Chico Hamilton on drums and Chet Baker on trumpet, in the fifties to his pianoless concert band in the sixties and his quartet with piano in the seventies and eighties, Mulligan has explored a variety of approaches to writing and composing. In the set on this tape recorded at Eric's in New York in 1981, a little before the release of his *Little Big Horn* album, he explores new avenues of arranging for quartet while maintaining a strong melody line to make the music accessible to the audience. "People have always said that I played the baritone like a little horn," Gerry explains. "I've attempted to create the illusion that it's not playing in the low register that it is by concentrating on its qualities as a melodic instrument. There are many basic ways of hearing jazz—mine will always be the melodic." Gerry and his quartet start their set off with "The 17 Mile Drive," a song named after the scenic

17-mile drive between Monterey and Carmel, California. During "An Unfinished Woman" pianist Harold Danko puts some of Gerry's new ideas about arranging for quartet into practice by strumming the wires inside the piano during the performance. Gerry plays cornet for the title tune from his Grammy-winning album, "Walk on the Water." The group again picks up on the theme of transportation in "The North Atlantic Run," a composition dedicated to the Boeing 747 pilots who fly across the North Atlantic. The quartet changes tempo and Mulligan changes back to his baritone for "Song for Strayhorn," a tribute to the arranger for the Duke Ellington band and composer of "Take the A Train," Billy Strayhorn. The final tune of the set, "K4 Pacific," is named after the large steam locomotives that pulled railroad trains on the New York to Chicago route in the forties. Mulligan relives those memories in this composition, using a variety of tempos to reproduce the feeling of the different speeds traveled during the trip.

JONI MITCHELL: SHADOWS AND LIGHT ★★★

JAZZ. 1979. Artists: Joni Mitchell, Pat Metheny, Jaco Pastorius, Lyle Mays, Michael Brecker, Don Alias, and The Persuasions. 60 min. Beta, VHS. Warner ($49.95)

Joni Mitchell has come a long way in 15 years, both geographically and musically. She started out as a folk singer in her native Canada, in Saskatoon and Toronto, moved to Detroit with her first husband, and there began to gain recognition for her songwriting. Judy Collins had a hit with her "Both Sides Now" and several folkies recorded her "Circle Game." After a couple of albums of mostly folk-inflected songs, she moved to Los Angeles to consciously restructure her music and image. By 1974, with the success of her *Court and Spark* album, Joni had found mass acceptance as a pop singer, using jazz phrasing in her highly polished vocals and introducing a more layered sound to her backing instrumentation. Seemingly uncomfortable with her MOR status, she began a musical evolution that has effectively taken her out of the mainstream of commercial recording and radio. This concert, recorded at the County Bowl in Santa Barbara, California, in September of 1979, features Joni's first concrete foray into the area of pop jazz, as she employs such well-known musicians as guitarist Pat Metheny, bassist Jaco Pastorius (Weather Report), and saxophonist Michael Brecker, all solid citizens in L.A.'s session society. Going beyond the stuff she had already done with Tom Scott on *Miles of Aisles,* this was intended to be an experiment in electronic jazz. It succeeds fitfully because Mitchell's strong suit is not her voice, light and airy enough for the reedy vocals of her folk music roots but too brittle and limited for the kind of jazz singing she wants to do. The concert is at its best when she lays back and allows the musicians to play. Pat Metheny, quite a star in his own right now, has some brilliant moments, most notably on "Pat's Solo," a set piece for his brand of

Joni Mitchell, singing electronic jazz in *Shadows and Light*.

guitar pyrotechnics. Also of interest are two songs Joni recorded with jazz great Charles Mingus shortly before his untimely death, "Dry Cleaner from Des Moines" and "Goodbye Porkpie Hat." Other numbers include "In France They Kiss on Main Street," "Edith and the King Pin," "Coyote," "Free Man in Paris," "Jaco's Solo," "Amelia," "Black Crow," "Furry Sings the Blues," "Raised on Robbery," "Why Do Fools Fall in Love?" (with The Persuasions), and "Shadow and Light." Directed by Joni Mitchell.

THE KING OF JAZZ ★★★

JAZZ. 1930. Artists: Paul Whiteman and his Orchestra, The Rhythm Boys. 93 min. Beta, VHS Stereo. MCA ($39.95)

The King of Jazz is a musical revue built around the most popular dance band of the twenties, the Whiteman Orchestra, and its leader, the "King of Jazz" himself, Paul

The Paul Whiteman orchestra performing Gershwin's "Rhapsody in Blue" atop a 40-foot piano in *The King of Jazz*.

Whiteman. The movie is notable as being the first musical film in color. The early technicolor process used renders everything in turquoise and rose, but that should not stop the home video audience from searching for a few surprises. Animator Walter Lantz, who later created Woody Woodpecker, animated "My Lord Delivered Daniel," a cartoon short at the beginning of the film that features Paul Whiteman as a big game hunter. The vocal group The Rhythm Boys sing "Mississippi Mud" and "The Bluebird and the Blackbird." If you keep your eyes peeled, you'll smile when you see a young Bing Crosby in their ranks. Although called the King of Jazz, Whiteman wrote his band's arrangements so that they were more symphonic orchestrations than real jazz. However, he did employ a number of fine improvisational jazz musicians in his orchestra, including violinist Joe Venuti, who can be seen in "Oh! How I Would Like to Own a Fish Store!" The highlight and most memorable moment of the film is the orchestra's performance of George Gershwin's *Rhapsody in Blue,* a composition Paul Whiteman premiered at Aeolian Hall in New York in February of 1924. The orchestra is set on top of a giant blue piano in a sequence that predates the giant production numbers of the dynamic director Busby Berkeley. It must be seen to be believed. *The King of Jazz* is a time capsule that will forever hold the exuberance and charm of the roaring twenties on tape.

THE LAST OF THE BLUE DEVILS   ★★★↙

JAZZ. 1979. Artists: Count Basie, Joe Turner, Jay McShann, Jimmy Forrest, Buddy Anderson, Ernie Williams, Eddie Durham, Curtis Foster, Paul Gunther, Jo Jones, Baby Lovett, Paul Quinichette, Buster Smith, and Gene Ramey. 90 min. Beta, VHS. Rhapsody ($90.00)

Over a 5-year-period, 1974 to 1979, New York filmmaker Bruce Ricker ventured to Kansas City to film the last members of the Oklahoma City Blue Devils, the seminal dance band with a highly distinctive sound that later formed the nucleus of the Bennie Moten band and even later the Count Basie Orchestra. Instead of the elegy to a bygone era that one would expect to see in a documentary of this type, Ricker's film is a celebration of the Kansas City sound of the thirties, forties, and fifties. Using a camera that intimately caresses some of the giants of jazz, the film immediately draws the audience in and makes us participants in an informal gathering at the Mutual Musicians Hall, formerly the Black Musicians' Union Hall in Kansas City. Big Joe Turner ambles in with cane in hand. Some of the older men are helped to their places by attendants. But, once the music starts, the years seem to fall away as these musicians play, blow, and wail with the same power that they did 40 years before. Watching this film is exciting because the music lives. Big Joe Turner and boogie pianist Jay McShann play an electrifying version of "Piney Top Blues." Big Joe claims he invented rock and roll. The film tries to prove his point by showing a TV performance of his "Shake, Rattle, and Roll" from the fifties and compares it to his performance of the song for the movie. The Count sits down at the piano and plays two Basie standards, "One O'Clock Jump" and "Jumping at the Woodside." A must-see movie.

Jay McShann and Big Joe Turner, featured performers on *The Last of the Blue Devils.*

MAX ROACH ★★★♩

JAZZ. 1981. Artists: Max Roach, Calvin Hill, Cecil Bridgewater, and Odean Pope. 19 min. Beta Hifi, VHS Stereo. Sony ($19.95)

Max Roach sits back and provides the firm rhythmic foundation on which trumpet player Cecil Bridgewater and tenor saxophonist Odean Pope build the melodies and beautiful solos on "Effie" and "Six Bits," the two pieces provided on this short tape recorded in March of 1981 at Blues Alley in Washington, D.C. Aided by superior sound quality, this performance tape sounds as good as it looks. Recommended.

ONE NIGHT STAND ★★

JAZZ. 1981. Artists: Eubie Blake, Kenny Barron, Bobby Hutcherson, Bob James, Hubert Laws, Ron Carter, George Duke, Herbie Hancock, Charles Earland, Buddy Williams, Roland Hanna, and Rodney Franklin. 98 min. Beta, VHS. CBS/Fox ($49.95)

On January 20, 1981, Carnegie Hall in New York was sold out for *One Night Stand,* an "unprecedented all-star evening of keyboard wizardry" for which a number of first-class jazz musicians were brought together.

Eubie Blake, the 98-year-old pianist-songwriter whose life's work was being celebrated at the time on Broadway in the stage show *Eubie!,* opens the show with a piano solo rendition of his own compositions "Sounds of Africa" and "Memories of You." Pianist Kenny Barron takes the stage with vibraphonist Bobby Hutcherson to play "Sunshower." "Winding River" is played in turn by Bob James on piano and Ron Carter on bass. Keyboard player George Duke sits at an organ for the first time in 20 years to play an organ duet with Charles Earland of "When Johnny Comes Marching Home Again." Alto saxophonist Arthur Blythe and pianist Sir Roland Hanna join forces to perform "A Common Cause." Six grand pianos, Herbie Hancock, Rodney Franklin, George Duke, Bob James, Kenny Barron, Roland Hanna, Eubie Blake, Ron Carter, and Buddy Williams appear on stage together to play an original piece, "Hexagon," composed by Jay Chattaway for the *One Night Stand* concert.

This is most notable as a recording of a number of quality jazz musicians playing together rather than musicians brought together to play quality jazz. The performances are too short and do not allow the keyboardists the time to develop their improvisations. The audience is supposed to be impressed by the magnitude of collected talent rather than the individual performances.

PLAYBOY JAZZ FESTIVAL, VOLUME I ★★

JAZZ. 1982. Artists: McCoy Tyner Quartet (Ron Carter, Elvin Jones, Freddie Hubbard, and McCoy Tyner), Red Norvo/Tal Farlow Trio, Benny Golson, Art Farmer, Nancy Wilson, Pieces of a Dream, Grover Washington, Jr., Maynard Ferguson and his Orchestra, and Lionel Hampton's All-Star Jam Session. 91 min. Beta Hifi, VHS Stereo. RCA/Columbia ($29.95)

Volume I of the Fourth Annual Playboy Jazz Festival is presented here live from the Hollywood Bowl as more of a quick sampler of some fine jazz performances than a complete tape of a full-length festival. The producer of this, the first volume of a two-volume series, would do better service to himself, the music, and the home video audience by releasing extended performances in more than two volumes than by cramming fourteen acts into a 90-minute tape. The highlights include The McCoy Tyner Quartet, a summit meeting of jazz masters with former John Coltrane sidemen McCoy Tyner on piano, Elvin Jones on drums, Freddie Hubbard on trumpet, and Ron Carter on bass. Electric guitarist Tal Farlow comes out of self-imposed semiretirement to join vibraphonist Red Norvo on a jaunty version of Sonny Rollins' "The Everywhere Calypso." Trumpeter Art Farmer and saxophonist Benny Golson reunite for the first time in 20 years to back up singer Nancy Wilson on "I'll Remember April," "I Want You to Save Your Love for Me," and "I Thought about You." Grover Washington, Jr., plays the pop hit "Just the Two of Us" with the members of Pieces of a Dream, the Philadelphia-based group that he helped mold into a professional trio. As the finale of the first volume of the Playboy Jazz Festival, bandleader and vibraphonist Lionel Hampton leads an all-star jam session that includes Freddie Hubbard on trumpet and master of ceremonies Bill Cosby on drums.

PLAYBOY JAZZ FESTIVAL, VOLUME II ★★♪

JAZZ. 1982. Artists: Free Flight, Dave Brubeck Quintet, Ornette Coleman, Weather Report, Manhattan Transfer, Dexter Gordon, Woody Shaw, Maynard Ferguson and his Orchestra, O. C. Smith, and Sarah Vaughan. 91 min. Beta Hifi, VHS Stereo. RCA/Columbia ($29.95)

This second of two volumes of the Fourth Annual Playboy Jazz Festival suffers from a lack of proper editing. In a concession to popular taste, a large percentage of the tape is given over to the fusion group Weather Report, which performs a total of four songs including Joe Zawinul's "Birdland" with vocals provided by the pop group Manhattan Transfer. In contrast, jazz vocalist Sarah Vaughan is given scant attention with one song, "Send in the Clowns." The editor of this tape needs a sense of balance. The tape has its high points. Dave Brubeck plays his signature tune, "Take Five."

Longtime expatriate saxophonist Dexter Gordon joins vibraphonist Milt Jackson to play Milt's "Bag's Groove." Pop singer O. C. Smith ("Little Green Apples") sings a blues number, "I'm Trying a Woman Who Wants to Grow Old with Me," with Gordon and Jackson playing backup. Between and during the individual performances, the tape cuts back to *Playboy* publisher Hugh Hefner in the audience at a table covered with bottles of wine and gourmet delicacies and surrounded by an entourage of beautiful models from his magazine. He is responsible for paying for this festival and he wants you to know it. The frequent cutting back to his approving expression is annoying. It links Mr. Hefner with his ostentatious display of abundant good taste. If this tape had concentrated more on the fine musicianship on stage, we would all have benefited.

ROB McCONNELL AND THE BOSS BRASS ★★

JAZZ. 1981. Artists: Rob McConnell and the Boss Brass. 26 min. Beta Hifi, VHS Stereo. Sony ($19.95)

Leonard Feather, noted jazz historian, named the Boss Brass the best jazz band of 1981. Based in Toronto, Rob McConnell's big-band re-creation has attracted surprisingly large audiences throughout North America. Apparently, there is still quite a demand for what Artie Shaw has called "America's classical music." Here, caught live at Howard Rumsey's Concerts By The Sea in Redondo Beach, California, the Boss Brass play three standards from the forties, using arrangements that closely recreate the charts of that era: "The Waltz I Blew for You," "My Man Bill," and "Street of Dreams." McConnell stands in front of the band like a symphony conductor with a baton. His players are veterans of such big bands as Count Basie's, Woody Herman's Thundering Herd, and Stan Kenton's. It all sounds a bit too well rehearsed, almost calculated. There's not a lot of spontaneity. The shot of Jimmy Dale, the pianist, reading a music stand full of charts as he plays speaks volumes about the "authenticity" of the sound. There are a few nice chops from Moe Koffman on saxophone, Ian McDougall on trombone, and Terry Clarke on drums. Directed by William Cosel.

THE SACRED MUSIC OF DUKE ELLINGTON ★★★

JAZZ. 1982. Artists: Rod Steiger, Douglas Fairbanks, Jr., Tony Bennett, McHenry Boatwright, Will Gaines, Adelaide Hall, Phyllis Hyman, and Jacques Loussier. 90 min. Beta Hifi, VHS Stereo. MGM/UA ($49.95)

In a dramatic departure from his popular secular jazz music, Duke Ellington wrote three concerts of sacred music in the last decade of his life. Ellington said about his

The Sacred Music of Duke Ellington.

sacred concerts, "Every man prays to God in his own language. There is no language that God does not understand." Definitely written in the familiar Ellingtonian jazz idiom, these sacred concerts were intended for cathedral and church performance. Based on his earlier jazz suites, they transcend his big-band composition, and incorporate orchestral church music, jazz, gospel, song, dance, choir, and narration to create a body of church music that might seem unusual to the uninitiated, but becomes completely appropriate to its ecclesiastical setting after a few minutes. At a gala concert in St. Paul's Cathedral, London, Douglas Fairbanks, Jr., in an opening narration, introduces the music of the first sacred concert with a few words about its history and significance. McHenry Boatwright, baritone, provides the concert's theme in "In the Beginning God," based on the first four words of the King James Version of the Bible, six syllables, or six notes, that are used in variation throughout the concert. This is followed by a scat singing of the names of the books of the Old and New Testaments by the Swingle Singers called "Rocks of the Bible." Jacques Loussier plays solo piano on "Meditations." Pop/jazz singer Tony Bennett adds his renditions of "Somebody Cares (And You Know Who)," and "Just One." Tap dancer Will Gaines closes the first concert with a tap devotional called "David Danced." The second concert, which premiered at the Cathedral of St. John the Divine in New York in January of 1968, starts with longtime Ellington associate Adelaide "Adie" Hall singing "Come Sunday" from the Duke's jazz suite, "Black, Brown, and Tan," and "Lord, Dear God of Love." The third and final concert, first performed in 1973, features Kenny Baker on trumpet and the Alan Cohen Orchestra playing "The Shepherd," and the sermon "Fire and Brimstone" read by the distinguished actor Rod Steiger. These concerts are as captivating as they are moving.

SPYRO GYRA ★★★

JAZZ. 1980. Artists: Spyro Gyra (Jay Beckenstein, Chet Catallo, Tom Schuman, Eli Konikoff, Gerardo Velez, and Jim Kurzdorfer). 56 min. Beta, VHS. Warner ($39.95)

When Miles Davis revolutionized the sound of jazz by introducing electronic instruments (piano, bass, guitar) and employing a rock drumbeat on his landmark LP, *Bitches Brew,* in 1969, he would not have guessed that jazz would undergo a revival in the seventies as the muzak of the under-forty generation. Inspired by his work, bands like Weather Report and Mahavishnu Orchestra reacquainted rock audiences with strictly instrumental music—but not necessarily true jazz. Spyro Gyra, an amalgamation of New York studio musicians, is part of that second generation of electric jazz groups that have become quite popular for their impeccably well played mood music. It is no coincidence that this music which makes one summon up images in one's mind turns out to be perfect for video. In this long-form video, part concert (at Park West in Chicago) and part video graphics display, the group plays "Percolator," "Shaker Song," "Autumn of Our Love," "Cockatoo," "Catching the Sun," "Laser Material," "Morning Dance," and "Lovin' You." Slightly better than musical wallpaper but only recommended if your tastes run that way.

STAGE SHOW ★★

JAZZ. 1955. Artists: Jimmy and Tommy Dorsey, Gene Krupa, Gordon McRae, Connie Francis, and Kim Novak. 29 min. Beta, VHS. Video Yesteryear ($29.95)

Stage Show was a television show sponsored by Nestlé coffee that was broadcast on NBC in the fifties. Here you have a typical show with commercials intact, featuring Connie Francis singing "My Treasure," Gene Krupa, the drummer and band leader, playing "Well, Git It," and *Oklahoma* star Gordon McRae singing "If I Loved You" from Rodgers and Hammerstein's *Carousel.*

SUN RA: A JOYFUL NOISE ★★★

JAZZ. 1980. Artists: Sun Ra, John Gilmore, Elo Omoe, and James Jacson. 60 min. Beta, VHS. Rhapsody ($70.00)

Sun Ra (born Herman Blount), who dresses in costumes inspired by the clothing of ancient Egypt, claims to be a descendant of the sun put on this earth to spread the word and music of celestial wisdom. His avant-garde music, a free mixture of big-band jazz, African, eastern, and electronic music, really defies any formal classification.

Sun Ra and his Solar Arkestra.

The followers of Sun Ra, a ten- to twenty-five–piece band known as the Solar Arkestra, a very professional ensemble featuring the solo work of world famous saxophonist John Gilmore, play in a style that sounds somewhat like an atonal Jimmy Lunceford band. On a rooftop in downtown Philadelphia, they play "Astro Black," part jazz composition, part religious chant, spotlighting vocalist June Tyson. Sun Ra reveals his insights into the nature of the universe, his views on contemporary civilization and ancient Egypt, and his impressions of modern music in an interview that follows. Later, at the Left Bank Jazz Society in Baltimore, Maryland, the Arkestra performs a set that includes "Saturn," and Thelonious Monk's "Round Midnight" with Sun Ra playing stride piano. A treat for the Sun Ra aficionado and a very good introduction for the uninitiated.

TALMAGE FARLOW ★★★♪

JAZZ. 1981. Artists: Talmage Farlow, Red Mitchell, Tommy Flanagan, Lenny Breau, and George Benson. 58 min. Beta, VHS. Rhapsody ($70.00)

Talmage Farlow is a film biography of the legendary jazz guitarist who left the music scene in 1958 at the height of his musical powers and popularity. A quiet, unassuming

Legendary jazz guitarist Talmage Farlow.

man with an enormous musical talent and "a wild sense of harmony," Farlow went into semiretirement in Sea Bright, New Jersey, to reassume the responsibilities of his first profession, sign painting. Today he still plays a limited number of club dates and concerts, as can be seen in the concert footage filmed at Joseph Papp's Public Theater in New York at the end of this tape and in his short performance with Red Norvo on RCA/Columbia's *Playboy Jazz Festival, Volume I.* As Tal says about his reluctance to play full time, "I don't want to be a star. I want to be a participant." *Talmage Farlow* also spotlights a jam session in pianist Tommy Flanagan's apartment with Tal on guitar, Tommy on piano, and Red Mitchell on bass. A variety of Tal's admirers, including pop-jazz guitarist George Benson, talk about his talent and reminisce about his arrival in New York in the fifties and his departure. A very incisive look into the life and career of a mysterious man.

A TRIBUTE TO BILLIE HOLIDAY   ★★

JAZZ. 1979. Artists: Billie Holiday, Morgana King, Carmen McRae, Esther Phillips, Nina Simone, and Maxine Weldon. 60 min. Beta, VHS. Media ($45.95)

Five very accomplished jazz singers, Morgana King, Carmen McRae, Esther Phillips, Nina Simone, and Maxine Weldon, salute *the* jazz singer, Billie Holiday, in a concert at the Hollywood Bowl. Ray Ellis conducts his orchestra as Morgana King performs "As Time Goes By" and "Easy Living," Carmen McRae sings her version of "Good Morning, Heartache," Esther Phillips sings the classic "Lover Man," Nina Simone performs "I Love You, Porgy," and Maxine Weldon sings "Sometimes I'm Happy." They appear on stage together to sing "God Bless the Child." Although each sings with grace and feeling, they do not approach the spine-tingling vocal magic that was the trademark of the great Lady Day. Perhaps musical numbers for which Billie made the definitive recordings, such as "Lover Man" and "God Bless the Child," should be retired in the same way a great baseball player's uniform number is retired at the end of his career. The highlights of this concert are the rare bits of film of Billie singing "Lost Man Blues" in 1935 and "God Bless the Child" in 1950.

FAMILY ENTERTAINMENT

BABES IN TOYLAND ★★✦

FAMILY ENTERTAINMENT. 1961. Cast: Ray Bolger, Tommy Sands, Annette Funicello, Ed Wynn, and Ann Jillian. 105 min. Beta, VHS. Disney ($69.95)

Based on the operetta *March of the Wooden Soldiers* by Victor Herbert and Glen McDonough, *Babes in Toyland* is a Disney Studios update with new songs and a slightly less menacing tone. Tommy Sands, who looks a lot like Frankie Avalon, and Annette Funicello play Tom and Mary, two denizens of Mother Goose Village who are scheduled to be married. But Barnaby (Ray Bolger), who wants Mary's inheritance, tricks her into agreeing to marry him. Only with the help of the Toymaker (Ed Wynn) and his wooden soldiers can Tom and Mary be reunited. The storybook backdrops, scenery, and costumes will delight the kids. There are eleven songs including "We Won't Be Happy 'Til We Get It," "Castle in Spain," "Gypsies," "No Way Out," "Toyland," and "Come and Marry."

BUGSY MALONE ★★↓

FAMILY ENTERTAINMENT. 1976. Cast: Scott Baio, Flossie Dugger, Jodie Foster, and John Cassisi. 94 min. Beta, VHS. Paramount ($69.95)

Some interesting names were responsible for this bizarre musical that uses children to play adult roles. Robert Stigwood financed it, David Puttnam (*Chariots of Fire*) produced it, Alan Parker (*Shoot the Moon*) directed it, and a very young Scott Baio and Jodie Foster starred in it. The concept, which turns out to be as strange as it sounds, is this: have children play the roles of mobsters and their molls in New York during the roaring twenties while singing and dancing to Paul Williams' original songs. Scott is Bugsy Malone, an undersized George Raft, Flossie Dugger plays chorus girl Blousey Brown, John Cassisi is the overweight and obnoxious gang leader, Fat Sam, and Jodie Foster plays Talullah, a flapper with a heart of pewter. The gang war that occupies most of the film is fought with "splurge guns" that spray the intended target with what looks like whipped cream. Kids might like this, but it's a bit too arch for us. Jodie displays the kind of precocious sensuality that made her performance in *Taxi Driver* so startling, and Flossie Dugger matches Jodie pout for pout and sly smile for sly smile. The forgettable Paul Williams songs include "Fat Sam's Grand Slam Speakeasy," "Tomorrow," "Bad Guys," "My Name Is Talullah," "Things That You Say and Do," and "Only a Fool."

Pint-size mobsters in *Bugsy Malone*.

THE CHRISTMAS RACCOONS ★★

FAMILY ENTERTAINMENT. 1980. Cast: Rita Coolidge, Rupert Holmes, and Rich Little. 30 min. Beta, VHS. Embassy ($39.95)

Rich Little narrates this animated episode of *The Raccoons* TV series. Chief park ranger Rupert Holmes investigates the sudden disappearance of evergreen trees from the forest. Meanwhile, his son and daughter discover that a trio of raccoons who have been displaced from their home after it's been chopped down are living in their Christmas tree. The children and their dog, Schaeffer, help the raccoons track down the man responsible for the wholesale destruction of the forest, Cyril Sneer, a lumber magnate. In the end, Sneer learns a lesson about forest conservation. Rita Coolidge sings "Lost Angels" and "Lake Freeze." Rupert Holmes (of "Escape" ("Pina Colada Song") fame) sings "Perfect Tree" and "Shake the Sun."

DICK DEADEYE ★★♪

FAMILY ENTERTAINMENT. 1976. 80 min. Beta, VHS. FHE ($39.95)

Dick Deadeye is a dim-witted sailor in Her Majesty's Navy called upon by Queen Victoria to recover Britain's "Ultimate Secret," which has been stolen by a sorcerer and a band of bloodthirsty pirates. In this rousing, fun, fast-paced animated film, drawn by British cartoonist Ronald Searle, we see and hear a host of favorite characters from Gilbert and Sullivan's comic operettas sing rock versions of the great duo's most famous songs. In a complicated plot that would make Sir Arthur gasp and would take pages to explain, Dick Deadeye recovers the "Ultimate Secret." Songs include "Sweet Little Buttercup," "A Wand'ring Minstrel I," "The Pirate King," and "I'm the Very Model of a Modern Major General."

DOCTOR DOOLITTLE ★★

FAMILY ENTERTAINMENT. 1967. Cast: Rex Harrison, Samantha Eggar, Anthony Newley, Geoffrey Holder, and Richard Attenborough. 152 min. Beta, VHS. CBS/Fox ($69.95)

Rex Harrison stars as Doctor Doolittle in this uneven musical based on Hugh Lofting's children's tales about a Victorian veterinarian who has the unique ability to communicate with animals. The other human inhabitants of his hometown of Puddleby on the Marsh, England, believe his linguistic talents are the fabrications of a deranged mind and that the doctor is nothing more than a harmless eccentric. Doctor Doolittle decides to leave this unsympathetic environment and go on a sea voyage in search of the great pink sea snail, a mythical creature the doctor is almost certain exists. The good doctor raises the necessary funds to pay for the expedition by exhibiting the rare Himalayan pushme-pullyu, a dancing two-headed llama, at a nearby carnival run by Mr. Blossom, played by Richard Attenborough. Trouble presents itself when Doolittle helps a lovesick seal escape to the rocky seacoast so that she can swim to the north pole to join her husband who is waiting for her. When local farmers see Doctor Doolittle throw the seal into the ocean, they think he is throwing a young woman to her death. He is put on trial on the charge of murder and tried by a jury of his peers. He defends himself by calling the judge's dog as a witness. The jury acquits him of the charge of murder, but, thinking him mad, commits him to an insane asylum. The animals in town cleverly execute the Doctor's escape and he is soon at sea in search of the great pink sea snail. The Doctor and his three human friends, the 11-year-old Tommy Stubbins, the town milkman, Matt, and the lovely daughter of the town judge, Emma Fairfax, are shipwrecked on the world's only floating island, a small piece of Africa that has been set adrift on the Atlantic by catastrophic forces. With the help of a passing whale they push the island back into its original continental resting place to the applause of the island's chief William Shakespeare X, played by Geoffrey Holder. Soon, the great pink sea snail, having heard of the great animal doctor's whereabouts, shows up complaining of a head cold. The film *Doctor Doolittle* is burdened by a plot that is so complicated and slow-moving that even the light, cheery songs of Leslie Bricuse and the choreography of Herbert Ross cannot lift its ailing spirits. Rex Harrison tries to carry some of the load with his rendition of "If I Could Talk to the Animals," the Las Vegas saloon standard for years afterward, and "I'm a Devoted Vegetarian," "When I Look into Your Eyes," and "Why Do We Treat Animals Like Animals." Anthony Newley, who plays Matt, the village milkman, adds his efforts: "My Friend the Doctor Says," and "After Today Nothing Will Be the Same." Together they fail to breathe life into this poorly conceived musical.

DOOZER MUSIC ★★★♪

FAMILY ENTERTAINMENT. 1984. Cast: Jerry Nelson, Dave Goelz, Steve Whitmire, Kathryn Mullen, Karen Prell, and Richard Hunt. 16 min. Beta Hifi, VHS Stereo. Disney ($29.95)

Irresistible puppetry from the Jim Henson studio, the best music videos and characters from the HBO series *Fraggle Rock,* and definitely worth a look-see for the kids and children of all ages. The Doozers are an industrious, insect-sized race of creatures

Two of Jim Henson's minuscule Doozers from *Doozer Music*.

who spend their days building crystalline structures that are beautiful to look at and delicious to eat (the Fraggles consider the Doozers' works delicacies). Green Pillsbury doughboys wearing boots and hardhats, the Doozers have their own little society, governed by their need to create, build, and repair their intricate edifices. Philip Balsam and Dennis Lee wrote the songs: "Doozer Marching Song," "Why?," "Doozer Work Theme," "Doozer Knitting Song," "The Way I've Got to Go," and "Yes We Can." Jim Henson's cute and cuddly salute to the American work ethic.

FRAGGLE SONGS, VOLUME I ★★♪

FAMILY ENTERTAINMENT. 1983. Cast: Jerry Nelson, Dave Goelz, Steve Whitmire, Kathryn Mullen, Karen Prell, and Richard Hunt. 51 min. Beta Hifi, VHS Stereo. Disney ($49.95)

A compilation of music videos from Jim Henson's HBO series, *Fraggle Rock,* this outgrowth of his famous Muppet characters is slightly off the mark. While the attempt to create a wholly imaginary topography inhabited by four species of creatures, the

Fraggles, the Gorgs, the Doozers, and a trash heap named Marjory, is solidly in the tradition of children's fantasy literature, the creatures are oddly frightening rather than cute and cuddly (except for the Doozers). As usual, the songs are really quite uninspired; the tunes are written by Philip Balsam and Dennis Lee. Twenty-eight tunes in all, some of the better ones being: "Workin', Workin'," "I Seen Trouble," "I Can Do It on My Own," "Get Blue," "Catch a Tail by the Tiger," "Friendship Song," and "Fraggle Rock Rock." Directed by Henson and George Bloomfield.

GOLDEN OLDIES ★★★

FAMILY ENTERTAINMENT. 1984. Artists: The Supremes, Spike Jones, Tennessee Ernie Ford, Barrett Strong, Burl Ives, Marvin Gaye, Annette Funicello, Smokey Robinson and the Miracles, The Coasters, Stevie Wonder, Lena Horne, The Beach Boys, and Louis Prima and Keely Smith. 45 min. Beta Hifi, VHS Stereo. Disney ($29.95)

This is another volume of music videos originally broadcast on the Disney Cable Channel. Produced by Chuck Braverman and edited by Ted Herrman, *Golden Oldies* is a

Huey, Dewey, and Louie performing in Disney's *Golden Oldies*.

compendium of songs ranging from Motown classics to Burl Ives folk ballads. Not as successful as *Pop and Rock* but filled, nevertheless, with great Disney cartoon characters in footage culled from the Disney film library. Some of the songs heard are: "Baby Love," done by the Supremes, "Blue Danube" and "Holiday for Strings" by Spike Jones, "That Old Black Magic" by Louis Prima and Keely Smith, "Can I Get a Witness" by Marvin Gaye, "Sixteen Tons" by Tennessee Ernie Ford, "Lavender Blue" by Burl Ives, "Mickey's Monkey" and "You Really Got a Hold on Me" by Smokey Robinson and the Miracles, "Stormy Weather" by Lena Horne, and "Stranded in the Jungle" by The Cadets.

HANS BRINKER ★★

FAMILY ENTERTAINMENT. 1979. Cast: Eleanor Parker, John Gregson, Richard Basehart, Cyril Ritchard, and Robin Askwith. 103 min. Beta, VHS. Warner ($59.95)

This British production was originally broadcast on NBC-TV. It is a remounting of the Hans Brinker story about a Dutch boy who wants to win the silver skates that are the first prize in the annual Christmas Day race in Amsterdam so that he can pay for a medical education. In this version, Hans' father suffers from an emotional imbalance caused by a fall many years ago. Since then he's been a basket case. Richard Basehart plays a noted surgeon who might be able to cure Mr. Brinker. There are songs amidst the melodrama and, of course, a happy ending. Hans doesn't win the silver skates, but Basehart cures his father and offers Hans a medical apprenticeship. "Holland, You Are Home," "There Is a Way," "Free," "I Don't Hear a Thing," and "Golden Tomorrow" are the tunes performed by the cast, including Eleanor Parker playing Hans' mother.

THE HAPPIEST MILLIONAIRE ★★

FAMILY ENTERTAINMENT. 1967. Cast: Fred MacMurray, Tommy Steele, Greer Garson, Geraldine Page, Hermione Baddeley, Paul Peterson, Lesley Ann Warren, and John Davidson. 144 min. Beta Hifi, VHS Stereo. Disney ($69.95)

In the late sixties, after the era of *Mary Poppins* and *The Absentminded Professor,* the Disney studio floundered with off-target efforts like this incredibly long, quite boring musical film. The film is set in 1916, and Fred MacMurray is an eccentric millionaire with an avid interest in boxing. Lesley Ann Warren is his beautiful daughter, who finds it difficult to reconcile her father's odd behavior with the exigencies of the real world. She falls in love with John Davidson, the scion of a wealthy New York family. Although the movie is over two hours long, it's anybody's guess what the whole thing is about. Is it a period piece, meant to provide an opportunity to glimpse some of the costumes and settings of pre-World War I Philadelphia? Is it some sort of elaborate extension of a wacky family sitcom from TV? Is it a try at making an eccentric musical for kids? Tommy Steele's presence is the only thing that's vaguely entertaining in this disappointing epic. He sings "Fortuosity" and "I'll Always Be Irish." Lesley Ann is lovely, singing "Valentine Candy or Boxing Gloves," "Are We Dancing?," and "Detroit." They don't make 'em like this anymore. A film ahead of its time; they didn't have cable then.

HAVE I GOT A STORY FOR YOU ★★✦

FAMILY ENTERTAINMENT. 1984. Cast: Shari Lewis, Lamb Chop, Charley Horse, Hush Puppy, and Honey Chile. 60 min. Beta, VHS. MGM/UA ($29.95)

In the first of a projected series, Shari Lewis, who entertained millions of kids on TV with her hand puppets in the early sixties, tells stories through words and music written by Lan O'Kun and Norman Martin. Traditional fairy tales make up the bulk of Lewis' stories. Essentially a one-woman show, she shares the stage with her hand-puppet characters, Lamb Chop, Hush Puppy, and the rest of the crew. The tape has the look of a PBS children's show, only slightly more intimate. The songs are: "A Quick, Little Lullabye," "Rumpelstilskin," "The Pied Piper," "The Boy Who Cried Wolf," "The Sorcerer's Apprentice," "The Tortoise and the Hare," "The Lion and the Mouse," "The Dog and His Bone," "Little Red Riding Hood," "Jack and the Beanstalk," "I Love a Happy Ending," and the title tune. Directed and choreographed by Walter Painter.

THE LAST UNICORN ★★★

FAMILY ENTERTAINMENT. 1982. Cast: Mia Farrow, Alan Arkin, Jeff Bridges, Tammy Grimes, Angela Lansbury, Christopher Lee, Keenan Wynn, and Robert Klein. 95 min. Beta Hifi, VHS Stereo. CBS/Fox ($49.95)

An animated film from the Rankin/Bass studio, *The Last Unicorn* is based on the children's novel by Peter S. Beagle and features the music of America, performing the compositions of Jim Webb. Mia Farrow is the voice of "the last unicorn," who embarks on a quest for the rest of her tribe. They have all been imprisoned in the surf by the evil King Haggard (Christopher Lee). Things get complicated when the unicorn is magically turned into a human, Lady Amalthia, who then falls in love with the king's well-meaning and handsome son, Lear (Jeff Bridges). This lyrical film was animated by a crack Japanese production team. With its pleasant songs and myth-and-magic story, *The Last Unicorn* should more than satisfy children.

MR. T'S BE SOMEBODY OR BE SOMEBODY'S FOOL ★★★

FAMILY ENTERTAINMENT. 1984. Cast: Mr. T, Valerie Landsburg, and New Edition. 52 min. Beta Hifi, VHS Stereo. MCA ($39.95)

Depending on your point of view, Mr. T, that human cartoon character with the mohawk who catapulted to fame in *Rocky III* and *The A-Team,* is a shrewdly sculpted media personality or someone whose bag of marbles has a large hole in it. In this

Mr. T offers advice to youngsters in *Be Somebody.*

video program, Mr. T is the emcee for what amounts to a children's version of their parents' motivational seminars. This homage to self-esteem and assertiveness has its bizarre charms and it's harmless enough. A cast of talented youngsters help Mr. T illustrate his lessons about shyness, roots, frustration, styling, peer pressure, recouping, creating, treating your mother right, working out, being somebody, friendship, and daydreaming. Valerie Landsburg (*Fame*) appears to sing "Try" and New Edition is seen performing "Peer Pressure." Mr. T raps and "breakdances" to the songs, "Be Somebody," "Love Each Other," "Treat Your Mother Right," "Work the Body Electric," and "I Am Somebody." Directed by Jeff Margolis.

THE MUPPET MOVIE ★★★

FAMILY ENTERTAINMENT. 1979. Cast: Miss Piggy, Kermit the Frog, Fozzie Bear, Rowlf the Dog, Dom DeLuise, James Coburn, Madeline Kahn, Telly Savalas, Carol Kane, Charles Durning, Milton Berle. 94 min. Beta Hifi, VHS Stereo. CBS/Fox ($59.95)

The first of Jim Henson and Frank Oz's Muppets films, this is a typical example of their sense of humor—bad puns, slightly bizarre jokes, and adorably absurd characters. Supported by a veritable parade of cameos (Elliot Gould, Bob Hope, Richard Pryor, Orson Welles, Cloris Leachman, Edgar Bergen, Steve Martin, and Mel Brooks in addition to those mentioned above), Kermit the Frog, Henson's Everyman (or is it Everyfrog?), travels to Hollywood from his home in the swamp in order to make it big in show business. Along the way, he picks up an entire entourage including Miss Piggy, Fozzie Bear, Rowlf the Dog, and the Electric Mayhem, a rock group with an improbable assortment of members, and is pursued hotly by Charles Durning, the owner of a chain of fast-food restaurants that serve frog's legs. The music, by Paul Williams and Kenny Ascher, receives an aggressively bad interpretation from the Muppets cast. "Rainbow Connection," "Moving Right Along," "Can You Picture That?," "Never Before," "I Hope Something Better Comes Along," and "I'm Going to Go Back There Someday" won't soon be seen on anyone's Top 40. Ultimately, what makes the Muppets entertaining, in spite of the terrible puns, ancient jokes, and silly songs, are the uniquely inventive puppets themselves—each a masterpiece of childish whimsy. Directed by James Frawley, who once won an Emmy Award for directing an episode of *The Monkees*.

THE NIGHT BEFORE CHRISTMAS/SILENT NIGHT ★★

FAMILY ENTERTAINMENT. 1968. 57 min. Beta, VHS. Media ($39.95)

These two very average animated television specials tell the story of the creation of two of the staples of the American Christmas tradition, the song "Silent Night" and the poem "The Night before Christmas." In *Silent Night,* the choirmaster of the church of the Austrian town of Obendorf writes the song for the town's Christmas festival. In *The Night before Christmas,* Clement Clark Moore writes the poem as a Christmas present for his ailing daughter.

THE NIGHTINGALE   ★★

FAMILY ENTERTAINMENT. 1983. Cast: Mick Jagger, Barbara Hershey, Bud Cort, Edward James Olmos, and Mako. 60 min. Beta, VHS. CBS/Fox ($39.95)

It seems like everyone in show business wants to get in on the action. Shelley Duvall's *Faerie Tale Theatre* cable series for children has attracted actors, writers, and directors of the highest caliber to work on it. It has won several awards and deservedly so, but the fact that it features such names as Mick Jagger has contributed greatly to its reputation. A series like this is particularly welcome since, in show business, children's programming gets the same lip service as God and country, and is usually warmed over and quite smarmy. In *The Nightingale,* the king of rock and roll plays the Emperor of Cathay, an Oriental kingdom in the mythic past. Jagger's problem is that he hasn't learned his limitations. When he hears of the beautiful singing of the nightingale, he orders his chamberlains to capture it and imprison it in the royal palace so that he can enjoy its songs at his leisure. Soon, though, the Emperor throws over the nightingale for a mechanical bird whose predictable melody seems sweeter. But only the nightingale's nonpareil song can save the Emperor when he falls mysteriously ill. Van Dyke Parks is the music director, Joan Micklin Silver wrote the script, and Ivan Passer directed. Bud Cort is absolutely perverse as one of Jagger's chamberlains; use parental discretion on whether your child should see him. Mick doesn't sing.

THE NUTCRACKER SUITE   ★♪

FAMILY ENTERTAINMENT. 1983. Cast: The Voices of Michelle Lee, Melissa Gilbert, Lurene Tuttle, Christopher Lee, Jo Anne Worley, Dick Van Patten, Roddy McDowall, and Eva Gabor. 90 min. Beta, VHS. RCA/Columbia ($39.95)

Screenwriter Shintaro Tsuji liberally interprets the story of the ballet *The Nutcracker,* for this Japanese animated puppet feature that uses the music of Tchaikovsky and the voices of several well-known British and American television actors. In the confused tale of *The Nutcracker Suite,* Uncle Drosselmeyer (Christopher Lee), the town magician

Scene from the animated feature *The Nutcracker Suite.*

and clockmaker, gives his niece Clara (Melissa Gilbert), a nutcracker doll that is stolen by evil mice whose Queen Morphia (Jo Anne Worley) has put a curse on the Kingdom of the Dolls' Princess Mary. King Goodwin (Dick Van Patten) is distraught and appeals to Clara for help. The Queen of Time (Eva Gabor) tells Clara that Queen Morphia holds her power in the Shell of Darkness that can only be broken with the Pearls of Light Sword. Clara seeks the aid of Franz, the brave young soldier who leads the dolls into battle against the mice and destroys the Shell of Darkness. But Queen Morphia uses her last breath to cast a spell on Franz, turning him into a nutcracker. The Puppeteer (Christopher Lee) tells Clara only unconditional love can free Franz from his wooden fate. Queen Morphia's son, Gar, returns to seek revenge. Clara offers her life to spare her love. Franz' curse is broken when Clara proves her love and returns to life. Clara and Franz fall into each other's arms. In addition to the music of Tchaikovsky played by the New Nihon Philharmonic Symphony Orchestra, *The Nutcracker Suite* features Randy Bishop and Marty Gwinn's "Dance of the Dolls," "In Your Heart of Hearts," and "Click Clock Fantasy."

PETE'S DRAGON ★★♪

FAMILY ENTERTAINMENT. 1977. Cast: Helen Reddy, Mickey Rooney, Shelley Winters, Jim Dale, Sean Marshall, Jim Backus, Red Buttons. 128 min. Beta, VHS. Disney ($84.95)

Elliott, a green dragon invisible to everyone except his companion, a little boy named Pete, helps Pete escape from a foster home governed by Shelley Winters, a rude backwoods woman. They make their way to the town of Passamaquoddy, and are eventually taken in by a lighthouse keeper (Mickey Rooney) and his daughter (Helen Reddy). Jim Dale, as Dr. Terminus, a medicine show charlatan passing through town, learns of the existence of Elliott the Dragon and wants him for use in making his medicinal preparations. Shelley Winters arrives in town and, seeing their mutual interests, joins forces with Dr. Terminus to entrap Elliott and Pete. This inconsistently entertaining movie, featuring a rather charming animated Elliott the Dragon, tries to make use of Helen Reddy's popularity; unfortunately the songs, by Al Kasha and Joel Hirschhorn, are pretty weak. "The Happiest Home in These Hills," "I Love You Too," "A Dragon," "It's So Easy," "Passamaquoddy," "Candle on the Water," "There's Room for Everyone," "Money by the Pound," "It's a Brazzle Dazzle Day," and "Bill of Sale" are performed by the cast.

POP AND ROCK ★★★♪

FAMILY ENTERTAINMENT. 1984. Artists: Martha and the Vandellas, Little Richard, Tommy Roe, The Diamonds, Stevie Wonder, the Supremes, Elvis Presley, Danny and the Juniors, Sheb Wooley, Johnny Burnette, Jan and Dean, The Four Tops, The Dovells, and The Beach Boys. 45 min. Beta Hifi, VHS Stereo. Disney ($29.95)

This volume in the series of compilations of music videos originally broadcast on the Disney Cable Channel as DTV is the best melding of images and music executed by Chuck Braverman and his supervising editor Ted Herrman. Cut to the beat, using visual and verbal puns set against the lyrical content of the songs, these videos are fun, often very funny, and musically diverting. The list of songs used in this volume is an eclectic one, chosen from golden oldies of the fifties and sixties. Parents can relive nostalgic memories while their children can enjoy the glimpses of such Disney cartoon favorites as Mickey Mouse, Donald Duck, Goofy, Pluto, Chip and Dale, Dumbo, and Willie the Whale. Some of the music: "Dancing in the Streets" by Martha and the Vandellas, "Tutti Frutti" and "Long Tall Sally" by Little Richard, "Stuck on You" and "Hound Dog" by Elvis Presley, "Uptight" and "I Was Made to Love Her" by Stevie Wonder, "Dreamin'" by Johnny Burnette, and "Reach Out (I'll Be There)" by The Four Tops.

POPEYE ★★

FAMILY ENTERTAINMENT. 1980. Cast: Robin Williams, Shelley Duvall, Ray Walston, and Paul Dooley. 114 min. Beta, VHS. Paramount ($24.95)

Before Robert Altman retreated to making low-budget films for a highbrow cult audience (*Streamers* and *Come Back to the 5 and Dime*), he attempted a last ditch effort to regain his mainstream position by directing this strange retelling of the Popeye story, based not on Max Fleischer's hugely popular animated cartoons but on Charles Segar's early newspaper comic strips. Famed cartoonist Jules Feiffer and Altman completely miss the spirit of the Popeye character, transforming the faintly surreal goings-on of the cartoons into a Freudian tale of paternal love/hate. Williams is too grotesquely made up as Popeye to elicit anything but bewilderment from the audience when he garbles his lines, trying to sound like the spinach eating sailor. Shelley Duvall is actually quite good as Olive Oyl, but she can't sing any of the Harry Nilsson songs in the film's rather unimpressive score. Ray Walston, playing Popeye's long lost Pappy, does a better Popeye impression than Williams, less mannered and more broadly cartoonlike. This film didn't garner big box office because it's incredibly depressing, grotesque, and irrelevant to the image of Popeye that we all have. The Nilsson songs include "Everything Is Food," "Sweet Sweethaven," "I'm Mean," "I Yam What I Yam," "He Needs Me," and "Popeye the Sailor Man."

THE RACCOONS: LET'S DANCE ★★♪

FAMILY ENTERTAINMENT. 1984. Cast: John Schneider, Rita Coolidge, Dottie West, and Leo Sayer. 23 min. Beta Hifi, VHS Stereo. Embassy ($29.95)

The animated characters from *The Raccoons* cartoon TV series are featured in this compilation of excerpts from past episodes augmented by songs sung by John Schneider, Rita Coolidge, Leo Sayer, and Dottie West. Director-producer Kevin Gillis' attempt to fashion a set of rock videos for children is not very successful. The notion of a rock concert in the forest attended by a whole host of woodland creatures is not even novel by kid-vid standards. And the music ("Calling You" and "Shining" by John Schneider, "You Can Do It" and "Takin' My Time" by Leo Sayer, "To Have You" by Rita Coolidge and Leo Sayer, "Lions and Tigers" by Dottie West, and "Friends" by Dottie and John Schneider) is barely recognizable as pop music. All in all, light years away from Disney's far more likeable children's music videos, *DTV*.

Classic Disney animation cut to favorite hit tunes performed by the original artists.

ROCK, RHYTHM, AND BLUES ★★ↄ

FAMILY ENTERTAINMENT. 1984. Artists: Hall and Oates, Jimmy Cliff, Richard Thompson, Jackson 5, Gladys Knight and the Pips, Doobie Brothers, the Supremes, Marvin Gaye and Tammi Terrell, Stevie Wonder, and Burning Sensation. 45 min. Beta Hifi, VHS Stereo. Disney ($29.95)

One volume of the three-volume collection of music video clips originally broadcast on the Disney Cable Channel under the rubric DTV, *Rock, Rhythm, and Blues* is the least successful of Chuck Braverman's fast-paced film collages drawn from the vaults of the Disney Studio. Using Disney cartoon characters to illustrate and/or comment on popular songs, these music videos are a wholesome alternative to the bizarre, often salacious images presented on MTV and other rock video compendia. In this particular case, songs by a predominantly R&B roster of musical artists are accompanied by edited snippets of classic Disney shorts. Perhaps it is the odd rhythmic pattern or the eccentric lyrical content of these songs, but Braverman's crew had a great deal of trouble matching images to the music. The cutting is against the beat, not with it, and many of the cartoon segments are just inappropriate in mood or tone. Some of the music used: "Kiss on My List" and "Private Eyes" by Hall and Oates, "Dancing Machine" by the Jackson 5, "Stop in the Name of Love" by the Supremes, "It Keeps You Running" by the Doobie Brothers, "Signed, Sealed, Delivered" by Stevie Wonder, and "Ain't No Mountain High Enough" by Marvin Gaye and Tammi Terrell.

SCROOGE ★ʃ

FAMILY ENTERTAINMENT. 1970. Cast: Albert Finney, Alec Guinness, Edith Evans, and Kenneth More. 115 min. Beta Hifi, VHS Stereo. CBS/Fox ($59.95)

Four of the best actors in British cinema try to breathe life into this boring musical rendition of Charles Dickens' *A Christmas Carol.* Most of the humor inherent in the scenario, even if unintentional on Dickens' part, has been lost by Ronald Neame's by-the-numbers direction of a pedestrian script, filled with sub-par Leslie Bricuse songs. Albert Finney plays Ebenezer Scrooge, the legendary miser and misanthrope, Alec Guinness plays Jacob Marley, Scrooge's late business partner, Edith Evans plays the Ghost of Christmas Past, and Kenneth More plays the Spirit of Christmas Present. Although Albert Finney attacks the script with his usual ferocity and originality, it's all for naught. When you have to sing songs like "I Hate People" and "The Minister's Cat," you're facing an insurmountable obstacle. The other songs are "Christmas Is for Children," "Father Christmas," "Happiness Is," "You," "I Like Life," "The Beautiful Day That I Dream About," and "Thank You Very Much."

STANLEY ★★ʃ

FAMILY ENTERTAINMENT. 1984. 30 min. Beta, VHS. I.M.A. ($29.95)

In this parable about self-esteem, Stanley, an ugly duckling, desperately wants to become something other than a duck. He tries his hand at being a dog, a turkey, and, finally, a member of the rough and tough Hell's Eagles before realizing that being a duck isn't so bad after all. Along the way, he is helped by his friend, a fox. There are four songs performed, including "I Am Definitely Not a Duck" and "I Like Myself." Passable animated short film.

SWAN LAKE ★★ɟ

FAMILY ENTERTAINMENT. 1981. Artists: The Vienna Symphony Orchestra conducted by Stefan Soltesz. 75 min. Beta, VHS. Media ($49.95)

Another of the distinctive full-length efforts from Japan's Toei Animation studio, *Swan Lake* is a loose retelling of the fairytale content of Tchaikovsky's classic ballet. Throughout, we can hear Tchaikovsky's music being performed by the Vienna Symphony Orchestra, as conducted by Stefan Soltesz. The story of Prince Siegfried's love for the swan/woman, Odette/Odille, and the evil deeds of the monstrous magician, Rothbart, all set in the magic forest, should be familiar to viewers. Children may find this typical Toei production weird and oddly menacing. The Japanese certainly make more intense cartoons than their American counterparts, and this one is filled with scary, stylized images. But it's not somber and dark all the time. There are, in fact, some charming aspects of *Swan Lake,* especially the pair of helpful chipmunks. Recommended with some reservations.

TOM THUMB ★★ɟ

FAMILY ENTERTAINMENT. 1958. Cast: Russ Tamblyn, Alan Young, Terry-Thomas, Peter Sellers. 92 min. Beta, VHS. MGM/UA ($29.95)

George Pal (*War of the Worlds*) brought his pioneering special effects magic to this children's fable about a 5-inch-tall boy who is magically conjured by the Queen of the Forest for a childless old woodsman and his wife when the woodsman agrees not to chop down the oldest tree in the forest. The Grimms' fairy tale is elaborated by the addition of the characters played by British funnymen Terry-Thomas and Peter Sellers, who are criminals with small minds but plenty of ambition. Only Alan Young (*Mr. Ed*) and the powers of the Queen of the Forest can save Tom Thumb from falling into their evil hands. Russ Tamblyn displays his acrobatic dancing skills to their fullest in many of the clever scenes using miniaturization and animation. Pal won an Oscar for his special effects. The songs, written by Douglas Gamley and Ken Jones, include "After All These Years," "This Is My Song," "Dancing Shoes," "Yawning Man," and "Tell Me It's True."

Russ Tamblyn as the tiny *Tom Thumb*.

WILLIE WONKA AND THE CHOCOLATE FACTORY ★★

FAMILY ENTERTAINMENT. 1971. Cast: Gene Wilder, Jack Albertson, Peter Ostrum, and Julie Dawn Cole. 100 min. Beta, VHS. Warner ($59.95)

You can't trust adults to make a children's movie, it seems. Roald Dahl's *Charlie and the Chocolate Factory* was a lot more fun than the movie that's based on it. In the film version, Willie Wonka, the mysterious owner of a candy factory, is given an ambivalent portrayal by Gene Wilder, so that we're never quite sure whether he's just a sicko or a man with a secret mission. Peter Ostrum plays Charlie, the boy who is lucky enough to find a gold certificate in a Wonka candy bar that allows him to take a guided tour of the factory, along with a select few. The factory is a surreal hall of mirrors, strange scenes, and unpredictable topography. It might be a little too scary for kids—rather strange for a children's film. The Leslie Bricuse-Anthony Newley score did produce a hit . . . for Sammy Davis, Jr.: "Candy Man." Other tunes include "Cheer Up Charlie," "I've Got a Golden Ticket," "Pure Imagination," "I Want It Now!," and others.

ZIGGY'S GIFT   ★★★

FAMILY ENTERTAINMENT. 1984. Artist: Harry Nilsson. 26 min. Beta, VHS. Vestron ($29.95)

Harry Nilsson, the pop singer-songwriter, wrote "Give Joy" for use throughout *Ziggy's Gift,* the animated Christmas special based on Tom Wilson's pudgy comic strip character Ziggy. In a very loosely scripted story, Ziggy foils some meanies who want to make Christmas a time for taking. Ziggy teaches them Christmas is a time for giving.

PERFORMING ARTS

ALL THE BEST FROM RUSSIA! ★⌐

PERFORMING ARTS. 1977. Artists: The Bolshoi Ballet, The Armenian Folk Ensemble, and the Moscow Circus. 60 min. Beta, VHS. Mastervision ($59.95)

If you like dancing bears, you'll love *All the Best from Russia!* If not, you still might like this aimless travelogue through portions of the Soviet Union that visits certain sites of cultural interest. Our host Bruno Gerussi takes us to a performance of the Armenian Folk Dance Ensemble before a whirlwind tour of Moscow and a brief glimpse of the wonders of the Moscow Circus. After a dash through the under-construction track and field stadium for the yet-to-be-boycotted 1980 Summer Olympic Games, we see a bit of the Bolshoi Ballet in production before a long and involved visit with Soviet actor Misha Kasakov, who performs Shakespeare's *Hamlet* in his native Russian. The Hermitage is next on the schedule. The tape is complete with a quick peek at the Bolshoi's performance of *Swan Lake.* Maybe in future through major advances in video technology it will be possible to simulate the experience of visiting foreign lands; until then watching television is going to prove a paltry second place to the real thing.

ARTUR RUBINSTEIN ★★★

PERFORMING ARTS. Artists: Artur Rubinstein, Jascha Heifetz, and Gregor Piatigorsky. 88 min. Beta, VHS Stereo. Kultur ($59.95)

This black and white tape is composed of three short films made in the forties and the fifties that try to dramatize Artur Rubinstein's piano artistry by placing him in artificially created situations that allow him to play before the camera. In the first film, a film producer asks Mr. Rubinstein if the producer can make a film recording of Rubinstein playing Mendelssohn's "Spinning Song" and Liszt's "Liebestraum" at his home in New York. In the second, Mr. Rubinstein plays Chopin for a few friends in his den. In the third, an unnamed screenwriter from an unnamed film studio arrives at Mr. Rubinstein's house in California just as Artur Rubinstein, Jascha Heifetz, and Gregor Piatigorsky sit down to play Shubert's Trio in B-Flat and the first, second, and third movements of Mendelssohn's Trio in D-Minor. The screenwriter is intrigued, convinced that there is a way to dramatize the situation. For some reason, it dawns on him only in the last part of the film to let the drama of the music and the artistry of the musicians speak for themselves. If the viewer can overlook these unnecessary dramatizations, he or she will be rewarded with the work of a great pianist interpreting the masters.

BACKSTAGE AT THE KIROV ★★★♪

PERFORMING ARTS. 1983. 80 min. Beta, VHS. Pacific Arts ($29.95)

This beautifully photographed film examines the illustrious history and backstage activities of what is arguably the world's best ballet company, the Kirov of Leningrad. Founded under the aegis of the Tsar as the Imperial Ballet, the Kirov has attracted and fostered such formidable talents as choreographers Marius Petipa and Michel Fokine, and dancers Anna Pavlova, Vaslav Nijinsky, and Mikhail Baryshnikov. It could be argued that without the Kirov there would be no ballet. Following the activities of every tier of the company from the ballet director, to the instructors, to the soloists, to the corps de ballet, down to the 10-year-old students in their first year at the company's ballet school, the viewer is struck by the constant, almost superhuman effort each member of the company exerts for the good of the company as a whole. Every dancer has a full day of classes with the corps. The soloists work additional backbreaking hours practicing their parts to achieve a fleeting moment of physical perfection and beauty on stage during a performance before returning to class the next day to repeat the process. The camerawork in *Backstage* is superb. During one memorable moment, the camera follows the swans on stage during a performance of *Swan Lake* to give the home video spectator the visual sensation of being a performer. As a look at the workings of a ballet company, this film is unparalleled.

BALLERINA: KAREN KAIN ★★★

PERFORMING ARTS. 1977. Artists: Karen Kain, Roland Petit, and Frank Augustyn. 60 min. Beta, VHS. Mastervision ($59.95)

Canadian dancer Karen Kain, the winner of the 1973 silver medal at the International Ballet Competition in Moscow, the first North American to dance as a guest artist with the Bolshoi Ballet, and the principal dancer with the National Ballet of Canada since 1971, performs with the Ballet de Roland Petit of Marseilles in a 1977 tour across Canada in this tape. Intercut with various stages of her rehearsal and performance of *Carmen* are interviews with Roland Petit, Canadian critic Clement Crisp, Kain's dance partner Frank Augustyn, principal of the National Ballet School of Canada Betty Oliphant, and Kain herself. One is immediately struck by Kain's natural talent for classical ballet and her importance to Canadian dance as a whole. In addition to the excerpts from her performance in *Carmen,* Karen Kain can also be seen in sections of Petit's *Coppelia* and *Romeo and Juliet.*

BALLERINA: LYNN SEYMOUR ★★★♪

PERFORMING ARTS. 1979. Artists: Lynn Seymour, Rudolph Nureyev, Christopher Gable, and Stephen Jeffries. 60 min. Beta, VHS. Mastervision ($59.95)

Ballerina: Lynn Seymour follows the busy life and career of Canadian ballerina Lynn Seymour over a 4-month period in 1979. The film begins in the rehearsal studio with Lynn Seymour and Rudolf Nureyev before Lynn rushes off to celebrate the birthday of her son Damion. Next it's off to Edmonton, Alberta, for the premiere of her pas de deux *Mac and Polly,* which she dances with her partner Stephen Jeffries in honor of the Commonwealth Games. Back in her position of guest dancer with the Royal Ballet in London, Lynn practices Sir Frederick Ashton's *Two Pigeons* with longtime partner Christopher Gable, who came out of retirement for this one performance. During the rehearsal they remember and reconstruct the ballet that they had premiered almost twenty years beforehand. Lynn dances in performance with David Wall in the pas de deux from Kenneth MacMillan's *Romeo and Juliet,* before leaving the Royal Ballet to take up the post of director and principal ballerina with the Ballet of the Bayerische Staatsoper in Munich.

BOLSHOI BALLET ★★◗

PERFORMING ARTS. 1967. Artists: Nina Timofeyeva, Ekaterina Maximova, and dancers of the Bolshoi Ballet. 90 min. Beta, VHS. Kultur ($59.95)

Bolshoi Ballet provides a cursory look at the Bolshoi Ballet Company circa 1967. After brief glimpses at the structure of the company and the ballet school, the film concentrates on eight scenes from eight well-known ballets in the Bolshoi's classical repertoire. The dazzling technique of the great Timofeyeva is presented in a short scene from *Laurencia.* Nina Sorokina is seen in an excerpt from *Giselle.* Yuroselv Sekh and Ekaterina Maximova dance to the music of Serge Rachmaninoff in *Paganini.* Scenes from Ravel's *Bolero* and *Waltz* are presented along with Prokofiev's *Stone Flower.* The color and lighting of this film are rather crude by American standards, but the brilliant dancing makes up for any technical deficiencies.

BUJONES/COPPELIA ★★★

PERFORMING ARTS. 1980. Cast: Fernando Bujones, Ana Maria Castañon. 110 min. Beta, VHS. Kultur ($59.95)

Fernando Bujones, featured dancer in Mikhail Baryshnikov's American Ballet Theater, joins Ana Maria Castañon, principal soloist of the Ballets de San Juan, and the rest of the company in a delightful performance of Leo Delibes' comedy *Coppelia.* Taped before an audience of mostly happy children giggling at the antics of Franz (Fernando Bujones) and Swanilda and Coppelia, both danced by Ana Maria Castañon, this *Coppelia* should entertain even the youngest member of the family. In the story, Swanilda breaks off her engagement with Franz when she discovers that he has eyes for Coppelia, the daughter of Dr. Coppelius, the town magician. Later, after Dr. Coppelius leaves his house, Swanilda breaks in with some of her friends to confront the flirt Coppelia, but they discover to their dismay and to the audience's delight that Coppelia is a mechanical doll. The girls wind up the other toys in the workshop and each does its own dance. Coppelius returns and in a rage sends the girls fleeing. Swanilda hides behind the curtain in which Coppelia is kept and puts on her clothes. At that very moment, Franz enters looking for Coppelia and finds her "father," Dr. Coppelius, who proceeds to get him drunk. Franz passes out and Dr. Coppelius casts a spell on Swanilda, who is dressed in Coppelia's clothes, and brings her to life. In a scene that amuses the audience to no end, Swanilda mimics the mechanical movements of Coppelia and ushers the drunk Franz out of Dr. Coppelius' house. In act three, Franz and Coppelia are to be wed during a public festival. Dr. Coppelius barges in on the festivities, demanding compensation for damage done to his workshop. Swanilda claims responsibility and offers her dowry as payment. The Count, who is responsible for the feast, is touched by Swanilda's sacrifice and pays Dr. Coppelius himself with a bag of gold.

THE COMPETITION ★★ﺟ

PERFORMING ARTS. 1980. Cast: Richard Dreyfuss, Amy Irving, Lee Remick, Sam Wanamaker, and James B. Sikking. 129 min. Beta, VHS. RCA/Columbia ($69.95)

Based on a *New Yorker* magazine article on the annual Leventritt piano competition, this attempt at a *Rocky* movie for classical music fans misses the mark dramatically with its very unlikeable lead characters and smarmy atmosphere of musical politics. Richard Dreyfuss, giving another of his smartalec performances, plays Paul, a classical pianist who has one last chance to gain a professional career—win the gold medal at the Arabella Hillman Piano Competition in San Francisco. His most serious competition comes from Heidi (Amy Irving), a little rich girl who travels with her obsessed coach (Lee Remick). Of course, the two fall in love, much to Lee Remick's dismay and against Paul's own better judgement. Other complications include a Russian competitor whose coach decides to defect right in the middle of the rehearsals, causing a lengthy delay in the competition that intensifies the cutthroat pressures surrounding success and failure. The whole thing is a bit too predictable from the very beginning and you know that Dreyfuss will never win the gold medal. If the Lee Remick character is meant to represent the typical piano coach, then Earl Weaver obviously picked the wrong field to be a coach in. This film parades past the viewer every cliché associated with concert musicians. The pieces for piano played are Ginastera's Sonata for Piano (Eduardo Delgado, soloist), Brahms' Piano Concerto No. 1 (Ralph Grierson), Chopin's Piano Concerto in E Minor (Lincoln Mayorga), Prokofiev's Piano Concerto No. 3 (Daniel Pollack), and Beethoven's Piano Concerto No. 9 (Chester B. Swiatkowski). Lalo Schifrin conducts the Los Angeles Philharmonic.

DIVA ★★★ﺟ

PERFORMING ARTS. 1982. Cast: Wilhelmenia Wiggins Fernandez, Frederic Andrei, Richard Bohringer, Thuy An Luu, and Jacques Fabbri. 123 min. Beta, VHS Stereo. MGM/UA ($69.95)

Diva, the French thriller that was director Jean-Jacques Beineix's debut film, charmed art house audiences across North America with its visual style and dazzling, sometimes overpowering, technique. Jules (Frederic Andrei) is a Parisian mailman who is such an opera fanatic that he makes an illegal tape recording of American diva Christine Hawkins (Wilhelmenia Wiggins Fernandez) singing "La Wally" by Catalani. Although Hawkins is one of the world's leading opera singers, she has never made a recording. Jules steals her gown out of her dressing room, and at the same time, accidentally comes into possession of a cassette that could incriminate the head of the Parisian police detectives, who is also the head of a secret drug smuggling and prostitution ring. While evading a pair of crooks, who want the tape that could convict their boss, and some Taiwanese record pirates, who want the only recording of Christine Hawkins in existence, Jules befriends the diva whose physical beauty equals the beauty of her voice. He returns her robe and the illegal tape recording of her concert, and with the help of Gorodish (Jacques Fabbri), a Zen-influenced latter-day French cowboy, and his teenage Vietnamese girlfriend (Thuy An Luu), saves the day. Wilhelmenia Wiggins Fernandez also performs Shubert's "Ave Maria." Vladimir Cosma wrote the atmospheric score.

THE FOUR SEASONS   ★★

PERFORMING ARTS. 1983. Artists: Lorin Maazel, Patrice Fontanarosa, Regis Pasquier, Jacques Duhem, Roland Pidoux, Tasso Adamopoulos, Gaby Lavrindon, and Emerson Buckley. 46 min. Beta Hifi, VHS Stereo. MGM/UA ($39.95)

Antonio Vivaldi's composition *The Four Seasons* is presented here beautifully played by Lorin Maazel and the members of his ensemble. Intercut with shots of the musicians in a bare blue television studio are sections of film that are intended to illustrate each season of Vivaldi's piece in turn.

Paris is the setting of the Spring section. New York is used as the setting of Summer. Autumn is filmed in Venice. Moscow is the setting of Winter. Only Winter in Moscow gives the viewer a sense of the season with shots of snow, ice covered rivers, frozen landscapes, etc. The other three vignettes concentrate completely on the architectural wonders in each city and leave the audience to guess the season of the year in which the film was shot. In addition, the editor of this tape cuts back and forth between the musicians and the urban portraits, jerking the audience from the studio to the four corners of the globe. Is this a film of musicians performing, a music video using film of the four cities to illustrate Vivaldi, or a musical portrait of the change of seasons throughout the world?

Lorin Maazel and his ensemble performing *The Four Seasons*.

JOAN SUTHERLAND IN THE MAKING OF "LAKME"   ★★★

PERFORMING ARTS. 1976. Cast: Joan Sutherland, Richard Bonynge, Henri Wilden, and Isabel Buchanan. 60 min. Beta Hifi, VHS Stereo. Mastervision ($59.95)

Joan Sutherland in the Making of "Lakme" covers in great detail the years of painstaking work by hundreds of singers, artists and technicians, required to stage an opera. The 1976 Australian Opera production of *Lakme,* Leo Delibes' French opera about cultural conflict in nineteenth-century India under the British Raj, starts more than a year beforehand with the preliminary costume and set sketches. After the necessary administrative approval, the sets are built, the costumes are sewn, and Desmond Digby, the Australian Opera's theatrical designer, flies halfway around the world, from Sydney to New York, to fit Joan Sutherland, the star, with the costumes that she will wear in half a year in Australia. With six months to go before the premiere of *Lakme,* the chorus is taught its parts for the production and nine other operas. Three weeks before curtain call, the principals arrive in Sydney and go through final rehearsals for the parts that they have spent six months learning. After the final staging rehearsal and a last checking of lighting cues, the Australian Opera production of *Lakme* is a complete success.

LA TRAVIATA ★★★★

PERFORMING ARTS. 1984. Cast: Placido Domingo, Teresa Stratas, Cornell MacNeil, Allan Monk, Axell Gail, Maurizio Barbaracini, Ekaterina Maximova, and Vladimir Vasiliev. 105 min. Beta Hifi, VHS Stereo. MCA ($69.95)

Franco Zeffirelli's filmed version of Giuseppe Verdi's *La Traviata* features an outstanding cast with one of the world's all-time great tenors, Placido Domingo, in the role of

Tenor Placido Domingo as Alfredo in Verdi's *La Traviata*.

Alfredo, critically acclaimed Metropolitan Opera soprano Teresa Stratas in the role of Violetta, and baritone Cornell MacNeil in the role of Alfredo's father Germont. Ekaterina Maximova and Vladimir Vasiliev of the Bolshoi Ballet appear in the film as well. Zeffirelli brings his years of experience in the theater and as a film director (such memorable films as *Brother Sun, Sister Moon, Romeo and Juliet,* and *The Taming of the Shrew*) to bear, creating a movie that strikes a balance between theater and film. In *La Traviata,* Zefferelli releases opera from the confines of the stage and places the action on location in and around Paris. At the same time, he reduces the scale of the work, making it less theatrical, staging the movements of each singer for the camera instead of an opera hall audience. The result is a *La Traviata* that can entertain and thrill a movie audience as opera and as film and should appeal to the opera buff and novice alike. Well worth the attention of anyone with a VCR.

THE LITTLE HUMPBACKED HORSE   ★★★

PERFORMING ARTS. 1961. Cast: Maya Plisetskaya, Vladimir Vasiliev, and Alexander Radunsky. 85 min. Beta, VHS. VAI ($59.95)

The Little Humpbacked Horse was the first classical ballet to be based on a Russian folk tale. It was first choreographed by Arthur Saint-Leon to music by Cesare Pugni for the Russian Imperial Ballet in 1864. This production was choreographed by Alexander Radunsky in 1960 for the Bolshoi Ballet. Based on a story by Pyotr Vershov, the ballet tells the old folk tale of Ivan (Vladimir Vasiliev), an intelligent young man who is taken for a simpleton. His father asks Ivan and his two brothers to guard his wheat fields at night to see who has been trampling them every evening. The two brothers fall asleep; Ivan stays awake and discovers that an enchanted mare has been foraging through his father's crop. Ivan captures the horse, who tells him that she will give him three horses in exchange for her release. One of the horses Ivan receives is a little humpbacked horse who has the magic power to grant any of Ivan's desires. His two brothers steal the two other horses and bring them to the King (Alexander Radunsky), who wants to buy them, but the horses will obey only Ivan, so the King hires him as stablemaster of the palace. Ivan dances with the Queen Maiden whom the King wants to marry immediately. She tries to fend off his royal advances by declaring that she will only marry the man who can bring her a special ring that is kept at the bottom of the sea. Ivan retrieves the ring with the help of the humpbacked horse and marries the Queen. The beautiful dancing in this film is complemented by animation and special effects that recall drawings of Russian folk motifs and give the filmed performance of the ballet even more of a fairytale atmosphere. Very enjoyable.

LUCIA DI LAMMERMOOR ★↲

PERFORMING ARTS. 1971. Cast: Anna Moffo, Giulio Fioravanti, Pietro di Vietri, and the Rome Symphony Orchestra. 108 min. Beta, VHS. VAI ($69.95)

This film production of *Lucia di Lammermoor* was moved from the opera house stage to the actual setting of the opera, the castles and moors of Scotland. The director of this film forgot to ask the principals to tone down their stage mannerisms and remember that they are performing for a camera not in a production at La Scala. The soloists mouth their parts to the playback of a tape of Donizetti's work that they had recorded with the Rome Symphony Orchestra back in Italy. Quite often there is a delay in the tape between what is heard on the audio track and what is seen on the television screen. If one wants more than a Scottish travelogue then one should skip this version of *Lucia.*

THE MEDIUM ★★↲

PERFORMING ARTS. 1950. Cast: Marie Powers, Leo Coleman, Anna Maria Alberghetti, Beverly Dame, and Donald Morgan. 80 min. Beta, VHS. VAI ($69.95)

Composer Gian Carlo Menotti first displayed *The Medium* on Broadway in 1946. It was avoided by opera buffs as too commercial and by Broadway theatergoers who refused to see anything labeled "opera." Menotti himself directed this filmed version on location in Italy in 1950. Sung in English, it tells the story of Madame Flora (Marie Powers), who with the help of her daughter Monica (Anna Maria Alberghetti) and Toby (Leo Coleman), her deaf assistant, tricks her clients into believing that they can contact deceased relatives through Madame's seances. Mrs. Nolan and Mr. and Mrs. Gobineau visit Madame Flora's seance parlor regularly to listen to the disguised voice of Monica, thinking that it is the voice of their long lost children. As usual Madame's clients are satisfied. But Madame becomes disturbed when she suddenly hears "other" voices. She accuses Toby, the deaf boy, of "putting" the voices in her head. As the opera progresses, she descends into madness, and in the end, accidentally shoots Toby. The dark and eerie look of the film and the shrill piercing singing of

Marie Powers and Anna Maria Alberghetti give this version of the opera the feel of an early fifties anthology television show.

PAVAROTTI ★★★

PERFORMING ARTS. 1984. Artists: Luciano Pavarotti, Andrea Griminelli, Emerson Buckley and the Las Vegas Symphony Orchestra. 78 min. Beta Hifi, VHS. U.S.A. ($29.95)

In his efforts to popularize opera in the tradition of Enrico Caruso and Mario Lanza, Luciano Pavarotti has used every medium available to enlarge his audience. He has performed in a comedy film and sung at Madison Square Garden. On this tape, he is seen at the Riviera Hotel in Las Vegas, where he gives a recital of Italian arias. Emerson Buckley conducts the Las Vegas Symphony Orchestra. Mr. Andrea Griminelli plays flute on a number of selections that are interspersed among the aria performances. Before an audience that includes Hollywood stars and Las Vegas headliners, Mr. Pavarotti sings ten well-known selections from various operas, including Verdi's "De miei bollenti spiriti" from his *La Traviata,* his "Ma se m'e forza perderti" from the opera *Un ballo in maschera,* and Verdi's "Ingemisco" from the *Messa da Requiem.* Mr. Pavarotti adds two selections from Puccini, "Che Gelinda Manila" from *La Bohème* and the famous aria from *Turandot,* "Nessun dorma." Mr. Griminelli performs the very popular "Flight of the Bumblebee" by Rimsky-Korsakov and the Concertino for Flute and Orchestra in D Major by Chaminade. Mr. Pavarotti closes the concert with renditions of the popular "Torna a surriento" by de Curtis and "O sole mio" by Di Capua.

PAVAROTTI IN LONDON ★★★★

PERFORMING ARTS. 1982. Artists: Luciano Pavarotti and the Royal Philharmonic Orchestra. 78 min. Beta Hifi, VHS Stereo. RCA/Columbia ($29.95)

Luciano Pavarotti, who has been called the world's greatest tenor by many critics, performs with the Royal Philharmonic Orchestra in an unforgettable gala concert for Her Majesty Queen Elizabeth, the Queen Mother, and an applauding and cheering crowd at the Royal Albert Hall in London. Videotaped on April 13, 1982, *Pavarotti in London* will stand as a record of the artist at the height of his powers. After the orchestra pays tribute to the Queen Mother by playing "God Save the Queen" and a performance of the overture from Verdi's *La forza del destino,* Mr. Pavarotti sings three selections from Puccini, "Recondita armonia" and "E lucevan le stelle" from *Tosca* and Mr. Pavarot-

Tenor Luciano Pavarotti.

ti's personal favorite, "Nessun dorma" from *Turandot.* The orchestra plays an interlude from Moussorgsky's *Khovanschina,* "The Dance of the Persian Slaves," before Mr. Pavarotti returns to sing the aria "La mia Letizia infondere" from Verdi's *I Lombardi alla prima crociata* and the beautiful "Quando le sere al placido" from Verdi's *Luisa Miller.* The audience is thrilled by the great tenor's renditions of "Fra poco a me ricovero" from Donizetti's *Lucia di Lammermoor* and "Lamento di Frederico" from Cilea's *L'Arlesiana.* Mr. Pavarotti performs the aria from Donizetti's *L'elisir d'amore,* "Una furtiva lagrima," before closing the concert with the perennial favorite, "Torna a surriento" by de Curtis. A tape worth watching again and again.

RUSSIAN FOLK SONG AND DANCE ★★♪

PERFORMING ARTS. 1977. Cast: Pyatnitsky Song and Dance Ensemble, Uzbekistan National Song and Dance Ensemble, Siberian Dancers and Singers of Omsk, and The Moldavian National Song and Dance Ensemble. 70 min. Beta, VHS. Kultur ($59.95)

Russian Folk Song and Dance is a misnomer. The dances presented on this tape are from four Soviet republics outside of what is traditionally known as Russia. The first section presents the Pyatnitsky Song and Dance Ensemble and the folk songs and dances of the Ukraine. The members of this company, named after the man who singlehandedly saved the folk traditions of the Ukrainian people, travel all over the Soviet Union as the representatives of a living art form. Next, the film travels to central Asia, to the Soviet republic of Uzbekistan, to record an Uzbek feast, traditional Uzbek dances as performed by the Uzbekistan National Song and Dance Ensemble, and a concert played by the Uzbek Philharmonic Orchestra on Uzbek folk instruments. Omsk in central Siberia is the setting for the third section of this tape. The Siberian Dancers and Singers of Omsk perform a folk opera about the loves of three Siberian teenagers on a colorful interior set. The last section of the tape was filmed in Moldavia, the Soviet republic that borders Rumania. The Moldavian National Song and Dance Ensemble, dressed in Moldavian folk costumes, perform traditional dances that have been part of the Moldavian national heritage since Roman times.

THE SOLDIER'S TALE ★★★★

PERFORMING ARTS. 1984. Cast: André Gregory, Max Von Sydow, Galina Panova, Dusan Makavejev, and Brother Theodore. 56 min. Beta Hifi, VHS Stereo. MGM/UA ($39.95)

Cartoonist R. O. Blechman, best known for his *New Yorker* magazine covers and his Perrier "caveman" commercials, created this Emmy Award-winning animated film, based on Igor Stravinsky's musical composition "The Soldier's Tale." The music was originally produced in 1918 to accompany a theater piece written by Swiss poet C. F. Ramuz. Blechman's film fully complements and even surpasses the intensity of Stravinsky's composition. With an imaginative and dazzling command of the art of animation, R. O. Blechman choreographs cut-outs, collages, photos, drawings in ink, colored pencil, and crayon to the pulsating music of the composer. In the Faust-like story, Vertov, a Russian soldier, unwittingly gives his violin to Satan in exchange for the pleasures and riches of the secular world. The film's wonderful cast of voices includes Max Von Sydow as Satan and Yugoslav film director Dusan Makavejev as Vertov. The narration is provided by André Gregory, *the* André from Louis Malle's

Scene from R. O. Blechman's animated *Soldier's Tale*.

My Dinner with André. MGM/UA adds the incredibly crisp and clear sound of Video-phonic sound processing to the audio track. All in all a great tape.

SOVIET ARMY CHORUS, BAND, AND DANCE ENSEMBLE   ★★♪

PERFORMING ARTS. 1977. Artists: The Soviet Army Chorus, Band, and Dance Ensemble. 70 min. Beta, VHS. Kultur ($59.95)

The Soviet Army Chorus and Band are stiffly composed in a clearing in a birch forest and in a light-blue television studio to sing classic Russian and Ukranian folk songs. They sing the traditional Russian folk melody, "The Birch Tree," which Tchaikovsky wove into the last movement of his Fourth Symphony. A balalaika provides the accompaniment for the Soviet Army Chorus' rendition of "Karaminska," which is followed by "Stenkarazen," "Meadowland," "The Piterskaia Road," "The Volga Boatmen," and "The Grey Cookoo." The real value of this tape is the limited exposure that it gives the Soviet Army Dance Ensemble. To the music of Alexandrov, the members of the ensemble recreate the energetic and dazzling Dance of the Soldiers high above Moscow in the Lenin Hills. Dressed in the colorful costumes of the Cossacks, the ensemble dances the Dance of the Cossacks, which has the same exuberance as the earlier dance. The chorus returns to close the tape with "Kalinka" and "Tender Moonlit Night."

STARS OF THE RUSSIAN BALLET: GALINA ULANOVA AND MAYA PLISETSKAYA ★★★

PERFORMING ARTS. 1953. Cast: Galina Ulanova, Maya Plisetskaya, Natalia Dudinskaya, and Konstantin Sergeyev. 80 min. Beta, Hifi. VAI ($59.95)

Stars of the Russian Ballet presents the leading lights of Russian ballet during the fifties, the stars of the Bolshoi and Kirov companies, in excerpts from three ballets. In Sergeyev's version of Tchaikovsky's *Swan Lake,* the Bolshoi's Galina Ulanova, often called the greatest dancer of this century, stars in the role of Odette to contrast with the Kirov's Natalia Dudinskaya's dancing in the role of Odille. Konstantin Sergeyev of the Kirov takes the role of Siegfried. The second selection on this tape is a section from Asafyev's *The Fountain of Bakhtchisarai.* Galina Ulanova as Maria dances in a classical style opposite the other great Bolshoi soloist, Maya Plisetskaya, who dances with more Oriental movement in the role of Zarema. In the story, a Tatar prince falls in love with Maria, a Russian princess, who dies at the hands of the jealous Zarema. In the third excerpt, taken from Asafyev's *The Flames of Paris,* French peasants attack the palace of the king who is plotting to quash the Revolution.

THE TCHAIKOVSKY COMPETITION: VIOLIN AND PIANO ★★★♪

Performing Arts. 1982. Artists: Vikoria Mullova, Kerry McDermott, Andres Cardenes, Stephanie Chase, Ralph Evans, Peter Donohoe, Anthony Ross, James Barbagallo, Sergei Stadler, Jonathan Shames, and Vladimir Ovchinnikov. 90 min. Beta Hifi, VHS Stereo. Mastervision ($69.95)

Over a 3-week period, as 250 contestants are narrowed down to only 12 for the finals in violin and 13 for the finals in piano, one question stays on the minds of the competitors, the judges, and the worldwide audience: who will win? *The Tchaikovsky Competition* from Moscow covers the progress of a small number of very talented competitors as they deliver technically brilliant performances and make their way closer with each round to the all-important finals. In various interviews with competing artists from various countries, the home video audience becomes acquainted with the contestants and soon can feel the tension that each performer must feel in the midst of the competition. In the finals of the violin competition, the home video viewer is treated to American Andres Cardenes' performance of Tchaikovsky's Violin Concerto in D Major. James

Barbagallo, also of the U.S., plays Rachmaninoff's *Rhapsody on a Theme of Paganini.* The United Kingdom's Peter Donohoe gives a flawless rendition of Rachmaninoff's Piano Concerto No. 3.

TURANDOT ★★★✦

PERFORMING ARTS. 1984. Cast: Eva Marton, José Carreras, Katia Ricciarelli, Waldmar Kmentt, John Paul Bogart, Robert Kerns, Helmut Wildhaber, Heinz Zednik, Kurt Rydl, and Bela Perencz. 138 min. Beta Hifi, VHS Stereo. MGM/UA ($79.95)

The Vienna Staatoper under the direction of Lorin Maazel brings *Turandot* (in Italian with English subtitles) to the Viennese stage in a production that emphasizes the tension, suspense, and drama of Giacomo Puccini's opera with lavish costumes and a spectacular set. In the story, a mysterious foreigner named Calif (José Carreras) enters the ancient city of Peking to find its inhabitants loathe to carry out the morbid wishes of the cold and heartless Chinese princess Turandot. The lone Turandot will marry and transfer the throne only to the man of royal blood who can answer her three cryptic riddles. The penalty for one incorrect answer is death. Many have tried, failed, and been executed by the reluctant population of Peking. Calif discovers his father, the exiled

José Carreras and Eva Marton in *Turandot.*

Tatar king, Timur, and his slave wandering among the disenchanted in the Chinese capital. Calif falls in love with Turandot at first sight and dares to take the challenge of the three riddles to become her husband. Calif sings the memorable aria "Nessun dorma" as night falls and the restless people of Peking nervously await what they anticipate to be his certain death. The next day, Calif answers the questions, reveals his royal lineage, and wins Turandot's love as well as her hand and frees the city from its odious responsibility.

VERDI'S RIGOLETTO AT VERONA ★★★

PERFORMING ARTS. 1981. Cast: Garbis Bovagian, Alida Ferrarini, and Vincenzo Bello. 115 min. Beta Hifi, VHS Stereo. Mastervision ($69.95)

Presented as part of the 1981 opera season at the ancient Roman amphitheater in Verona, Italy (for other productions in the 1981 Verona series see Thorn-EMI's *Aida* and *Madama Butterfly*), Giuseppe Verdi's *Rigoletto* tells the tragic story of the cursed court jester (Garbis Bovagian) and his daughter Gilda (Alida Ferrarini.) The acoustics in the 2000-year-old amphitheater are next to perfect. The ancient open air site provides the ideal setting for Verdi's opera, allowing the room required to build the enormous two-tiered stage used for the production. In the same way that the famous quartet from the last act of *Rigoletto* combines four voices simultaneously to create a heightened sense of drama, the two tiers of the stage permit the opera to project new dramatic power by dividing the opera's action and singing and presenting them simultaneously. With this new staging the third act takes on new dramatic emphasis. For example, when Gilda waits dressed as a man by the river on the upper tier, Maddalena argues with Sparafucile on the lower tier. This production is worth watching.

WHO'S AFRAID OF OPERA? VOLUME I ★★✦

PERFORMING ARTS. 1973. Artist: Joan Sutherland. 57 min. Beta Hifi, VHS Stereo. MGM/UA ($29.95)

The three volumes of *Who's Afraid of Opera?*, an English television show for children hosted by diva Joan Sutherland, are intended as light introductions to some of the world's great operas. In each volume, Ms. Sutherland, acting as narrator and performer, presents highlights from two famous works. She explains the plot of each opera and the motivations of each character to three puppets, a wise old goat named Sir William, his nephew Billy, and a wisecracking young lion named Rudy. In between the explanations, Ms. Sutherland sings great arias in the languages in which they were written,

Joan Sutherland in *Who's Afraid of Opera? Volume II.*

and with the help of a fine supporting cast, rushes through condensed versions of six great operas. The first volume is composed of scenes from Gounod's *Faust* and Verdi's *Rigoletto.* At times it appears that the cast is lip-synching to a recording of the music as played by conductor Richard Bonynge and the London Symphony Orchestra. Even so, each presentation immediately draws the home video viewer into the drama of the opera. Who can resist being captivated by the story of Faust's pact with Satan or the tale of Rigoletto's suffering the consequences of his fatal curse? This first volume might be too frightening for small children, but it should be a big success with their older siblings.

WHO'S AFRAID OF OPERA? VOLUME II ★★↓

PERFORMING ARTS. 1973. Artist: Joan Sutherland. 57 min. Beta Hifi, VHS Stereo. MGM/UA ($29.95)

The second volume of *Who's Afraid of Opera?* presents international opera star Joan Sutherland introducing two more great stage works to her puppet friends, Sir William,

Billy, and Rudy, and the children of her home video audience. Excerpts from Guiseppe Verdi's timeless classic *La Traviata* and Gaetano Donizetti's *Daughter of the Regiment* are included in this tape. Ms. Sutherland takes the starring role of Violetta in *La Traviata,* singing Violetta's song of freedom, "Sempre libera," from the opening scene, and "Addio del passato" (Farewell to Bright Visions) the aria Violetta sings in the last scene as she is dying of tuberculosis. Tenor Ian Caley sings the part of Alfredo and is given the opportunity to toast a happy and gay Violetta in the first act with the famous drinking song "Libiamo." The libretto of Donizetti's *Daughter of the Regiment* was written in French by Bayard and Jules Vernoy. In this story of misplaced patrimony, which takes place during the Napoleonic wars, Joan Sutherland plays the part of Marie, "the daughter of the regiment," and sings "Au Bruit de la guerre," "Chacun le sait, Chacun le dit," "Il faut partir, mes bons compagnons," and "Tous les trois, réunis." Spiro Malas sings the part of Suplice. Tenor Ramon Remedios sings the part of Tonio. The part of the Marchioness of Birkenfeld is sung by Monica Sinclair.

WHO'S AFRAID OF OPERA? VOLUME III ★★⌐

PERFORMING ARTS. 1973. Artist: Joan Sutherland. 57 min. Beta Hifi, VHS Stereo. MGM/UA ($29.95)

In the third volume of *Who's Afraid of Opera?,* Joan Sutherland and her small television company perform scenes from Gioacchino Rossini's comedy, *The Barber of Seville,* and Gaetano Donizetti's tragedy, *Lucia di Lammermoor.* As in the other two volumes of the series, Ms. Sutherland gives the home video audience the threads of the plot of each opera by discussing them with Larry Berthelson's puppets. The abbreviated production of *The Barber of Seville* is very comical—at times hilarious. Joan Sutherland sings the part of Rosina. Tom McDonnell sings the title role of the barber-matchmaker, Figaro. He opens the first scene with the famous aria "Largo al factorum." Clifford Grant plays Dr. Bartolo, the old man who wants to marry Rosina for her dowry. In *Lucia di Lammermoor,* Ms. Sutherland stars as the ill-fated Lucia, a woman caught in the middle of a political rivalry. This shortened version of the opera opens with the ending of *Lucia di Lammermoor,* in which Edgardo, played by John Brecknock, sings the aria "Tu che a Dio spegasti l'ali" after stabbing himself over the tomb of his beloved Lucia. This performance also features the famous wedding scene in which the six principals sing the famous sextet, "Chi mi freba."

YES, GIORGIO ★★

PERFORMING ARTS. 1983. Cast: Luciano Pavarotti, Kathryn Harrold, and Eddie Albert. 111 min. Beta, VHS. MGM/UA ($69.95)

Yes, Giorgio bombed at the box office when it was released at theaters across the country in 1983. Movie audiences stayed away in droves. The film careers of Luciano Pavarotti, Kathryn Harrold, and Eddie Albert were put on ice. Kathryn Harrold later found a role on TV's *MacGruder and Loud.* Eddie Albert was soon on Broadway in a revival of George S. Kaufman's *You Can't Take It with You.* Luciano Pavarotti returned to the opera circuit, bearing the brunt of the film critics' wrath. The criticism of Luciano's performance was misplaced. The script of *Yes, Giorgio* put him in the role of an Italian opera superstar, Giorgio Fini, a dislikeable character who is an arrogant, selfish, and manipulative adulterer. The screenwriter failed to sculpt his screenplay around Mr. Pavarotti's natural buoyant good humor, and created a lackluster, inept vehicle for the great tenor. Perhaps Mr. Pavarotti will be given another chance in the future. In the film, Giorgio Fini leaves his native Italy to perform a recital featuring "Una Furtiva Lagrima" from Donizetti's *L'elisir d'amore,* "La donna e mobile" from Verdi's *Rigoletto,* and Shubert's "Ave Maria," on the banks of the Charles River in Boston where he develops a psychosomatic case of laryngitis when he hears that he will have to sing the part of Calif in Puccini's *Turandot* with the Metropolitan Opera in New York. It seems that Fini had been part of a disastrous production of *La Gioconda* at the Met 7 years earlier. Fini's manager, Mr. Pollack (Eddie Albert), calls the leading throat specialist in New England, Dr. Pamela Taylor (Kathryn Harrold), who declares that there is nothing wrong with Giorgio Fini and gives him a placebo that cures nervousness and throat "problem" instantly. Fini's gratitude turns to infatuation and he shamelessly chases Dr. Taylor around Boston. She reminds him that he is married. He says it doesn't matter and whisks her off for what is supposed to be a romantic weekend in San Francisco. They fly to New York where he triumphs at the Met and she says goodbye. Pavarotti sings "Cielo e mar" from Ponchielli's *La Gioconda,* "Donna non vidi mai" from Puccini's *Manon Lescaut,* and "Nessun dorma" from Puccini's *Turandot.*

APPENDIX

Video Distributors

Blackhawk Films
1235 West 5th Street
P.O. Box 3990
Davenport, Iowa 52808

CBS/Fox Video
1211 Avenue of the Americas
2nd Floor
New York, NY 10036

Continental Video
2320 Cotner
Los Angeles, CA 90064

Embassy Home Entertainment
1901 Avenue of the Stars
Los Angeles, CA 90067

Independent United Distributors
430 West 54th Street
New York, NY 10019

International Video Entertainment
7920 Alabama Avenue
Canoga Park, CA 91304–4991

Kultur Video
1340 Ocean Avenue
Suite 12B
Sea Bright, NJ 07760

Mastervision
969 Park Avenue
New York, NY 10028

MCA Home Video
70 Universal City Plaza
Universal City, CA 91608

Media Home Entertainment
5730 Buckingham Parkway
Culver City, CA 90230

MGM/UA Home Video
1350 Avenue of Americas
New York, NY 10019

New Video
90 University Place
New York, NY 10003

NTA (Republic Pictures Corp.)
12636 Beatrice Street
P.O. Box 66930
Los Angeles, CA 90066

Paramount Home Video
5555 Melrose Avenue
Los Angeles, CA 90038

Rhapsody Films
30 Charlton Street
New York, NY 10014

Sony Corp. of America
9 West 57th Street
New York, NY 10019

Tower Video
900 Enterprise Drive
Sacramento, CA 95825

Unicorn Video
20822 Dearborn Street
Chatsworth, CA 91311

Vestron Video
1011 High Ridge Road
P.O. Box 4000
Stamford, CT 06907

Vid America
235 East 55th Street
New York, NY 10022

Walt Disney Home Video
500 South Buena Vista Street
Burbank, CA 91522

Warner Home Video
4000 Warner Boulevard
Burbank, CA 91522

Thorn EMI Home Video
1370 Avenue of the Americas
New York, NY 10019

Photo Credits

p. xxi	Arnold Browne	p. 123	David Alexander
p. 24	Steve Rapport	p. 127	Richard Haughton
p. 27	Sam Emerson	p. 132	Anton Corbijn
p. 30	Jean Pagliuso	p. 269	Bob Blakeman
p. 31	E. J. Camp	p. 288	Bret Lopez
p. 42	Steve Meisel	p. 298	Francesco Scavullo
p. 64	Michael Rutland	p. 304	Adrian Boot
p. 65	Malcolm Heywood	p. 308	Randy Bachman
p. 78	Norman Seeff	p. 315	Annie Leibovitz
p. 81	Henry Diltz	p. 317	Paul Cox
p. 85	Chris Walter	p. 339	Norman Seeff
p. 96	Jean Pagliuso	p. 340	Beverly Parker
p. 106	Lynn Goldsmith	p. 351	Stuart Math

Photo Copyrights

pp.	2, 34, 46, 71, 113, 116, 117, 125, 175, 255, 275, 291, 330, 382, 401	RCA/Columbia Pictures Home Video
p.	4	The This Is the Week That Beatlemania Was Co., Inc.
p.	15	Four Star International, Inc.
pp.	36, 60, 173, 211, 242, 280, 314	Warner Bros., Inc.
p.	80	MCA Home Video
pp.	81, 90, 122, 132, 149, 176, 191, 194, 220, 262, 294, 296, 311, 320, 324, 327, 332, 336, 360, 397	Universal City Studios, Inc.
p.	139	Sprint N.V.
pp.	150, 151, 218, 219, 227, 231, 243, 343	Paramount Pictures Corporation
p.	180	Stigwood Group, Ltd.
pp.	228, 297	Columbia Pictures Industries, Inc.
p.	264	Associated Film Distribution
p.	301	Allarco Productions, Ltd.
p.	316	CPII
p.	372	National Film Trustee Co., Ltd.
p.	375	Henson Associates, Inc.
p.	377	Walt Disney Productions
p.	380	MCA Videocassette, Inc.